LENIN

COLLECTED WORKS

33

THE RUSSIAN EDITION WAS PRINTED
IN ACCORDANCE WITH A DECISION
OF THE NINTH CONGRESS OF THE R.C.P.(B.)
AND THE SECOND CONGRESS OF SOVIETS
OF THE U.S.S.R.

ИНСТИТУТ МАРКСИЗМА-ЛЕНИНИЗМА при ЦК КПСС

В. И. ЛЕНИН

СОЧИНЕНИЯ

Издание четвертое

ГОСУДАРСТВЕННОЕ ИЗДАТЕЛЬСТВО
ПОЛИТИЧЕСКОЙ ЛИТЕРАТУРЫ

МОСКВА

V. I. LENIN

COLLECTED WORKS

VOLUME
33

August 1921 — March 1923

PROGRESS PUBLISHERS
MOSCOW

TRANSLATED FROM THE RUSSIAN

EDITED BY DAVID SKVIRSKY
AND THE LATE GEORGE HANNA

First printing 1965
Second printing 1973
Third printing 1976

11-17-78

Printed in the Union of Soviet Socialist Republics

$$\text{Л} \frac{10102 - 72}{014\,(01) - 76} \; 22 - 76$$

CONTENTS

	Page
Preface	17

1921

NEW TIMES AND OLD MISTAKES IN A NEW GUISE	21
LETTERS TO THE CENTRAL STATISTICAL BOARD	30
1. To the Manager of the Central Statistical Board, *August 16*	30
2. To the Manager of the Central Statistical Board or His Deputy, *September 1*	33
LETTER TO THE EDITORS OF *EKONOMICHESKAYA ZHIZN, September 1*	36
PURGING THE PARTY	39
TASKS OF THE WORKERS' AND PEASANTS' INSPECTION AND HOW THEY ARE TO BE UNDERSTOOD AND FULFILLED	42
TO THE PRESIDIUM OF THE EIGHTH ALL-RUSSIA CONGRESS OF ELECTRICAL ENGINEERS	49
FOURTH ANNIVERSARY OF THE OCTOBER REVOLUTION	51
THE NEW ECONOMIC POLICY AND THE TASKS OF THE POLITICAL EDUCATION DEPARTMENTS. *Report to the Second All-Russia Congress of Political Education Departments, October 17*	60
Abrupt Change of Policy of the Soviet Government and the R.C.P.	60

The 1918 Decision of the All-Russia Central Execu-
tive Committee on the Role of the Peasantry   61
Our Mistake   62
A Strategical Retreat   63
Purport of the New Economic Policy   64
Who Will Win, the Capitalist or Soviet Power? . . .   65
The Fight Will Be Even Fiercer   66
Is This the Last Fight?   68
We Must not Count on Going Straight to Communism   69
The Principle of Personal Incentive and Responsibil-
ity   70
Shall We Be Able to Work for Our Own Benefit? .   71
Obsolete Methods   73
The Greatest Miracle of All   74
Tasks of Political Educationalists   76
The Three Chief Enemies   77
    The First Enemy—Communist Conceit   77
    The Second Enemy—Illiteracy   78
    The Third Enemy—Bribery   78
Difference Between Military and Cultural Problems .   78

SEVENTH MOSCOW GUBERNIA CONFERENCE OF THE RUS-
SIAN COMMUNIST PARTY, October 29-31, 1921   81

    1. REPORT ON THE NEW ECONOMIC POLICY, Octo-
       ber 29   83

    2. CLOSING SPEECH, October 29   102

THE IMPORTANCE OF GOLD NOW AND AFTER THE COMPLETE
VICTORY OF SOCIALISM   109

SPEECH AT A MEETING OF THE PROKHOROV TEXTILE MILLS
WORKERS, HELD TO MARK THE FOURTH ANNIVERSARY OF
THE OCTOBER REVOLUTION, November 6, 1921. Brief News-
paper Report   117

SPEECH AT A MEETING OF WORKING MEN AND WOMEN,
RED ARMY MEN AND YOUNG PEOPLE OF KHAMOVNIKI
DISTRICT, MOSCOW, HELD TO MARK THE FOURTH ANNI-
VERSARY OF THE OCTOBER REVOLUTION, November 7,
1921   118

SPEECH AT A WORKERS' MEETING AT THE ELEKTROSILA
PLANT No. 3 (FORMERLY DYNAMO PLANT) TO MARK THE
FOURTH ANNIVERSARY OF THE OCTOBER REVOLUTION,
November 7, 1921. Brief Newspaper Report   120

PREFACE TO THE PAMPHLET: THE PROBLEM OF THE NEW
ECONOMIC POLICY (TWO OLD ARTICLES AND A STILL
OLDER POSTSCRIPT)   121

TELEGRAM TO NARIMANOV, CHAIRMAN OF THE COUNCIL OF PEOPLE'S COMMISSARS OF AZERBAIJAN, *Baku*   124

A CAPABLY WRITTEN LITTLE BOOK   125

MEMO TO J. V. STALIN WITH THE DRAFT DECISION OF THE POLITICAL BUREAU OF THE C.C., R.C.P.(B.) ON THE FORMATION OF A FEDERATION OF TRANSCAUCASIAN REPUBLICS, *November 28*   127

SPEECH AT THE FIRST MOSCOW GUBERNIA AGRICULTURAL CONGRESS, *November 29, 1921*   128

THE THESES ON THE AGRARIAN QUESTION ADOPTED BY THE COMMUNIST PARTY OF FRANCE   131

LETTER TO P. A. ZALUTSKY, A. A. SOLTS AND ALL MEMBERS OF THE POLITICAL BUREAU RE THE PARTY PURGE AND THE CONDITIONS OF ADMISSION INTO THE PARTY, *December 19*   138

LETTER TO THE POLITICAL BUREAU RE THE RESOLUTION OF THE NINTH ALL-RUSSIA CONGRESS OF SOVIETS ON THE INTERNATIONAL SITUATION, *DECEMBER 22*   139

NINTH ALL-RUSSIA CONGRESS OF SOVIETS, December 23-28, 1921   141

   1. THE HOME AND FOREIGN POLICY OF THE REPUBLIC. *Report of the All-Russia Central Executive Committee and the Council of People's Commissars, December 23*   143

   2. INSTRUCTIONS BY THE NINTH ALL-RUSSIA CONGRESS OF SOVIETS ON QUESTIONS OF ECONOMIC ACTIVITIES, *December 28*   178

BRITISH LABOUR PARTY POLICY   182

THE ROLE AND FUNCTIONS OF THE TRADE UNIONS UNDER THE NEW ECONOMIC POLICY   184

   1. The New Economic Policy and the Trade Unions   184

   2. State Capitalism in the Proletarian State and the Trade Unions.   185

   3. The State Enterprises That Are Being Put on a Profit Basis and the Trade Unions   185

4. The Essential Difference Between the Class Struggle of the Proletariat in a State Which Recognises Private Ownership of the Land, Factories, etc., and Where Political Power Is in the Hands of the Capitalist Class, and the Economic Struggle of the Proletariat in a State Which Does not Recognise Private Ownership of the Land and the Majority of the Large Enterprises and Where Political Power Is in the Hands of the Proletariat   186

5. Reversion to Voluntary Trade Union Membership   188

6. The Trade Unions and the Management of Industry   188

7. The Role and Functions of the Trade Unions in the Business and Administrative Organisations of the Proletarian State   189

8. Contact With the Masses—the Fundamental Condition for All Trade Union Activity   192

9. The Contradictions in the Status of the Trade Unions Under the Dictatorship of the Proletariat   193

10. The Trade Unions and the Specialists   194

11. The Trade Unions and Petty-Bourgeois Influence on the Working Class   195

1922

DRAFT DIRECTIVE OF THE POLITICAL BUREAU ON THE NEW ECONOMIC POLICY   197

TO THE WORKING PEOPLE OF DAGHESTAN   199

LETTER TO G. K. ORJONIKIDZE ON THE STRENGTHENING OF THE GEORGIAN RED ARMY, *February 13*   200

LETTER TO D. I. KURSKY WITH NOTES ON THE DRAFT CIVIL CODE, *February 28*   202

NOTES OF A PUBLICIST. *On Ascending a High Mountain; the Harm of Despondency; the Utility of Trade; Attitude Towards the Mensheviks. etc.*   204

I. By Way of Example   204

II. Without Metaphors   205

III. Catching Foxes; Levi and Serrati   207

THE INTERNATIONAL AND DOMESTIC SITUATION OF THE SOVIET REPUBLIC. *Speech Delivered to a Meeting of the Communist Group at the All-Russia Congress of Metalworkers, March 6, 1922*   212

ON THE SIGNIFICANCE OF MILITANT MATERIALISM 227

TO COMRADE MOLOTOV FOR THE MEMBERS OF THE POLITICAL BUREAU. *Re Comrade Preobrazhensky's Theses, March 16* 237

MEMO TO G. Y. ZINOVIEV WITH THE DRAFT OF THE SOVIET GOVERNMENT'S REPLY TO E. VANDERVELDE, *March 17* . . 243

PREFACE TO I. I. STEPANOV'S *THE ELECTRIFICATION OF THE R.S.F.S.R. AND THE TRANSITIONAL PHASE OF WORLD ECONOMY* 245

LETTER TO J. V. STALIN ON THE FUNCTIONS OF THE DEPUTY CHAIRMEN OF THE COUNCIL OF PEOPLE'S COMMISSARS AND OF THE COUNCIL OF LABOUR AND DEFENCE, *March 21* 247

FOURTH ANNIVERSARY OF *BEDNOTA* 249

LETTER TO V. M. MOLOTOV FOR THE PLENARY MEETING OF THE C.C., R.C.P.(B.) WITH THE PLAN OF THE POLITICAL REPORT FOR THE ELEVENTH PARTY CONGRESS, *March 23* 251

THE CONDITIONS FOR ADMITTING NEW MEMBERS TO THE PARTY. *Letters to V. M. Molotov* 254

    1. 254

    2. 256

ELEVENTH CONGRESS OF THE R.C.P.(B.), March 27-April 2, 1922 259

    1. SPEECH IN OPENING THE CONGRESS. *March 27* 261

    2. POLITICAL REPORT OF THE C.C., R.C.P.(B.), *March 27* 263

    3. CLOSING SPEECH ON THE POLITICAL REPORT OF THE C.C., R.C.P.(B.), *March 28* 310

    4. SPEECH IN CLOSING THE CONGRESS, *April 2* 325

ON THE DRAFT OF THE ELEVENTH PARTY CONGRESS RESOLUTION ON WORK IN THE COUNTRYSIDE. *Letter to Comrade Osinsky, April 1* 327
WE HAVE PAID TOO MUCH 330

DECREE ON THE FUNCTIONS OF THE DEPUTY CHAIRMEN OF THE COUNCIL OF PEOPLE'S COMMISSARS AND OF THE COUNCIL OF LABOUR AND DEFENCE   335

I. The General and Main Functions of the Deputy Chairmen   335

II. Specific Questions Concerning the Work of the Deputy Chairmen   336

III. The Deputy Chairmen's Methods of Work. Their Staffs   339

IV. Co-ordinating the Work of the Two Deputy Chairmen   341

V. Distribution of Functions Between the Deputy Chairmen   341

LETTER TO J. V. STALIN. *To Comrade Stalin (for the Political Bureau), April 15*   344

PREFACE TO THE PAMPHLET *OLD ARTICLES ON ALMOST NEW SUBJECTS. Preface to the 1922 Edition*   345

TELEGRAM TO THE WORKERS AND ENGINEERS OF THE AZNEFT TRUST, *Baku, April 28*   348

ON THE TENTH ANNIVERSARY OF *PRAVDA*   349

REPLY TO REMARKS CONCERNING THE FUNCTIONS OF THE DEPUTY CHAIRMEN OF THE COUNCIL OF PEOPLE'S COMMISSARS   353

DRAFT DECISION OF THE ALL-RUSSIA CENTRAL EXECUTIVE COMMITTEE ON THE REPORT OF THE DELEGATION TO THE GENOA CONFERENCE   356

LETTER TO D. I. KURSKY, *May 17*   358

LETTERS TO J. V. STALIN FOR MEMBERS OF THE POLITICAL BUREAU OF THE C.C., R.C.P.(B.) ON THE PROMOTION OF RADIO ENGINEERING   360

1. *May 19*   360

2. *May 19*   362

"DUAL" SUBORDINATION AND LEGALITY, *May 20*   363

A FLY IN THE OINTMENT 368

LETTER TO **THE FIFTH** ALL-RUSSIA CONGRESS OF TRADE UNIONS, *September 17* 370

MEMO TO THE POLITICAL BUREAU ON COMBATING DOMINANT NATION CHAUVINISM, *October 6* 372

TO THE WORKERS OF BAKU, *October 6* 373

TO THE FIFTH CONGRESS OF THE YOUNG COMMUNIST LEAGUE OF RUSSIA, *October 11* 374

LETTER TO J. V. STALIN FOR MEMBERS OF THE C.C., R.C.P.(B.) RE THE FOREIGN TRADE MONOPOLY, *October 13* . . 375

TO THE ALL-RUSSIA CONGRESS OF FINANCIAL WORKERS, *October 20* 379

TO THE SOCIETY OF FRIENDS OF SOVIET RUSSIA (IN THE UNITED STATES), *October 20* 380

TO THE SOCIETY FOR TECHNICAL AID FOR SOVIET RUSSIA, *October 20* 381

GREETINGS TO THE LIBERATED PRIMORYE TERRITORY, *October 26* 382

INTERVIEW GIVEN TO MICHAEL FARBMAN, *OBSERVER* AND *MANCHESTER GUARDIAN* CORRESPONDENT 383

SPEECH AT THE FOURTH SESSION OF THE ALL-RUSSIA CENTRAL EXECUTIVE COMMITTEE, NINTH CONVOCATION, *October 31* 390

TO *PETROGRADSKAYA PRAVDA*, *November 1* 396

TO *PRAVDA*, *November 2* 397

TO THE FIRST INTERNATIONAL CONFERENCE OF COMMUNIST CO-OPERATORS, *November 2* 398

TO THE ALL-RUSSIA CONGRESS OF STATISTICIANS, *November 4* 399

INTERVIEW WITH ARTHUR RANSOME, *MANCHESTER GUARDIAN* CORRESPONDENT 400
    First Version 400
    Second Version (Unfinished) 406

TO THE NON-PARTY CONFERENCE OF WOMEN WORKERS AND PEASANTS OF MOSCOW CITY AND MOSCOW GUBERNIA, *November 6*   410

TO THE WORKERS OF THE FORMER MICHELSON PLANT, *November 7*   411

TO THE WORKERS AND EMPLOYEES AT THE STATE ELEK-TROPEREDACHA POWER STATION, *November 7*   412

TO THE WORKERS AT THE STODOL CLOTH MILL IN KLINTSI, *November 8*   413

FOURTH CONGRESS OF THE COMMUNIST INTERNATION-AL, November 5-December 5, 1922   415

1. TO THE FOURTH CONGRESS OF THE COMMUNIST INTERNATIONAL AND TO THE PETROGRAD SOVIET OF WORKERS' AND RED ARMY DEPUTIES, *November 4* . .   417

2. FIVE YEARS OF THE RUSSIAN REVOLUTION AND THE PROSPECTS OF THE WORLD REVOLUTION. *Report to the Fourth Congress of the Communist International, November 13, 1922*   418

GREETINGS TO THE ALL-RUSSIA AGRICULTURAL EXHIBI-TION, *November 14*   433

TO THE *CLARTÉ* GROUP, *November 15*   434

SPEECH AT A PLENARY SESSION OF THE MOSCOW SOVIET, *November 20, 1922*   435

TO THE PRESIDIUM OF THE FIFTH ALL-RUSSIA CONGRESS OF THE SOVIET EMPLOYEES' UNION   444

TO THE EDUCATIONAL WORKERS' CONGRESS, *November 26* .   445

TO THE THIRD CONGRESS OF THE YOUNG COMMUNIST INTERNATIONAL, MOSCOW, *December 4*   446

NOTES ON THE TASKS OF OUR DELEGATION AT THE HAGUE   447

A FEW WORDS ABOUT N. Y. FEDOSEYEV   452

TO THE ALL-UKRAINE CONGRESS OF SOVIETS, *December 10* .   454

RE THE MONOPOLY OF FOREIGN TRADE, *December 13* . . .   455

LETTER TO J. V. STALIN FOR MEMBERS OF THE C.C., R.C.P.(B.), *December 15*   460

1923

PAGES FROM A DIARY   462

ON CO-OPERATION   467

    I.   467

    II.   472

OUR REVOLUTION (*Apropos of N. Sukhanov's Notes*) . . .   476

    I.   476

    II.   480

HOW WE SHOULD REORGANISE THE WORKERS' AND PEAS-
ANTS' INSPECTION (*Recommendation to the Twelfth Party
Congress*)   481

BETTER FEWER, BUT BETTER   487

Notes   503

The Life and Work of V. I. Lenin. Outstanding Dates . . .   539

———

ILLUSTRATIONS

Portrait of V. I. Lenin. 1921 . . . .   **16-17**
First page of Lenin's manuscript "Fourth Anniversary of
the October Revolution", October 14, 1921 . . . .   **44-45**

———

V. I. LENIN
1921

PREFACE

Volume 33 contains articles, reports, speeches and letters written by Lenin in the period from August 16, 1921 to March 2, 1923.

In them he sums up the first results of economic rehabilitation under the New Economic Policy and substantiates the possibility of and outlines a plan for the building of socialism in Soviet Russia.

In the articles "New Times and Old Mistakes in a New Guise", "Fourth Anniversary of the October Revolution", "The Importance of Gold Now and After the Complete Victory of Socialism", the reports "The Home and Foreign Policy of the Republic" at the Ninth All-Russia Congress of Soviets on December 23, 1921, "Political Report of the Central Committee of the R.C.P.(B.)" on March 27, 1922 at the Eleventh Party Congress, "Five Years of the Russian Revolution and the Prospects of the World Revolution" at the Fourth Congress of the Communist International on November 13, 1922, "Speech at a Plenary Session of the Moscow Soviet" on November 20, 1922, and in other works, Lenin traces the restoration and revival of large-scale socialist industry and the strengthening of the alliance between the workers and peasants on a new economic foundation. He outlines the ways of combating capitalist elements and expresses the firm conviction that "NEP Russia will become socialist Russia".

Some of the speeches, articles and documents in this volume deal with the building up of the Party, the purging of the Party and the improvement of its social composition, criticism and self-criticism, and the leadership of local government bodies, the trade unions and the co-operatives.

These include the article "Purging the Party", the letters "The Conditions for Admitting New Members to the Party", "Political Report of the Central Committee of the R.C.P.(B.)" at the Eleventh Party Congress, and the decision of the C. C., R.C.P.(B.) on "The Role and Functions of the Trade Unions Under the New Economic Policy".

Considerable space is taken up in this volume by works showing Lenin's activity in strengthening and improving the state apparatus. These include "Tasks of the Workers' and Peasants' Inspection and How They Are to Be Understood and Fulfilled", "Letter to J. V. Stalin on the Functions of the Deputy Chairmen of the Council of People's Commissars and of the Council of Labour and Defence", "Decree on the Functions of the Deputy Chairmen of the Council of People's Commissars and of the Council of Labour and Defence," "'Dual' Subordination and Legality" and "Speech at the Fourth Session of the All-Russia Central Executive Committee, Ninth Convocation" on October 31, 1922.

In many of the speeches, articles and documents in this volume Lenin sets forth the fundamental principles of the Soviet Government's foreign policy. On the premise that the Soviet Republic could coexist peacefully with capitalist states, Lenin considered that Soviet foreign policy should be founded on the struggle for peace and the defence of the independence and sovereignty of the Soviet state.

In the works dealing with the international working-class and communist movement, Lenin formulates the key objectives of the united front tactics and speaks of the prospects for the development of the world revolution. He emphasises that the mounting national liberation movement and revolutionary struggle in the East, in India and China, which together with Soviet Russia have the overwhelming majority of the world's population, are of tremendous importance for the final triumph of socialism on a world scale.

This volume contains Lenin's last articles: "Pages From a Diary", "On Co-operation", "Our Revolution", "How We Should Reorganise the Workers' and Peasants' Inspection" and "Better Fewer, but Better". In these articles he sums up the results of the work that has been done, outlines a plan for building socialism in Soviet Russia by drawing the peasants into socialist construction, and puts forward his co-operative plan for bringing the peasants into the work of building socialism. He defines the tasks in the cultural revolution and suggests concrete measures aimed at reorganising the state apparatus.

Included in this volume is Lenin's well-known article "On the Significance of Militant Materialism", in which he sets forth a programme of work in the sphere of Marxist philosophy.

The works and letters in this volume clearly show Lenin's struggle against the enemies of the Party—the Trotskyites and Bukharinites, against great-Russian chauvinism and local nationalism, and for strengthening friendship among nations.

Also in this volume are 20 works published in the *Collected Works* for the first time. "Letters to the Central Statistical Board", "Speech at a Meeting of Working Men and Women, Red Army Men and Young People of Khamovniki District, Moscow, Held to Mark the Fourth Anniversary of the October Revolution" on November 7, 1921 and "Draft Directive of the Political Bureau on the New Economic Policy" (the latter two documents are published for the first time) deal with the implementation of the New Economic Policy.

In "Letter to P. A. Zalutsky, A. A. Solts and All Members of the Political Bureau Re the Party Purge and the Conditions of Admission into the Party" Lenin suggests instituting stricter conditions for admission into the Party.

In "Reply to Remarks Concerning the Functions of the Deputy Chairmen of the Council of People's Commissars" Lenin sharply criticises Trotsky's hostile, anti-Party stand on the question of the role and functions of the Workers' and Peasants' Inspection and the State Planning Commission.

For the first time the *Collected Works* include Lenin's letter to D. I. Kursky on the Soviet Civil Code; "Memo to the Political Bureau on Combating Dominant Nation Chauvinism"; "Letter to J. V. Stalin for Members of the C. C., R.C.P.(B.) Re the Foreign Trade Monopoly" on October 13, 1922 (published for the first time) in which Lenin upholds the immutability of the monopoly on foreign trade against the attempts of Bukharin, Sokolnikov and others to wreck

the foundations of that monopoly; "Letter to J. V. Stalin
for Members of the C.C., R.C.P.(B.)" on December 15,
1922, on the question of the report to the Tenth All-Russia
Congress of Soviets; two letters to the Political Bureau on
the promotion of radio engineering, and a letter for the Political Bureau on April 15, 1922 (published for the first time).

In the "Letter to the Political Bureau Re the Resolution
of the Ninth All-Russia Congress of Soviets on the International Situation" Lenin emphasises the international role
of the Soviet state as the first country to have actually
implemented the policy of self-determination of nations.

The "Draft Decision of the All-Russia Central Executive
Committee on the Report of the Delegation to the Genoa
Conference" defines the basic objectives of Soviet foreign policy; in the "Memo to G. Y. Zinoviev with the Draft of
the Soviet Government's Reply to E. Vandervelde" Lenin
exposes the treachery of the leaders of the Second and
Two-and-a-Half Internationals who came out in defence
of the counter-revolutionary Menshevik and Socialist-
Revolutionary parties (both documents are published
for the first time).

Published for the first time in the *Collected Works* are
Lenin's greetings to various congresses and organisations:
"Telegram to Narimanov, Chairman of the Council of People's
Commissars of Azerbaijan" (published for the first time), "To
the Working People of Daghestan", "Telegram to the Workers
and Engineers of the Azneft Trust", "To the Workers of
the Former Michelson Plant" and "To the Workers and Employees at the State Elektroperedacha Power Station".

NEW TIMES AND OLD MISTAKES
IN A NEW GUISE

Every specific turn in history causes some change in the form of petty-bourgeois wavering, which always occurs alongside the proletariat, and which, in one degree or another, always penetrates its midst.

This wavering flows in two "streams": petty-bourgeois reformism, i. e., servility to the bourgeoisie covered by a cloak of sentimental democratic and "Social"-Democratic phrases and fatuous wishes; and petty-bourgeois revolutionism—menacing, blustering and boastful in words, but a mere bubble of disunity, disruption and brainlessness in deeds. This wavering will inevitably occur until the taproot of capitalism is cut. Its form is now changing owing to the change taking place in the economic policy of the Soviet government.

The leitmotif of the Mensheviks[1] is: "The Bolsheviks have reverted to capitalism; that is where they will meet their end. The revolution, including the October Revolution, has turned out to be a bourgeois revolution after all! Long live democracy! Long live reformism!" Whether this is said in the purely Menshevik spirit or in the spirit of the Socialist-Revolutionaries,[2] in the spirit of the Second International or in the spirit of the Two-and-a-Half International,[3] it amounts to the same thing.

The leitmotif of semi-anarchists like the German "Communist Workers' Party",[4] or of that section of our former Workers' Opposition[5] which has left or is becoming estranged from the Party, is: "The Bolsheviks have lost faith in the working class." The slogans they deduce from this are more or less akin to the "Kronstadt" slogans of the spring of 1921.[6]

In contrast to the whining and panic of the philistines from among reformists and of the philistines from among revolutionaries, the Marxists must weigh the alignment of actual class forces and the incontrovertible facts as soberly and as accurately as possible.

Let us recall the main stages of our revolution. The first stage: the purely political stage, so to speak, from October 25 to January 5, when the Constituent Assembly[7] was dissolved. In a matter of ten weeks we did a hundred times more to actually and completely destroy the survivals of feudalism in Russia than the Mensheviks and Socialist-Revolutionaries did during the eight months *they* were in power—from February to October 1917. At that time, the Mensheviks and Socialist-Revolutionaries in Russia, and all the heroes of the Two-and-a-Half International abroad, acted as miserable accomplices of reaction. As for the anarchists, some stood aloof in perplexity, while others helped us. Was the revolution a bourgeois revolution at that time? Of course it was, insofar as our function was to complete the bourgeois-democratic revolution, insofar as there was as yet no class struggle among the "peasantry". But, at the same time, we accomplished a great deal *over and above* the bourgeois revolution *for* the socialist, proletarian revolution: 1) we developed the forces of the working class for *its* utilisation of state power to an extent never achieved before; 2) we struck a blow that was felt all over the world against the fetishes of petty-bourgeois democracy, the Constituent Assembly and bourgeois "liberties" such as freedom of the press for the rich; 3) we created the Soviet *type* of state, which was a gigantic step in advance of 1793 and 1871.

The second stage: the Brest-Litovsk peace.[8] There was a riot of revolutionary phrase-mongering against peace—the semi-jingoist phrase-mongering of the Socialist-Revolutionaries and Mensheviks, and the "Left" phrase-mongering of a certain section of the Bolsheviks. "Since you have made peace with imperialism you are doomed," argued the philistines, some in panic and some with malicious glee. But the Socialist-Revolutionaries and the Mensheviks made peace with imperialism as participants in the bourgeois robbery of the workers. We "made peace", surrendering to the robbers part of our property, only in order to save the workers' rule, and in order to be able to strike heavier blows at the robbers later on. At that time we heard no end of talk about our having "lost faith in the forces of the working class"; but we did not allow ourselves to be deceived by this phrase-mongering.

The third stage: the Civil War, beginning with the Czecho-slovaks[9] and the Constituent Assembly crowd and ending with Wrangel,[10] from 1918 to 1920. At the beginning of the war our Red Army was non-existent. Judged as a material force, this army is even now insignificant compared with the army of any of the Entente powers. Nevertheless, we emerged victorious from the struggle against the mighty Entente. The alliance between the peasants and the workers led by proletarian rule—this achievement of epoch-making importance—was raised to an unprecedented level. The Mensheviks and Socialist-Revolutionaries acted as the accomplices of the monarchy overtly (as Ministers, organisers and propagandists) and covertly (the more "subtle" and despicable method adopted by the Chernovs and Martovs, who pretended to wash their hands of the affair but actually used their pens against us). The anarchists too vacillated helplessly, one section of them helping us, while another hindering us by their clamour against military discipline or by their scepticism.

The fourth stage: the Entente is compelled to cease (for how long?) its intervention and blockade. Our unprecedent-edly dislocated country is just barely beginning to recover, is only just realising the full depth of its ruin, is suffering the most terrible hardships—stoppage of industry, crop failures, famine, epidemics.

We have risen to the highest and at the same time the most difficult stage of our historic struggle. Our enemy at the present moment and in the present period is not the same one that faced us yesterday. He is not the hordes of whiteguards commanded by the landowners and supported by all the Mensheviks and Socialist-Revolutionaries, by the whole international bourgeoisie. He is everyday economics in a small-peasant country with a ruined large-scale industry. He is the petty-bourgeois element which surrounds us like the air, and penetrates deep into the ranks of the proletariat. And the proletariat is declassed, i. e., dislodged from its class groove. The factories and mills are idle—the proletariat is weak, scattered, enfeebled. On the other hand, the petty-bourgeois element within the country is backed by the whole international bourgeoisie, which still retains its power throughout the world.

Is this not enough to make people quail, especially heroes like the Mensheviks and Socialist-Revolutionaries, the knights of the Two-and-a-Half International, the helpless anarchists and the lovers of "Left" phrases? "The Bolsheviks are reverting to capitalism; the Bolsheviks are done for. Their revolution, too, has not gone beyond the confines of a bourgeois revolution." We hear plenty of wails of this sort.

But we have grown accustomed to them.

We do not belittle the danger. We look it straight in the face. We say to the workers and peasants: The danger is great; more solidarity, more staunchness, more coolness; turn the pro-Menshevik and pro-Socialist-Revolutionary panic-mongers and tub-thumpers out with contempt.

The danger is great. The enemy is far stronger than we are economically, just as yesterday he was far stronger than we were militarily. We know that; and in that knowledge lies our strength. We have already done so tremendously much to purge Russia of feudalism, to develop all the forces of the workers and peasants, to promote the world-wide struggle against imperialism and to advance the international proletarian movement, which is freed from the banalities and baseness of the Second and Two-and-a-Half Internationals, that panicky cries no longer affect us. We have more than fully "justified" our revolutionary activity, we have shown the whole world by our deeds what proletarian revolutionism is capable of in contrast to Menshevik-Socialist-Revolutionary "democracy" and cowardly reformism decked with pompous phrases.

Anyone who fears defeat on the eve of a great struggle can call himself a socialist only out of sheer mockery of the workers.

It is precisely because we are not afraid to look danger in the face that we make the best use of our forces for the struggle—we weigh the chances more dispassionately, cautiously and prudently—we make every concession that will strengthen us and break up the forces of the enemy (now even the biggest fool can see that the "Brest peace" was a concession that strengthened us and dismembered the forces of international imperialism).

The Mensheviks are shouting that the tax in kind, the freedom to trade, the granting of concessions and state capitalism signify the collapse of communism. Abroad, the ex-Communist Levi has added his voice to that of the Mensheviks. This same Levi had to be defended as long as the mistakes he had made could be explained by his reaction to some of the mistakes of the "Left" Communists, particularly in March 1921 in Germany[11] ; but this same Levi cannot be defended when, instead of admitting that he is wrong, he slips into Menshevism all along the line.

To the Menshevik shouters we shall simply point out that as early as the spring of 1918 the Communists proclaimed and advocated the idea of a bloc, an alliance with state capitalism against the petty-bourgeois element. That was three years ago! In the first months of the Bolshevik victory! Even then the Bolsheviks took a sober view of things. And since then nobody has been able to challenge the correctness of our sober calculation of the available forces.

Levi, who has slipped into Menshevism, advises the Bolsheviks (whose defeat by capitalism he "forecasts" in the same way as all the philistines, democrats, Social-Democrats and others had forecast our doom if we dissolved the Constituent Assembly!) to appeal for aid to the *whole* working class! Because, if you please, up to now only *part* of the working class has been helping us!

What Levi says here remarkably coincides with what is said by those semi-anarchists and tub-thumpers, and also by certain members of the former "Workers' Opposition", who are so fond of talking large about the Bolsheviks now having "lost faith in the forces of the working class". Both the Mensheviks and those with anarchist leanings make a fetish of the concept "forces of the working class"; they are incapable of grasping its actual, concrete meaning. Instead of studying and analysing its meaning, they declaim.

The gentlemen of the Two-and-a-Half International pose as revolutionaries; but in every serious situation they prove to be counter-revolutionaries because they shrink from the violent destruction of the old state machine; they have no faith in the forces of the working class. It was not a mere catch-phrase we uttered when we said this about the Social-ist-Revolutionaries and Co. Everybody knows that the Octo-ber Revolution actually brought new forces, a new class, to the forefront, that the best representatives of the proletar-iat are now governing Russia, built up an army, led that army, set up local government, etc., are running industry, and so on. If there are some bureaucratic distortions in this administration, we do not conceal this evil; we expose it, combat it. Those who allow the struggle against the distor-tions of the new system to obscure its content and to cause them to forget that the working class has created and is guid-ing a state of the Soviet type are incapable of thinking, and are merely throwing words to the wind.

But the "forces of the working class" are not unlimited. If the flow of fresh forces from the working class is now feeble, sometimes very feeble, if, notwithstanding all our decrees, appeals and agitation, notwithstanding all our orders for "the promotion of non-Party people", the flow of forces is still feeble, then resorting to mere declamations about having "lost faith in the forces of the working class" means descending to vapid phrase-mongering.

Without a certain "respite" these new forces will not be forthcoming; they can only grow slowly; and they can grow only on the basis of restored large-scale industry (i. e., to be more precise and concrete, on the basis of electrification). They can be obtained from *no other* source.

After an enormous, unparalleled exertion of effort, the working class in a small-peasant, ruined country, the work-ing class which has very largely become declassed, needs an interval of time in which to allow new forces to grow and be brought to the fore, and in which the old and worn-out forces can "recuperate". The creation of a military and state machine capable of successfully withstanding the trials of 1917-21 was a great effort, which engaged, absorbed and exhausted real "forces of the working class" (and not such as exist merely in the declamations of the tub-thumpers). One must understand this and reckon with the necessary, or rather, inevitable *slackening* of the rate of growth of *new* forces of the working class.

When the Mensheviks shout about the "Bonapartism" of

the Bolsheviks (who, they claim, rely on troops and on the machinery of state against the will of "democracy"), they magnificently express the tactics of the bourgeoisie; and Milyukov, from his own standpoint, is right when he supports them, supports the "Kronstadt" (spring of 1921) slogans. The bourgeoisie quite correctly takes into consideration the fact that the *real* "forces of the working class" now consist of the mighty vanguard of that class (the Russian Communist Party, which—not at one stroke, but in the course of twenty-five years—won for itself by deeds the role, the name and the power of the "vanguard" of the only revolutionary class) plus the elements which have been most weakened by being declassed, and which are most susceptible to Menshevik and anarchist vacillations.

The slogan "more faith in the forces of the working class" is now being used, *in fact*, to increase the influence of the Mensheviks and anarchists, as was vividly proved and demonstrated by Kronstadt in the spring of 1921. Every class-conscious worker should expose and send packing those who shout about our having "lost faith in the forces of the working class", because these tub-thumpers are actually the accomplices of the bourgeoisie and the landowners, who seek to weaken the proletariat for their benefit by helping to spread the influence of the Mensheviks and the anarchists.

That is the crux of the matter if we dispassionately examine what the concept "forces of the working class" really means.

Gentlemen, what are you really doing to promote non-Party people to what is the main "front" today, the economic front, for the work of economic development? That is the question that class-conscious workers should put to the tub-thumpers. That is how the tub-thumpers always can and should be exposed. That is how it can always be proved that, actually, they are not assisting but hindering economic development; that they are not assisting but hindering the proletarian revolution; that they are pursuing not proletarian, but petty-bourgeois aims; and that they are serving an alien class.

Our slogans are: Down with the tub-thumpers! Down with the unwitting accomplices of the whiteguards who are repeating the mistakes of the hapless Kronstadt mutineers of the spring of 1921! Get down to business-like, practical work that will take into account the specific features of the present situation and its tasks! We need not phrases but deeds.

A sober estimation of these specific features and of the real, not imaginary, class forces tells us:

The period of unprecedented proletarian achievements in the military, administrative and political fields has given way to a period in which the growth of new forces will be much slower; and that period did not set in by accident, it was inevitable; it was due to the operation not of persons or parties, but of objective causes. In the economic field, development is inevitably more difficult, slower, and more gradual; that arises from the very nature of the activities in this field compared with military, administrative and political activities. It follows from the specific difficulties of this work, from its being more deep-rooted, if one may so express it.

That is why we shall strive to formulate our tasks in this new, higher stage of the struggle with the greatest, with treble caution. We shall formulate them as moderately as possible. We shall make as many concessions as possible within the limits, of course, of what the proletariat *can* concede and yet remain the ruling class. We shall collect the moderate tax in kind as quickly as possible and allow the greatest possible scope for the development, strengthening and revival of peasant farming. We shall lease the enterprises that are not absolutely essential for us to lessees, including private capitalists and foreign concessionaires. We need a bloc, or alliance, between the proletarian state and state capitalism against the petty-bourgeois element. We must achieve this alliance skilfully, following the rule: "Measure your cloth seven times before you cut." We shall leave ourselves a smaller field of work, only what is absolutely necessary. We shall concentrate the enfeebled forces of the working class on something *less*, but we shall consolidate ourselves all the more and put ourselves to the test of practical experience not once or twice, but over and over again. Step by step, inch by inch—for at present the "troops" we have at our command *cannot* advance any other way on the difficult road we have to travel, in the stern conditions under which we are living, and amidst the dangers we have to face. Those who find this work "dull", "uninteresting" and "unintelligible", those who turn up their noses or become panic-stricken, or who become intoxicated with their own declamations about the absence of the "previous elation", the "previous enthusiasm", etc., had better be "relieved of their jobs" and given a back seat, so as to prevent them from causing harm; for they will not or cannot understand the specific features of the present stage, the present phase of the struggle.

Amidst the colossal ruin of the country and the exhaustion of the forces of the proletariat, by a series of almost superhuman efforts, we are tackling the most difficult job: laying the foundation for a really socialist economy, for the regular exchange of commodities (or, more correctly, exchange of products) between industry and agriculture. The enemy is still far stronger than we are; anarchic, profiteering, individual commodity exchange is undermining our efforts at every step. We clearly see the difficulties and will systematically and perseveringly overcome them. More scope for independent local enterprise; more forces to the localities; more attention to their practical experience. The working class can heal its wounds, its proletarian "class forces" can recuperate, and the confidence of the peasantry in proletarian leadership can be strengthened *only* as real success is achieved in restoring industry and in bringing about a regular exchange of products through the medium of the state that benefits both the peasant and the worker. And as we achieve this we shall get an influx of new forces, not as quickly as every one of us would like, perhaps, but we shall get it nevertheless.

Let us get down to work, to slower, more cautious, more persevering and persistent work!

August 20, 1921

Pravda No. 190, August 28, 1921
Signed: *N. Lenin*

Published according to
the *Pravda* text checked
with proofs corrected by Lenin

LETTERS TO THE CENTRAL STATISTICAL BOARD

1

TO THE MANAGER OF THE CENTRAL STATISTICAL BOARD

August 16

Comrade Popov,

The correspondence with the Central Statistical Board, particularly the data supplied to me on August 3 on current industrial statistics, has made it perfectly clear to me that my instructions (in the letter of June 4, 1921) are not being carried out at all and that the entire work, the entire organisation of the Central Statistical Board is wrong.

The data given to me on August 3 as current industrial statistics are obsolete and were supplied *multa non multum* — of considerable volume but small content! That is exactly like the "bureaucratic institutions", from which you said in your letter of June 11, 1921 you want to separate the Central Statistical Board.

Ekonomicheskaya Zhizn[12] has already *printed much* fuller data in the supplement to its No. 152 issue, i. e., in *July*!

From the same *Ekonomicheskaya Zhizn* I have *already had* data for the first quarter of 1921!

The Central Statistical Board, which *lags behind* an unofficial group of writers, is a model bureaucratic institution. In about two years' time it may provide a heap of data for research, but that is not what we want.

Nearly two and a half months have passed since my letter of June 4, 1921, but nothing has changed. The same shortcomings are in evidence. There is no sign of your promised "calendar programme" and so forth (letter of June 11).

Once more I draw your attention to the incorrectness of

all this and to the need to *accelerate* the *reorganisation* of the work of the Central Statistical Board.

In particular:

1) the chairman or manager of the Central Statistical Board must work in *closer* contact with the State Planning Commission and in accordance with the *direct instructions* of and tasks set by the Chairman of the State Planning Commission and its Presidium;

2) current statistics (both industrial and agricultural) must give summarised, practical key data (postponing academic analyses of "full" data) never later but necessarily *earlier* than our press.

You must learn to pick out what is *practically* important and urgent, and shelve data of academic value;

3) together with the State Planning Commission, a kind of index-number* must be prepared by which to appraise the state of our entire economy; it must be done at least once a month and must be given in comparison with pre-war figures and then with the figures for 1920 and, where possible, for 1917, 1918 and 1919.

Approximate, presumed, preliminary data (with a special reservation on each such or similar category) must be given where exact figures are unobtainable.

For our practical work we *must* have figures and the Central Statistical Board *must* have them *before anybody else*. Let the checking of the accuracy of the figures, the determining of the percentage of error and so forth be postponed for some time.

The figures to be used for the index-number must be determined by the Central Statistical Board and the State Planning Commission. (Roughly: main, key figures—population, territory, output of principal products, main results of the work of transport, and so forth—at least 10-15 figures conformably with the way these "index-numbers" have for a long time been compiled by statisticians abroad.)

4) Immediately, without any red tape (for it was absolutely impermissible to have done nothing about it for two and a half months) organise the prompt delivery of data on the eight questions I indicated on June 4 in my

---

* The words "index-number" are in English in the original.—*Ed.*

"approximate list" and also a summary report both general and in particular:

—without delay on Moscow (Moscow must be exemplary);

—then on Petrograd,

—and on each gubernia (singling out those gubernias where the people do their work quickly, without red tape, not in accordance with old academic customs).

Have nine-tenths of the available personnel at the Central Statistical Board and the Gubernia Statistical Bureaus put at once to the job of processing these eight questions correctly and rapidly, and put one-tenth on the academic work of studying complete and all-embracing data. If that cannot be done, ninety-nine per cent of the personnel must be put on processing data practically and urgently required for our economy, and the rest of the work should be postponed until better times, until the time when there will be surplus personnel.

5) Every month the Central Statistical Board must submit to the Council of Labour and Defence[13] —it must be done before it is in the press—*preliminary* data on *key* problems of the economy (with a compulsory comparison with the preceding year). These key problems, key figures, both those that go into the "index-number" and those that do not, must be worked on immediately.

Please send me the programme of these questions and the reply on other points without delay.

V. Ulyanov (Lenin),
Chairman of the Council
of People's Commissars

2

TO THE MANAGER OF THE CENTRAL STATISTICAL BOARD
OR HIS DEPUTY

September 1, 1921

The undated "programme" of work sent to me boils down to a request for additional funds.

We cannot afford it at present.

The *entire* programme must, therefore, be *cut down in such a way* as to enable the necessary work to be continued (more regularly and completed faster) with the funds *at present* available.

I suggest that this cut be made at once; while the question of additional funds be postponed *to approximately November*.

I suggest that the programme be cut in such a way as to leave (until more funds are available) only the *most necessary* processes. They must include:

1. Monthly reports on the distribution of food by the state.

Forms for obtaining information must be established jointly with the People's Commissariat of Food roughly as follows:

a) the number of people receiving bread (I think that as a start it would be more prudent to limit the data to bread if no personnel is available to add data on all other issued products, both foodstuffs and non-foodstuffs)

> 1/4 lb each
> 1/2 „   „
> 3/4 „   „
> 1 „   „   and so forth;

b) their grades by profession, occupation and so on;

c) summary: total number of recipients and total quantity of bread issued.

The data for Moscow and Petrograd are the most urgent; then for Moscow and Petrograd gubernias, the *key industrial gubernias* (Ivanovo-Voznesensk, Donbas, Baku, the Urals and so on) and, lastly, the other gubernias.

2. Monthly reports on enterprises transferred to collective supply.

While there are not many of them, all must be kept under observation (as you have suggested in your memo, p. 2, paragraph 1). Later, when there are very many, inspect *in detail* one-fifth or one-tenth selectively.

In short—all enterprises on collective supply.

The reports you require from these enterprises are far too sweeping (end of p. 2, paragraph 2). They can and must be shorter and show only what is most important.

3. Current industrial statistics for monthly reports must be reduced, with first place given, as absolutely essential, to data on the *quantity of articles produced*, specifically on the most important items.

These data are absolutely necessary every month.

The rest are not absolutely essential and may be compiled not so urgently, as the personnel and funds of the Central Statistical Board permit.

4. Production, distribution and consumption of fuel. This must be in the report every month.

The programme must be drawn up jointly with the Central Fuel Board with as few changes as possible in the forms now in operation.

5. Monthly summaries of commodity exchanges (Commissariat of Food and the Central Council of Co-operative Societies) in the briefest possible form: such-and-such a quantity of such-and-such products issued to uyezds in exchange for such-and-such a quantity of bread.

6. As you indicate in Supplement No. 1, paragraph IV, it is of course difficult to keep an account of the work of Soviet institutions. But difficulty is not impossibility. If not monthly reports, then reports once in two or three months are absolutely necessary at least, as a start, on "available personnel" as compared with the pre-war staff or that of other departments, other gubernias and so on,

with a rational subdivision of all employees into grades (responsible posts, purely office workers, service staff—an *approximate* list of certain grades).

A comparison of the largest and smallest staffs by gubernias and so on. First and foremost, for Moscow and Petrograd.

The decisions of the last Congress of Soviets make it obligatory for the Central Statistical Board to *tackle* the statistical study of the work of our Soviet offices, the number of employees, and so forth.[14]

7. Selection for study of a *small* number of typical enterprises (factories, state farms) and *institutions*—a) the best, exemplary, b) middling and c) worst.

Cut down all the rest, except these seven paragraphs.

Inform me of your conclusion on the substance of the programme of work and the time limit for its compilation.

Lenin,
Chairman of the Council
of Labour and Defence

First published in 1933   Published according to
                                            the manuscript

LETTER TO THE EDITORS
OF *EKONOMICHESKAYA ZHIZN*

September 1

The conversion of *Ekonomicheskaya Zhizn* into the official organ of the Council of Labour and Defence should not be a simple and empty formality.

The paper must become a militant organ that not only, first, provides regular and truthful information on our economy but, secondly, analyses the information, processes it scientifically to arrive at the right conclusions for the management of industry, etc., and, thirdly and lastly, *tightens up the discipline* of all workers on the economic front, ensures punctuality in reporting, approves good work and exposes inaccurate, backward and incompetent workers in a certain factory, office, branch of economy, etc., to the judgement of all.

The paper provides a mass of valuable, especially statistical, material on our economy. That material, however, suffers from two faults—it is casual, incomplete, unsystematic and, what is more, not processed, not analysed.

I will give you examples to explain this.

The article "The Moscow Basin in July" (No. 188) is one of the best because it analyses the data, compares them with the past and compares the enterprises one with another. The analysis, however, is incomplete. There is no explanation of why one enterprise (the Tovarkovo mines) has solved a problem others have not solved. No practical deduction is made. There is no comparison with annual data.

In issue No. 190, on page 2, there is an abundance of statistical details, usual for the paper, but they are not "digested" at all, they are casual, raw, without a suggestion of analysis and are not compared (with the past or with other enterprises), etc.

The following changes must be made if the paper is to be the real organ of the Council of Labour and Defence, and not its organ in words alone.

(1) Keep a strict check on unpunctual and incomplete reports sent to relevant organisations and publicly list those that are inaccurate; at the same time *work to ensure* (through the People's Commissariat concerned or through the directorate of the Council of Labour and Defence) precise reporting.

(2) All statistical data must be much more strictly, that is, more carefully and thoroughly, systematised, and data must be obtained for comparison, always using the data for past years (past months, etc.); always select material for analysis that will explain the *reasons* for failure, and will *make prominent* some successfully operating enterprises or, at least, those that are ahead of the rest, etc.

(3) Organise a network of local correspondents, both Communists *and non-Party people*; allot greater space to local correspondence from factories, mines, state farms, railway depots and workshops, etc.

(4) Publish returns on the most important problems of our economy as special supplements. The returns absolutely must be processed, with an all-round analysis and practical conclusions.

Since we are short of newsprint, we must economise. And we probably can. For instance, reduce the number of copies from 44,000 to 30,000 (quite enough if correctly distributed, allowing two copies to each of 10,000 volosts, four to each of 1,000 uyezds, ten to each of 100 gubernias and 5,000 extra —all of them to go only to libraries, editorial offices and a few institutions). That will leave enough newsprint for eight supplements, each of two pages, a month.

That would be sufficient for monthly returns on a large number of important points (fuel; industry—two or three supplements; transport; food supplies; state farms, etc.).

These supplements should provide summarised statistics on the most important branches of the economy and they should be processed and analysed, and practical conclusions should be drawn from them.

The entire statistical material in the daily paper—there is a great deal of it but it is fragmentary—should be *adjusted* to the monthly reports and shorn of all details and trivialities, etc.

Since, in many cases, *Ekonomicheskaya Zhizn* and the *Central Statistical Board* use the same sources, the supplements to the newspaper should (for the time being) replace the publications of the *Central Statistical Board*.

(5) All current statistical material should be divided between (a) employees of *Ekonomicheskaya Zhizn*, (b) members of the *State Planning Commission* and (c) members or employees of the *Central Statistical Board* in such a way that each should be in charge of *one* branch of the economy, and should be *responsible for*—

(aa) the timely receipt of reports and summaries; for a successful "struggle" to get them; for repeated demands for them, etc.;

(bb) for the summarising and analysis of data, and
(cc) for practical conclusions.

(6) *Ekonomicheskaya Zhizn* must keep track of enterprises granted as concessions and those *leased*, as far as their reporting is concerned and also by way of supervision and the drawing of conclusions, *in the same way* as it keeps track of all others.

Please arrange for a conference to include an editor of *Ekonomicheskaya Zhizn*, one member of the Central statistical Board and one member of the State Planning Commission to discuss these questions and measures to be taken. Please inform me of the decisions of the conference.

Lenin,
Chairman of the Council of Labour and Defence

P. S. Will that conference please discuss the question of elaborating an index-number* to determine the general state of our economy. This index should be published every month.

First published
on November 6, 1923 in
Ekonomicheskaya Zhizn No. 31

Published according to
the manuscript

* These words are in English in the original.—*Ed.*

PURGING THE PARTY[15]

The purging of the Party has obviously developed into a serious and vastly important affair.

In some places the Party is being purged mainly with the aid of the experience and suggestions of non-Party workers; these suggestions and the representatives of the non-Party proletarian masses are being heeded with due consideration. That is the most valuable and most important thing. If we really succeed in purging our Party from top to bottom *in this way*, without exceptions, it will indeed be an enormous achievement for the revolution.

The achievements of the revolution cannot now be the same as they were previously. Their nature inevitably changes in conformity with the transition from the war front to the economic front, the transition to the New Economic Policy, the conditions that primarily demand higher productivity of labour, greater labour discipline. At such a time improvements at home are the major achievements of the revolution; a neither salient, striking, nor immediately perceptible improvement in labour, in its organisation and results; an improvement from the viewpoint of the fight against the influence of the petty-bourgeois and petty-bourgeois-anarchist element, which corrupts both the proletariat and the Party. To achieve such an improvement, the Party must be purged of those who have lost touch with the masses (let alone, of course, those who discredit the Party in the eyes of the masses). Naturally. we shall not submit to every thing the masses say, because the masses, too, sometimes—particularly in time of exceptional weariness and exhaustion resulting from excessive hardship and suffering—yield to sentiments that are in no way advanced. But in appraising persons, in the negative attitude to those who have "attached" themselves to us for selfish motives, to those who have become "puffed-up commissars" and "bureaucrats", the suggestions of the non-Party proletarian masses and, in many cases, of the non-Party peasant masses, are extremely valuable. The working masses have a fine intuition, which enables them to distinguish honest and devoted Communists from those who arouse the disgust of people earning their bread by the sweat of their brow, enjoying no privileges and having no "pull".

To purge the Party it is very important to take the suggestions of the non-Party working people into consideration. It will produce big results. It will make the Party a much stronger vanguard of the class than it was before; it will make it a vanguard that is more strongly bound up with the class, more capable of leading it to victory amidst a mass of difficulties and dangers.

As one of the specific objects of the Party purge, I would point to the combing out of ex-Mensheviks. In my opinion, of the Mensheviks who joined the Party after the beginning of 1918, not more than a hundredth part should be allowed to remain; and even then, every one of those who are allowed to remain must be tested over and over again. Why? Because, as a trend, the Mensheviks have displayed in 1918-21 the two qualities that characterise them: first, the ability skilfully to adapt, to "attach" themselves to the prevailing trend among the workers; and second, the ability even more skilfully to serve the whiteguards heart and soul, to serve them in action, while dissociating themselves from them in words. Both these qualities are the logical outcome of the whole history of Menshevism. It is sufficient to recall Axelrod's proposal for a "labour congress",[16] the attitude of the Mensheviks towards the Cadets[17] (and to the monarchy) in words and action, etc., etc. The Mensheviks "attach" themselves to the Russian Communist Party not only and even not so much because they are Machiavellian (although ever since 1903 they have shown that they are past masters in the art of bourgeois diplomacy), but because they are so "adaptable" Every opportunist is distinguished for his adaptability (but not all adaptability is opportunism); and the Mensheviks, as opportunists, adapt themselves "on principle"

so to speak, to the prevailing trend among the workers and
assume a protective colouring, just as a hare's coat turns
white in winter. This characteristic of the Mensheviks must
be kept in mind and taken into account. And taking it into
account means purging the Party of approximately
ninety-nine out of every hundred Mensheviks who joined the
Russian Communist Party after 1918, i. e., when the victory
of the Bolsheviks first became probable and then certain.

The Party must be purged of rascals, of bureaucratic,
dishonest or wavering Communists, and of Mensheviks who
have repainted their "façade" but who have remained Mensheviks at heart.

September 20, 1921

Pravda No. 210, September 21, 1921
Signed: *N. Lenin*

Published according **to**
the *Pravda* text

TASKS OF THE WORKERS' AND PEASANTS' INSPECTION AND HOW THEY ARE TO BE UNDERSTOOD AND FULFILLED[18]

It is more the duty of the Workers' and Peasants' Inspection to *be able to improve* things than to merely "detect" and "expose" (that is the function of the courts with which the Workers' and Peasants' Inspection is in close contact but with which it is not to be identified).

Timely and skilful rectification—this is the prime function of the Workers' and Peasants' Inspection.

To be able to correct it is necessary, first, to make a *complete* study of the methods by which the affairs of a given office, factory, department, and so forth, are conducted; second, to *introduce* in good time the necessary practical changes and to see that they are actually put into effect.

There is much that is similar, basically similar, in the methods by which the affairs of different and diverse factories, institutions, departments, etc., are conducted. The function of the Workers' and Peasants' Inspection is to train, on the basis of practical inspection work, a group of leading, experienced and well-informed persons, who would be capable of presenting problems (for the skilful and correct *presentation* of problems in itself predetermines the success of an investigation and makes it possible to rectify mistakes); to direct investigations or inspections; to see that improvements are introduced, and so forth.

The proper organisation of accounting and reporting, for example, is a fundamental function of all departments and offices of the most diverse types. The Workers' and

Peasants' Inspection should study and make itself thoroughly familiar with this; it should be able to investigate at the shortest notice (by sending a man to a given office for half an hour or an hour) whether a system of accounting exists and, if so, whether it is properly organised, what defects there are in the system, how these defects may be eliminated, etc.

The Workers' and Peasants' Inspection should study, analyse and summarise the methods of accounting, the penalties for inefficiency, the methods of "detecting" fraud, and the methods of executive control. It should have a *list* of offices, departments and gubernias where the system of accounting is tolerably well *organised*. There will be nothing tragic if these constitute one in a hundred, or even one in a thousand, as long as *systematic*, undeviating, persistent and unflagging efforts are made to enlarge the sphere where proper methods are employed. The Workers' and Peasants' Inspection should have a chronological table showing what *progress* is being made in these efforts, the successes and reverses.

Acquaintance with the preliminary draft of the report on the work of the fuel supply organisations and on the growing crisis (fuel) in the autumn of 1921, makes me feel that *basically* the work of the Workers' and Peasants' Inspection is not organised on proper lines. This draft report contains *neither* evidence that the subject has been *studied, nor even a hint at suggestions for improvement.*

For example, a comparison is made between a three-week period in 1921 and a similar period in 1920. Bare totals are taken. It is wrong to make such a comparison, because allowances are not made for (1) the difference in the food supply (in the spring of 1921 and throughout the first half of that year *special* conditions prevailed as a consequence of the *transition* to the tax in kind), or for (2) the crop failure in 1921.

Danishevsky states that the gubernias that were unaffected by the crop failure fulfilled their three-week programme in 1921 *over one hundred per cent*; the affected gubernias fell very short of fulfilment.

There is no evidence in the report that the subject has been *studied*.

The defects in accounting employed at the Central Timber Board are, evidently, correctly pointed out in the preliminary report of the Workers' and Peasants' Inspection. Danishevsky admits it. It has been proved. The methods of accounting are faulty.

But it is exactly on this *fundamental* question that the Workers' and Peasants' Inspection cannot, in its preliminary report, *confine* itself to the "thesis" that "accounting is faulty, that there is no accounting". What have the comrades of the Workers' and Peasants' Inspection done to *improve* those methods? In the winter and spring of 1921 many prominent officials of the Workers' and Peasants' Inspection *personally* took part in a *vast number* of conferences and commissions on the fuel crisis. In the spring of 1921 (I think it was in *March* 1921) a *new* chief was appointed to the Central Timber Board. Consequently, *new methods of accounting* should have been introduced in it in *March* 1921.

Danishevsky did that; but he did it *unsatisfactorily*. His methods of accounting are faulty. He is to blame, undoubtedly.

But to find the guilty party in the person of the chief is only a very minor part of the task.

Has the Workers' and Peasants' Inspection carried out its task and done its duty? *Does it properly understand its task*? That is the main question. The reply to this must be negative.

Knowing the critical fuel situation, knowing that firewood is the most important, knowing that under the former Director of the Central Timber Board (Lomov) accounting was bad, the Workers' and Peasants' Inspection,

> in *March* 1921, should have *officially advised* them in writing: organise your accounting in *such-and-such a way*;
>
> in *April* 1921, it should have investigated how the new Director (Danishevsky) had *organised* accounting and should have

few lines to give total figures (of the amount of timber felled, in cubic sazhens[19]; the amount carted; the amount of grain, fodder, etc., received and issued);

(3) give Danishevsky legal authority to arrest any person who fails to send in reports punctually

or (if that is impossible, if it does not go through for some reason) apply to the Presidium of the All-Russia Central Executive Committee for a warrant to *arrest* any person who fails to send in reports; the Central Committee of the Russian Communist Party to issue instructions accordingly; verify fulfilment;

(4) methods of personal and direct *inspection on the spot*: Is this being practised? How? What are the difficulties?

Danishevsky says that he has appointed *travelling* inspectors all over Russia, and that these have already visited *all* the gubernias; that they have delved down to the lowest units, are tightening things up, and in many gubernias have already succeeded in tightening things up.

Is that true? Is not Danishevsky being misled by his clerks?

Very probably he is.

But what about the Workers' and Peasants' Inspection? It should go into the matter and ascertain the facts. There is not a word about this in the preliminary report. When were the travelling inspectors appointed? How many? What is their standard of efficiency? What are the results of their activities? How can matters be improved if they are not satisfactory? These are the essentials; but it is just these essentials that the inspector of the Workers' and Peasants' Inspection is silent about.

I repeat: the organisation of a system of accounting is the fundamental problem. It has not been studied by the Workers' and Peasants' Inspection, which has not fulfilled—and evidently does *not understand*—its task, which is to investigate the methods of accounting and to strive for and secure an improvement.

It must be able, through the All-Russia Central Executive Committee, through the Central Committee of the Russian Communist Party, through every possible channel, to

again officially advised th[e]
in writing: introduce the f[ol-]
lowing changes, otherwi[se]
things will not run smoothly[;]
in *May* 1921, it should have inves[-]
tigated again;

and so forth, *month after month*,
until accounting had been tolerably well organised.

In the spring of 1921, the Workers' and Peasants' Inspection should have appointed a definite inspector (a *single* person is better than a "department", although in practice it is probable that the Workers' and Peasants' Inspection has a whole "department" for auditing and inspecting matters concerning firewood and fuel in general) to keep his eye on accounting at the Central Timber Board, to *study* it and to report every month to a definite member of the Collegium, or else submit a monthly return (giving a list of gubernias in which accounting is tolerably well organised, in which there is no accounting, and so on. What measures have been taken? by the Central Committee of the Russian Communist Party? by the All-Russia Central Executive Committee? What results?).

Danishevsky is to blame for the bad organisation of accounting.

The Workers' and Peasants' Inspection, i.e., the *particular* responsible *auditor* or inspector, etc., whose name I do not know, is guilty of failing to perform his duty *as from March 1921.*

The practical, business-like, non-bureaucratic question i[s:] How can accounting at the Central Timber Board be *improved[?]*

Failing to find an answer to this (extremely importan[t] question in the preliminary report of the Workers' a[nd] Peasants' Inspection—whose *duty* it was to provide [the] answer—I am seeking for an answer myself; but I m[ay] easily go wrong, for I have not studied the subject. [My] proposals are the following, and I will gladly amend t[hem] if better ones are suggested:

(1) introduce a system of accounting (once a fortn[ight]) not by post, as hitherto, but by wire;

(2) draw up for this purpose a sort of "code" consi[sting] of seven to nine figures and letters so as to be able

"bring the matter" before the highest bodies,
Party and Soviet, and to secure an improvement in the system of accounting.

I have dealt at length with the most important (and
simplest) question, viz., the system of accounting; but
there are other important and more complicated questions,
as, for example, contract work (executive control, accounting, etc.), and so forth.

One particularly interesting question is *broached* in
the preliminary report, but only broached and not dealt
with in a business-like fashion. Namely, the author of
the preliminary report writes: "The responsible leaders
are so overwhelmed with work that they are on the verge
of exhaustion, while the technical staffs of the subordinate organisations" (organisations subordinated to the
Central Fuel Board—the Central Coal Board, the Central
Timber Board, etc.) *"are full of idle employees."*

I am sure that this is a valuable and absolutely correct
observation, and that it applies not only to the Central
Fuel Board, but to *all* or ninety-nine per cent of the offices
and departments.

That evil is to be found everywhere.

In March, when the (new) organisation was being set
up, or at the latest in April, when it had already been set
up, the Workers' and Peasants' Inspection should have
made the official proposal in writing:

improve matters in such-and-such a way.

That was not done.

How can the evil be eliminated?

I haven't the faintest idea. The Workers' and Peasants'
Inspection should know, because it is its business to study
the subject, compare different departments, make practical
proposals, see how they work out in practice, etc.

When I say "Workers' and Peasants' Inspection" I mean
primarily the author of this preliminary report; but I am
perfectly well aware that it applies not only to this author.

Several absolutely conscientious, capable and experienced officials of the Workers' and Peasants' Inspection
should be chosen, if only two or three (I am sure that that
number can be found), and instructed to draw up a rational
plan of work for inspectors, beginning at least with the

system of accounting. It is better to start with a small job and finish it.

The author of the preliminary report touches upon a host of subjects, but not one of them has been studied; they have been hastily jumbled together and the whole thing is pointless. This is simply playing at "parliamentary reports". It is of no use to us. What we need is *actual improvement*.

How inadequately the subjects have been studied can be seen, for example, from question 52 (39): make a special list of exemplary mines only. That is exactly the conclusion the commission of the Council of Labour and Defence (Smilga and Ramzin) arrived at after visiting the Donets Basin in September 1921. It is exactly the conclusion that the State Planning Commission arrived at.

Why do I know about the work of the State Planning Commission and of Smilga's commission, while the *special inspector* who sat down to draw up a report on the Central Fuel Board does not know about it?

Because the work is not properly organised.

To sum up, I make the following practical proposals:

(1) make a special feature of at least the question of properly organising accounting and pursue it to the end;

(2) appoint definite persons for this job and send me their names;

(3) send me the name of the inspector in charge of Timber Board affairs.

Lenin

September 27, 1921

First published on February 6, 1927
in *Pravda* No. 30

Published according to
the manuscript

TO THE PRESIDIUM
OF THE EIGHTH ALL-RUSSIA CONGRESS
OF ELECTRICAL ENGINEERS[20]

I regret very much that I am unable to greet your Congress in person.

I have on more than one occasion expressed my opinion on the importance of the book *A Plan for Electrification* and still more so of electrification itself. Large-scale machine industry and its extension to agriculture is the only possible economic basis for socialism, the only possible basis for a successful struggle to deliver mankind from the yoke of capital, to save mankind from the slaughter and mutilation of tens of millions of people in order to decide whether the British or German, the Japanese or American, etc., vultures are to have the advantage in dividing up the world.

The Workers' and Peasants' Soviet Republic has initiated the planned and systematic electrification of the country. However meagre and modest the beginning may be, however enormous the difficulties may be for the country which the landowners and capitalists have reduced to ruin in the course of four years of imperialist war and three years of civil war, and which the bourgeoisie of the whole world is watching, ready to pounce upon and convert into their colony, however slow, painfully slow, the progress in the electrification of our country may be, progress is nevertheless being made. With the assistance of your Congress, with the assistance of all the electrical engineers in Russia, and of a number of the best and progressive scientists in all parts of the world, by the heroic efforts of the vanguard of the workers and working peasants, we shall cope with this task, and our country will be electrified.

I greet the Eighth All-Russia Congress of Electrical Engineers and wish you every success.

> *V. Ulyanov (Lenin)*,
> Chairman of the Council of People's
> Commissars

Written on October 8, 1921

Published on October 11, 1921
in the *Bulleten VIII Vserossiiskogo
elektrotekhnicheskogo syezda* (Bulletin of the 8th All-Russia Congress
of Electrical Engineers) No. 3

Published according to
the manuscript

FOURTH ANNIVERSARY OF THE OCTOBER REVOLUTION

The fourth anniversary of October 25 (November 7) is approaching.

The farther that great day recedes from us, the more clearly we see the significance of the proletarian revolution in Russia, and the more deeply we reflect upon the practical experience of our work as a whole.

Very briefly and, of course, in very incomplete and rough outline, this significance and experience may be summed up as follows.

The direct and immediate object of the revolution in Russia was a bourgeois-democratic one, namely, to destroy the survivals of medievalism and sweep them away completely, to purge Russia of this barbarism, of this shame, and to remove this immense obstacle to all culture and progress in our country.

And we can justifiably pride ourselves on having carried out that purge with greater determination and much more rapidly, boldly and successfully, and, from the point of view of its effect on the masses, much more widely and deeply, than the great French Revolution over one hundred and twenty-five years ago.

Both the anarchists and the petty-bourgeois democrats (i.e., the Mensheviks and the Socialist-Revolutionaries, who are the Russian counterparts of that international social type) have talked and are still talking an incredible lot of nonsense about the relation between the bourgeois-democratic revolution and the socialist (*that is*, proletarian) revolution. The last four years have proved to the hilt that our interpretation of Marxism on this point, and our estimate of the experience of former revolutions were correct. We have *consummated* the bourgeois-democratic revolution as nobody had done before. We are *advancing* towards the socialist revolution consciously, firmly and unswervingly, knowing that it is not separated from the bourgeois-democratic revolution by a Chinese Wall, and knowing too that (in the last analysis) *struggle alone* will determine how far we shall advance, what part of this immense and lofty task we shall accomplish, and to what extent we shall succeed in consolidating our victories. Time will show. But we see even now that a tremendous amount—tremendous for this ruined, exhausted and backward country—has already been done towards the socialist transformation of society.

Let us, however, finish what we have to say about the bourgeois-democratic content of our revolution. Marxists must understand what that means. To explain, let us take a few striking examples.

The bourgeois-democratic content of the revolution means that the social relations (system, institutions) of the country are purged of medievalism, serfdom, feudalism.

What were the chief manifestations, survivals, remnants of serfdom in Russia up to 1917? The monarchy, the system of social estates, landed proprietorship and land tenure, the status of women, religion, and national oppression. Take any one of these Augean stables, which, incidentally, were left largely uncleansed by all the more advanced states when they accomplished *their* bourgeois-democratic revolutions one hundred and twenty-five, two hundred and fifty and more years ago (1649 in England); take any of these Augean stables, and you will see that we have cleansed them thoroughly. In a matter of *ten weeks*, from October 25 (November 7), 1917 to January 5, 1918, when the Constituent Assembly was dissolved, we accomplished a thousand times more in this respect than was accomplished by the bourgeois democrats and liberals (the Cadets) and by the petty-bourgeois democrats (the Mensheviks and the Socialist-Revolutionaries) *during the eight months* they were in power.

Those poltroons, gas-bags, vainglorious Narcissuses and petty Hamlets brandished their wooden swords—but did not even destroy the monarchy! We cleansed out all that monarchist muck as nobody had ever done before. We left not a stone, not a brick of that ancient edifice, the social-estate system (even the most advanced countries, such as Britain, France and Germany, have not completely eliminated the survivals of that system to this day!), standing. We tore out the deep-seated roots of the social-estate system, namely, the remnants of feudalism and serfdom in the system of landownership, to the last. "One may argue" (there are plenty of quill-drivers, Cadets, Mensheviks and Socialist-Revolutionaries abroad to indulge in such arguments) as to what "in the long run" will be the outcome of the agrarian reform effected by the Great October Revolution. We have no desire at the moment to waste time on such controversies, for we are deciding this, as well as the mass of accompanying controversies, by struggle. But the fact cannot be denied that the petty-bourgeois democrats "compromised" with the landowners, the custodians of the traditions of serfdom, for eight months, while we completely swept the landowners and all their traditions from Russian soil in a few weeks.

Take religion, or the denial of rights to women, or the oppression and inequality of the non-Russian nationalities. These are all problems of the bourgeois-democratic revolution. The vulgar petty-bourgeois democrats talked about them for eight months. In not a *single* one of the most advanced countries in the world have *these* questions been *completely* settled on *bourgeois-democratic* lines. In our country they have been settled completely by the legislation of the October Revolution. We have fought and are fighting religion in earnest. We have granted *all* the non-Russian nationalities *their own* republics or autonomous regions. We in Russia no longer have the base, mean and infamous denial of rights to women or inequality of the sexes, that disgusting survival of feudalism and medievalism, which is being renovated by the avaricious bourgeoisie and the dull-witted and frightened petty bourgeoisie in every other country in the world without exception.

All this goes to make up the content of the bourgeois-democratic revolution. A hundred and fifty and two hundred and fifty years ago the progressive leaders of that revolution (or of those revolutions, if we consider each national variety of the one general type) promised to rid mankind of medieval privileges, of sex inequality, of state privileges for one religion or another (or "religious *ideas*",

"the church" in general), and of national inequality. They
promised, but did not keep their promises. They could
not keep them, for they were hindered by their "respect"—
for the "sacred right of private property". Our proletarian
revolution was not afflicted with this accursed "respect"
for this thrice-accursed medievalism and for the "sacred
right of private property".

But in order to consolidate the achievements of the
bourgeois-democratic revolution for the peoples of Russia,
we were obliged to go farther; and we did go farther. We
solved the problems of the bourgeois-democratic revolution
in passing, as a "by-product" of our main and genuinely
proletarian-revolutionary, socialist activities. We have
always said that reforms are a by-product of the revolutionary class struggle. We said—and proved it by deeds—
that bourgeois-democratic reforms are a by-product of the
proletarian, i.e., of the socialist revolution. Incidentally,
the Kautskys, Hilferdings, Martovs, Chernovs, Hillquits,
Longuets, MacDonalds, Turatis and other heroes of "Two-
and-a-Half" Marxism were incapable of understanding *this*
relation between the bourgeois-democratic and the prole-
tarian-socialist revolutions. The first develops into the
second. The second, in passing, solves the problems of the
first. The second consolidates the work of the first. Struggle,
and struggle alone, decides how far the second succeeds
in outgrowing the first.

The Soviet system is one of the most vivid proofs, or
manifestations, of how the one revolution develops into
the other. The Soviet system provides the maximum of
democracy for the workers and peasants; at the same time,
it marks a break with *bourgeois* democracy and the rise of
a *new*, epoch-making *type* of democracy, namely, proletarian democracy, or the dictatorship of the proletariat.

Let the curs and swine of the moribund bourgeoisie and
of the petty-bourgeois democrats who trail behind them heap
imprecations, abuse and derision upon our heads for our
reverses and mistakes in the work of building up *our* Soviet
system. We do not forget for a moment that we have committed and are committing numerous mistakes and are
suffering numerous reverses. How can reverses and mistakes
be avoided in a matter so new in the history of the world

as the building of an unprecedented *type* of state edifice! We shall work steadfastly to set our reverses and mistakes right and to improve our practical application of Soviet principles, which is still very, very far from being perfect. But we have a right to be and are proud that to us has fallen the good fortune to *begin* the building of a Soviet state, and thereby to *usher in* a new era in world history, the era of the rule of a *new* class, a class which is oppressed in every capitalist country, but which everywhere is marching forward towards a new life, towards victory over the bourgeoisie, towards the dictatorship of the proletariat, towards the emancipation of mankind from the yoke of capital and from imperialist wars.

The question of imperialist wars, of the international policy of finance capital which now dominates the whole world, a policy that must *inevitably* engender new imperialist wars, that must inevitably cause an extreme intensification of national oppression, pillage, brigandry and the strangulation of weak, backward and small nationalities by a handful of "advanced" powers—that question has been the keystone of all policy in all the countries of the globe since 1914. It is a question of life and death for millions upon millions of people. It is a question of whether 20,000,000 people (as compared with the 10,000,000 who were killed in the war of 1914-18 and in the supplementary "minor" wars that are still going on) are to be slaughtered in the next imperialist war, which the bourgeoisie are preparing, and which is growing out of capitalism before our very eyes. It is a question of whether in that future war, which is inevitable (if capitalism continues to exist), 60,000,000 people are to be maimed (compared with the 30,000,000 maimed in 1914-18). In this question, too, our October Revolution marked the beginning of a new era in world history. The lackeys of the bourgeoisie and its yes-men—the Socialist-Revolutionaries and the Mensheviks, and the petty-bourgeois, allegedly "socialist", democrats all over the world—derided our slogan "convert the imperialist war into a civil war". But that slogan proved to be the *truth*—it was the only truth, unpleasant, blunt, naked and brutal, but nevertheless the *truth*, as against the host of most refined jingoist and pacifist lies. Those lies are being dispelled. The Brest peace has been exposed. And with every passing day the significance and consequences of a peace that is even worse than the Brest peace— the peace of Versailles—are being more relentlessly exposed. And the millions who are thinking about the causes of the recent war and of the approaching future war are more and more clearly realising the grim and inexorable truth that it is impossible to escape imperialist war, and imperialist peace (if the old orthography were still in use, I would have written the word *mir* in two ways, to give it both its meanings)* which inevitably engenders imperialist war, that it is impossible to escape that inferno, *except by a Bolshevik struggle and a Bolshevik revolution.*

Let the bourgeoisie and the pacifists, the generals and the petty bourgeoisie, the capitalists and the philistines, the pious Christians and the knights of the Second and the Two-and-a-Half Internationals vent their fury against that revolution. No torrents of abuse, calumnies and lies can enable them to conceal the historic fact that for the first time in hundreds and thousands of years the slaves have replied to a war between slave-owners by openly proclaiming the slogan: "Convert this war between slave-owners for the division of their loot into a war of the slaves of all nations against the slave-owners of all nations."

For the first time in hundreds and thousands of years that slogan has grown from a vague and helpless waiting into a clear and definite political programme, into an effective struggle waged by millions of oppressed people under the leadership of the proletariat; it has grown into the first victory of the proletariat, the first victory in the struggle to abolish war and to unite the workers of all countries against the united bourgeoisie of different nations, against the bourgeoisie that makes peace and war at the expense of the slaves of capital, the wage-workers, the peasants, the working people.

This first victory is *not yet the final victory*, and it was achieved by our October Revolution at the price of incredible difficulties and hardships, at the price of unprecedented suffering, accompanied by a series of serious reverses

---

* In Russian, the word *mir* has two meanings (*world* and *peace*) and had two different spellings in the old orthography.—*Tr.*

and mistakes on our part. How could a single backward people be expected to frustrate the imperialist wars of the most powerful and most developed countries of the world without sustaining reverses and without committing mistakes! We are not afraid to admit our mistakes and shall examine them dispassionately in order to learn how to correct them. But the fact remains that for the first time in hundreds and thousands of years the promise "to reply" to war between the slave-owners by a revolution of the slaves directed *against* all the slave-owners *has been completely fulfilled*—and is being fulfilled despite all difficulties.

We have made the start. When, at what date and time, and the proletarians of which nation will complete this process is not important. The important thing is that the ice has been broken; the road is open, the way has been shown.

Gentlemen, capitalists of all countries, keep up your hypocritical pretence of "defending the fatherland"—the Japanese fatherland against the American, the American against the Japanese, the French against the British, and so forth! Gentlemen, knights of the Second and Two-and-a-Half Internationals, pacifist petty bourgeoisie and philistines of the entire world, go on "evading" the question of how to combat imperialist wars by issuing new "Basle Manifestos" (on the model of the Basle Manifesto of 1912[21]). *The first Bolshevik revolution* has wrested *the first hundred million people* of this earth from the clutches of imperialist war and the imperialist world. Subsequent revolutions will deliver the rest of mankind from such wars and from such a world.

Our last, but most important and most difficult task, the one we have done least about, is economic development, the laying of economic foundations for the new, socialist edifice on the site of the demolished feudal edifice and the semi-demolished capitalist edifice. It is in this most important and most difficult task that we have sustained the greatest number of reverses and have made most mistakes. How could anyone expect that a task so new to the world could be begun without reverses and without mistakes! But we have begun it. We shall continue it. At this very moment we are, by our New Economic Policy, correct-

ing a number of our mistakes. We are learning how to
continue erecting the socialist edifice in a small-peasant
country without committing such mistakes.

The difficulties are immense. But we are accustomed
to grappling with immense difficulties. Not for nothing do
our enemies call us "stone-hard" and exponents of a "firm-
line policy". But we have also learned, at least to some
extent, another art that is essential in revolution, namely,
flexibility, the ability to effect swift and sudden changes
of tactics if changes in objective conditions demand them,
and to choose another path for the achievement of our goal
if the former path proves to be inexpedient or impossible
at the given moment.

Borne along on the crest of the wave of enthusiasm,
rousing first the political enthusiasm and then the military
enthusiasm of the people, we expected to accomplish economic tasks just as great as the political and military
tasks we had accomplished by relying directly on this
enthusiasm. We expected—or perhaps it would be truer
to say that we presumed without having given it adequate
consideration—to be able to organise the state production
and the state distribution of products on communist lines
in a small-peasant country directly as ordered by the proletarian state. Experience has proved that we were wrong.
It appears that a number of transitional stages were necessary—state capitalism and socialism—in order to *prepare*—
to prepare by many years of effort—for the transition to
communism. Not directly relying on enthusiasm, but aided
by the enthusiasm engendered by the great revolution, and
on the basis of personal interest, personal incentive and
business principles, we must first set to work in this small-
peasant country to build solid gangways to socialism by
way of state capitalism. Otherwise we shall never get to
communism, we shall never bring scores of millions of
people to communism. That is what experience, the objective course of the development of the revolution, has
taught us.

And we, who during these three or four years have learned
a little to make abrupt changes of front (when abrupt
changes of front are needed), have begun zealously, attentively and sedulously (although still not zealously,

attentively and sedulously enough) to learn to make a new change of front, namely, the New Economic Policy. The proletarian state must become a cautious, assiduous and shrewd "businessman", a punctilious *wholesale merchant*— otherwise it will never succeed in putting this small-peasant country economically on its feet. Under existing conditions, living as we are side by side with the capitalist (for the time being capitalist) West, there is no other way of progressing to communism. A wholesale merchant seems to be an economic type as remote from communism as heaven from earth. But that is one of the contradictions which, in actual life, lead from a small-peasant economy via state capitalism to socialism. Personal incentive will step up production; we must increase production first and foremost and at all costs. Wholesale trade economically unites millions of small peasants: it gives them a personal incentive, links them up and leads them to the next step, namely, to various forms of association and alliance in the process of production itself. We have already started the necessary changes in our economic policy and already have some successes to our credit; true, they are small and partial, but nonetheless they are successes. In this new field of "tuition" we are already finishing our preparatory class. By persistent and assiduous study, by making practical experience the test of every step we take, by not fearing to alter over and over again what we have already begun, by correcting our mistakes and most carefully analysing their significance, we shall pass to the higher classes. We shall go through the whole "course", although the present state of world economics and world politics has made that course much longer and much more difficult than we would have liked. No matter at what cost, no matter how severe the hardships of the transition period may be—despite disaster, famine and ruin—we shall not flinch; we shall triumphantly carry our cause to its goal.

October 14, 1921

Pravda No. 234,
October 18, 1921
Signed: *N. Lenin*

Published according to
the manuscript

THE NEW ECONOMIC POLICY AND THE TASKS OF THE POLITICAL EDUCATION DEPARTMENTS

REPORT TO THE SECOND ALL-RUSSIA CONGRESS OF POLITICAL EDUCATION DEPARTMENTS OCTOBER 17, 1921[22]

Comrades, I intend to devote this report, or rather talk, to the New Economic Policy, and to the tasks of the Political Education Departments arising out of this policy, as I understand them. I think it would be quite wrong to limit reports on questions that do not come within the scope of a given congress to bare information about what is going on generally in the Party or in the Soviet Republic.

ABRUPT CHANGE OF POLICY OF THE SOVIET GOVERNMENT AND THE R.C.P.

While I do not in the least deny the value of such information and the usefulness of conferences on all questions, I nevertheless find that the main defect in the proceedings of most of our congresses is that they are not directly and immediately connected with the practical problems before them. These are the defects that I should like to speak about both in connection with and in respect of the New Economic Policy.

I shall speak about the New Economic Policy briefly and in general terms. Comrades, the overwhelming majority of you are Communists, and although some of you are very young, you have worked magnificently to carry out our general policy in the first years of our revolution. Having done a large part of this work you cannot help seeing the abrupt change made by our Soviet government and our

Communist Party in adopting the economic policy which we call "new", new, that is, in respect of our previous economic policy.

In substance, however, this new policy contains more elements of the old than our previous economic policy did.

Why? Because our previous economic policy, if we cannot say counted on (in the situation then prevailing we did little counting in general), then to a certain degree assumed—we may say uncalculatingly assumed—that there would be a direct transition from the old Russian economy to state production and distribution on communist lines.

If we recall the economic literature that we ourselves issued in the past, if we recall what Communists wrote before and very soon after we took power in Russia—for example, in the beginning of 1918, when the first political assault upon old Russia ended in a smashing victory, when the Soviet Republic was created, when Russia emerged from the imperialist war, mutilated, it is true, but not so mutilated as she would have been had she continued to "defend the fatherland" as she was advised to do by the imperialists, the Mensheviks and Socialist-Revolutionaries—if we recall all this we shall understand that in the initial period, when we had only just completed the first stage in the work of building up the Soviet government and had only just emerged from the imperialist war, what we said about our tasks in the field of economic development was much more cautious and circumspect than our actions in the latter half of 1918 and throughout 1919 and 1920.

THE 1918 DECISION OF THE ALL-RUSSIA CENTRAL EXECUTIVE COMMITTEE ON THE ROLE OF THE PEASANTRY

Even if all of you were not yet active workers in the Party and the Soviets at that time, you have at all events been able to make, and of course have made, yourselves familiar with decisions such as that adopted by the All-Russia Central Executive Committee at the end of April 1918.[23] That decision pointed to the necessity to take peasant farming into consideration, and it was based on a report which made allowance for the role of state capitalism in building socialism in a peasant country; a report which emphasised the importance of personal, individual, one-man responsibility; which emphasised the significance of that factor in the administration of the country as distinct from the political tasks of organising state power and from military tasks.

OUR MISTAKE

At the beginning of 1918 we expected a period in which peaceful construction would be possible. When the Brest peace was signed it seemed that danger had subsided for a time and that it would be possible to start peaceful construction. But we were mistaken, because in 1918 a real military danger overtook us in the shape of the Czechoslovak mutiny and the outbreak of civil war, which dragged on until 1920. Partly owing to the war problems that overwhelmed us and partly owing to the desperate position in which the Republic found itself when the imperialist war ended—owing to these circumstances, and a number of others, we made the mistake of deciding to go over directly to communist production and distribution. We thought that under the surplus-food appropriation system the peasants would provide us with the required quantity of grain, which we could distribute among the factories and thus achieve communist production and distribution.

I cannot say that we pictured this plan as definitely and as clearly as that; but we acted approximately on those lines. That, unfortunately, is a fact. I say unfortunately, because brief experience convinced us that that line was wrong, that it ran counter to what we had previously written about the transition from capitalism to socialism, namely, that it would be impossible to bypass the period of socialist accounting and control in approaching even the lower stage of communism. Ever since 1917, when the problem of taking power arose and the Bolsheviks explained it to the whole people, our theoretical literature has been definitely stressing the necessity for a prolonged, complex transition through socialist accounting and control from capitalist society (and the less developed it is the longer the transition will take) to even one of the approaches to communist society.

A STRATEGICAL RETREAT

At that time, when in the heat of the Civil War we had to take the necessary steps in economic organisation, it seemed to have been forgotten. In substance, our New Economic Policy signifies that, having sustained severe defeat on this point, we have started a strategical retreat. We said in effect: "Before we are completely routed, let us retreat and reorganise everything, but on a firmer basis." If Communists deliberately examine the question of the New Economic Policy there cannot be the slightest doubt in their minds that we have sustained a very severe defeat on the economic front. In the circumstances it is inevitable, of course, for some people to become very despondent, almost panic-stricken, and because of the retreat, these people will begin to give way to panic. That is inevitable. When the Red Army retreated, was its flight from the enemy not the prelude to its victory? Every retreat on every front, however, caused some people to give way to panic for a time. But on each occasion—on the Kolchak front, on the Denikin front, on the Yudenich front, on the Polish front and on the Wrangel front—once we had been badly battered (and sometimes more than once) we proved the truth of the proverb: "A man who has been beaten is worth two who haven't." After being beaten we began to advance slowly, systematically and cautiously.

Of course, tasks on the economic front are much more difficult than tasks on the war front, although there is a general similarity between the two elementary outlines of strategy. In attempting to go over straight to communism we, in the spring of 1921, sustained a more serious defeat on the economic front than any defeat inflicted upon us by Kolchak, Denikin or Pilsudski. This defeat was much more serious, significant and dangerous. It was expressed in the isolation of the higher administrators of our economic policy from the lower and their failure to produce that development of the productive forces which the Programme of our Party regards as vital and urgent.

The surplus-food appropriation system in the rural districts—this direct communist approach to the problem of urban development—hindered the growth of the productive forces and proved to be the main cause of the profound economic and political crisis that we experienced in the spring of 1921. That was why we had to take a step which from the point of view of our line, of our policy, cannot be called anything else than a very severe defeat and retreat. Moreover, it cannot be said that this retreat is—like retreats of the Red Army—a completely orderly retreat to previously prepared positions. True, the positions for our present retreat were prepared beforehand. That can be proved by comparing the decisions adopted by our Party in the spring of 1921 with the one adopted in April 1918, which I have mentioned. The positions were prepared beforehand; but the retreat to these positions took place (and is still taking place in many parts of the country) in disorder, and even in extreme disorder.

PURPORT OF THE NEW ECONOMIC POLICY

It is here that the task of the Political Education Departments to combat this comes to the forefront. The main problem in the light of the New Economic Policy is to take advantage of the situation that has arisen as speedily as possible.

The New Economic Policy means substituting a tax for the requisitioning of food; it means reverting to capitalism to a considerable extent—to what extent we do not know. Concessions to foreign capitalists (true, only very few have been accepted, especially when compared with the number we have offered) and leasing enterprises to private capitalists definitely mean restoring capitalism, and this is part and parcel of the New Economic Policy; for the abolition of the surplus-food appropriation system means allowing the peasants to trade freely in their surplus agricultural produce, in whatever is left over after the tax is collected—and the tax takes only a small share of that produce. The peasants constitute a huge section of our population and of our entire economy, and that is why capitalism must grow out of this soil of free trading.

That is the very ABC of economics as taught by the rudiments of that science, and in Russia taught, furthermore, by the profiteer, the creature who needs no economic or political science to teach us economics with. From the point of view of strategy the root question is: who will take advantage of the new situation first? The whole question is—whom will the peasantry follow? The proletariat, which wants to build socialist society? Or the capitalist, who says, "Let us turn back; it is safer that way; we don't know anything about this socialism they have invented"?

WHO WILL WIN, THE CAPITALIST OR SOVIET POWER?

The issue in the present war is—who will win, who will first take advantage of the situation: the capitalist, whom we are allowing to come in by the door, and even by several doors (and by many doors we are not aware of, and which open without us, and in spite of us), or proletarian state power? What has the latter to rely on economically? On the one hand, the improved position of the people. In this connection we must remember the peasants. It is absolutely incontrovertible and obvious to all that in spite of the awful disaster of the famine—and leaving that disaster out of the reckoning for the moment—the improvement that has taken place in the position of the people has been due to the change in our economic policy.

On the other hand, if capitalism gains by it, industrial production will grow, and the proletariat will grow too. The capitalists will gain from our policy and will create an industrial proletariat, which in our country, owing to the war and to the desperate poverty and ruin, has become declassed, i.e., dislodged from its class groove, and has ceased to exist as a proletariat. The proletariat is the class which is engaged in the production of material values in large-scale capitalist industry. Since large-scale capitalist industry has been destroyed, since the factories are at a standstill, the proletariat has disappeared. It has sometimes figured in statistics, but it has not been held together economically.

The restoration of capitalism would mean the restoration of a proletarian class engaged in the production of socially useful material values in big factories employing machinery, and not in profiteering, not in making cigarette-lighters for sale, and in other "work" which is not very useful, but which is inevitable when our industry is in a state of ruin.

The whole question is who will take the lead. We must face this issue squarely—who will come out on top? Either the capitalists succeed in organising first—in which case they will drive out the Communists and that will be the end of it. Or the proletarian state power, with the support of the peasantry, will prove capable of keeping a proper rein on those gentlemen, the capitalists, so as to direct capitalism along state channels and to create a capitalism that will be subordinate to the state and serve the state. The question must be put soberly. All this ideology, all these arguments about political liberties that we hear so much of, especially among Russian émigrés, in Russia No. 2, where scores of daily newspapers published by all the political parties extol these liberties in every key and every manner—all these are mere talk, mere phrase-mongering We must learn to ignore this phrase-mongering.

THE FIGHT WILL BE EVEN FIERCER

During the past four years we have fought many hard battles and we have learnt that it is one thing to fight hard battles and another to talk about them—something onlookers particularly indulge in. We must learn to ignore all this ideology, all this chatter, and see the substance of things. And the substance is that the fight will be even more desperate and fiercer than the fight we waged against Kolchak and Denikin. That fighting was war, something we were familiar with. There have been wars for hundreds, for thousands of years. In the art of human slaughter much progress has been made.

True, nearly every landowner had at his headquarters Socialist-Revolutionaries and Mensheviks, who talked loudly about government by the people, the Constituent Assembly, and about the Bolsheviks having violated all liberties.

It was, of course, much easier to solve war problems than those that confront us now; war problems could be solved by assault, attack, enthusiasm, by the sheer physical force of the hosts of workers and peasants, who saw the landowners marching against them. Now there are no avowed landowners. Some of the Wrangels, Kolchaks and Denikins have gone the way of Nicholas Romanov, and some have sought refuge abroad. The people no longer see the open enemy as they formerly saw the landowners and capitalists. The people cannot clearly picture to themselves that the enemy is the same, that he is now in our very midst, that the revolution is on the brink of the precipice which all previous revolutions reached and recoiled from—they cannot picture this because of their profound ignorance and illiteracy. It is hard to say how long it will take all sorts of extraordinary commissions to eradicate this illiteracy by extraordinary means.

How can the people know that instead of Kolchak, Wrangel and Denikin we have in our midst the enemy who has crushed all previous revolutions? If the capitalists gain the upper hand there will be a return to the old regime. That has been demonstrated by the experience of all previous revolutions. Our Party must make the masses realise that the enemy in our midst is anarchic capitalism and anarchic commodity exchange. We ourselves must see clearly that the issue in this struggle is: Who will win? Who will gain the upper hand? and we must make the broadest masses of workers and peasants see it clearly. The dictatorship of the proletariat is the sternest and fiercest struggle that the proletariat must wage against the whole world, for the whole world was against us in supporting Kolchak and Denikin.

Now the bourgeoisie of the whole world are supporting the Russian bourgeoisie, and they are still ever so much stronger than we are. That, however, does not throw us into a panic. Their military forces were stronger than ours. Nevertheless, they failed to crush us in war, although, being immeasurably superior to us in artillery and aircraft, it should have been very easy for them to do so. Perhaps they would have crushed us had any of the capitalist states that were fighting us mobilised a few army corps in time, and had they not grudged a loan of several millions in gold to Kolchak.

However, they failed because the rank-and-file British soldiers who came to Archangel, and the sailors who compelled the French fleet to leave Odessa, realised that their rulers were wrong and we were right. Now, too, we are being attacked by forces that are stronger than ours; and to win in this struggle we must rely upon our last source of strength. That last source of strength is the mass of workers and peasants, their class-consciousness and organisation.

Either organised proletarian power—and the advanced workers and a small section of the advanced peasants will understand this and succeed, in organising a popular movement around themselves—in which case we shall be victorious; or we fail to do this—in which case the enemy, being technologically stronger, will inevitably defeat us.

IS THIS THE LAST FIGHT?

The dictatorship of the proletariat is fierce war. The proletariat has been victorious in one country, but it is still weak internationally. It must unite all the workers and peasants around itself in the knowledge that the war is not over. Although in our anthem we sing: "The last fight let us face", unfortunately it is not quite true; it is not our last fight. Either you succeed in uniting the workers and peasants in this fight, or you fail to achieve victory.

Never before in history has there been a struggle like the one we are now witnesses of; but there have been wars between peasants and landowners more than once in history, ever since the earliest times of slavery. Such wars have occurred more than once; but there has never been a war waged by a government against the bourgeoisie of its own country and against the united bourgeoisie of all countries.

The issue of the struggle depends upon whether we

succeed in organising the small peasants on the basis of the development of their productive forces with proletarian state assistance for this development, or whether the capitalists gain control over them. The same issue has arisen in scores of revolutions in the past; but the world has never witnessed a struggle like the one we are waging now. The people have had no way of acquiring experience in wars of this kind. We ourselves must create this experience and we can rely only on the class-consciousness of the workers and peasants. That is the keynote and the enormous difficulty of this task.

WE MUST NOT COUNT
ON GOING STRAIGHT TO COMMUNISM

We must not count on going straight to communism. We must build on the basis of peasants' personal incentive. We are told that the personal incentive of the peasants means restoring private property. But we have never interfered with personally owned articles of consumption and implements of production as far as the peasants are concerned. We have abolished private ownership of land. Peasants farmed land that they did not own—rented land, for instance. That system exists in very many countries. There is nothing impossible about it from the standpoint of economics. The difficulty lies in creating personal incentive. We must also give every specialist an incentive to develop our industry.

Have we been able to do that? No, we have not! We thought that production and distribution would go on at communist bidding in a country with a declassed proletariat. We must change that now, or we shall be unable to make the proletariat understand this process of transition. No such problems have ever arisen in history before. We tried to solve this problem straight out, by a frontal attack, as it were, but we suffered defeat. Such mistakes occur in every war, and they are not even regarded as mistakes. Since the frontal attack failed, we shall make a flanking movement and also use the method of siege and undermining.

THE PRINCIPLE OF PERSONAL INCENTIVE
AND RESPONSIBILITY

We say that every important branch of the economy must be built up on the principle of personal incentive. There must be collective discussion, but individual responsibility. At every step we suffer from our inability to apply this principle. The New Economic Policy demands this line of demarcation to be drawn with absolute sharpness and distinction. When the people found themselves under new economic conditions they immediately began to discuss what would come of it, and how things should be reorganised. We could not have started anything without this general discussion because for decades and centuries the people had been prohibited from discussing anything, and the revolution could not develop without a period in which people everywhere hold meetings to argue about all questions.

This has created much confusion. This is what happened—this was inevitable, but it must be said that it was not dangerous. If we learn in good time to separate what is appropriate for meetings from what is appropriate for administration we shall succeed in raising the position of the Soviet Republic to its proper level. Unfortunately, we have not yet learnt to do this, and most congresses are far from business-like.

In the number of our congresses we excel all other countries in the world. Not a single democratic republic holds as many congresses as we do; nor could they permit it.

We must remember that ours is a country that has suffered great loss and impoverishment, and that we must teach it to hold meetings in such a way as not to confuse, as I have said, what is appropriate for meetings with what is appropriate for administration. Hold meetings, but govern without the slightest hesitation; govern with a firmer hand than the capitalist governed before you. If you do not, you will not vanquish him. You must remember that government must be much stricter and much firmer than it was before.

After many months of meetings, the discipline of the Red Army was not inferior to the discipline of the old army. Strict, stern measures were adopted, including capital punishment, measures that even the former government did not apply. Philistines wrote and howled, "The Bolsheviks have introduced capital punishment." Our reply is, "Yes, we have introduced it, and have done so deliberately."

We must say: either those who wanted to crush us—and who we think ought to be destroyed—must perish, in which case our Soviet Republic will live, or the capitalists will live, and in that case the Republic will perish. In an impoverished country either those who cannot stand the pace will perish, or the workers' and peasants' republic will perish. There is not and cannot be any choice or any room for sentiment. Sentiment is no less a crime than cowardice in wartime. Whoever now departs from order and discipline is permitting the enemy to penetrate our midst.

That is why I say that the New Economic Policy also has its educational aspect. You here are discussing methods of education. You must go as far as saying that we have no room for the half-educated. When there is communism, the methods of education will be milder. Now, however, I say, education must be harsh, otherwise we shall perish.

SHALL WE BE ABLE TO WORK FOR OUR OWN BENEFIT?

We had deserters from the army, and also from the labour front. We must say that in the past you worked for the benefit of the capitalists, of the exploiters, and of course you did not do your best. But now you are working for yourselves, for the workers' and peasants' state. Remember that the question at issue is whether we shall be able to work for ourselves, for if we cannot, I repeat, our Republic will perish. And we say, as we said in the army, that either those who want to cause our destruction must perish, or we must adopt the sternest disciplinary measures and thereby save our country—and our Republic will live.

That is what our line must be, that is why (among other things) we need the New Economic Policy.

Get down to business, all of you! You will have capitalists beside you, including foreign capitalists, concessionaires and leaseholders. They will squeeze profits out of you amounting to hundreds per cent; they will enrich themselves, operating alongside of you. Let them. Meanwhile you will learn from them the business of running the economy, and only when you do that will you be able to build up a communist republic. Since we must necessarily learn quickly, any slackness in this respect is a serious crime. And we must undergo this training, this severe, stern and sometimes even cruel training, because we have no other way out.

You must remember that our Soviet land is impoverished after many years of trial and suffering, and has no socialist France or socialist England as neighbours which could help us with their highly developed technology and their highly developed industry. Bear that in mind! We must remember that at present all their highly developed technology and their highly developed industry belong to the capitalists, who are fighting us.

We must remember that we must either strain every nerve in everyday effort, or we shall inevitably go under.

Owing to the present circumstances the whole world is developing faster than we are. While developing, the capitalist world is directing all its forces against us. That is how the matter stands! That is why we must devote special attention to this struggle.

Owing to our cultural backwardness we cannot crush capitalism by a frontal attack. Had we been on a different cultural level we could have approached the problem more directly; perhaps other countries will do it in this way when their turn comes to build their communist republics. But we cannot do it in the direct way.

The state must learn to trade in such a way that industry satisfies the needs of the peasantry, so that the peasantry may satisfy their needs by means of trade. We must see to it that everyone who works devotes himself to strengthening the workers' and peasants' state. Only then shall we be able to create large-scale industry.

The masses must become conscious of this, and not only conscious of it, but put it into practice. This, I say, suggests what the functions of the Central Political Education Department should be. After every deep-going political

revolution the people require a great deal of time to assimilate the change. And it is a question of whether the
people have assimilated the lessons they received. To my
deep regret, the answer to this question must be in the
negative. Had they assimilated the lessons we should
have started creating large-scale industry much more
quickly and much earlier.

After we had solved the problem of the greatest political
revolution in history, other problems confronted us, cultural problems, which may be called "minor affairs".
This political revolution must be assimilated; we must
help the masses of the people to understand it. We must
see to it that the political revolution remains something
more than a mere declaration.

OBSOLETE METHODS

At one time we needed declarations, statements, manifestos and decrees. We have had enough of them. At one
time we needed them to show the people how and what
we wanted to build, what new and hitherto unseen things
we were striving for. But can we go on showing the people
what we want to build? No. Even an ordinary labourer
will begin to sneer at us and say: "What use is it to keep
on showing us what you want to build? Show us that you
can build. If you can't build, we're not with you, and
you can go to hell!" And he will be right.

Gone is the time when it was necessary to draw political
pictures of great tasks; today these tasks must be carried
out in practice. Today we are confronted with cultural
tasks, those of assimilating that political experience,
which can and must be put into practice. Either we lay
an economic foundation for the political gains of the Soviet
state, or we shall lose them all. This foundation has not
yet been laid—that is what we must get down to.

The task of raising the cultural level is one of the most
urgent confronting us. And that is the job the Political
Education Departments must do, if they are capable of
serving the cause of "political education", which is the
title they have adopted for themselves. It is easy to adopt

a title; but how about acting up to it? Let us hope that after this Congress we shall have precise information about this. A Commission for the Abolition of Illiteracy was set up on July 19, 1920. Before coming to this Congress I purposely read the decree establishing that commission. It says: All-Russia Commission for the Abolition of Illiteracy.... More than that—Extraordinary Commission for the Abolition of Illiteracy. Let us hope that after this Congress we shall receive information about what has been done in this field, and in how many gubernias, and that the report will be concrete. But the very need to set up an Extraordinary Commission for the Abolition of Illiteracy shows that we are (what is the mildest term I can use for it?), well, something like semi-savages because in a country that was not semi-savage it would be considered a disgrace to have to set up an Extraordinary Commission for the Abolition of Illiteracy. In such countries illiteracy is abolished in schools. There they have tolerably good schools where people are taught. What are they taught? First of all they are taught to read and write. If we have not yet solved this elementary problem it is ridiculous to talk about a New Economic Policy.

THE GREATEST MIRACLE OF ALL

What talk can there be of a new policy? God grant that we manage to stick to the old policy if we have to resort to extraordinary measures to abolish illiteracy. That is obvious. But it is still more obvious that in the military and other fields we performed miracles. The greatest miracle of all, in my opinion, would be if the Commission for the Abolition of Illiteracy were completely abolished, and if no proposals, such as I have heard here, were made for separating it from the People's Commissariat of Education. If that is true, and if you give it some thought, you will agree with me that an extraordinary commission should be set up to abolish certain bad proposals.

More than that—it is not enough to abolish illiteracy, it is necessary to build up Soviet economy, and for that literacy alone will not carry us very far. We must raise culture to a much higher level. A man must make use of his ability to read and write; he must have something to read, he must have newspapers and propaganda pamphlets, which should be properly distributed and reach the people and not get lost in transit, as they do now, so that no more than half of them are read, and the rest are used in offices for some purpose or other. Perhaps not even one-fourth reach the people. We must learn to make full use of the scanty resources we do possess.

That is why we must, in connection with the New Economic Policy, ceaselessly propagate the idea that political education calls for raising the level of culture at all costs. The ability to read and write must be made to serve the purpose of raising the cultural level; the peasants must be able to use the ability to read and write for the improvement of their farms and their state.

Soviet laws are very good laws, because they give everyone an opportunity to combat bureaucracy and red tape, an opportunity the workers and peasants in any capitalist state do not have. But does anybody take advantage of this? Hardly anybody! Not only the peasants, but an enormous percentage of the Communists do not know how to utilise Soviet laws to combat red tape and bureaucracy, or such a truly Russian phenomenon as bribery. What hinders the fight against this? Our laws? Our propaganda? On the contrary! We have any number of laws! Why then have we achieved no success in this struggle? Because it cannot be waged by propaganda alone. It can be done if the masses of the people help. No less than half our Communists are incapable of fighting, to say nothing of those who are a hindrance in the fight. True, ninety-nine per cent of you are Communists, and you know that we are carrying out an operation on these latter Communists. The operation is being carried out by the Commission for Purging the Party, and we have hopes of removing a hundred thousand or so from our Party. Some say two hundred thousand, and I much prefer that figure.

I hope very much that we shall expel a hundred thousand to two hundred thousand Communists who have attached themselves to the Party and who are not only incapable of fighting red tape and bribery, but are even a hindrance in this fight.

TASKS OF POLITICAL EDUCATIONALISTS

If we purge the Party of a couple of hundred thousand it will be useful, but that is only a tiny fraction of what we must do. The Political Education Departments must adapt all their activities to this purpose. Illiteracy must be combated; but literacy alone is likewise not enough. We also need the culture which teaches us to fight red tape and bribery. It is an ulcer which no military victories and no political reforms can heal. By the very nature of things, it cannot be healed by military victories and political reforms, but only by raising the cultural level. And that is the task that devolves upon the Political Education Departments.

Political educationalists must not understand their job as that of functionaries, as often seems to be the case when people discuss whether representatives of Gubernia Political Education Departments should or should not be appointed to gubernia economic conferences.[24] Excuse me for saying so, but I do not think you should be appointed to any office; you should do your job as ordinary citizens. When you are appointed to some office you become bureaucrats; but if you deal with the people, and if you enlighten them politically, experience will show you that there will be no bribery among a politically enlightened people. At present bribery surrounds us on all sides. You will be asked what must be done to abolish bribery, to prevent so-and-so on the Executive Committee from taking bribes. You will be asked to teach people how to put a stop to it. And if a political educationalist replies that it does not come within the functions of his department, or that pamphlets have been published and proclamations made on the subject, the people will say that he is a bad Party member. True, this does not come within the functions of your department, we have the Workers' and Peasants' Inspection for that; but are you not members of the Party? You have adopted the title of political educationalists. When you were about to adopt that title you were warned not to choose such a pretentious one, to choose something more modest. But you wanted the title of political educationalists, and that title implies a great deal. You did not take the title of general educationalists, but of political educationalists. You may be told, "It is a good thing that you are teaching the people to read and write and to carry on economic campaigns; that is all very well, but it is not political education, because political education is the sum total of everything."

We are carrying on propaganda against barbarism and against ulcers like bribery, and I hope you are doing the same, but political education is much more than this propaganda—it means practical results, it means teaching the people how to achieve these results, and setting an example to others, not as members of an Executive Committee, but as ordinary citizens who, being politically better educated, are able not only to hurl imprecations at red tape—that is very widely practised among us—but to show how this evil can really be overcome. This is a very difficult art, which cannot be practised until the general level of culture is raised, until the mass of workers and peasants is more cultured than now. It is to this function that I should like most of all to draw the attention of the Central Political Education Department.

I should now like to sum up all that I have said and to suggest practical solutions for the problems that confront the Gubernia Political Education Departments.

THE THREE CHIEF ENEMIES

In my opinion, three chief enemies now confront one, irrespective of one's departmental functions; these tasks confront the political educationalist, if he is a Communist—and most of the political educationalists are. The three chief enemies that confront him are the following: the first is communist conceit; the second—illiteracy, and the third—bribery.

THE FIRST ENEMY—COMMUNIST CONCEIT

A member of the Communist Party, who has not yet been combed out, and who imagines he can solve all his problems by issuing communist decrees, is guilty of communist conceit. Because he is still a member of the ruling party and is employed in some government office, he imagines this entitles him to talk about the results of political education. Nothing of the sort! That is only communist conceit. The point is to learn to impart political knowledge; but that we have not yet learnt; we have not yet learnt how to approach the subject properly.

THE SECOND ENEMY—ILLITERACY

As regards the second enemy, illiteracy, I can say that so long as there is such a thing as illiteracy in our country it is too much to talk about political education. This is not a political problem; it is a condition without which it is useless talking about politics. An illiterate person stands outside politics, he must first learn his ABC. Without that there can be no politics; without that there are rumours, gossip, fairy-tales and prejudices, but not politics.

THE THIRD ENEMY—BRIBERY

Lastly, if such a thing as bribery is possible it is no use talking about politics. Here we have not even an approach to politics; here it is impossible to pursue politics, because all measures are left hanging in the air and produce absolutely no results. A law applied in conditions which permit of widespread bribery can only make things worse. Under such conditions no politics whatever can be pursued; the fundamental condition for engaging in politics is lacking. To be able to outline our political tasks to the people, to be able to say to the masses what things we must strive for (and this is what we should be doing!), we must understand that a higher cultural level of the masses is what is required. This higher level we must achieve, otherwise it will be impossible really to solve our problems.

DIFFERENCE BETWEEN MILITARY AND CULTURAL PROBLEMS

A cultural problem cannot be solved as quickly as political and military problems. It must be understood that conditions for further progress are no longer what they were. In a period of acute crisis it is possible to achieve a political victory within a few weeks. It is possible to obtain victory in war in a few months. But it is impossible to achieve a cultural victory in such a short time. By its very nature it requires a longer period; and we must adapt ourselves to this longer period, plan our work accordingly, and display the maximum of perseverance, persistence and method. Without these qualities it is impossible even to start on the work of political education. And the only criterion of the results of political education is the improvement achieved in industry and agriculture. We must not only abolish illiteracy and the bribery which persists on the soil of illiteracy, but we must get the people really to accept our propaganda, our guidance and our pamphlets, so that the result may be an improvement in the national economy.

Those are the functions of the Political Education Departments in connection with the New Economic Policy, and I hope this Congress will help us to achieve greater success in this field.

Published in the *Vtoroi Vserossiisky syezd politprosvetov. Bulleten syezda* (Bulletin of the Second All-Russia Congress of Political Education Departments) No. 2, October 19, 1921

Published according to the *Bulleten* proofs corrected by Lenin

SEVENTH MOSCOW GUBERNIA CONFERENCE
OF THE RUSSIAN COMMUNIST PARTY [25]

OCTOBER 29-31, 1921

Published in *Pravda*
Nos. 248 and 249,
November 3 and 4, 1921

Published according to
the *Pravda* text

1

REPORT ON THE NEW ECONOMIC POLICY
OCTOBER 29

Comrades, in reporting on the New Economic Policy, I must start with the reservation that I understand this subject differently from what many of you here, perhaps, expect; or rather, that I can deal with only one small part of this subject. Naturally, on this question interest centres mainly on the explanation and assessment of the recent laws and decisions of the Soviet government on the New Economic Policy. The larger the number of these decisions and the more urgent the need for their formulation, regulation and summation, the more legitimate the interest in such a subject, and as far as I can judge from my observations in the Council of People's Commissars, this need is now felt very, very acutely. No less legitimate is the desire to learn the facts and figures already available on the results of the New Economic Policy. The number of confirmed and tested facts is still very small, of course, but nonetheless such facts are available. Undoubtedly, to become familiar with the New Economic Policy it is absolutely necessary to keep up to date on these facts and to try to summarise them. But I cannot undertake to deal with either of these subjects, and if you are interested in them I am sure you will be able to find reporters on them. What interests me is another subject, namely, the tactics, or, if one may so express it, the revolutionary strategy we have adopted in connection with our change of policy; the extent, on the one hand, to which that policy corresponds to our general conception of our tasks, and, on the other hand, the extent to which the Party knows and appreciates the necessity for the New Economic Policy. This is the special question to which I should like to devote my talk exclusively.

What interests me first of all is this. In appraising our New Economic Policy, in what sense can we regard our former economic policy as a mistake? Would it be correct to say that it was a mistake? And lastly, if it was a mistake, is it useful and necessary to admit it?

I think this question is important for an assessment of the extent to which agreement prevails in our Party on the most fundamental issues of our present economic policy.

Should the Party's attention be now concentrated exclusively on certain definite aspects of this economic policy, or should it be devoted, from time to time, at least, to appraising the general conditions of this policy, and to the question of whether Party political consciousness, Party interest and Party attention conform to these general conditions? I think the position today is that our New Economic Policy is not yet sufficiently clear to large numbers of our Party members; and unless the mistake of the previous economic policy is clearly understood we cannot successfully accomplish our task of laying the foundations and of finally determining the direction of our New Economic Policy.

To explain my views and to indicate in what sense we can, and in my opinion should, say that our previous economic policy was mistaken, I would like to take for the purpose of analogy an episode from the Russo-Japanese War, which, I think, will enable us to obtain a clearer picture of the relationship between the various systems and political methods adopted in a revolution of the kind that is taking place in our country. The episode I have in mind is the capture of Port Arthur by the Japanese General Nogi. The main thing that interests me in this episode is that the capture of Port Arthur was accomplished in two entirely different stages. The first stage was that of furious assaults; which ended in failure and cost the celebrated Japanese commander extraordinarily heavy losses. The second stage was the extremely arduous, extremely difficult and slow method of siege, according to all the rules of the art. Eventually, it was by this method that the problem of capturing the fortress was solved. When we examine these facts we naturally ask in what way was the Japanese general's first mode of operation against the fortress of Port Arthur mistaken? Were the direct assaults on the fortress a mistake? And if they were, under what circumstances should the Japanese army have admitted that it was mistaken so as to achieve its object; and to what extent should it have admitted that the assaults were mistaken?

At first sight, of course, the answer to this question would seem to be a simple one. If a series of assaults on Port Arthur proved to be ineffective—and that was the case—if the losses sustained by the assailants were extremely heavy —and that, too, was undeniably the case—it is evident that the tactics of immediate and direct assault upon the fortress of Port Arthur were mistaken, and this requires no further proof. On the other hand, however, it is easy to understand that in solving a problem in which there are very many unknown factors, it is difficult without the necessary practical experience to determine with absolute certainty the mode of operation to be adopted against the enemy fortress, or even to make a fair approximation of it. It was impossible to determine this without ascertaining in practice the strength of the fortress, the strength of its fortifications, the state of its garrison, etc. Without this it was impossible for even the best of commanders, such as General Nogi undoubtedly was, to decide what tactics to adopt to capture the fortress. On the other hand, the successful conclusion of the war called for the speediest possible solution of the problem. Furthermore, it was highly probable that even very heavy losses, if they were inevitable in the process of capturing the fortress by direct assault, would have been more than compensated for by the result; for it would have released the Japanese army for operations in other theatres of war, and would have achieved one of the major objects of the war before the enemy (the Russian army) could have dispatched large forces to this distant theatre of war, improved their training and perhaps gained immense superiority

If we examine the course of the military operations as a whole and the conditions under which the Japanese army operated, we must come to the conclusion that these assaults on Port Arthur were not only a display of supreme heroism on the part of the army which proved capable of enduring such huge losses, but that they were the only possible tactics that could have been adopted under the conditions then prevailing, i.e., at the opening of hostilities. Hence, these tactics were necessary and useful; for without a test of strength by the practical attempt to carry the fortress by assault, without testing the enemy's power of resistance, there would have been no grounds for adopting the more prolonged and arduous method of struggle, which, by the very fact that it was prolonged, harboured a number of other dangers. Taking the operations as a whole, we cannot but regard the first stage, consisting of direct assaults and attacks, as having been a necessary and useful stage, because, I repeat, without this experience the Japanese army could not have learnt sufficiently the concrete conditions of the struggle. What was the position of this army when the period of fighting against the enemy fortress by means of direct assault had drawn to a close? Thousands upon thousands of men had fallen, and thousands more would fall, but the fortress would not be taken in this way—such was the position when some, or the majority, began to realise that the tactics of direct assault had to be abandoned and siege tactics adopted. Since the previous tactics had proved mistaken, they had to be abandoned, and all that was connected with them had to be regarded as a hindrance to the operations and dropped. Direct assaults had to cease; siege tactics had to be adopted; the disposition of the troops had to be changed, stores and munitions redistributed, and, of course, certain methods and operations had to be changed. What had been done before had to be resolutely, definitely and clearly regarded as a mistake in order to remove all obstacles to the development of the new strategy and tactics, to the development of operations which were now to be conducted on entirely new lines. As we know, the new strategy and tactics ended in complete victory, although it took much longer to achieve than was anticipated.

I think this analogy can serve to illustrate the position in which our revolution finds itself in solving its socialist problems of economic development. Two periods stand out very distinctly in this connection. The first, the period from approximately the beginning of 1918 to the spring of 1921; and the other, the period from the spring of 1921 to the present.

If you recall the declarations, official and unofficial, which our Party made in late 1917 and early 1918, you will see that even at that time we were aware that the revolution, the struggle, might proceed either by a relatively short road, or by a very long and difficult road. But in estimating the prospects of development we in most cases —I can scarcely recall an exception—started out with the assumption—perhaps not always openly expressed but always tacitly taken for granted—that we would be able to proceed straight away with socialist construction. I have purposely read over again all that was written, for example, in March and April 1918 about the tasks of our revolution in the sphere of socialist construction,[26] and I am convinced that that was really the assumption we made.

This was the period when we accomplished the essential, and from the political point of view necessarily the preliminary, task of seizing power, setting up the Soviet state system in place of the former bourgeois parliamentary system, and then the task of getting out of the imperialist war. And this withdrawal from the war was, as you know, accompanied by extremely heavy losses, by the signing of the unbelievably humiliating Treaty of Brest, which imposed almost impossible terms upon us. After the conclusion of that peace we had a period—from March to the summer of 1918—in which war problems appeared to have been solved. Subsequent events showed that this was not the case. In March 1918, after the problem of the imperialist war was solved, we were just approaching the beginning of the Civil War, which in the summer of 1918 was brought closer and closer by the Czechoslovak mutiny. At that time—March or April 1918—in discussing our tasks, we began to consider the prospect of passing from methods of gradual transition to such modes of operation as a struggle mainly for the expropriation of the expropriators, and this, in the main, characterised the first months of the revolution—the end of 1917 and the beginning of 1918. Even at that time we were obliged to say that our organisation of accounting and control lagged considerably behind our work and activities in connection with the expropriation of the expropriators. That meant we had expropriated more than we could take account of, control, manage, etc., and thus the question was raised of transferring our activities from the task of expropriating, of smashing the power of the exploiters and expropriators, to that of organising accounting and control, to the, so to speak, prosaic tasks of actual economic development. Even at that time we had to retreat on a number of points. For example, in March and April 1918, the question was raised of remunerating specialists at rates that conformed, not to socialist, but to bourgeois relationships, i.e., at rates that corresponded, not to the difficulty or arduousness of the work performed, but to bourgeois customs and to the conditions of bourgeois society. Such exceptionally high—in the bourgeois manner—remuneration for specialists did not originally enter into the plans of the Soviet government, and even ran counter to a number of decrees issued at the end of 1917. But at the beginning of 1918 our Party gave direct instructions to the effect that we must step back a bit on this point and agree to a "compromise" (I employ the term then in use). On April 29, 1918, the All-Russia Central Executive Committee adopted a decision to the effect that it was necessary to make this change in the general system of payment.[27]

We regarded the organisational, economic work, which we put in the forefront at that time, from a single angle. We assumed that we could proceed straight to socialism without a preliminary period in which the old economy would be adapted to socialist economy. We assumed that by introducing state production and state distribution we had established an economic system of production and distribution that differed from the previous one. We assumed that the two systems—state production and distribution and private commodity production and distribution—would compete with each other, and meanwhile we would build up state production and distribution, and step by step win them away from the hostile system. We said that our task now was not so much to expropriate the expropriators as to introduce accounting and control, increase the productivity of labour and tighten up discipline. We said this in March and April 1918; but we did not ask ourselves in what relation our economy would stand to the market, to trade. When in the spring of 1918, for example, in our polemics with a number of comrades, who were opposed to concluding the Brest peace, we raised the question of state capitalism, we did not argue that we were going back to state capitalism, but that our position would be alleviated and the solution of our socialist problems facilitated if state capitalism became the predominant economic system in Russia. I want to draw your particular attention to this, because I think it is necessary to bear it in mind in order to understand the present change in our economic policy and how this change should be interpreted.

I shall give you an example which may illustrate more concretely and vividly the conditions under which our struggle has evolved. In Moscow recently I saw a copy of the privately owned publication *Listok Obyavleni*.[28] After three years of our old economic policy this *Listok Obyavleni* seemed to me to be something very unusual, very new and strange. Looking at it from the point of view of the general methods of our economic policy, however, there was nothing queer about it. Taking this slight but rather typical example you must remember how the struggle was developing, and what were its aims and methods in our revolution in general. One of the first decrees at the end of 1917 was that which established a state monopoly of advertising. What did that decree imply? It implied that the proletariat, which had won political power, assumed that there would be a more gradual transition to the new social and economic relations—not the abolition of the private press, but the establishment of a certain amount of state control that would direct it into the channels of state capitalism. The decree which established a state monopoly of advertising thereby assumed that privately owned newspapers would continue to exist as a general rule, that an economic policy requiring private advertisements would continue, and that private property would remain—that a number of private establishments which needed advertising and advertisements would continue to exist. That is what the decree on the state monopoly of private advertising meant, and it could have meant nothing else. There was

something analogous to this in the decrees on banking, but
I shall not go into that, for it would only complicate my
example.

What was the fate of the decree establishing a state
monopoly of private advertising issued in the first weeks of
the Soviet government? It was soon swept away. When we
now recall the course of the struggle and the conditions
under which it has proceeded since then, it is amusing to
think how naïve we were to talk then, at the close of 1917,
about introducing a state monopoly of private advertising.
What sort of private advertising could there have been in a
period of desperate struggle? The enemy, i.e., the capitalist world, retaliated to that Soviet government decree by
continuing the struggle and by stepping it up to the
limit. The decree assumed that the Soviet government,
the proletarian dictatorship, was so firmly established
that no other system of economy was possible; that the
necessity to submit to it would be so obvious to the mass
of private entrepreneurs and individual owners that they
would accept battle where we, as the state power, chose. We
said in effect: "We will allow your private publications
to continue; private enterprises will remain; the freedom
to advertise, which is necessary for the service of these
private enterprises, will remain, except that the state will
impose a tax on advertisements; advertising will be concentrated in the hands of the state. The private advertising
system, as such, will not be abolished; on the contrary,
you will enjoy those benefits which always accrue from
the proper concentration of publicity." What actually
happened, however, was that we had to wage the struggle on
totally different terrain. The enemy, i.e., the capitalist
class, retaliated to this decree of the state power by completely repudiating that state power. Advertising ceased
to be the issue, for all the remnants of what was bourgeois
and capitalist in our system had already concentrated their
forces on the struggle against the very foundations of state
power. We, who had said to the capitalists, "Submit to
state regulation, submit to state power, and instead of
the complete abolition of the conditions that correspond
to the old interests, habits and views of the population,
changes will be gradually made by state regulation"—we

found our very existence in jeopardy. The capitalist class had adopted the tactics of forcing us into a desperate and relentless struggle, and that compelled us to destroy the old relations to a far larger extent than we had at first intended.

Nothing came of the decree establishing state monopoly of private advertising; it remained a dead letter, while actual events, i.e., the resistance of the capitalist class, compelled our state to shift the struggle to an altogether different plane; not to the petty, ridiculously petty, issues we were naïve enough to dabble in at the end of 1917, but to the issue of "To be or not to be?"—to smash the sabotage of the former salaried class; to repel the white-guard army, which was receiving assistance from the bourgeoisie of the whole world.

I think that this episode with the decree on advertising provides useful guidance on the fundamental question of whether the old tactics were right or wrong. Of course, when we appraise events in the light of subsequent historical development, we cannot but regard our decree as naïve and, to a certain extent, mistaken. Nevertheless, it did contain something that was right, in that the state power—the proletariat—made an attempt to pass, as gradually as possible, breaking up as little of the old as possible, to the new social relations while adapting itself, as much as possible, one may say, to the conditions then prevailing. But the enemy, i.e., the bourgeois class, went to all ends to provoke us into an extremely desperate struggle. Was this strategically correct from the enemy's point of view? Of course it was; for how could the bourgeoisie be expected to submit to an absolutely new, hitherto unprecedented proletarian power without first testing its strength by means of a direct assault? The bourgeoisie said to us, in effect, "Excuse us, gentlemen, we shall not talk to you about advertisements, but about whether we can find in our midst another Wrangel, Kolchak or Denikin, and whether they will obtain the aid of the international bourgeoisie in deciding, not whether you are going to have a State Bank or not, but an entirely different issue." Quite a lot was written about the State Bank at the end of 1917 but as in the case with advertisements it all remained largely a dead letter.

At that time the bourgeoisie retaliated with a strategy that was quite correct from its point of view. What it said was, "First of all we shall fight over the fundamental issue of whether you are really the state power or only think you are; and this question will not be decided by decrees, of course, but by war, by force; and in all probability this war will be waged not only by us, the capitalists who have been expelled from Russia, but by all those who want the capitalist system. And if it turns out that the rest of the world is sufficiently interested, we Russian capitalists will receive the assistance of the international bourgeoisie." From the standpoint of its own interests, the bourgeoisie acted quite rightly. If it had had even a crumb of hope of settling the fundamental issue by the most effective means—war—it could not and should not have agreed to the partial concessions the Soviet government offered it while contemplating a more gradual transition to the new system. "We don't want your transition, we don't want your new system," was the reply of the bourgeoisie.

That is why events developed in the way they did. On the one hand, we had the victory of the proletarian state accompanied by a struggle of extraordinary magnitude amidst unprecedented popular enthusiasm, which character-ised the whole period of 1917 and 1918. On the other hand, the Soviet government attempted to introduce an economic policy that was originally calculated to bring about a num-ber of gradual changes, to bring about a more cautious transi-tion to the new system. This policy was expressed, among other things, by the little example I have just given you. In retaliation, the enemy camp proclaimed its determination to wage a relentless struggle to decide whether Soviet power could, as a state, maintain its position in the international system of economic relations. That issue could be decided only by war, which, being civil war, was very fierce. The sterner the struggle became, the less chance there was of a cautious transition. As I have said, in the logic of the strug-gle the bourgeoisie was right from its own point of view. But what could we say? We said to the capitalists, "You will not frighten us, gentlemen. In addition to the thrashing we gave you and your Constituent Assembly in the polit-ical field, we shall give you a thrashing in this field too."

We could not act otherwise. Any other way would have meant the complete surrender of our positions.

If you recall the conditions under which our struggle developed you will understand what this seemingly wrong and fortuitous change meant; why—relying upon the general enthusiasm and on ensured political power—we were so easily able to disperse the Constituent Assembly; why we at the same time had to try a number of measures that meant the gradual and cautious introduction of economic reforms; and why, finally, the logic of the struggle and the resistance of the bourgeoisie compelled us to resort to the most extreme, most desperate and relentless civil war, which devastated Russia for three years.

By the spring of 1921 it became evident that we had suffered defeat in our attempt to introduce the socialist principles of production and distribution by "direct assault", i.e., in the shortest, quickest and most direct way. The political situation in the spring of 1921 revealed to us that on a number of economic issues a retreat to the position of state capitalism, the substitution of "siege" tactics for "direct assault", was inevitable.

If this transition calls forth complaints, lamentations, despondency and indignation among some people, we must say that defeat is not as dangerous as the fear to admit it, fear to draw all the logical conclusions from it. A military struggle is much simpler than the struggle between socialism and capitalism; and we defeated Kolchak and Co. because we were not afraid to admit our defeats, we were not afraid to learn the lessons that these defeats taught us and to do over and over again what had been left unfinished or done badly.

We must act in the same way in the much more complicated and difficult field of struggle between socialist and capitalist economy. Don't be afraid to admit defeat. Learn from defeat. Do over again more thoroughly, more carefully, and more systematically what you have done badly. If any of us were to say that admission of defeat—like the surrender of positions—must cause despondency and relaxation of effort in the struggle, we would reply that such revolutionaries are not worth a damn.

I hope that, except in isolated cases, nobody will be able to say that about the Bolsheviks, who have been steeled

by the experience of three years of civil war. Our strength
lay and will lie in our ability to evaluate the severest
defeats in the most dispassionate manner and to learn from
them what must be changed in our activities. That is why
we must speak plainly. This is interesting and important
not only from the point of view of correct theory, but also
from the practical point of view. We cannot learn to solve
our problems by new methods today if yesterday's experience has not opened our eyes to the incorrectness of the
old methods.

The New Economic Policy was adopted because, in the
spring of 1921, after our experience of direct socialist construction carried on under unprecedentedly difficult conditions, under the conditions of civil war, in which the
bourgeoisie compelled us to resort to extremely hard forms
of struggle, it became perfectly clear that we could not
proceed with our direct socialist construction and that in a
number of economic spheres we must retreat to state capitalism. We could not continue with the tactics of direct
assault, but had to undertake the very difficult, arduous and
unpleasant task of a long siege accompanied by a number of
retreats. This is necessary to pave the way for the solution
of the economic problem, i.e., that of the economic transition to socialist principles.

I cannot today quote figures, data, or facts to show the
results of this policy of reverting to state capitalism. I
shall give only one small example. You know that one of
our principal industrial centres is the Donets Basin. You
know that there we have some of the largest of the former
capitalist enterprises, which are in no way inferior to the
capitalist enterprises in Western Europe. You know also
that our first task there was to restore the big industrial
enterprises; it was easier for us to start the restoration
of the Donets industry because we had a relatively small
number of workers there. But what do we see there now,
after the change of policy last spring? We see the very
opposite, viz., that the development of production is
particularly successful in the small mines which we have
leased to peasants. We see the development of state capitalist relations. The peasant mines are working well and
are delivering to the state, by way of rent, about thirty

per cent of their coal output. The development of production in the Donets Basin shows a considerable general improvement over last summer's catastrophic position; and this is largely due to the improvement of production in small mines, to their being exploited along the lines of state capitalism. I cannot here go into all the data on the question, but this example should clearly illustrate to you some of the practical results that have been achieved by the change of policy. A revival of economic life—and that is what we must have at all costs—and increased productivity—which we must also have at all costs—are what we are beginning to obtain as a result of the partial reversion to the system of state capitalism. Our ability, the extent to which we shall be able to apply this policy correctly in the future, will determine to what extent we shall continue to get good results.

I shall now go back and develop my main idea. Is our transition to the New Economic Policy in the spring, our retreat to the ways, means and methods of state capitalism, sufficient to enable us to stop the retreat and prepare for the offensive? No, it is not yet sufficient. And for this reason. To go back to the analogy I gave at the beginning (of direct assault and siege in war), we have not yet completed the redeployment of our forces, the redistribution of our stores and munitions, etc.; in short, we are not yet fully prepared for the new operations, which must be conducted on different lines in conformity with the new strategy and tactics. Since we are now passing to state capitalism, the question arises of whether we should try to prevent the methods which were suitable for the previous economic policy from hindering us now. It goes without saying, and our experience has proved it, that that is what we must secure. In the spring we said that we would not be afraid to revert to state capitalism, and that our task was to organise commodity exchange. A number of decrees and decisions, a vast number of newspaper articles, all our propaganda and all the laws passed since the spring of 1921 have been directed to the purpose of stimulating commodity exchange. What was implied by that term? What plan of development, if one may so express it, did it imply? It implied a more or less socialist exchange throughout the country of the products of industry for the products of agriculture, and by means of that commodity exchange the restoration of large-scale industry as the sole basis of socialist organisation. But what happened? You are all now well aware of it from your own practical experience, and it is also evident from our press, that this system of commodity exchange has broken down; it has broken down in the sense that it has assumed the form of buying and selling. And we must now admit this if we do not want to bury our heads in the sand, if we do not want to be like those who do not know when they are beaten, if we are not afraid of looking danger straight in the face. We must admit that we have not retreated far enough, that we must make a further retreat, a further retreat from state capitalism to the creation of state-regulated buying and selling, to the money system. Nothing came of commodity exchange; the private market proved too strong for us; and instead of the exchange of commodities we got ordinary buying and selling, trade.

Take the trouble to adapt yourselves to this; otherwise, you will be overwhelmed by the wave of spontaneous buying and selling, by the money system!

That is why we find ourselves in the position of having to retreat still further, in order, eventually, to go over to the offensive. That is why we must all admit now that the methods of our previous economic policy were wrong. We must admit this in order to be able to understand the nature of the present position, the specific features of the transition that now lies ahead of us. We are not now confronted with urgent problems of foreign affairs; nor are we confronted with urgent war problems. We are now confronted mainly with economic problems, and we must bear in mind that the next stage cannot be a transition straight to socialist construction.

We have not been able to set our (economic) affairs in order in the course of three years. The devastation, impoverishment and cultural backwardness of our country were so great that it proved impossible to solve the problem in so short a time. But, taken as a whole, the assault left its mark and was useful.

Now we find ourselves in the position of having to retreat even a little further, not only to state capitalism, but to the state regulation of trade and the money system. Only in this way, a longer way than we expected, can we restore economic life. Unless we re-establish a regular system of economic relations, restore small-peasant farming, and restore and further expand large-scale industry by our own efforts, we shall fail to extricate ourselves from the crisis. We have no other way out; and yet there are many in our ranks who still do not understand clearly enough that this economic policy is necessary. When we say, for example, that the task that confronts us is to make the state a wholesale merchant, or that it must learn to carry on wholesale trade, that our task is commercial, some people think it is very queer and even very terrible. They say: "If Communists have gone to the length of saying that the immediate task is to engage in trade, in ordinary, common, vulgar, paltry trade, what can remain of communism? Is this not enough to make anyone throw up his hands in despair and say, 'All is lost'?" If we look round, I think we shall find people who express sentiments of this kind, and such sentiments are very dangerous, because if they become widespread they would give many people a distorted view of things and prevent them from appraising our immediate tasks soberly. If we concealed from ourselves, from the working class, from the masses the fact that we retreated in the economic field in the spring of 1921, and that we are continuing the retreat now, in the autumn and winter of 1921-22, we would be certifying to our own lack of political consciousness; it would prove that we lacked the courage to face the present situation. It would be impossible to work and fight under such conditions.

If an army which found that it was unable to capture a fortress by direct assault declared that it refused to leave the old positions and occupy new ones, refused to adopt new methods of achieving its object, one would say that that army had learnt to attack, but had not learnt to retreat when certain severe conditions made it necessary, and would, therefore, never win the war. There has never been a war in history that was an uninterrupted victorious advance from beginning to end—at any rate, such wars are very rare exceptions. This applies to ordinary wars—but what about wars which decide the fate of a whole class, which decide the issue of socialism or capitalism? Are there reasonable grounds for assuming that a nation which is attempting to solve this problem for the first time can immediately find the only correct and infallible method? What grounds are there for assuming that? None whatever! Experience teaches the very opposite. Of the problems we tackled, not one was solved at the first attempt, every one of them had to be taken up a second time. After suffering defeat we tried again, we did everything all over again; if we could not find an absolutely correct solution to a problem we tried to find one that was at least satisfactory. That is how we acted in the past, and that is how we must continue to act in the future. If, in view of the prospects before us, there were no unanimity in our ranks it would be a very sad sign that an extremely dangerous spirit of despondency had lodged itself in the Party. If, however, we are not afraid to speak the sad and bitter truth straight out, we shall learn, we shall unfailingly and certainly learn to overcome all our difficulties.

We must take our stand on the basis of existing capitalist relations. Will this task scare us? Shall we say that it is not communist? If so, then we have failed to understand the revolutionary struggle, we have failed to understand that the struggle is very intense and is accompanied by extremely abrupt changes, which we cannot brush aside under any circumstances.

I shall now sum up.

I shall touch upon the question that occupies many people's minds. If today, in the autumn and winter of 1921, we are making another retreat, when will the retreat stop? We often hear this question put directly, or not quite directly. This question recalls to my mind a similar question that was asked in the period of the Brest peace. When we concluded the Brest peace we were asked, "If you concede this, that and the other to German imperialism, when will the concessions stop? And what guarantee is there that they will stop? And in making these concessions, are you not making the position more dangerous?" Of course, we are making our position more dangerous; but you must not forget the fundamental laws of every war. War itself is always dangerous. There is not a moment in time of war when you are not surrounded by danger. And what is the dictatorship of the proletariat? It is war, much more cruel, much more prolonged and much more stubborn than any other war has ever been. Here danger threatens us at every step.

The position which our New Economic Policy has created —the development of small commercial enterprises, the leasing of state enterprises, etc.—entails the development of capitalist relations; and anybody, who fails to see this shows that he has lost his head entirely. It goes without saying that the consolidation of capitalist relations in itself increases the danger. But can you point to a single path in revolution, to any stage and method that would not have its dangers? The disappearance of danger would mean that the war had come to an end, and that the dictatorship of the proletariat had ceased. Of course, not a single one among us thinks that anything like that is possible at the present moment. Every step in this New Economic Policy entails a series of dangers. When we said in the spring that we would substitute the tax in kind for requisitioning, that we would pass a decree granting freedom to trade in the surplus grain left over after the tax in kind had been paid, we thereby gave capitalism freedom to develop. Failure to understand this means losing sight of the fundamental economic relations; and it means that you are depriving yourself of the opportunity to look round and act as the situation demands. Of course, the methods of struggle have changed; the dangers spring from other sources. When the question of establishing the power of the Soviets, of dissolving the Constituent Assembly was being decided, political danger threatened us. That danger proved to be insignificant. When the period of civil war set in—civil war backed by the capitalists of the whole world—the military danger, a far more formidable danger, arose. And when we changed our economic policy, the danger became still greater, because, consisting as it does of a vast number of economic, workaday trifles, which one usually becomes accustomed to and fails to notice, economics calls for special attention and effort and more peremptorily demands that we learn the proper methods of overcoming this danger. The restoration of capitalism, the development of the bourgeoisie, the development of bourgeois relations in the sphere of trade, etc.—this constitutes the danger that is peculiar to our present period of economic development, to our present gradual approach to the solution of problems that are far more difficult than previous problems have been. There must not be the slightest misunderstanding about this.

We must understand that the present concrete conditions call for the state regulation of trade and the money system, and it is precisely in this field that we must show what we are capable of. There are more contradictions in our economic situation now than there were before the New Economic Policy was adopted; there is a partial, slight improvement in the economic position of some sections of the population, of the few; there is an extreme disproportion between economic resources and the essential needs of other sections, of the majority. Contradictions have increased. And it goes without saying that in making this very sharp change we cannot escape from these contradictions at one bound.

In conclusion, I should like to emphasise the three main points of my report. First, the general question—in what respect must we admit that our Party's economic line in the period preceding the New Economic Policy was wrong? By quoting the example of what had occurred during a certain war I tried to explain the necessity of passing from assault to siege tactics, the inevitability of assault tactics at first, and the need to realise the importance of new fighting methods after the assault tactics have failed.

Next, the first lesson, the first stage which we had reached by the spring of 1921—the development of state capitalism on new lines. Here certain successes can be recorded; but there are still unprecedented contradictions. We have not yet mastered this sphere of activity.

And third, after the retreat from socialist construction to state capitalism, which we were obliged to make in the spring of 1921, we see that the regulation of trade and the money system are on the order of the day. Remote from communism as the sphere of trade may seem to be, it is here that a specific problem confronts us. Only by solving that problem can we get down to the problem of meeting economic needs that are extremely urgent; and only in that way shall we be able to restore large-scale industry—by a longer and surer way, the only way now open to us.

These are the main factors in the New Economic Policy that we must always bear in mind. In solving the problems of this policy we must clearly see the fundamental lines of development so as to be able to keep our bearings in the seeming chaos in economic relations we now observe, when, simultaneously with the break up of the old, we see the still feeble shoots of the new, and often employ methods that do not conform to the new conditions. Having set ourselves the task of increasing the productive forces and of restoring large-scale industry as the only basis for socialist society, we must operate in a way that will enable us to approach this task properly, and to solve it at all costs.

2

CLOSING SPEECH
OCTOBER 29

Comrades! Before replying to the observations submitted in writing I should like to say a few words in reply to the comrades who have spoken here. I should like to point to what I think is a misunderstanding in Comrade Larin's speech. Either I did not express myself clearly, or else he did not understand me properly; but he linked the question of regulation, which I dealt with in my speech, with the question of regulating industry. That is obviously wrong. I spoke about regulating trade and the money system and compared it with commodity exchange. To this I must add that if we want our policy, our decisions and our propaganda and agitation to be effective, and if we want to secure an improvement in our propaganda, agitation and decrees, we must not turn our backs on recent experience. Is it not true that we spoke about commodity exchange in the spring of 1921? Of course, it is; you all know it. Is it not true that commodity exchange, as a system, proved to be unsuited to the prevailing conditions, which have given rise to the money system, to buying and selling for money, instead of commodity exchange? There can be no doubt about this; the facts prove it. This answers both Comrade Stukov and Comrade Sorin, who spoke here about people imagining mistakes. Here is a striking example not of an imaginary, but of a real mistake.

The experience of our economic policy during the recent period, that commenced with the spring, has shown that in the spring of 1921 nobody challenged the New Economic Policy and that the whole Party, at congresses and conferences and in the press, had accepted it absolutely unanimously. The controversies that had raged previously did not affect the new, unanimous decision in the least. This decision was based on the assumption that by means of commodity exchange we could achieve a more direct transition to socialist construction. But at present it is clear that we must go by a roundabout way—through trade.

Comrades Stukov and Sorin complained that there was a lot of talk about mistakes and begged us to refrain from inventing them. Of course, it is a very bad thing to invent mistakes; but it is utterly wrong to brush practical problems aside, as Comrade Gonikman does. He delivered quite an oration on the theme that "historical phenomena could not assume any other shape than they have done". That is absolutely incontrovertible, and, of course, we have all learnt this from the ABC of communism, the ABC of historical materialism, and the ABC of Marxism. Here is an argument based on these lines. Was Comrade Semkov's speech a historical phenomenon, or not? I maintain that it was. The very fact that this historical phenomenon could not assume any other shape than it did proves that nobody has invented mistakes and that nobody maliciously wanted members of the Party to give way—or maliciously wanted to permit them to give way—to despondency, dismay and dejection. Comrades Stukov and Sorin were very much afraid that the admission of mistakes would be harmful in one way or another, wholly or partly, directly or indirectly, because it would spread despondency and dejection. The purpose I had in mind in giving these examples was to show that the crux of the matter is this—has the admission of mistakes any practical significance at the moment? Should anything be changed after what has happened, and had to happen? First we launched an assault; and only after that did we commence a siege. Everybody knows that; and now the application of our economic policy is being hindered by the erroneous adoption of methods that would, perhaps, be excellent under other conditions, but which are harmful today. Nearly all the comrades who spoke here entirely avoided this subject although this, and this alone, is the point at issue. My best ally here proved to be Comrade Semkov, because his speech was a vivid example of this mistake. Had Comrade Semkov not been here, or had he not spoken here today, the impression might have remained that Lenin was inventing mistakes. But Comrade Semkov very definitely said: "What's the use of talking to us about state trade! They didn't teach us to trade in prison." Comrade Semkov, it is quite true that we were not taught to trade in prison! But were we taught to fight in prison? Were we taught how to administer a state in prison? Were we ever taught the very unpleasant business of reconciling the different People's Commissariats and of co-ordinating their activities? We were not taught that anywhere. We were not taught anything in prison. At best, we studied ourselves. We studied Marxism, the history of the revolutionary movement, and so forth. In that respect, for many of us the time we spent in prison was not lost. When we are told: "They did not teach us to trade in prison", it clearly shows that those who say it have a mistaken idea of the practical objects of the Party's struggle and activities today. And this is the mistake of employing methods suitable for an "assault" when we are in the period of "siege". Comrade Semkov revealed the mistake that is being made in the ranks of the Party. This mistake must be admitted and rectified.

If we could rely on military and political enthusiasm— which undoubtedly has been a gigantic historical force and has played a great role that will affect the international working-class movement as well for many years to come; if this enthusiasm—with a certain degree of culture, and with our factories in a better condition—could help us to pass straight on to socialist construction, we would not now engage in anything so unpleasant as business calculation and the art of commerce. It would not be necessary. As things are, however, we must engage in these matters. Why? Because we are directing, and must direct, economic development. Economic development has brought us to the position where we must resort not only to such unpleasant things as leasing, but also to this unpleasant business of trading. It was to be expected that this unpleasant situation would give rise to despondency and dejection. But who is to blame for that? Is it not those who have given way to dejection and despondency? If the economic situation in which we find ourselves as a result of the sum total of conditions, economic and political, international and Russian, is such that the money system and not commodity exchange has become a fact, if it has become necessary to regulate the trade and defective money system that exist today, shall we Communists say that it has nothing to do with us? That would indeed be the most pernicious despondency, would express a mood of utter despair, and would make all further work impossible.

The situation in which we are carrying on our work has not been created by ourselves alone; it is bound up with the economic struggle and our relations with other countries. Things so turned out that last spring we had to discuss the question of leasing, and today we have to discuss the question of trade and the money system. To shirk this question by arguing "that they did not teach us to trade in prison" means to give way to inexcusable despondency, means shirking our economic task. It would be much more pleasant to capture capitalist trade by assault, and under certain circumstances (if our factories were not ruined and if we had a developed economy and culture) it would not be a mistake to launch an "assault", i.e., to pass straight on to commodity exchange. In the present circumstances, however, the mistake we make is that we refuse to understand that another method of approach is necessary and inevitable. Nobody is inventing this mistake; it is not a mistake taken from history—it is a lesson that will help us to understand what can and must be done at the present time. Can the Party successfully accomplish the task that confronts it if it approaches it on the principle that "they did not teach us to trade in prison" and that we don't want any commercial calculations? There are lots of things that we did not learn in prison, but which we had to learn after the revolution; and we learnt them very well.

I think it is our duty to learn to understand commercial relations and trade; and we shall begin to learn this, and finally master it, when we begin to talk about it without beating about the bush. We have had to retreat so far that the question of trade has become a practical question for the Party, a question of economic development. What dictates our transition to a commercial basis? Our environ-

ment, our present conditions. This transition is essential
to enable us speedily to restore large-scale industry, link
it up speedily with agriculture and organise a correct
exchange of products. In a country with a better developed
industry all this would take place much quicker; in our
country this follows a longer, circuitous road, but in the
end we shall attain our goal. And today we must be guided
by the tasks that the present and immediate future pose
before us, before our Party, which has to direct the whole
state economy. We can no longer speak of commodity
exchange today because we have lost it as a sphere of struggle.
That is an incontrovertible fact, no matter how unpleasant
it may be to us. Does that mean we must say there is nothing else for us to do? Nothing of the sort. We must learn.
We must acquire the knowledge needed for the state to
regulate commercial relations—it is a difficult task but
not an impossible one. And we shall carry it out because
we have carried out tasks that were just as new, necessary
and difficult. The co-operative trade is something difficult
but not impossible; we have to understand this thoroughly
and get down to serious work. That is what our new policy
boils down to. To date we have already put a small number
of enterprises on a commercial footing; at these enterprises
wages are paid according to the prices on the open market,
and they have gone over to gold in their settlements. But
the number of such economic units is insignificant; in most
of the others there is chaos, a serious discrepancy between
wages and living conditions; state supplies for some have
ceased and for others have been reduced. What is the way
out? The only way is to learn, adapt ourselves and resolve
these problems properly, i.e., in conformity with the conditions obtaining.

That is my reply to the comrades who have spoken about
today's talk, and now I shall reply briefly to some of the
notes submitted.

One of them reads: "You refer to Port Arthur. But don't
you see the possibility of our being Port Arthur besieged
by the international bourgeoisie?"

Yes, comrades. I have already said that war itself is
always dangerous; that we must never embark on war without
bearing in mind the possibility of defeat. If we are defeated,

then, of course, we shall find ourselves in the deplorable position of Port Arthur. But in my speech I had in mind the Port Arthur of international capitalism, which is being besieged, and other armies besides our own are taking part in this siege. In every capitalist country there is a steadily growing army that is besieging this Port Arthur of international capitalism.

A comrade asks: "What will be our tactics on the morrow of the social revolution if it breaks out next year, or the year after?" If it were possible to answer such questions it would be quite easy to make revolutions, and we would make any number of them all over the place. But such questions cannot be answered, because we cannot say what will happen in six months' time, let alone next year, or the year after. It is as useless to put such questions as to attempt to decide which of the belligerents will find itself in the deplorable position of the fortress of Port Arthur. The only thing we know is that in the long run the fortress of the international Port Arthur must inevitably be captured, because the forces that will capture it are growing in all countries. The main problem that confronts us today is how to retain the possibility of restoring large-scale industry under the extremely difficult conditions in which we now find ourselves. We must not shun commercial accounting, but must understand that only on this basis can we create tolerable conditions that will satisfy the workers as regards wages, employment, etc. Only on this commercial basis will it be possible for us to build up our economy. This is being hindered by prejudice and by reminiscences of yesterday. Unless we take this into account we shall fail to carry out the New Economic Policy properly.

Questions like the following are also asked, "Where is the last line of retreat?" I have other questions of the same type, "How far can we retreat?" I anticipated this question and said a few words about it in my report. This question reflects a mood of despondency and dejection, and is absolutely groundless. We heard the same sort of question at the time we concluded the Brest-Litovsk peace. It is wrong to put such a question, because only when we have pursued our new policy for some time shall we have material on which to base our reply to it. We shall go on retreating

until we have completed our education; until we have
made our preparations for a definite offensive. I cannot
say more than that. It is very unpleasant to retreat. But
when heavy blows are being struck, nobody stops to ask
whether it is pleasant or unpleasant: the troops retreat,
and nobody is surprised. Nothing useful will come of asking
how long we shall go on retreating. Why anticipate hopeless situations? Instead of doing that, we must get down
to definite work. We must closely examine the concrete
conditions, the concrete situation, decide what position we
can hold—a river, a hill, a bog, a railway station. Because
only when we are able to hold our ground shall we be able
to pass to the offensive. We must not give way to despondency; we must not shirk the problem by shouting propaganda slogans, which are all very well in their proper place,
but which in the present case can do nothing but harm.

THE IMPORTANCE OF GOLD NOW AND AFTER THE COMPLETE VICTORY OF SOCIALISM

The best way to celebrate the anniversary of a great revolution is to concentrate attention on its unsolved problems. It is particularly appropriate and necessary to celebrate the revolution in this way at a time when we are faced with fundamental problems that the revolution has not yet solved, and when we must master something new (from the point of view of what the revolution has accomplished up to now) for the solution of these problems.

What is new for our revolution at the present time is the need for a "reformist", gradual, cautious and roundabout approach to the solution of the fundamental problems of economic development. This "novelty" gives rise to a number of questions, perplexities and doubts in both theory and practice.

A theoretical question. How can we explain the transition from a series of extremely revolutionary actions to extremely "reformist" actions in the same field at a time when the revolution as a whole is making victorious progress? Does it not imply a "surrender of positions", an "admission of defeat", or something of that sort? Of course, our enemies—from the semi-feudal type of reactionaries to the Mensheviks or other knights of the Two-and-a-Half International—say that it does. They would not be enemies if they did not shout something of the sort on every pretext, and even without any pretext. The touching unanimity that prevails on this question among all parties, from the feudal reactionaries to the Mensheviks, is only further proof that all these parties constitute "one reactionary mass" opposed to the proletarian revolution (as Engels foresaw in his letters to Bebel of 1875 and 1884—be it said in parenthesis).[29]

But there is "perplexity", shall we say, among friends, too.

Restore large-scale industry, organise the direct exchange of its goods for the produce of small-peasant farming, and thus assist the socialisation of the latter. For the purpose of restoring large-scale industry, borrow from the peasants a certain quantity of foodstuffs and raw materials by requisitioning—this was the plan (or method, system) that we followed for more than three years, up to the spring of 1921. This was a revolutionary approach to the problem—to break up the old social-economic system completely at one stroke and to substitute a new one for it.

Since the spring of 1921, instead of this approach, plan, method, or mode of action, we have been adopting (we have not yet "adopted" but are still "adopting", and have not yet fully realised it) a totally different method, a reformist type of method: not to *break up* the old social-economic system—trade, petty production, petty proprietorship, capitalism—but to *revive* trade, petty proprietorship, capitalism, while cautiously and gradually getting the upper hand over them, or making it possible to subject them to state regulation *only to the extent* that they revive.

That is an entirely different approach to the problem.

Compared with the previous, revolutionary, approach, it is a reformist approach (revolution is a change which breaks the old order to its very foundations, and not one that cautiously, slowly and gradually remodels it, taking care to break as little as possible).

The question that arises is this. If, after trying revolutionary methods, you find they have failed and adopt reformist methods, does it not prove that you are declaring the revolution to have been a mistake in general? Does it not prove that you should not have started with the revolution but should have started with reforms and confined yourselves to them?

That is the conclusion which the Mensheviks and others like them have drawn. But this conclusion is either sophistry, a mere fraud perpetrated by case-hardened politicians, or it is the childishness of political tyros. The greatest, perhaps the only danger to the genuine revolutionary is that of exaggerated revolutionism, ignoring the limits and conditions in which revolutionary methods are appropriate and can be successfully employed. True revolutionaries have mostly come a cropper when they began to write "revolution" with a capital R, to elevate "revolution" to something almost divine, to lose their heads, to lose the ability to reflect, weigh and ascertain in the coolest and most dispassionate manner at what moment, under what circumstances and in which sphere of action you must act in a revolutionary manner, and at what moment, under what circumstances and in which sphere you must turn to reformist action. True revolutionaries will perish (not that they will be defeated from outside, but that their work will suffer internal collapse) only if they abandon their sober outlook and take it into their heads that the "great, victorious, world" revolution can and must solve all problems in a revolutionary manner under all circumstances and in all spheres of action. If they do this, their doom is certain.

Whoever gets such ideas into his head is lost because he has foolish ideas about a fundamental problem; and in a fierce war (and revolution is the fiercest sort of war) the penalty for folly is defeat.

What grounds are there for assuming that the "great, victorious, world" revolution can and must employ only revolutionary methods? There are none at all. The assumption is a pure fallacy; this can be proved by purely theoretical propositions if we stick to Marxism. The experience of our revolution also shows that it is a fallacy. From the theoretical point of view—foolish things are done in time of revolution just as at any other time, said Engels,[30] and he was right. We must try to do as few foolish things as possible, and rectify those that are done as quickly as possible, and we must, as soberly as we can, estimate which problems can be solved by revolutionary methods at any given time and which cannot. From the point of view of our practical experience the Brest peace was an example of action that was not revolutionary at all; it was reformist, and even worse, because it was a retreat, whereas, as a general rule, reformist action advances slowly, cautiously, gradually, and does not move backward. The proof that our tactics in concluding the Brest peace were correct is now so complete, so obvious to all and generally admitted, that there is no need to say any more about it.

Our revolution has completed only its bourgeois-democratic work; and we have every right to be proud of this. The proletarian or socialist part of its work may be summed up in three main points: (1) The revolutionary withdrawal from the imperialist world war; the exposure and *halting* of the slaughter organised by the two world groups of capitalist predators—for our part we have done this in full; others could have done it only if there had been a revolution in a number of advanced countries. (2) The establishment of the Soviet system, as a form of the dictatorship of the proletariat. An epoch-making change has been made. The era of bourgeois-democratic parliamentarism has come to an end. A new chapter in world history—the era of proletarian dictatorship—has been opened. The Soviet system and all forms of proletarian dictatorship will have the finishing touches put to them and be completed only by the efforts of a number of countries. There is still a great deal we have not done in this field. It would be unpardonable to lose sight of this. Again and again we shall have to improve the work, redo it, start from the beginning. Every step onward and upward that we take in developing our productive forces and our culture must be accompanied by the work of improving and altering our Soviet system—we are still low in the scale of economics and culture. Much will have to be altered, and to be "embarrassed" by this would be absurd (if not worse). (3) The creation of the economic basis of the socialist system; the main features of what is most important, most fundamental, have not yet been completed. This, however, is our soundest basis, soundest from the point of view of principle and from the practical point of view from the point of view of the R.S.F.S.R. today and from the international point of view.

Since the main features of this basis have not yet been completed we must concentrate all our attention upon it. The difficulty here lies in the form of the transition.

In April 1918, in my *Immediate Tasks of the Soviet Government*,[31] I wrote:

"It is not enough to be a revolutionary and an adherent of socialism or a Communist in general. You must be able at each particular moment to find the particular link in the chain which you must grasp with all your might in order to hold the whole chain and to prepare firmly for the transition to the next link; the order of the links, their form, the manner in which they are linked together, their difference from each other in the historical chain of events are not as simple and not as senseless as those in an ordinary chain made by a smith."

At the present time, in the sphere of activity with which we are dealing, this link is the revival of home *trade* under proper state regulation (direction). Trade is the "link" in the historical chain of events, in the transitional forms of our socialist construction in 1921-22, which we, the proletarian government, we, the ruling Communist Party, *"must grasp with all our might"*. If we "grasp" this link firmly enough *now* we shall certainly control the *whole* chain in the very near future. If we do not, we shall not control the whole chain, we shall not create the foundation for socialist social and economic relations.

Communism and trade?! It sounds strange. The two seem to be unconnected, incongruous, poles apart. But if we study it from the point of view of *economics*, we shall find that the one is no more remote from the other than communism is from small-peasant, patriarchal farming.

When we are victorious on a world scale I think we shall use gold for the purpose of building public lavatories in the streets of some of the largest cities of the world. This would be the most "just" and most educational way of utilising gold for the benefit of those generations which have not forgotten how, for the sake of gold, ten million men were killed and thirty million maimed in the "great war for freedom", the war of 1914-18, the war that was waged to decide the great question of which peace was the worst, that of Brest or that of Versailles; and how, for the sake of this same gold, they certainly intend to kill twenty million men and to maim sixty million in a war, say, in 1925, or 1928, between, say, Japan and the U.S.A., or between Britain and the U.S.A., or something like that.

But however "just", useful, or humane it would be to utilise gold for this purpose, we nevertheless say that we must work for another decade or two with the same intensity and with the same success as in the 1917-21 period, only in a much wider field, in order to reach this stage. Meanwhile, we must save the gold in the R.S.F.S.R., sell it at the highest price, buy goods with it at the lowest price. When you live among wolves, you must howl like a wolf, while as for exterminating all the wolves, as should be done in a rational human society, we shall act up to the wise Russian proverb: "Boast not before but after the battle".

Trade is the only possible economic link between the scores of millions of small farmers and large-scale industry *if... if* there is not alongside these farmers an excellently equipped large-scale machine industry with a network of power transmission lines, an industry whose technical equipment, organisational "superstructures" and other features are sufficient to enable it to supply the small farmers with the best goods in larger quantities, more quickly and more cheaply than before. On a world scale this "if" *has already been achieved*, this condition already exists. But the country, formerly one of the most backward capitalist countries, which tried alone directly and at one stroke to create, to put into use, to organise practically the *new* links between industry and agriculture, failed to achieve this task by "direct assault", and must now try to achieve it by a number of slow, gradual, and cautious "siege" operations.

The proletarian government can control trade, direct it into definite channels, keep it within certain limits. I shall give a small, a very small example. In the Donets Basin a slight, still very slight, but undoubted revival in the economy has commenced, partly due to a rise in the productivity of labour at the large state mines, and partly due to the leasing of small mines to peasants. As a result, the proletarian government is receiving a small additional quantity (a miserably small quantity compared with what is obtained in the advanced countries, but an appreciable quantity considering our poverty-stricken condition) of coal at a cost of, say, 100; and it is selling this coal to various government departments at a price of, say, 120, and to private individuals at a price of, say, 140. (I must say in parenthesis that my figures are quite arbitrary, first because I do not know the exact figures, and, secondly, I would not now make them public even if I did.) This looks as if we are *beginning*, if only in very modest dimensions, to control *exchange* between industry and agriculture, to control wholesale trade, to cope with the task of taking in hand the available, small, backward industry, or large-scale but weakened and ruined industry; of reviving trade on the *present* economic basis; of making the ordinary middle peasant (and that is the typical peasant, the peasant in the mass, the true representative of the petty-bourgeois milieu) feel the benefit of the economic revival; of taking advantage of it for the purpose of more systematically and persistently, more widely and successfully restoring large-scale industry.

We shall not surrender to "sentimental socialism", or to the old Russian, semi-aristocratic, semi-muzhik and patriarchal mood, with their supreme contempt for trade. We can use, and, since it is necessary, we *must* learn to use, all transitional economic forms for the purpose of strengthening the link between the peasantry and the proletariat, for the purpose of immediately reviving the economy of our ruined and tormented country, of improving industry, and facilitating such future, more extensive and more deep-going, measures as electrification.

Marxism alone has precisely and correctly defined the relation of reforms to revolution, although Marx was able to see this relation only from one aspect—under the conditions preceding the first to any extent permanent and lasting victory of the proletariat, if only in one country. Under those conditions, the basis of the proper relation was that reforms are a by-product of the revolutionary class struggle of the proletariat. Throughout the capitalist world this relation is the foundation of the revolutionary tactics of the proletariat—the ABC, which is being distorted and obscured by the corrupt leaders of the Second International and the half-pedantic and half-finicky knights of the Two-and-a-Half International. After the victory of the proletariat, if only in one country, something new enters into the relation between reforms and revolution. In principle, it is the same as before, but a change in form takes place, which Marx himself could not foresee, but which can be appreciated only on the basis of the philosophy and politics of Marxism. Why were we able to carry out the Brest retreat successfully? Because we had advanced so far that we had room in which to retreat. At such dizzy speed, *in a few weeks,* from October 25, 1917, to the Brest peace, we built up the Soviet state, withdrew from the imperialist war in a revolutionary manner and completed the bourgeois-democratic revolution so that *even* the great backward movement (the Brest peace) left us sufficient room in which to take advantage of the "respite" and to march forward victoriously against Kolchak, Denikin, Yudenich, Pilsudski and Wrangel.

Before the victory of the proletariat, reforms are a by-product of the revolutionary class struggle. After the victory (while still remaining a "by-product" on an international scale) they are, in addition, for the country in which victory has been achieved, a necessary and legitimate breathing space when, after the utmost exertion of effort, it becomes obvious that sufficient strength is lacking for the revolutionary accomplishment of some transition or another. Victory creates such a "reserve of strength" that it is possible to hold out even in a forced retreat, hold out both materially and morally. Holding out materially means preserving a sufficient superiority of forces to prevent the enemy from inflicting utter defeat. Holding out morally means not allowing oneself to become demoralised and disorganised, keeping a sober view of the situation, preserving vigour and firmness of spirit, even retreating a long way, but not too far, and in such a way as to stop the retreat in time and revert to the offensive.

We retreated to state capitalism, but we did not retreat too far. We are now retreating to the state regulation of trade, but we shall not retreat too far. There are visible signs that the retreat is coming to an end; there are signs that we shall be able to stop this retreat in the not too distant future. The more conscious, the more unanimous, the more free from prejudice we are in carrying out this necessary retreat, the sooner shall we be able to stop it, and the more lasting, speedy and extensive will be our subsequent victorious advance.

November 5, 1921

Pravda No. 251,
November 6-7, 1921
Signed: *N. Lenin*

Published according to
the *Pravda* text

SPEECH AT A MEETING
OF THE PROKHOROV TEXTILE MILLS WORKERS, HELD TO MARK THE FOURTH ANNIVERSARY OF THE OCTOBER REVOLUTION NOVEMBER 6, 1921[32]

BRIEF NEWSPAPER REPORT

(*The entire audience rises. Prolonged applause.*) If we glance back over the past four years we see that in no country of the world but Russia have the proletariat won complete victory over the bourgeoisie. But if we have been successful it is only because the peasants and workers knew they were fighting for their land and their rule. The war against Denikin, Wrangel and Kolchak was the first occasion in history when the working people fought successfully against their oppressors. The second cause of our victory is that the Entente could not fling sufficient numbers of loyal troops against Russia, as the soldiers of France and the sailors of Britain did not want to go and oppress their brothers.

Four years have enabled us to perform a miracle without parallel, in that a starving, weak and half-ruined country has defeated its enemies—the mighty capitalist countries.

We have won a strong position for ourselves in the world, one without parallel and totally unforeseen. What still remains is the tremendous task of setting our national economy going. All that we have achieved goes to show that we base ourselves on the most wonderful force in the world—that of the workers and peasants. This makes us confident that we shall meet our next anniversary with victory on the labour front.

Pravda No. 252,
November 9, 1921

Published according to
the *Pravda* text

SPEECH AT A MEETING
OF WORKING MEN AND WOMEN,
RED ARMY MEN AND YOUNG PEOPLE
OF KHAMOVNIKI DISTRICT, MOSCOW,
HELD TO MARK THE FOURTH ANNIVERSARY
OF THE OCTOBER REVOLUTION
NOVEMBER 7, 1921

(*The orchestra plays "The Internationale". General applause.*) Comrades, I cannot share with you reminiscences that would be as instructive and interesting as those of the comrades who were present in Moscow and personally engaged in this or that struggle. I was not in Moscow at the time, so I think I shall confine myself to a brief message of greetings.

One of the previous comrades finished his speech with an appeal for the workers themselves to work hard in trade union and Soviet bodies and to put all their energies into that work. I should like to support that appeal.

Comrades, during these four years we have experienced an unparalleled struggle. And had we been told four years ago that the foreign worker was not so near to world revolution, that we would have to wage bitter civil war for three years, nobody at that time would have believed that we would withstand it. However, even though we were attacked on all sides, we withstood the onslaught, and if we succeeded in doing so it was not because some miracle took place (for intelligent people don't believe in miracles), but because the troops that were sent against us were unreliable. Had the British not departed from Archangel and the French sailors not left Odessa, and had the foreign worker dressed in soldier's uniform and sent against us not become a sympathiser of Soviet rule, we would not be guaranteed even now against the possibility of an offensive against us. But we are not afraid of that, because we know that we have many allies in every country. And the comrade who appealed to you here to work as a team was right, and I whole-heartedly support him, because you know that famine has attacked us at our most difficult hour, and the capitalists of the whole world are trying to use this situation to drive us into bondage. But there are masses of workers who are making it possible for us to carry on the fight against them.

Take, for example, the seed help being given to the peasants. You know that the surplus-food appropriation system has been replaced by a tax in kind, and you can now see how well that tax and the seed loan are coming in.

The other day we discussed how to help the peasants of the famine-stricken areas to sow the spring-crop fields, and we found that the quantity of seeds possessed by the state is far from enough to sow even as much as was sown this year. To do that the state needs 30 million poods of grain, whereas the tax in kind will only yield us 15 million poods, so that we shall have to buy the remaining 15 million poods abroad. Lately we have seen that the British bourgeoisie are campaigning for the cancellation of the trade agreement with Soviet Russia, but the British workers are opposed to that. We know that agreements are being concluded with other countries, and difficult as it may be to purchase 15 million poods of grain, we shall be able to do so.

In all foreign countries we see industrial crises and unemployment on a huge scale. Germany, crushed by the shameless Versailles Treaty, has been forced for long out of the international arena. She has been crushed to such an extent by the Versailles peace that she cannot trade. The Allies concluded the unprecedented Versailles peace, and in spite of it are perishing themselves.

Our economic position is improving with every passing day.

What I would ask is that you respond to the previous comrade's appeal and work harder inside our country. The necessity for doing so must be fully appreciated, for we are working to improve the peasants' husbandry, and that requires far greater effort than before. We are confident that we shall be able to do this. (*Applause. The orchestra plays "The Internationale".*)

Published for the first time
from the stenographic record

SPEECH AT A WORKERS' MEETING AT THE ELEKTROSILA PLANT No. 3 (FORMERLY DYNAMO PLANT) TO MARK THE FOURTH ANNIVERSARY OF THE OCTOBER REVOLUTION NOVEMBER 7, 1921

BRIEF NEWSPAPER REPORT

Comrade Lenin cited vivid examples showing that Soviet power was day by day gaining ever greater significance in the minds of the working people and was giving them ever greater proof that it is the power of the working people themselves.

"The man with a gun—who was the terror of the working people in the past," said Comrade Lenin, "is no longer a terror for he is now a representative of the Red Army, and is their protector."

Pravda No. 254,
November 11, 1921

Published according to
the *Pravda* text

PREFACE TO THE PAMPHLET:
THE PROBLEM OF THE NEW ECONOMIC
POLICY (TWO OLD ARTICLES AND A STILL
OLDER POSTSCRIPT)[33]

In the spring of 1919 I spoke at a meeting of Petrograd workers. As usual, a verbatim report of the speech was taken, and, as usual, it was taken very badly—or perhaps the report was not so bad, but I, as usual, spoke badly. Be that as it may—reported badly or delivered badly—the speech was published, as usual.

Knowing and feeling all these "badlies" and "as usuals" only too well, I, soon after, sent the Petrograd comrades the following "postscript" to my speech (which, if I remember rightly, was published under the title of *Achievements and Difficulties of the Soviet Government*[34]):

"POSTSCRIPT

"After spending no little effort in correcting the verbatim report of my speech, I am compelled to make the following urgent request to all comrades who want to report my speeches for the press.

"My request is that they should never rely on the shorthand or any other verbatim reports of my speeches, never make any endeavour to obtain such reports, and never publish such reports of my speeches.

"Instead of publishing the verbatim reports of my speeches, let them, if necessary, publish summaries of them. I have seen such summaries of my speeches in the newspapers that were satisfactory; but I have never seen a single verbatim report of my speech that was at all satisfactory. Whether

this is due to the fact that I speak too fast, or that I do not
construct my sentences properly, or to some other reason, I
will not undertake to say; but the fact remains that I have
never seen a single satisfactory shorthand or any other verbatim report of my speech.

"A good summary of a speech is better than a bad verbatim report. That is why I request that no verbatim reports of
my speeches should ever be published. April 17, 1919.
N. Lenin."

I sent this postscript to Petrograd with the following note:
"I earnestly request the Petrograd comrades to publish
the enclosed as a *preface*, or *postscript*, to my speech, at least
in the smallest type. April 17. *Lenin.*"

The reader will note the polite, almost pleading tone in
which I begged the Petrograd comrades to publish these few
lines "at least in the smallest type". As usual, the Petrograd
comrades—headed by Comrade Zinoviev—"let me down",
to use the mildest term I can think of. As usual, the Petrograd
comrades are extremely fond of doing everything they can
to display their self-reliance and independence—even going
to the length of not granting an author's request, which is
considered an obligatory duty by all people, comrades and
citizens in all countries and in all republics, including even
Soviet republics (with the exception of independent Petrograd). When I found that the Petrograd comrades had not
fulfilled my request, I complained bitterly to Comrade
Zinoviev; but the latter, as usual, answered, "It's done now
and cannot be changed. Besides, how could we publish a
postscript in which you *discredit* your own pamphlet." Thus
... "independence" was augmented by cunning, and I was
made to feel foolish.

Recently I had other cases of badly delivered or (perhaps
I should say "and") badly recorded speeches. These were
the speeches I made at the Second All-Russia Congress of
Political Education Departments and at the Moscow
Gubernia Party Conference. Taught by bitter experience I
have now decided to act in a less "pleading" manner. Among
my papers I have found my old preface of April 17, 1919, and
am publishing it as a preface to my two articles. I am not
publishing the two speeches mentioned for the reasons I have
already stated.

Let truth prevail—better late than never. And it will prevail in many respects; in that the Petrograd comrades will be punished, even if to some slight degree, considering their offence, for their excessive "independence" and cunning; in that the reading public will at last realise most precisely, vividly and palpably how bad the verbatim reports of my speeches are; and in that those who are interested to learn my opinion about one of the most important tasks of the day in the sphere of our New Economic Policy will obtain an exact text of what I really wanted to say, and really did say.

N. Lenin

November 16, 1921

First published in 1930

Published according to proofs corrected by Lenin

TELEGRAM TO NARIMANOV,
CHAIRMAN OF THE COUNCIL
OF PEOPLE'S COMMISSARS OF AZERBAIJAN

Baku

My wish to the newly-opened Azerbaijan State Bank is that it should be a firm bulwark of the New Economic Policy in the hands of the workers and peasants of the fraternal Soviet republic. The donation of 40 millions to the famine victims on the Volga and in Kurdistan is the best proof of the preparedness to march under the banner of the Red International of working people.

Lenin,
Chairman of the Council
of People's Commissars of the R.S.F.S.R.

Written not earlier than
November 17, 1921
Published for the first time

Published according to
the manuscript signed by Lenin

A CAPABLY WRITTEN LITTLE BOOK

A Dozen Knives in the Back of the Revolution, Paris,
1921. This small volume of stories was written by the whiteguard Arkady Averchenko, whose rage rises to the pitch of
frenzy. It is interesting to note how his burning hatred brings
out the remarkably strong and also the remarkably weak
points of this extremely capably written book. When the
author takes for his stories subjects he is unfamiliar with, they
are inartistic. An example is the story showing the home
life of Lenin and Trotsky. There is much malice, but little
truth in it, my dear Citizen Averchenko! I assure you that
Lenin and Trotsky have many faults in all respects, including their home life. But to describe them skilfully one must
know what they are. This you do not know.

But most of the stories in the book deal with subjects
Arkady Averchenko is very familiar with, has experienced,
given thought to and felt. He depicts with amazing skill
the impressions and moods of the representative of the old,
rich, gorging and guzzling Russia of the landowners and capitalists. That is exactly what the revolution must look like
to the representatives of the ruling classes. Averchenko's
burning hatred makes some—in fact most—of his stories
amazingly vivid. There are some really magnificent stories,
as, for example, "Grass Trampled by Jackboots", which
deals with the psychology of children who have lived and
are living through the Civil War.

But the author shows real depth of feeling only when he
talks about food; when he relates how the rich people fed
in old Russia, how they had snacks in Petrograd—no, not
in Petrograd, in St. Petersburg—costing fourteen and a
half rubles, fifty rubles, etc. He describes all this in really

voluptuous terms. These things he knows well; these things he has experienced; here he makes no mistakes. His knowledge of the subject and his sincerity are most extraordinary.

In his last story, "Fragments of the Shattered", he describes an ex-Senator in the Crimea, in Sevastopol, who was "rich, generous and well-connected", but who is "now a day labourer at the artillery dumps, unloading and sorting shells", and an ex-director of a "vast steel plant which was considered to be the largest works in Vyborg District. Now he is a salesman at a shop which sells second-hand goods on commission, and has lately even acquired a certain amount of experience in fixing the price of ladies' second-hand robes and plush teddy-bears that people bring to be sold on commission."

The two old fogies recall the old days, the St. Petersburg sunsets, the streets, the theatres and, of course, the meals at the "Medved", "Vienna", "Maly Yaroslavets", and similar restaurants. And they interrupt their reminiscences to exclaim: "What have we done to deserve this? How did we get in anyone's way? Who did we interfere with?... Why did they treat Russia so?"...

Arkady Averchenko is not the one to understand why. The workers and peasants, however, seem to understand quite easily and need no explanations.

In my opinion some of these stories are worth reprinting. Talent should be encouraged.

Pravda No. 263,
November 22, 1921
Signed: *N. Lenin*

Published according to
the *Pravda* text

MEMO TO J. V. STALIN WITH THE DRAFT DECISION OF THE POLITICAL BUREAU OF THE C.C., R.C.P.(B.) ON THE FORMATION OF A FEDERATION OF TRANSCAUCASIAN REPUBLICS

November 28

Comrade Stalin, in the main I agree with you, but I feel that the wording should be somewhat amended.

1) While a federation of Transcaucasian republics is absolutely correct in principle, and should be implemented without fail, its immediate practical realisation must be regarded as premature, i. e., a certain period of time will be required for its discussion, propagation and adoption by lower Soviet bodies;

2) the Central Committees of Georgia, Armenia and Azerbaijan shall be instructed (through the Caucasian Bureau) to submit the federation question for broad discussion in the Party and by the *worker and peasant masses*, conduct vigorous propaganda *in favour* of a federation and secure *decisions* to that effect by the congresses of Soviets in each of these republics. Should serious opposition arise, the Political Bureau of the C.C., R.C.P. must be informed accurately and in good time.

Lenin

Written on November 28, 1921

First published, in abridged form, in 1923 in the book *Dvenadtsaty syezd R.K.P.(B.)* (Twelfth Congress of the Russian Communist Party [Bolsheviks]), April 17-25, 1923. Bulletins. Moscow, Publishing House at the All-Russia Central Executive Committee

Published in full for the first time, according to the manuscript

SPEECH AT THE FIRST MOSCOW GUBERNIA
AGRICULTURAL CONGRESS
NOVEMBER 29, 1921[35]

Comrades, permit me first of all to greet your Congress on behalf of the Council of People's Commissars. I very much regret that I am unable to deliver a comprehensive report to the Congress, as should be the case, and to stay behind to hear the reports and, in particular, the speeches that will be made here by representatives from the localities, by those who are directly engaged in farming, who are directly interested in promoting agriculture and are adle to give essential practical pointers. I shall therefore have to limit myself, in addition to conveying general greetings, to a brief statement on the exceptional importance of the work of your Congress.

You all know, comrades, that the fundamental problem, the problem that all present circumstances have made one of the cardinal problems of the home and foreign policy of our Republic, is that of promoting the economy in general and agriculture in particular. All the signs indicate that now, after the bitter years of the imperialist war and after the victorious Civil War, a deep-going change is taking place among the peasant masses, and that deep down among them there is the realisation that it is no longer possible to carry on in the old way. The principal task now confronting us is to make known to the peasant masses what has been achieved by a small number of peasants and to make available to tens of millions knowledge that under our low level of scientific farming has been inadequately disseminated among them. There are a number of signs indicating the desire to reorganise their farms and improve farming methods which the peasants feel more profoundly, widely and acutely than ever before; and we should see to it that agricultural congresses like the present one are held more frequently and that their results have a practical effect in the immediate future.

The greatest disaster that has befallen us this year is the famine in a number of gubernias and also the drought, which, evidently, may threaten us again, if not next year, then in the next few years. In this connection the key task, not only of agriculture but of the whole economy, is to secure a radical and immediate practical improvement of agriculture. That can be done only if the realisation that farming must be improved penetrates the mass of peasants engaged in farming. We shall be able to overcome and defeat the famine and secure an improvement of peasant farming only if the improvements that have been begun on a very large scale spread to all gubernias without exception. The work of a small number of specialists, a number that is insignificant compared with the masses of peasants, cannot be productive if it is not brought close to the practical tasks of agriculture. Congresses like yours must be held in all gubernias and must influence the peasant masses. The basic, I would even say political, necessity (because all political problems, inasmuch as our international position has improved, now run in a single channel) is now that of boosting farm productivity at all costs. An increase of its productivity must definitely result in an improvement in industry and in an improvement in the supplies of all necessary items to peasant farms— items of personal consumption and implements of production, machines, without which there can be no guaranteed living standard for the worker and peasant masses.

Comrades, you have heard here the report made by Comrade Osinsky on general economic policy and, as I have been told, the report of Comrade Mesyatsev on land tenure. I repeat that the practical suggestions that will be made by those directly engaged in farming, by the peasants themselves, are of the utmost value to us. The experience that you have brought with you and which will become available to the broadest masses is of extraordinary importance and value to us. Moscow Gubernia is, however, in an almost unique position because Moscow peasants can exchange

experiences with the central authorities and with farming
specialists—this exchange has been possible and easier for
them; the work and results of your Congress have an importance that goes far beyond the bounds of Moscow Gubernia.
The most formidable danger will arise if the link with science
is allowed to weaken; Moscow Gubernia peasants must,
therefore, regard their experiments and the improvements
in farming they have achieved as the first steps along that
road and bring them to the knowledge of all the peasants.
This is what I should like to draw your attention to: the
experiments and the conclusions which you will draw here
should not only enable you to make further progress on your
own farms but should be transmitted to the peasants of the
most remote gubernias.

All the questions that have been raised here: the questions of farmsteads, in short, all the questions connected
with land tenure, are important for a much broader field;
for us representatives of the centre, it is very important to
know your opinion on these questions. We plan to approach
them on the basis of practical experience. It is most important and basic for our peasant masses to realise the need to
improve peasant farming, and for you yourselves to discuss
thoroughly the practical steps that have been taken. We shall
take note of everything you say here and will take your
experience into account when we implement practical measures. I repeat, your experience must become known in the most
remote gubernias. That is what we regard as particularly
important in your work.

In conclusion let me once again convey greetings from the
Council of People's Commissars, and wish you every success
in your work. (*Applause.*)

Brief report published
in *Pravda* No. 270,
November 30, 1921

Published in full for the first
time, according to the stenographic record checked with the
newspaper text

THE THESES ON THE AGRARIAN QUESTION ADOPTED BY THE COMMUNIST PARTY OF FRANCE

Apropos of the *theses on the agrarian question* published over the signature of the Central Committee (*Le comité directeur*) of the Communist Party of France in *La Voix Paysanne* (Peasant Voice)[36] No. 95 of November 19, 1921, I may say the following:

It seems to me that the main ideas of the theses are quite correct, that they correspond to the decisions of the congresses of the Comintern, and that they are very well formulated. These ideas are: (1) that a revolution is necessary if new imperialist wars are to be averted; (2) that the pacifist and Wilson ideology has been defeated; (3) that it is absolutely necessary to draw up an agrarian "programme of transitional measures" (*un programme transitoire*) to communism, adapted to the peasants' *voluntary* transition to the socialisation of farming, that will, at the same time, ensure an *immediate* improvement in the condition of the vast majority of the rural population, the hired labourers and small peasants; (4) the immediate *confiscation*, i. e., expropriation without compensation (*sans indemnité*), both of lands lying fallow (*les terres arables en friche*) and of lands cultivated by the labour of *coloni*, tenant farmers or hired labourers (*les terres mises en valeur par les colons, fermiers ou salariés*); (5) the transfer of these lands to the whole body of workers who now cultivate them in order that these workers form "producers' co-operative societies" (*cooperatives de production*) in conformity with the provisions of the new agrarian legislation; (6) the unconditional permanent (and hereditary) tenure of their lands by the "small proprietors who cultivate their lands themselves" (*les petits propriétaires exploitant eux-mêmes*); (7) the need to ensure "continuous and increasing production" in agriculture (*"continuité et augmentation de la production"*); (8) the need for a number of measures for the systematic "communist education of the peasantry" (*"éducation communiste de la classe paysanne"*).

Being in complete agreement with these main ideas in the theses, I can only make the following few general observations about them.

1. The first part of the theses deals with the question: "war or revolution?" Here it says among other things, and quite rightly, that "the events of the last few years have killed the pacifist and Wilson ideology" (*"les événements des dernières années ont tué l'idéologie pacifiste et wilsonienne"*).

In order to dispel these pacifist illusions completely I think we should speak not only of war in general, but also of the specifically imperialist nature of the war of 1914-18, and of the war now in preparation between America and Japan with the probable participation of Great Britain and France.

There is no doubt that only the proletarian revolution can and certainly will put a stop to all war. But it would be a pacifist illusion to think that a victorious proletarian revolution in one country, say France, could put a stop to all war once and for all.

The experience of Russia has vividly dispelled this illusion. This experience has shown that only by means of a revolution were we able to extricate ourselves from the imperialist war, and that the Russian workers and peasants have gained immensely by their revolution *despite* the *Civil War* forced upon them by the capitalists of all countries. Just as reactionary wars, and imperialist wars in particular, are criminal and fatal (and among imperialist wars must be included the war France waged in 1914-18; the Treaty of Versailles has very vividly demonstrated this), so revolutionary wars are legitimate and just—i. e., wars waged against the capitalists in defence of the oppressed classes, wars against the oppressors in defence of the nations oppressed by the imperialists of a handful of countries, wars in defence of the socialist revolution against foreign invaders. The more

clearly the masses of workers and peasants of France understand this the less probable and less prolonged will be the
inevitable attempts of the French, British and other capitalists to crush the revolution of the workers and peasants
of France by means of war. In present-day Europe, after
the victory Soviet Russia has achieved over *all* the capitalist countries which supported Denikin, Kolchak, Wrangel,
Yudenich and Pilsudski—in present-day Europe, in view
of the outrageous and shameless throttling of Germany
by the Treaty of Versailles, a civil war waged by the French
capitalists against a victorious socialist revolution in France
can only be of very short duration and a thousand times less
arduous for the French workers and peasants than the Civil
War was for the Russians. Nevertheless, it is absolutely
necessary to distinguish clearly between imperialist wars—
wars for the division of capitalist loot, wars to strangle
small and weak nations—and revolutionary wars—wars of
defence against the counter-revolutionary capitalists, wars
to throw off the capitalist yoke.

In the light of the foregoing considerations I think that
instead of what is said in the theses about "war or revolution", it would be more correct to say approximately the
following.

The events of the last few years have revealed the utter
falsity and fraud of the pacifist and Wilson ideology. This
fraud must be thoroughly exposed. The war of 1914-18 was an
imperialist, predatory and reactionary war not only on
the part of Germany, but also on the part of France. This
has been most vividly demonstrated by the Treaty of Versailles, which is even more brutal and revolting than the
Treaty of Brest-Litovsk. The new war now in preparation
between America and Japan (or Great Britain), and which is
unavoidable if capitalism continues to exist, will inevitably involve capitalist France, for she is implicated in all
the imperialist crimes, atrocities and villainies of the present
imperialist era. Either another war or series of wars to
"defend" French imperialism, or a socialist revolution—
there is no other choice before the workers and peasants
of France. They will not allow themselves to be intimidated
by the tales of the counter-revolutionary capitalists about
the hardships of the Civil War which they forced upon

Soviet Russia. The workers and peasants of France proved that they were capable of waging a legitimate, just and revolutionary war against their feudal aristocracy when the latter wanted to crush the great French Revolution of the eighteenth century. They will be able to wage a similarly legitimate, just and revolutionary war against the French capitalists, when the latter become émigrés and organise foreign invasion against the French Socialist Republic. It will be easier for the French workers and peasants to crush their exploiters because the *whole* of Europe, exhausted, tormented and Balkanised by the atrocious Treaty of Versailles, will, directly or indirectly, be on their side.

2. I think that the statement in the next part of the theses that "the impending revolution in France (*cette révolution que nous devons faire*) will in a way be a premature revolution" (*sera en quelque sorte une révolution avant terme*) is wrong, as is also the following statement:

"The concentration of property proclaimed by Marxist theoreticians did not proceed according to rule in agriculture" (*La concentration de la propriété annoncée par les théoriciens du marxisme ne s'est pas produite avec régularité dans l'agriculture*).

That is wrong; and it is not the view of Marx or of Marxism, but the view of those "theoreticians" of *quasi*-"Marxism" who were responsible for the shameful breakdown of the Second International in 1914. It is the view of the pseudo-Marxists who in 1914 deserted to the side of "their" national bourgeoisie, and who were derided long ago by none other than Jules Guesde when he opposed Millerand in the press and said that the future Millerands would be on the side of "their" capitalists in the impending war for the division of the capitalist loot.

Marx did not regard concentration in agriculture as a simple and straightforward process. Proof of this will be found in Volume III of *Capital*, and in the article Engels wrote in the 1890s in opposition to the French agrarian programme[37] of that time. Marx did not consider that the proletarian revolution would be "opportune" only when the last peasant had been expropriated. Let us leave it to the Hyndmans, Renaudels, Vanderveldes and Südekums, to

Messieurs Turati and Serrati to interpret Marx's view in this way.

My advice would be to delete these statements for they are incorrect, unnecessary, and discredit the French Communists. They are not needed to prove the practically and theoretically important and correct main idea that the immediate application (*l'application immédiate*) of *integral* communism to *small-peasant farming* (by no means in France only, but in all countries where small-peasant husbandry exists) would be a *profound* error.

Instead of making these incorrect statements it would be better to explain in greater detail why the wealth the French peasants accumulated during the war cannot be lasting, why the money they accumulated during the war is depreciating, why the oppression of both the workers and the peasants of France by the big banks is increasing, what forms this increased oppression is taking, and so forth.

3. The theses go on to say that according to pre-war statistics there were in France 5,700,000 farms (*exploitations rurales*), of which 4,850,000 were small farms (up to 10 hectares) and 850,000 had over 10 hectares of land each. These figures show, state the theses, how unevenly the land is distributed in France. And they go on to say: "But these figures do not give us an exact idea (*"mais ils [ces chiffres] ne fournissent aucune précision..."*) of the ratio between the area of the lands cultivated by their owners and the lands that serve as a source of capitalist profit" (...*"sur le rapport qui existe entre l'étendue des terres travaillées par leurs propriétaires et des terres source de profit capitaliste"*).

Firstly, in France (as in every other capitalist country) the lands cultivated by their owners *also* serve as a "source of capitalist profit". Theoretically it would have been more correct, and practically more useful to have explained in the theses of the Communist Party of France the forms this profit takes rather than to have said that the concentration of property does not proceed "according to rule" (*"avec régularité"*) in agriculture.

Secondly, it is true that French farming statistics are poor, inferior to the German, U.S., Swiss and Danish, and that they do not give an *exact* idea of the *area* of land cultivated on capitalist lines. It is also true, as is stated further on in the

theses, that farms with less than 10 hectares of land sometimes employ hired labour and that peasant owners
sometimes cultivate by their own efforts "farms of 20, 30
and more hectares of land" ("des fermes de 20, 30 hectares et
au-dessus").

. Although from the French agrarian statistics one cannot
get an idea of the exact area of land cultivated on capitalist
lines, one can, nevertheless, obtain an *approximation*. I have
neither Compère-Morel's book, nor any other sources at
hand; but I remember that in the French statistics farms
with 40 and more hectares of land are given separately. It
would be very useful to quote these figures to show the small
peasants of France more strikingly what a vast amount of
land the French capitalists and landowners have grabbed
(from the workers and from them). In the agrarian theses one
can (and must, in my opinion) demonstrate more vividly
with the aid of French agrarian statistics (and the statistics
compiled by Compère-Morel—when he was still a socialist
and not a champion of the capitalists and of their predatory
war of 1914-18 and of their predatory Treaty of Versailles)
that the vast majority of the rural population of France
would gain at once, immediately and very considerably from
a proletarian revolution.

4. My last observation concerns the points of the theses
which speak of the need to increase the output of agricultural produce and the importance of modern machines (*des
machines modernes*), particularly threshing machines (*les
batteuses*), tractor ploughs (*les charrues à tracteur*), etc.

All these statements in the theses are undoubtedly correct
and necessary from the practical point of view. I think, however, that we should not confine ourselves to the ordinary
capitalist technique, but should take a step beyond that. A few
words should have been said about the need for planned
and complete electrification of the whole of France, and to
show that it is absolutely impossible to do this *for the benefit
of the workers and peasants* unless bourgeois rule is overthrown and power is seized by the proletariat. French literature contains no little data on the importance of electrification for France. I know that a small part of this data is
quoted in the plan for the electrification of Russia that was
drawn up by order of our government, and that since the

war considerable progress has been made in France towards the technical solution of the problem of electrification.

In my opinion it is extremely important both from the theoretical and from the practical propaganda point of view to say in the theses (and generally to enlarge on it in our communist literature) that modern advanced technology imperatively calls for *the electrification of the whole country—and of a number of neighbouring countries*—under a *single* plan; that this is quite feasible at the present time; that agriculture, and particularly the peasantry, stand to gain most from this; that as long as capitalism and private ownership of the means of production exist, the electrification of a whole country, or a series of countries, firstly, cannot be carried out speedily and according to plan, and secondly, *cannot benefit* the workers and peasants. Under capitalism, electrification will inevitably lead to increased *oppression* of the workers *and peasants* by the *big banks*. Even before the war, not a "narrow-minded Marxist", but none other than Lysis—who is now patriotically licking the boots of the capitalists—had proved that France was actually governed by a *financial oligarchy*.

France possesses splendid opportunities for electrification. After the victory of the proletariat in France, the *small peasants* particularly will benefit *enormously* from electrification carried out according to plan and unhindered by the private property of big landowners and capitalists. If the capitalists remain in power, however, electrification cannot possibly be planned and rapid; and in so far as it is carried out at all, it will be a means of imposing new fetters on the peasants, a new means of enslaving the peasants to the "financial oligarchy" which is robbing them today.

These are the few observations I am able to make on the French agrarian theses, which on the whole are, in my opinion, quite correct.

December 11, 1921

First published in 1922
in *The Communist
International* No. 20
Signed: *A Russian Communist*

Published according to
the manuscript

LETTER TO P. A. ZALUTSKY, A. A. SOLTS AND ALL MEMBERS OF THE POLITICAL BUREAU RE THE PARTY PURGE AND THE CONDITIONS OF ADMISSION INTO THE PARTY[38]

To Zalutsky, Solts and All Members of the Political Bureau

I would say that the facts published on the Party purge fully bear out the immense success of that measure despite the rather numerous individual mistakes. I think that the decision of the Party Conference should underline both these circumstances. I think no date should be set for a repeat purge, so as not to tie our hands in any way.

I would advise the Party Conference to pass a decision on stricter conditions for admission into the Party: a term of probation of one and a half years for a worker (regarding a person a worker if he worked at least ten years in large-scale industry as an ordinary wage-worker and has now been working for not less than two or three years) and three years for everybody else.

These periods may be halved in special cases, when devotion to the Party and communist self-restraint have been proved beyond doubt and when $4/5$ths of the membership in the Party bodies deciding the question are satisfied that such is the case.

The same probation period should be established for those who have been expelled from the Party under the present purge if they have not been expelled for a definite period and if they have not been expelled for shameful behaviour.

Show my letter to your immediate comrades, and if it won't be any trouble, send me, c/o Fotieva, your opinion in brief, even if it only underlines what you agree or disagree with in this letter.

Lenin

December 19, 1921

First published in 1945
in *Lenin Miscellany XXXV*

Dictated by telephone
Published according to
the stenographer's notes

LETTER TO THE POLITICAL BUREAU
RE THE RESOLUTION OF THE NINTH ALL-RUSSIA CONGRESS OF SOVIETS ON THE INTERNATIONAL SITUATION[39]

I ask that the question be discussed as to whether the Congress of Soviets ought to adopt a special resolution against the adventurist policy of Poland, Finland and Rumania (for a number of reasons it is better to say nothing about Japan). In the resolution it must be comprehensively explained that no government of Russia (except the Soviet Government) has ever recognised or could recognise the criminal nature of the imperialist policy in respect of the outlying regions of the former Russian Empire pursued both by tsarism and by the Provisional Government, which had the backing of the Mensheviks and Socialist-Revolutionaries. The resolution should state in detail how much we have shown by deeds that we value both the self-determination of nations and peaceful relations with the states that were once part of the Russian Empire. Say in detail that we fully anticipate a peaceful attitude, not only on the part of the workers and peasants of all the countries mentioned, but also on the part of a huge section of the reasonable bourgeoisie and the governments. In respect of the adventurist elements, end up with a sharp threat to the effect that if the adventurist fooling with gangs similar to the former Savinkov gangs does not stop, and if they continue to interfere with our peaceful work, we shall arise in a people's war, and those who take part in adventures and banditism will be completely crushed.

Instruct Trotsky and Chicherin to draw up a draft resolution.

A Congress resolution with such a content would be convenient for mass distribution in all languages.

December 22, 1921   *Lenin*

Dictated by telephone
on December 22

First published (abridged) in 1945 in
Lenin Miscellany XXXV

Published (unabridged)
according to the
stenographer's notes
(typewritten copy)

NINTH ALL-RUSSIA CONGRESS
OF SOVIETS

DECEMBER 23-28, 1921 [40]

1

THE HOME AND FOREIGN POLICY
OF THE REPUBLIC

REPORT OF THE ALL-RUSSIA CENTRAL EXECUTIVE COMMITTEE
AND THE COUNCIL OF PEOPLE'S COMMISSARS
DECEMBER 23

(*Stormy applause. Cries of* "Hurrah!", "Long live our leader, Comrade Lenin!", "Long live the leader of the world proletariat, Comrade Lenin!" *Prolonged applause.*) Comrades, I have to make a report on the foreign and home situation of the Republic. This is the first time I have been able to make such a report when a whole year has passed without one, at any rate large-scale, attack against our Soviet power by Russian or foreign capitalists. This is the first year that we have been able to enjoy a relative respite from attacks, even if for a limited period, and have been able in some measure to apply our energies to our chief and fundamental tasks, namely, the rehabilitation of our war-ravaged economy, healing the wounds inflicted on Russia by the exploiting classes that had been in power, and laying the foundations for socialist construction.

First and foremost, in dealing with the question of the international position of our Republic, I must repeat what I have already said, namely, that a certain equilibrium, though a highly unstable one, has been created in international relations. This is now evident. It is very strange for those of us who have lived through the revolution from its inception, who have experienced and observed our incredible difficulties in breaching the imperialist fronts, to see how things have now developed. At that time probably none of us expected or could have expected that things would shape out like this.

We imagined (and it is perhaps well worth remembering this now because it will help us in our practical conclusions on the main economic problems) that future development would take a more simple, a more direct form than the one it took. We told ourselves and we told the working class and all working people both of Russia and of other countries that there was no way out of the accursed, criminal imperialist slaughter except through revolution, and that by breaking off the imperialist war by revolution we were opening up the only possible way out of this criminal slaughter for all peoples. It seemed to us then, as it was bound to, that this was the obvious, direct and easiest path to take. This direct path, which, in fact, alone had enabled us to break free of imperialist ties, of imperialist crimes and of the imperialist war continuing to threaten the rest of the world, proved to be one which other nations were unable to take—at any rate not as quickly as we had thought they would. When, nevertheless, we now see what has taken place, when we see that there is only one Socialist Soviet Republic and that it is surrounded by a whole array of frenziedly hostile imperialist powers, we ask ourselves—how was it possible for this to happen?

One may reply without any exaggeration that this happened because our understanding of events was basically correct, our appraisal of the imperialist slaughter and the confusion in the relations between the imperialist powers was also basically correct. It is only due to this that such a strange situation, the unstable, inexplicable, and yet to a certain extent indisputable equilibrium that we witness, has arisen. The fact of the matter is that although completely surrounded by countries economically and militarily much more powerful than ourselves, whose open hostility to us quite often borders on frenzy, we nevertheless see that they were unable to destroy Soviet Russia directly and instantly—something on which they had been spending so much of their resources and their strength for three years. When we ask ourselves how this could have happened, how it could be that a state, undoubtedly one of the most backward and weakest, managed to repel the attacks of the openly hostile, most powerful countries in the world, when we try to examine this question, we see clearly that it was because we proved to be correct on the most fundamental issues. Our forecasts and calculations proved to be correct. It turned out that although we did not receive the swift and direct support of the working people of the world that we had counted on, and which we had regarded as the basis of the whole of our policy, we did receive support of another kind, which was not direct or swift—the sympathy of the workers and peasants, the farm workers, throughout the world, even in the countries most hostile to us, the sympathy that was great enough to be the final and most decisive source, the decisive reason for the complete failure of all the attacks directed against us. This sympathy consolidated the alliance of the working people of all countries which we had proclaimed and which had been implemented within the borders of our Republic, and which had its effect on all countries. No matter how precarious this support may be, as long as capitalism exists in other countries (this we must of course see clearly and frankly acknowledge), we may say that it is something we can rely on. Because of this sympathy and support, the intervention, which we endured in the course of three years, which caused us incredible destruction and suffering, is, I will not say impossible—one has to be very cautious and circumspect here—but, at any rate, has been made far more difficult for our enemies to carry out. And this, in the final analysis, explains the situation now obtaining and which at first glance appears so strange and incomprehensible.

When we calmly weigh up the sympathy felt for Bolshevism and the socialist revolution, when we survey the international situation from the point of view of the balance of forces, irrespective of whether these forces favour a just or an unjust cause, whether they favour the exploiting class or the working people—we shall ignore this aspect and attempt an appraisal of the alignment of these forces on an international scale—then we shall see that they are grouped in a manner that basically confirms our predictions and calculations: that capitalism is disintegrating and that since the war, which ended first with the Treaty of Brest-Litovsk and subsequently with the Treaty of Versailles—and I don't know which is worse—hatred and loathing for the war increase as time passes even in the countries which emerged as victors. And the farther we get from the war the clearer it becomes, not only to the working people, but to an extremely large extent also to the bourgeoisie of the victor countries, that capitalism is disintegrating, that the world economic crisis has created an intolerable situation from which there is no escape, despite all the victories. That is why, while being immeasurably weaker economically, politically and militarily than all the other powers, we are at the same time stronger, because we are aware of and correctly assess all that emerges and must emerge from this imperialist confusion, from this bloody tangle and from those contradictions (to take only the currency contradictions, I will not mention the others) in which they have become entangled and are becoming entangled still more deeply and from which they see no way out.

Today we see how the representatives of the most moderate bourgeoisie, who are definitely and without doubt far removed from socialist ideas, to say nothing of "that awful Bolshevism", change their tune; this concerns even people like the famous writer Keynes, whose book has been translated into all languages, who took part in the Versailles negotiations, and who devoted himself heart and soul to helping the governments—even he, subsequently, has had to change his tune, to give it up, although he continues to curse socialism. I repeat, he does not mention, nor does he wish even to think about Bolshevism—but he tells the capitalist world: "What you are doing will lead you into a hopeless situation", and he even proposes something like the annulment of all debts.

That is excellent, gentlemen! You should have followed our example long ago.

Only a few days ago we read a short report in the newspapers to the effect that one of the most experienced, exceedingly skilful and astute leaders of a capitalist government, Lloyd George, is, it appears, beginning to propose a similar step; and that seemingly the U.S.A. wishes to reply by saying: "Sorry, but we want to be repaid in full." That being so, we say to ourselves that things are not going too well in these advanced and mighty states since they are discussing such a simple measure so many years after the war. This was one of the easiest things we did—it was nothing to some of the other difficulties we overcame. (*Applause.*) When we see the growing confusion on this question we say that we are not afraid of their propaganda; although we by no means forget either the dangers surrounding us or our economic and military weakness compared to any one of these states, who, jointly, quite openly and frequently express their hatred for us. Whenever we express somewhat different views as to whether the existence of landowners and capitalists is justified they do not like it, and these views are declared to be criminal propaganda. I simply cannot understand this, for the same sort of propaganda is conducted legally in all states that do not share our economic views and opinions. Propaganda which calls Bolshevism monstrous, criminal, usurpatory—this monster defies description—this propaganda is conducted openly in all these countries. Recently I had a meeting with Christensen, who was a candidate for the U. S. Presidency on behalf of the farmers' and workers' party there. Do not be misled by this name, comrades. It does not in the least resemble the workers' and peasants' party in Russia. It is a purely bourgeois party, openly and resolutely hostile to any kind of socialism, and is recognised as being perfectly respectable by all bourgeois parties. This Danish-born American, who received almost a million votes at the presidential elections (and this, after all, is something in the United States), told me how in Denmark, when he tried to say among people "dressed like I am", and he was well dressed, like a bourgeois, that the Bolsheviks were not criminals, "they nearly killed me". They told him that the Bolsheviks were monsters, usurpers, and that they were surprised that anyone could mention such people in decent society. This is the type of propaganda atmosphere surrounding us.

We see, nevertheless, that a certain equilibrium has been created. This is the objective political situation, quite independent of our victories, which proves that we have fathomed the depth of the contradictions connected with the imperialist war, and that we are gauging them more correctly than ever before and more correctly than other powers, who, despite all their victories, despite all their strength, have not yet found a way out, nor see any. That is the substance of the international situation which accounts for what we now see. We have before us a highly unstable equilibrium but one that is, nevertheless, certain, obvious, indisputable. I do not know whether this is for long, and I do not think that anyone can know. That is why, for our part, we must display the utmost caution. And the first precept of our policy, the first lesson that emerges from our governmental activities for the past year, the lesson which must be learned by all workers and peasants, is to be on the alert, to remember that we are surrounded by people, classes, governments who openly express the utmost hatred for us. We must remember that we are always a hair's breadth away from invasion. We shall do all in our power to prevent this misfortune. It is doubtful that any nation has experienced such a burden of the imperialist war as we have. Then we bore the burden of the Civil War forced on us by the ruling classes, who fought for the Russia of the émigrés, the Russia of the landowners, the Russia of the capitalists. We know, we know only too well, the incredible misfortunes that war brings to the workers and peasants. For that reason our attitude to this question must be most cautious and circumspect. We are ready to make the greatest concessions and sacrifices in order to preserve the peace for which we have paid such a high price. We are ready to make huge concessions and sacrifices, but not any kind and not for ever. Let those, fortunately not numerous, representatives of the war parties and aggressive cliques of Finland, Poland and Rumania who make great play of this—let them mark it well. (*Applause.*)

Anyone who has any political sense or acumen will say that there has not been—nor can there be—a government in Russia other than the Soviet Government prepared to make such concessions and sacrifices in relation to nationalities within our state, and also to those which had joined the Russian Empire. There is not, and cannot be, another government which would recognise as clearly as we do and declare so distinctly to one and all that the attitude of old Russia (tsarist Russia, Russia of the war parties) to the nationalities populating Russia was criminal, that this attitude was impermissible, that it aroused the rightful and

indignant protest and discontent of the oppressed nationalities. There is not, and cannot be, another government which
would so openly admit this, which would conduct this anti-
chauvinist propaganda, a propaganda that recognises the
guilt of old Russia, tsarist Russia, Kerensky Russia—a
government which would conduct propaganda against the
forcible incorporation of other nationalities into Russia.
This is not mere words—this is an obvious political fact,
absolutely indisputable and plain for all to see. As long as
no nationalities engage in intrigues against us which bind
them to the imperialist oppression, as long as they do not
help to crush us, we shall not be deterred by formalities.
We shall not forget that we are revolutionaries. (*Applause.*)
But there are facts incontrovertibly and indisputably
showing that in Russia, that has defeated the Mensheviks
and Socialist-Revolutionaries, the smallest, completely
unarmed nationality, however weak it may be, may and
must absolutely rest assured that we have nothing but peaceful intentions towards it, that our propaganda about the
criminality of the old policy of the old governments is not
weakening, and that we are as firm as ever in our desire at
all costs, and at the price of enormous sacrifices and concessions, to maintain peace with all nationalities that belonged
to the former Russian Empire, but who did not wish
to remain with us. We have proved this. And we shall prove
this no matter how great the curses rained on us from all
sides. It seems to us that we have given excellent proof of
it, and we declare to the meeting of representatives of the
workers and peasants of Russia, to the many millions of
workers and peasants, that we shall do our utmost to preserve
peace in the future, that we shall not shrink from great
sacrifices and concessions in order to safeguard this peace.

There are, however, limits beyond which one cannot go.
We shall not permit peace treaties to be flouted. We shall
not permit attempts to interfere with our peaceful work. On
no account shall we permit this, and we shall rise to a man
to defend our existence. (*Applause.*)

Comrades, what I have just said is perfectly clear and
comprehensible to you, and you could not expect anything
else from anyone reporting to you on our policy. You know
that such, and no other, is our policy. But, unfortunately,

there are now two worlds: the old world of capitalism, that is in a state of confusion but which will never surrender voluntarily, and the rising new world, which is still very weak, but which will grow, for it is invincible. This old world has its old diplomacy, which cannot believe that it is possible to speak frankly and forthrightly. This old diplomacy thinks there must be a trap of some sort here. (*Applause, laughter.*) When this economically and militarily all-powerful old world sent us—that was some time ago—Bullitt, a representative of the United States Government, who came to us with the proposal that we should conclude peace with Kolchak and Denikin on terms that were most unfavourable to us—we said that we held so dear the blood of the workers and peasants shed for so long in Russia that although the terms were extremely unfavourable we were prepared to accept them, because we were convinced that the forces of Kolchak and Denikin would disintegrate from within. We said this quite frankly, with the minimum of diplomatic subtlety, and so they concluded that we must be trying to dupe them. And Bullitt, who had held these friendly, round-table conversations with us, was met with reproach and compelled to resign as soon as he got home. I am surprised that he has not yet been thrown into gaol, in keeping with the imperialist custom, for secretly sympathising with the Bolsheviks. (*Laughter, applause.*) But the upshot was that we, who at that time had proposed peace to our disadvantage, obtained peace on much more favourable terms. That was something of a lesson. I know that we can no more learn the old diplomacy than we can remould ourselves; but the lessons in diplomacy that we have given since then and that have been learned by the other powers must have had some effect; they must have remained in the memory of some people. (*Laughter.*) Hence, our straightforward statement that our workers and peasants prized above all the blessings of peace, but that there were limits to the concessions they were prepared to make to preserve it, was taken to mean that they had not for a moment, not for a second, forgotten the hardships they had suffered in the imperialist war and the Civil War. This reminder, which I am sure this Congress, and the whole mass of workers and peasants, all Russia, will endorse and express—

this reminder will surely have some effect and play a certain role, no matter how the powers take it, no matter what diplomatic ruse their old diplomatic habits make them suspect.

This, comrades, is what I think must be said about our international situation. A certain unstable equilibrium has been reached. Materially—economically and militarily—we are extremely weak; but morally—by which, of course, I mean not abstract morals, but the alignment of the real forces of all classes in all countries—we are the strongest of all. This has been proved in practice; it has been proved not merely by words but by deeds; it has been proved once and, if history takes a certain turn, it will, perhaps, be proved many times again. That is why we say that having started on our work of peaceful development we shall exert every effort to continue it without interruption. At the same time, comrades, be vigilant, safeguard the defence potential of our country, strengthen our Red Army to the utmost, and remember that we have no right to permit an instant's slackening where our workers and peasants and their gains are concerned. (*Applause.*)

Comrades, having thus briefly outlined the most essential features of our international position, I shall now deal with the manner in which economic relations are beginning to shape out in our country and in Western Europe, in the capitalist countries. The greatest difficulty here is that without definite relations between us and the capitalist countries we cannot have stable economic relations. Events very clearly show that neither can the capitalist countries have them. But today we are not in an altruistic mood. We are thinking more of how to continue in existence when other powers are hostile to us.

But is the existence of a socialist republic in a capitalist environment at all conceivable? It seemed inconceivable from the political and military aspects. That it is possible both politically and militarily has now been proved; it is a fact. But what about trade? What about economic relations? Contacts, assistance, the exchange of services between backward, ruined agricultural Russia and the advanced, industrially-developed group of capitalist countries—is all this possible? Did they not threaten

to surround us with a barbed wire fence so as to prevent
any economic relations with us whatever? "War did not
scare them, so we shall reduce them by means of a
blockade."

Comrades, during the past four years we have heard so
many threats, and such terrible ones, that none of them can
frighten us any more. As for the blockade, experience has
shown that it is an open question as to who suffers from
it most, the blockaded or the blockaders. Experience has
shown beyond doubt that during this first year, on which
I am able to report as a period of a relatively elementary
respite from direct brute force, we have not been recognised, we have been rejected, and relations with us have
been declared non-existent (let them be recognised as non-
existent by the bourgeois courts); but they nevertheless
exist. I deem it my right to report to you that this is, without
the slightest exaggeration, one of the main results achieved
in 1921, the year under review.

I do not know whether the report of the People's Commissariat of Foreign Affairs to the Ninth Congress of Soviets
has been, or will be, distributed to you today. In my opinion,
the defect in this report is that it is too bulky and is difficult to read right through. But, perhaps, this is my own
failing, and I have no doubt that the overwhelming majority of you, as well as all those who are interested in politics, will read it, even if not immediately. Even if you do
not read it all, but only glance through its pages, you will
see that Russia has sprouted, if one may so express it,
a number of fairly regular and permanent commercial
relations, missions, treaties, etc. True, we are not yet
recognised *de jure*. This is still important, because the
danger of the unstable equilibrium being upset, the danger
of new attempts at invasion has, as I have said, increased;
the relations, however, are a fact.

In 1921—the first year of trade with foreign countries—
we made considerable progress. This was partly due to
the improvement in our transport system, perhaps the
most important, or one of the most important sectors of
our economy. It is due also to our imports and exports.
Permit me to quote very brief figures. All our difficulties,
our most incredible difficulties—the burden of these diffi-

culties, the most crucial feature of them—lie in fuel and food, in the peasant economy, in the famine and calamities that have afflicted us. We know very well that all this is bound up with the transport problem. We must discuss this, and all comrades from the localities must know and repeat it over and over again to all their comrades there that we must strain every nerve to overcome the food and fuel crisis. It is from this that our transport system suffers, and transport is the material instrument of our relations with foreign countries.

The organisational improvements in our transport system over the past year are beyond doubt. In 1921 we transported by river much more than in 1920. The average run per vessel in 1921 was 1,000 pood-versts as compared with 800 pood-versts in 1920. We have definitely made some progress in organisation. I must say that for the first time we are beginning to obtain assistance from abroad. We have ordered thousands of locomotives, and we have already received the first thirteen from Sweden and thirty-seven from Germany. It is a very small beginning, but a beginning, nevertheless. We have ordered hundreds of tank cars, about 500 of which arrived here in the course of 1921. We are paying a high, an exorbitant price for these things, but still, it shows that we are receiving the assistance of the large-scale industry of the advanced countries; it shows that the large-scale industry of the capitalist countries is helping us to restore our economy, although all these countries are governed by capitalists who hate us heart and soul. All of these capitalists are united by governments which continue to make statements in their press about how matters stand with the *de jure* recognition of Soviet Russia, and about whether or not the Bolshevik Government is a legitimate one. Lengthy research revealed that it is a legitimate government, but it cannot be recognised. I have no right to conceal the sad truth that we are not yet recognised, but I must tell you that commercial relations are nevertheless developing.

All these capitalist countries are in a position to make us pay through the nose; we pay more for the goods than they are worth; but for all that, they are helping our economy. How did that happen? Why are they acting against their own inclinations and in contradiction to what they are constantly asserting in their press? And this press is more than a match for ours in respect of circulation, and the force and venom with which it attacks us. They call us criminals, and all the same they help us. And so it turns out they are bound up with us economically. It turns out as I have already said, that our calculations, made on a grand scale, are more correct than theirs. This is not because they lack people capable of making correct calculations—they have far more than we have—but because it is impossible to calculate properly when one is heading for destruction. That is why I would like to supplement my remarks with a few figures to show how our foreign trade is developing. I shall quote only very brief figures that are easy to remember. In three years—1918, 1919 and 1920—our total imports amounted to a little over 17,000,000 poods; in 1921 they amounted to 50,000,000 poods, that is to say, three times the total amount imported in the three preceding years. Our exports in the first three years totalled 2,500,000 poods; in 1921 alone, they amounted to 11,500,000 poods. These figures are infinitesimally, miserably, ridiculously small; any well-informed person will at once say that they are indicative of poverty. And that is what they do indicate. But for all that, it is a beginning. And we, who have experienced direct attempts to crush us, who for years have been hearing threats that everything will be done to prevent any relations with us as long as we remain what we are, nevertheless see that something has proved more potent than these threats. We see that their forecast of economic development was wrong and ours was right. We have made a start, and we must now exert all our efforts to continue this development without interruption. We must make it our primary concern, giving it all our attention.

I shall give you another little illustration of the progress we made in 1921. In the first quarter of 1921 imports amounted to about 3,000,000 poods, in the second quarter to 8,000,000 poods, in the third quarter to 24,000,000 poods. So we are making progress. These figures are infinitesimally small, but they nevertheless show a gradual increase. We see how they grew in 1921, which was a year of unprecedented difficulties. You know what that calamity, the famine, cost us, what incredible difficulties it is still causing on the farms, in industry and in our life generally. But although our country has been devastated by war, has suffered tremendous hardship as a result of all the wars and of the rule of tsars and capitalists, we are now on the road that offers us a prospect of improvement, in spite of the unceasing hostility towards us. That is the main factor. That is why, when we read recently about the Washington Conference,[41] when we heard the news that the countries hostile to us would be obliged to convene a second conference next summer and to invite Germany and Russia to discuss the terms of a genuine peace, we said that our terms are clear and definite; we have formulated them, we have published them. How much hostility shall we encounter? We have no illusions about that; but we know that the economic position of those who blockaded us has proved to be vulnerable. There is a force more powerful than the wishes, the will and the decisions of any of the governments or classes that are hostile to us. That force is world general economic relations, which compel them to make contact with us. The farther they proceed in this direction the more extensive and rapid will be the development of what in today's report for 1921 I have been able to indicate to you only by some scanty figures.

Now for our domestic economic situation; here, too, the important question that has priority is that of our economic policy. Our main task for 1921, the year under review, was to go over to the New Economic Policy, to take the first steps along this path, to learn how to make them, to adjust our legislation and administrative apparatus to it. The press has given you a lot of facts and information showing how this work has developed. You will not, of course, expect me to quote here additional facts or to give figures. It is only necessary to determine what the main thing was that united us most of all, that is more vital from the point of view of the most important and radical question of our entire revolution and of all future socialist revolutions (if viewed generally on a world scale).

The most basic, most vital question is that of the attitude of the working class to the peasants; this involves the alliance of the working class and the peasants; the ability of the advanced workers, who have passed through a lengthy, difficult but rewarding school of experience in a large factory, to do things in such a way that they attract to their side the mass of peasants, who were ground down by capitalism, by the landowners and by their old poverty-stricken, petty farms, to prove to them that only in alliance with the workers, no matter what the difficulties to be encountered on this path, and they are many, and we cannot close our eyes to this—only through this alliance can the peasants abolish the age-old oppression by the landowners and capitalists. Only by consolidating the alliance of the workers and peasants can mankind be saved from events such as the recent imperialist slaughter, from the barbarous contradictions to be seen in the capitalist world today, where a small number, a miserable handful of the richest powers are choking with wealth, while the huge population of the globe suffers privations, being unable to benefit from the culture and rich resources that lie before them but cannot be made use of because of insufficient commerce.

Unemployment is the chief calamity in the advanced countries. There is no way out of this situation other than through the firm alliance of the peasants with a working class that has passed through the difficult, but one reliable school of importance, the school of factory life, factory exploitation, factory solidarity—there is no other way out. We have tested this alliance in the political and military fields during our Republic's most difficult years. In 1921, for the first time, we tested this alliance in the economic field. So far we have handled things very, very badly in this field, as we must frankly admit. We must recognise this shortcoming and not gloss over it; we must do everything possible to eliminate it and understand that the foundation of our New Economic Policy lies in this alliance. There are only two ways in which proper relations between the working class and the peasants can be established. If large-scale industry is flourishing, if it can immediately supply the small peasants with a sufficient amount of goods, or more than previously, and in this way establish proper relations between manufactured goods and the supply of surplus agricultural goods coming from the peasants, then the peasants will be fully satisfied, then the mass of peasants, the non-Party peasants, will acknowledge, by virtue of experience, that this new system is better than the capitalist system. We speak of a flourishing large-scale industry, which is able to supply all the goods the peasants are in urgent need of, and this possibility exists; if we consider the problem on a world scale, we see that a flourishing large-scale industry capable of supplying the world with all kinds of goods exists, only its owners do not know how to use it for anything but the manufacture of guns, shells and other armaments, employed with such success from 1914 to 1918. Then industry was geared to war and supplied mankind with its products so abundantly that no fewer than 10 million people were killed and no fewer than 20 million maimed. This is something we have all seen, and, besides, war in the twentieth century is not like previous wars.

After this war, even among the victor countries, among those most hostile and alien to any kind of socialism, who ruthlessly oppose the slightest socialist idea, a large number of people have been heard to say quite definitely that even if there were no wicked Bolsheviks in the world, it is hardly likely that another war of this kind could be permitted. This is said by the representatives of the most wealthy countries. This is what this rich, advanced, large-scale industry was used for. It served to maim people, and it had no time to supply the peasants with its goods. All the same we have a right to say that such an industry exists on a world scale. There are countries whose large-scale industry is so advanced that it could instantly satisfy the needs of hundreds of millions of backward peasants. We make this the basis of our calculations. From your daily observations you know better than anyone else what has been left of our large-scale industry, which was weak anyway. In the Donets Basin, the main centre of our large-scale industry, for instance, the Civil War caused so much destruction, and so many imperialist governments established their rule there (how many of them did the Ukraine see!), that it was inevitable that next to nothing should remain of our large-scale industry. When, added to this, there is the misfortune of the 1921 crop failure, it becomes clear that the attempt to supply the peasants with goods from large-scale industry, which had been placed under state control, was unsuccessful. Once this attempt has failed, the only economic relation possible between the peasants and the workers, that is, between agriculture and industry, is exchange, trade. That is the crux of the matter. The substitution of the tax in kind for requisitioning—that, very simply, is the substance of our economic policy. When there is no flourishing large-scale industry which can be organised in such a way as to supply the peasants with goods immediately, then the gradual development of a powerful alliance of the workers and peasants is possible only through trade and the gradual advance of agriculture and industry above their present level, under the guidance and control of the workers' state. Sheer necessity has driven us to this path. And this is the sole basis and substance of our New Economic Policy.

At a time when the main attention and the main forces were diverted to political and military problems, we simply had to press forward with great speed along with the vanguard, knowing that it would have support. The alliance of the peasants and workers in the fight for great political changes, for our great achievements of the past three years, which put us at war with the dominant world powers, was made possible by a simple burst of political and military enthusiasm because every peasant realised, felt and sensed that he was confronted by his age-old enemy, the landowner, who in one way or another was being aided by representatives of other parties. That is why this alliance was so solid and invincible.

In the economic field the basis of this alliance has to be different. A change in the substance and form of the alliance is essential. If anyone from the Communist Party, from the trade unions, or merely anyone sympathetic to Soviet power has overlooked the need to change the form and substance of this alliance, then so much the worse for him. Such oversights in a revolution are impermissible. The change in the form of the alliance has become necessary because the political and military alliance could not continue intact in the realm of economics, when we have as yet no large-scale industry, when what we had has been ruined by a war such as no other country has ever experienced. Even in countries infinitely more wealthy than ours, in countries that had gained, not lost from the war, the level of industry has not yet risen. A change in the form and substance of the alliance of the workers and peasants has become essential. We went much further forward in the political and military period than the purely economic aspect of the alliance of the workers and peasants permitted us to do. We had to do this in order to defeat the enemy, and we had the right to do this. We were successful because we defeated our enemies in the field that existed at that time, in the political and military field, but we suffered a series of defeats in the economic field. There is no need to be afraid to admit this; on the contrary, we shall only learn how to win when we do not fear to acknowledge our defeats and shortcomings, when we look truth, even the saddest truth, straight in the face. We have a right to be proud of our achievements in the first field, that is, in the political and military field. They have gone down in history as an epoch-making victory, whose overall influence is yet to be felt. But economically, in the year under review, we only started the New Economic Policy and we are taking a step forward in this regard. At the same time, we are only just beginning to learn and are making very many more mistakes, looking back, being carried away by our past experience—splendid, lofty, magnificent, of world-wide significance, but which could not solve the economic problems now imposed on us in a country where large-scale industry has been devastated; in conditions which demand that we learn, in the first place, to establish the economic link now necessary and inevitable. That link is trade. This is a very unpleasant discovery for Communists. It is quite likely that this discovery is extremely unpleasant, in fact it is certain that it is unpleasant, but if we are swayed by ideas of pleasantness or unpleasantness we shall fall to the level of those would-be socialists of whom we saw plenty at the time of the Kerensky Provisional Government. It is hardly likely that "socialists" of this type still have any authority in our Republic. And our strength has always been our ability to take the actual balance of forces into consideration and not to be afraid of it no matter how unpleasant it might be for us.

Since large-scale industry exists on a world scale, there can be no doubt that a direct transition to socialism is possible—and nobody will deny this fact, just as nobody will deny that this large-scale industry either comes to a standstill and creates unemployment in the most flourishing and wealthy victor countries, or only manufactures shells for the extermination of people. And if, owing to the backwardness with which we came to the revolution, we have not reached the industrial development we need, are we going to give up, are we going to despair? No. We shall get on with the hard work because the path that we have taken is the right one. There is no doubt that the path of the alliance of the mass of the people is the sole path which will ensure that the workers and peasants work for themselves and not for the exploiters. In order to bring this about in our conditions we must have the only possible economic link, the link through the economy.

That is why we have retreated, that is why we have had to retreat to state capitalism, retreat to concessions, retreat to trade. Without this, proper relations with the peasants cannot be restored in the conditions of devastation, in which we now find ourselves. Without this, we are threatened with the danger of the revolution's vanguard getting swiftly so far ahead that it would lose touch with the peasants. There would be no contact between the vanguard and the peasants and that would mean the collapse of the revolution. Our approach to this must be particularly careful, first and foremost, because what we call our New Economic Policy follows from it. That is why we have unanimously declared that we shall carry out this policy in earnest and for a long time, but, of course, as has already been correctly noted, not for ever; it has been made necessary by our poverty and devastation and by the tremendous weakening of our large-scale industry.

I shall permit myself to quote a few figures in order to prove that despite the difficulties and the many mistakes we have made (and we have made a great number) we are nevertheless moving ahead. Comrades, I have not got the overall figures on the development of internal trade; I only wish to deal with information on the turnover of the Central Council of Co-operative Societies for three months. For September the turnover of these co-operatives amounted to one million gold rubles, for October three million and for November six million. Again, if taken as absolute, the figures are miserable, small; this must be frankly recognised, because it will be more harmful to harbour any illusions on this score. They are paltry figures, but in these conditions of devastation they undoubtedly show that there is an advance, and that we can fasten on to this economic basis. No matter how numerous the mistakes we make—the trade unions, the Communist Party and the administrative bodies—we are becoming convinced that we can rid ourselves of them, and are gradually doing so, and that we are taking the path that is sure to lead to the restoration of relations between agriculture and industry. The growth of the productive forces can and must be achieved even on the level of petty-peasant economy and, for the time being, on the basis of small-scale industry, since it is so difficult to rehabilitate large-scale industry. We must make headway, and we are beginning to, but we need to remember that in this field a different rate and different conditions of work obtain, that here victory will be more difficult. Here we cannot achieve our aims as quickly as we were able to in the political and military fields. Here we cannot proceed by leaps and bounds, and the periods involved are different—they are reckoned in decades. These are the periods in which we shall have to achieve successes in the economic war, in conditions of hostility instead of assistance from our neighbours.

This path of ours is the right one, for it is the path which, sooner or later, all other countries must inevitably take. We have begun to follow this right path; we must assess even the smallest step, take into account our slightest mistakes, and then we shall reach our goal by following this path.

I ought now, comrades, to say a few words about our main preoccupation, farming, but I believe that you are to hear a far more detailed and fuller report on this question than I could make, and also on the famine, to be made by Comrade Kalinin.

You are fully aware, comrades, of the incredible hardships of the 1921 famine. It was inevitable that the misfortunes of old Russia should have been carried over to our times, because the only way to avoid them is to restore the economy, but not on the old, paltry, petty basis. It must be rehabilitated on a new basis, the basis of large-scale industry and electrification. Only in that way shall we be rid of our poverty and of interminable famines. It can be seen at once that the periods by which we were able to measure our political and military victories do not apply here. Surrounded by hostile countries, we have, nevertheless, pierced the blockade: no matter how meagre the help, we did get something. In all, it amounts to 2,500,000 poods. That is all the help that we have received from abroad, that the foreign countries graciously presented to starving Russia. We were able to collect about 600,000 gold rubles in donations. It is a far too pitiful sum, and shows the mercenary attitude of the European bourgeoisie toward our famine. No doubt you have all read how, at the news of the famine, influential statesmen grandiloquently and solemnly declared that to take advantage of the famine in order to raise the question of old debts would be a devilish thing to do. I am not so sure that the devil is worse than modern imperialism. What I do know is that in actual fact, despite the famine, they did try to recover their old debts on particularly harsh conditions. We do not refuse to pay, and solemnly declare that we are prepared to discuss things in a business-like fashion. But you all understand, and there can be no doubt about this, that we shall never under any circumstances allow ourselves to be tied hand and foot in this matter without considering all its aspects, without taking into account reciprocal claims, without a business-like discussion.

I have to inform you that during recent days we have had considerable success in the struggle against the famine. You have no doubt read in the newspapers that the U.S.A. has allocated 20 million dollars for the relief of the starving in Russia, probably on the same conditions as A.R.A.—the American Relief Administration. Krasin sent us a telegram a few days ago saying that the U.S. Government is formally proposing to guarantee the dispatch to us over a period of three months of foodstuffs and seeds worth 20 million dollars, provided we, on our part, can agree to the expenditure of 10 million dollars (20 million gold rubles) for the same purpose. We immediately agreed to this and have telegraphed accordingly. And I think we may say that, during the first three months, we shall be able to supply the starving with seed and food worth 30 million dollars, that is, 60 million gold rubles. This is, of course, very little; it by no means covers the terrible losses we have suffered. You all understand this perfectly well. But at any rate this is aid which will undoubtedly help to relieve our desperate need and desperate famine. And since in autumn we were able to achieve certain successes in providing the starving areas with seed and in extending the sown areas in general, we now have hopes for far greater success in the spring.

In the autumn, approximately 75 per cent of the usual area was sown to winter crops in the famine-stricken gubernias, 102 per cent in the gubernias partially hit by the crop failure, 123 per cent in the producing gubernias and 126 per cent in the consuming gubernias. This, at any rate, proves that no matter how fantastically difficult our conditions, we were still able to give the peasants some help in enlarging the area sown to crops and in fighting the famine. Under present conditions we have every right to expect, without any exaggeration or fear of error, that we shall be able to help the peasants substantially with seed for the spring-crop area. This aid, I repeat, is by no means adequate. Under no circumstances shall we have enough for all our needs. This must be stated quite frankly. All the more reason, therefore, to do everything possible to extend this aid.

In this connection I must give you the final figures on our work to solve the food problem. Generally speaking, the tax in kind made things much easier for the peasants as a whole. This needs no proof. It is not simply a question of how much grain has been taken from the peasants, but that the peasant feels better provided for under the tax in kind, and has a greater interest in improving his farm. With increased productive forces the tax in kind has opened up wider horizons for an industrious peasant. On the whole, the results of the collection of the tax in kind for the year under review are such that we have to say that we must make every effort to avert failure.

Here, in brief, are the general results that I can give you based on the latest returns supplied by the People's Commissariat of Food. We need at least 230 million poods. Of these, 12 million are needed for the famine-stricken, 37 million for seed, and 15 million for the reserve fund. We can obtain 109 million through the tax in kind, 15 million from the milling tax, 12,500,000 from the repayment of the seed loan, 13,500,000 from trade, 27 million from the Ukraine and 38 million poods from abroad—38 million, reckoning the 30 million from the source I have already mentioned to you, and in addition the eight million poods we plan to buy. This makes a total of 215 million poods. So we still have a deficit, with not a single pood in reserve, nor is it certain that we shall be able to buy more abroad. Our food plan has been calculated to the narrowest margin so that the least possible burden falls on the peasants who have been victims of the famine. In the central Soviet organisations we have for a long time been making every effort to have the plan for food deliveries fulfilled to the maximum. In 1920 we estimated that the state maintained 38 million people; now we have reduced this figure to eight million. Such is the reduction we have made in this respect. This can lead to only one conclusion: there must be 100 per cent collection of the tax in kind, i.e., it must at all costs be collected in full. For the peasants that have suffered so much, this represents a great burden and we do not forget this. I am perfectly well aware that the comrades in the localities, who have themselves experienced all the difficulties of solving the food campaign problem, know better than I do what it means to collect the tax in full at this moment. But, as a result of our work during 1921, I must say on behalf of the government that this task, comrades, has to be carried out; this difficulty will have to be faced, this problem will have to be overcome. Otherwise we cannot meet the most basic, most elementary requirements of our transport and industry, we cannot ensure the very minimum, absolutely essential budget, without which we cannot exist in our present condition of hostile encirclement and the highly unstable international balance of forces.

Without the most tremendous efforts, there is and can be no way out of the situation in which we find ourselves after being tortured by the imperialist and civil wars and after being persecuted by the ruling classes of all countries. Therefore, not shunning the bitter truth, we must state quite definitely, and bring this home to the workers in the localities on behalf of the Congress: "Comrades, the entire existence of the Soviet Republic and our very modest plan for rehabilitating transport and industry are based on the assumption that we shall fulfil our general food procurement programme. It is vitally necessary, therefore, to collect the tax in full."

Speaking of the plan I shall now deal with the present position of the state plan. I shall begin with fuel, which is the food of industry and the basis of all our industrial work. Probably you have already received today, or will do so in a few days, a report on the work of our Gosplan, the State Planning Commission. You will receive a report on the Congress of Electrical Engineers, which made a valuable and important contribution and an examination by Russia's best technical and scientific personnel of the plan providing the only scientific short-cut to the rehabilitation of our large-scale industry, a plan that will take at least ten to fifteen years to fulfil. I have already said, and I shall not tire of repeating, that the periods we have to reckon with in our practical work today are different from those that we saw in the political and military sphere. Very many leading workers of the Communist Party and trade unions have understood this, but it is vital that everyone should do so. Incidentally, in Comrade Krzhizhanovsky's pamphlet—the report on the work of the State Planning Commission—which will be distributed to you tomorrow, you will see how the engineers and farming experts together regard the question of the state plan in general. You will see that their approach is not our usual one of viewing things from a general political or economic point of view, but of regarding matters in the light of their joint experience as engineers and farming experts and, incidentally, showing the limit to our retreat. In the pamphlet you will find an answer to this question from the point of view of the engineers and farming experts; its contents are all the more valuable because you will find there how our general state planning organisation tackles the question of transport and industry as a result of its work during the year under review. Naturally, I cannot outline the contents of this report here.

I should like to say a few words on the state of the fuel plan, as in this sphere we suffered the gravest setback at the beginning of 1921, the year under review. It was precisely here, basing ourselves on the improved situation at the end of 1920, that we made the serious miscalculation which led to the colossal crisis in transport in the spring of 1921, a crisis caused not only by a shortage of material resources, but by a miscalculation of the rate of development. The mistake of transferring the experience we had gained during the political and war periods to economic problems was already having its effect; it was an important, a fundamental mistake which, comrades, we still repeat at every step. Many mistakes are being made right now, and it must be said that if we do not realise this and rectify them at all costs, there can be no stable economic improvement. After the lesson we have had we have worked out the fuel plan for the second half of 1921 with far greater care, regarding as impermissible the slightest exaggeration, and doing all we can to prevent it. The figures given me by Comrade Smilga, who is in charge of all our fuel collection institutions, for the end of December, although still incomplete, show that there is a deficit, which is now insignificant and indicates an improvement in the internal structure of our fuel budget, or its mineralisation, as the technical experts put it, that is, considerable success in supplying Russia with mineral fuel; after all, a firm foundation for large-scale industry capable of serving as the basis for socialist society can only be built on mineral fuel.

This is how our fuel plan was calculated at the beginning of the second half of 1921. We hoped to obtain 297 million poods of fuel in firewood, i.e., 2,700,000 cubic sazhens converted into 7,000-calory conventional fuel in the way we usually do and in the way it is done on p. 40 of Krzhi-

zhanovsky's pamphlet, which will be distributed to you.
Our figures show that to date we have received nearly 234
million poods. This is an enormous deficiency to which
I must draw your attention. During the year under review
we have paid very careful attention to the work of our fuel
institutions in the matter of firewood. This is the work,
however, that is mainly connected with the state of the
peasant farms. It is the peasant and his horse that have
to bear the burden. The fuel and fodder shortage, etc.,
greatly affect their work. Hence the shortage. That is why
now, when we stand on the threshold of the winter fuel
campaign, I must say once again—comrades, you must take
to the localities the slogan that the greatest concentration
of effort is needed in this work. Our fuel budget has been
based on the absolute minimum required to raise the level
of industrial production, but it is vitally necessary that
this absolute minimum be achieved, no matter how difficult the conditions.

Further. We estimated that we would receive 143 million poods of coal; we received 184 million poods. That
is progress, progress in increasing the amount of mineral fuel,
progress made by the Donets coalfield and other enterprises,
where many comrades have worked selflessly and achieved
practical results in improving large-scale industry. I shall
give you a couple of figures concerning the Donets Basin,
because it is the basis, the main centre of all our industry.
Oil—we reckoned on receiving 80 million poods, which
if converted into conventional fuel would be 120 million
poods. Peat—we calculated at 40 million (19 million
poods of conventional fuel) and we received 50 million. So
we had reckoned on obtaining a total of 579 million poods,
but apparently we shall not succeed in getting more than
562 million poods. In general, there is a fuel shortage.
True, it is not very great, possibly 3-4 per cent short of
requirements, but nevertheless it is a shortage. In any case,
it has to be admitted that all this constitutes a direct threat
to large-scale industry, because some part of the minimum
requirements will not be met. I think I have proved to
you by this example, firstly, that our planning bodies
have not wasted their time, that the moment is approaching
when we shall be fulfilling our plans, and, at the same

time, that we are beginning to make just a little progress, and that the hardships and difficulties of our economic situation are still extremely great. Therefore, the main slogan, the main battle-cry, the main appeal with which this Congress must proceed in its work and with which it must conclude its work, which the delegates must carry to the localities is this: an all-out effort is still needed, no matter how difficult it may be, both in the industrial and in the agricultural field. An all-out effort is the only hope for the Republic, the only way in which the rule of the workers and peasants can be maintained, preserved and stabilised. That we have achieved notable successes has been shown particularly in the Donets Basin, where comrades such as Pyatakov in large-scale industry and Rukhimovich in small-scale industry have worked with great devotion and great success, with the result that for the first time the small-scale industry is in a position to produce something. In large-scale industry, output per coal-hewer reached the pre-war level, which had not been the case earlier. The total output of the Donets Basin for 1920 was 272 million poods, and in 1921 it is estimated at 350 million poods. This is a very, very small figure compared to the maximum pre-war figure—1,700 million. But still it is something. It proves that there is an important advance. It is, after all. a step forward in the rehabilitation of large-scale industry, and we cannot afford to grudge any sacrifice to this end.

Now a few words about the iron and steel industry. Here our situation is particularly difficult. We are producing possibly something like six per cent of the pre-war figure. That is. the extent of the ruin and poverty to which the imperialist and civil wars have reduced Russia. But we are, of course, making headway. We are building centres like Yugostal,[42] where Comrade Mezhlauk is working with the utmost devotion. Difficult as our position is, we nevertheless can see tremendous successes in this sphere. In the first half of 1921, 70,000 poods of iron were smelted monthly; in October, 130,000; in November, 270,000 or almost four times as much. We can see that there are no grounds for panic. We by no means close our eyes to the fact that the figures I have given represent a miserable, paltry level, but all the same they prove that no matter how exceptionally grave things were in 1921, no matter what extraordinary burdens have fallen to the lot of the working class and peasants, we are, nonetheless, progressing, we are on the right path, and by straining every nerve we can hope that there will be even greater improvement.

I should also like to give some figures on our progress in electrification. Unfortunately, so far, we have not been very successful. I counted on being able to congratulate the Ninth Congress on the opening of the second big electric power station built by the Soviet government; the first was Shatura, and the second the Kashira Station, which we had hoped to open in December.[43] It would have generated, and can generate, 6,000 kw at first, which, with the 18,000 kw we have in Moscow, would have been substantial help. But a number of obstacles prevented us from opening the station in December 1921; it will be opened very soon, in a few weeks at the latest. You have probably seen the report published in *Ekonomicheskaya Zhizn* a few days ago and signed by engineer Levi, one of the leading participants at the Eighth All-Russia Congress of Electrical Engineers and, in general, one of our most important workers. I shall give you a few figures from this report. Taking 1918 and 1919 together, 51 stations with a 3,500 kw capacity were commissioned. If we take 1920 and 1921 together, 221 stations with a 12,000 kw capacity were commissioned. Of course, when these figures are compared with Western Europe they seem extremely small and paltry. But they show that progress can be made even in face of difficulties such as no country has ever experienced. The building of small power stations throughout the countryside played an important role. It must be frankly admitted that they were very often too far apart, although there was some good in that, too. Thanks to these small stations new centres of modern large-scale industry were set up in the countryside. Although they may be of trifling significance, they show the peasants that Russia will not remain a country of manual labour, or of the primitive wooden plough, but will go forward to different times. And the peasant masses are gradually coming to understand that we must and can put Russia on a different footing. The periods involved, as I have already pointed out, are measured in decades, but the work has already commenced, and the realisation of this is spreading among the mass of the peasants, partly because the small stations grow faster than the larger ones. But if in 1921 there was a delay in the opening of one large electric power station, at the beginning of 1922 there will be two stations—at Kashira near Moscow, and at Utkina Zavod near Petrograd.[44] In this respect, at any rate, we have taken the path that ensures progress, provided we approach the fulfilment of our tasks with unrelaxed zeal.

A few words about yet another achievement—our success in peat production. Our peat output reached 93 million poods in 1920 and 139 million poods in 1921; this is, possibly, the only sphere in which we have far surpassed the pre-war level. Our peat resources are inexhaustible, greater than those of any other country. But there have always been gigantic difficulties, and to some extent they still remain, in the sense that this work, which is arduous in general, was especially arduous in Russia. The hydraulic method of peat-cutting, recommended by Comrades Radchenko, Menshikov and Morozov of the Central Peat Board, has made the work easier. There have been great achievements in this field. In 1921, we had in operation only two peat pumps, machines for the hydraulic extraction of peat, which relieve the workers of the back-breaking toil still involved in peat-cutting. Twenty of these machines have been ordered from Germany and will be received in 1922. Co-operation with an advanced European country has begun. We cannot ignore the possibilities for the development of peat-cutting which now open out before us. There are more bogs and peat deposits in Russia than anywhere else, and it is now possible to transform the back-breaking labour, which only a few workers were prepared to undertake, into more normal work. Practical co-operation with a modern, advanced state—Germany—has been achieved because her factories are already working on machines designed to lighten this labour, machines which will most certainly start to operate in 1922. We must take this fact into account. We can do a great deal in this sphere if we all understand and all spread the idea that, given intensified efforts and mechanised labour, we in Russia have a better opportunity to emerge from the economic crisis than any other country.

I want to emphasise another aspect of our economic policy. In assessing our New Economic Policy it is not enough to pay attention to what may be of particular importance. Of course, the essence of this policy is the alliance of the proletariat and the peasantry, the union of the vanguard of the proletariat with the broad mass of the peasants. Thanks to the New Economic Policy, the development of the productive forces—at all costs, and without delay—has begun. There is another aspect of the New Economic Policy, that of the possibility of learning. The New Economic Policy is a form that will enable us to begin learning how to manage our economy in real earnest; up to now we have been doing this very badly. Of course, it is difficult for a Communist leader, for a trade union leader of the working people to realise that at the moment trade is the touchstone of our economic life, the only possible basis for the alliance of the vanguard of the proletariat with the peasants, the only possible link which will permit us to begin economic development all along the line. If we take any merchant trading under state and legal control (our court is a proletarian one, and it can watch each private businessman in order to see that the laws are not interpreted for them as in bourgeois states; recently there was an example of this in Moscow,[45] and you all know that we shall multiply these examples, severely punishing any attempts by these private businessmen to contravene our laws), we shall see that all the same, this merchant, this private businessman, eager for his 100 per cent profit, will do business—for example, he will acquire raw material for industry in a way that most Communists or trade union workers would never be able to do. That is the significance of the New Economic Policy. Here is something you can learn. It is a very serious lesson, and we must all learn it. It is an extremely harsh one, not like listening to lectures or passing examinations. We are up against a difficult problem, a stern economic struggle, in circumstances of poverty, in circumstances of unparalleled difficulty, a bread shortage, famine and cold; this is the real school and we must graduate from it. Every attempt to brush this task aside, every attempt to turn a blind eye to it, to disregard it, would be the most criminal and most dangerous arrogance on the part of Communists and trade unionists. All of us, comrades, who are governing Soviet Russia, are apt to commit this sin, and we must admit it quite frankly in order to rid ourselves of this shortcoming.

We are undertaking economic development on the basis of yesterday's experience, and it is here that we make our main mistake. I shall quote a French proverb which says that people's faults are usually connected with their merits. A man's faults are, as it were, a continuation of his merits. But if the merits persist longer than they are needed, are displayed when and where they are no longer needed, they become faults. Very likely, almost all of you have observed this in private and public life, and we now note it in the development of our revolution, of our Party and of our trade unions, which are the mainstay of our Party; in the entire government machinery ruling Soviet Russia, we see this fault, which, as it were, is the continuation of our merits. Our great merit was that in the political and military fields we took a step of historic importance, that has gone down in world history as a change of epochs. What we have done cannot be taken from us, no matter what sufferings lie ahead. It was due to the proletarian revolution and to the fact that the Soviet system replaced the old system that we emerged from the imperialist war and got out of our misfortunes. This cannot be taken away from us—this is the undoubted, unalterable, inalienable merit, which no efforts or onslaughts of our enemies can take away from us, but which if it persists where it is no longer needed becomes a most dangerous fault.

A burst of enthusiasm on the part of the workers and peasants at their present level of class-consciousness was sufficient to solve political and military problems. They all understood that the imperialist war was crushing them— to understand this there was no need of a higher level of consciousness, of a new level of organisation. The enthusiasm, drive and heroism, which still remain and which will remain for ever as a monument to what a revolution can do and has done, helped to solve these problems. That is how we achieved our political and military successes, and this merit now becomes our most dangerous fault. We look back and we think that economic problems can be solved in the same manner. That, however, is the mistake; when the situation has changed and different problems have to be solved, we cannot look back and attempt to solve them by yesterday's methods. Don't try—you won't succeed! We must realise that this is a mistaken attitude. There are Communist Party and trade union workers who very often turn their backs on and wave aside the humble, many years' difficult work in economic management, which demands forbearance, bitter experiences, long effort, punctuality and perseverance, whether as government workers, or as yesterday's fighters; they excuse themselves with recollections of the great things they did yesterday. These people remind me of the fable of the geese[46] who boasted that they had "saved Rome", but to whom the peasant replied using a long switch, "Leave your ancestors in peace, and what good have *you* done, geese?" No one will deny that in 1917-18-19-20 we solved our political and military problems with the heroism and success that opened a new epoch in world history. That belongs to us, and there is no one, either in the Party or in the trade unions, who is attempting to take this away from us—but an entirely different task now faces government and trade union workers.

At the present moment you are surrounded by capitalist powers who will not help you, but will hamper you; at the present moment you work in conditions of poverty, ruin, famine and calamity. You must either learn to work at a different rate, calculating the work to be done in decades and not months, relying on the worn-out mass of the people who cannot keep pace with the revolutionary-heroic momentum in their daily work; either you learn to do this, or you will deserve to be called geese. When a trade union or a political worker makes the general statement that the trade unions, the Communist Party run things—that is good. In the political and military sphere we did this splendidly, but in the economic field we do it very badly. We have to admit this and do better. "Stop wagging your tongue" is what I will say to any trade union worker who puts the general question of whether the trade unions should take part in production. (*Applause*.) It would be better to give me a practical reply to the question and tell me (if you hold a responsible position, are a man in authority, a Communist Party or a trade union worker) where you have organised production well, how many years it took you to do it, how many people you have under you—a thousand or ten thousand. Give me a list of those whom you have assigned to the work of economic management which you have completed, instead of starting twenty different jobs without completing a single one because you had no time. It happens that we in Soviet Russia have not made a habit of completing economic tasks so as to be able to talk about our success for years to come, and of not fearing to learn from the merchant who makes one hundred per cent profit and a bit more; instead we write a wonderful resolution about raw materials and say that we are representatives of the Communist Party, the trade union, the proletariat. Forgive me, but what is the proletariat? It is the class which is working in large-scale industry. Where is your large-scale industry? What kind of proletariat is it? Where is your industry? Why is it at a standstill? Because there is no raw material? But did you succeed in collecting it? No. Write a resolution that it should be collected, and you will find yourself in a mess. And people will say, how stupid, and, consequently, you resemble the geese whose ancestors saved Rome.

History has allotted us the task of completing the great political revolution by slow, hard and laborious economic work, covering a very long period. Great political changes in history have always demanded a long period of assimilation. All great political changes have come about through the enthusiasm of the vanguard, whom the masses followed spontaneously, not quite consciously. There could be no other development in a society that was oppressed by tsars, landowners and capitalists. And we carried out this part of the work, the political revolution, in a manner that makes its epoch-making significance indisputable. Subsequently, following the great political revolution, however, another task arises which must be understood: this revolution has to be assimilated, has to be put into effect, and we must not plead that the Soviet system is bad, and that it must be rebuilt. We have a tremendous number of enthusiasts who want to rebuild in any kind of way, and these reconstructions lead to calamities of a kind which I have never known in all my life. I am very well aware of the faults of our government machinery in mass organisational work, and for every ten faults that any of you can point out to me, I can immediately point out a hundred more. The thing, however, is not that it should be improved by rapid reorganisation, but that this political transformation has to be assimilated to arrive at a different level of economic efficiency. That is the whole point. It is not necessary to rebuild, but, on the contrary, it is necessary to help correct the many faults present in the Soviet system and in the whole system of management, so as to help tens of millions of people. We need the aid of all the peasants to assimilate our great political victory. We need to look at things soberly and realise that victory has been won, but it has not yet become part and parcel of the economy of everyday life and of the living conditions of the people. This work will take many decades and will require colossal efforts. It cannot be carried out at the same rate, speed, and under the same conditions which existed during the war.

Before concluding, I want to apply this lesson—that faults are sometimes the continuation of our merits—to one of our institutions, namely, to the Cheka. You all know, comrades, the violent hatred towards this institution displayed by Russian émigrés and those numerous members of the ruling classes of the imperialist countries who live alongside these Russian émigrés. And no wonder! It was our effective weapon against the numerous plots and numerous attacks on Soviet power made by people who were infinitely stronger than us. The capitalists and landowners retained all their international ties and all the international support; they were supported by states incomparably more powerful than our state. You know from the history of these conspiracies how these people acted. You know that the only way in which we could reply to them was by merciless, swift and instant repression, with the sympathy and support of the workers and peasants. That is the merit of our Cheka. We shall always emphasise this whenever we hear, directly or indirectly, as we often do from abroad, the howls of those Russians who can say the word "Cheka" in all languages, and regard it as an example of Russian barbarism.

Gentlemen, Russian and foreign capitalists! We know

that you will never come to love this institution. No wonder! It was able to repulse your intrigues and plots better than anyone else, at a time when you throttled us, invaded us from all sides, when you organised internal plots and committed every possible crime in order to frustrate our peaceful work. Our only response is through an institution aware of the plotters' every move and able to retaliate immediately instead of engaging in persuasion. As long as there are exploiters in the world, who have no desire to hand over their landowner and capitalist rights to the workers on a platter, the power of the working people cannot survive without such an institution. We are keenly aware of this, but we also know that a man's merits may become his faults, and we know that prevailing conditions insistently demand that the work of this organisation be limited to the purely political sphere, that it concentrate its efforts on tasks in which it is aided by the situation and the circumstances. If the attempts of the counter-revolution resemble their previous attempts—and we have no proof that the mentality of our adversaries has altered in this respect, we have no grounds for believing this—we shall be able to reply in such a way that will make it clear that we are in earnest. The Soviet government grants admission to foreign representatives, who come here under the pretext of giving aid, but these same representatives turn round and help overthrow Soviet rule; there have been cases of this. Our government will not find itself in this position, because we shall value and make use of an institution like the Cheka. This we can guarantee to one and all. But, at the same time, we say categorically that it is essential to reform the Cheka, define its functions and powers, and limit its work to political problems. The task now confronting us is to develop trade, which is required by the New Economic Policy, and this demands greater revolutionary legality. Naturally, if we had made this the all-important task when we were attacked and Soviet power was taken by the throat, we would have been pedants; we would have been playing at revolution, but would not be making the revolution. The closer we approach conditions of unshakable and lasting power and the more trade develops, the more imperative it is to put forward the firm slogan of greater revolutionary legality, and the narrower becomes the sphere of activity of the institution which matches the plotters blow for blow. This conclusion results from the experience, observation and reflection of the government for the past year.

I must say in conclusion, comrades, that we have placed on a correct footing the problem we have been handling this year and which up to now we have handled so badly—that of forming a sound economic alliance of the workers and peasants, even under conditions of extreme poverty and devastation; we have taken the correct line, and there can be no doubt about this. And this is not merely a task for Russia alone, it is a world task. (*Stormy, prolonged applause.*)

This task which we are working on now, for the time being on our own, seems to be a purely Russian one, but in reality it is a task which all socialists will face. Capitalism is dying; in its death throes it can still condemn tens and hundreds of millions of people to unparalleled torment, but there is no power that can prevent its collapse. The new society, which will be based on the alliance of the workers and peasants, is inevitable. Sooner or later it will come— twenty years earlier or twenty years later—and when we work on the implementation of our New Economic Policy, we are helping to work out for this society the forms of alliance between the workers and peasants. We shall get this done and we shall create an alliance of the workers and peasants that is so sound that no power on earth will break it. (*Stormy, prolonged applause.*)

Pravda No 292,   Published according to
December 25, 1921   the verbatim report

2

INSTRUCTIONS BY THE NINTH ALL-RUSSIA CONGRESS
OF SOVIETS ON QUESTIONS OF ECONOMIC ACTIVITIES
DECEMBER 28

The Ninth All-Russia Congress of Soviets, having examined the reports of the People's Commissariats on their
economic activities during the year under review, supplements and summarises the decisions of the Congress of
Soviets on individual economic questions with the following
guiding points, which must be strictly adhered to by all
Soviet bodies at the centre and in the localities.

1. The Congress of Soviets orders· that the main and
immediate task of all the economic bodies must be to effect,
speedily and at all costs, stable practical improvements in
supplying the peasantry with large quantities of the goods
that are needed to raise the level of agriculture and improve
the living conditions of the working peasantry.

2. This being the main object, it must be kept in mind
by all industrial administrative bodies, allowing of course
no relaxation in the supply of the Red Army with everything it needs, a task which must remain primary in order
to maintain the Soviet Republic's defence potential.

3. The improvement of the conditions of the workers
should also depend on the achievement of this object, which
means that it is the duty of all workers' organisations (primarily the trade unions) to see to it that industry is so organised as to be able speedily and fully to satisfy the requirements of the peasantry; wage increases and improvement in
the conditions of industrial workers should be directly
determined by the degree to which success is achieved in this
field.

4. This object must also be pursued by the People's Commissariat of Finance; and the Ninth Congress of Soviets instructs it to make every effort to secure the speediest reduction of the issue of paper money, eventually put a stop to it and establish a sound currency backed by gold. The substitution of taxes for the issue of paper money must be pursued undeviatingly without any red tape.

5. The same object must be given priority by all bodies and organisations engaged in home and foreign trade, i. e., the Central Council of Co-operative Societies, the People's Commissariat of Foreign Trade, etc. The Congress of Soviets will judge—and instructs the leading bodies of the Soviet government to judge—the success of these organisations only by the rapid and practical results they achieve in developing exchange between agriculture and industry. In particular, the Congress instructs the various organisations to use private enterprises more widely for supplying raw materials, transporting these materials and for promoting trade in every way, while the function of state bodies is to control and direct this exchange, and sternly punish all deadening red tape and bureaucracy.

6. The Ninth Congress of Soviets calls upon all organisations and departments engaged in economic activities to devote infinitely more attention and energy than hitherto to the task of enlisting the services of all capable non-Party workers and peasants in this field of state activity.

The Congress declares that in this respect we are a long way behind requirements, that not enough method and perseverance are being displayed in this matter, that it is absolutely and urgently necessary to recruit business and government officials from a wider circle than hitherto; and, in particular, that every success achieved in rebuilding industry and agriculture should be more regularly encouraged by awards of the Order of the Red Banner of Labour, as well as by cash bonuses.

The Congress of Soviets draws the attention of all economic bodies and all mass organisations of a non-governmental, class character to the fact that it is absolutely essential still more perseveringly to enlist the services of specialists in economic organisation, to employ scientists and technicians, and men who by their practical activities have acquired experience and knowledge of trade, of organising large enterprises, of supervising business transactions, etc. The improvement of the material position of specialists and the training under their direction of a large number of workers and peasants must receive unflagging attention from the central and local government bodies of the R.S.F.S.R.

7. The Ninth Congress of Soviets calls upon the People's Commissariat of Justice to display far more energy than hitherto in two matters:

first, that the People's Courts of the Republic should keep close watch over the activities of private traders and manufacturers, and, while prohibiting the slightest restriction of their activities, should sternly punish the slightest attempt on their part to evade rigid compliance with the laws of the Republic. The People's Courts should encourage the masses of workers and peasants to take an independent, speedy and practical part in ensuring enforcement of the laws;

second, that the People's Courts should take more vigorous action against bureaucracy, red tape and mismanagement. Trials of such cases should be held not only for the purpose of increasing responsibility for the evil which it is so difficult to combat under present circumstances, but also for the purpose of focussing the attention of the masses of workers and peasants on this extremely important matter, and of securing a practical object, viz., greater success in the economic field.

The Ninth Congress is of the opinion that the task of the People's Commissariat of Education in this new period is to train, in the shortest possible period, specialists in all fields from among the peasants and workers; and it orders that school and extra-mural education should be more closely connected with the current economic tasks of the Republic as a whole, as well as of the given region and locality. In particular, the Ninth Congress of Soviets declares that far from enough has been done to fulfil the decision of the Eighth Congress of Soviets on the popularisation of the plan for the electrification of Russia, and requires that every electric power station mobilise all competent forces and arrange regular talks, lectures and practical studies to acquaint the workers and peasants with the importance of electricity and with the plan for electrification. In those uyezds where no power stations yet exist, at least small power stations should be built as speedily as possible and used as local centres for propaganda, education and the encouragement of every initiative in this field.

Written on December 25-27, 1921

Published in *Izvestia* No. 295,
December 30, 1921

Published according to
the manuscript

BRITISH LABOUR PARTY POLICY

(TO COMRADE CHICHERIN, A COPY TO COMRADE RADEK
AND ALL MEMBERS OF THE POLITICAL BUREAU)

The telegram about the British Labour Party shows how extraordinarily naïve Krasin is. As I see it, measures of two kinds should now be taken: 1) a series of articles signed by various people and ridiculing the views of so-called European democracy on the Georgian problem should be published in the press; 2) some caustic journalist should be immediately commissioned to draft for Chicherin a super-polite Note in reply to the British Labour Party. In this Note he should make it perfectly plain that the proposal that we withdraw our troops from Georgia and hold a referendum there would be quite reasonable and might be recognised as coming from people who have not gone out of their minds, and have not been bribed by the Entente, if it extended to all nations of the globe; specifically, in order to set the British Labour Party leaders thinking about the meaning of present-day imperialist relations in international politics, we suggest, in particular, that that party give favourable consideration to the following: first, that British troops be withdrawn from Ireland and that a referendum be held there; second, the same with regard to India; third, the same with regard to the withdrawal of Japanese troops from Korea; fourth, the same with regard to all countries in which there are troops of any of the big imperialist states. The Note should express, in superbly polite terms, the idea that people desirous of giving thought to these proposals of ours and to the system of imperialist relations in international politics may prove capable of understanding the "interesting" nature of the proposals made by us to the

British Labour Party. On the whole, the draft Note, couched in super-polite and extremely popular terms (to suit the intelligence of ten-year-olds), should deride the idiotic leaders of the British Labour Party.

I propose that the Political Bureau consider whether it ought to send a copy of this letter to Krasin. I personally am in favour.

Lenin

December 27, 1921

First published in *Pravda* No. 21,
January 21, 1930

Dictated by telephone
Published according to
a typewritten copy

THE ROLE AND FUNCTIONS OF THE TRADE UNIONS UNDER THE NEW ECONOMIC POLICY

DECISION OF THE C.C., R.C.P.(B.), JANUARY 12, 1922 [47]

1. THE NEW ECONOMIC POLICY AND THE TRADE UNIONS

The New Economic Policy introduces a number of important changes in the position of the proletariat and, consequently, in that of the trade unions. The great bulk of the means of production in industry and the transport system remains in the hands of the proletarian state. This, together with the nationalisation of the land, shows that the New Economic Policy does not change the nature of the workers' state, although it does substantially alter the methods and forms of socialist development for it permits of economic rivalry between socialism, which is now being built, and capitalism, which is trying to revive by supplying the needs of the vast masses of the peasantry through the medium of the market.

Changes in the forms of socialist development are necessary because the Communist Party and the Soviet government are now adopting special methods to implement the general policy of transition from capitalism to socialism and in many respects are operating differently from the way they operated before: they are capturing a number of positions by a "new flanking movement", so to speak; they are retreating in order to make better preparations for a new offensive against capitalism. In particular, a free market and capitalism, both subject to state control, are now being permitted and are developing; on the other hand, the socialised state enterprises are being put on what is called a profit basis, i. e., they are being reorganised on commercial

lines, which, in view of the general cultural backwardness
and exhaustion of the country, will, to a greater or lesser
degree, inevitably give rise to the impression among the
masses that there is an antagonism of interest between the
management of the different enterprises and the workers
employed in them.

2. STATE CAPITALISM IN THE PROLETARIAN STATE AND THE TRADE UNIONS

The proletarian state may, without changing its own
nature, permit freedom to trade and the development of
capitalism only within certain bounds, and only on the
condition that the state regulates (supervises, controls, deter-
mines the forms and methods of, etc.) private trade and private
capitalism. The success of such regulation will depend not
only on the state authorities but also, and to a larger
extent, on the degree of maturity of the proletariat and of
the masses of the working people generally, on their cultural
level, etc. But even if this regulation is completely successful, the antagonism of class interests between labour and
capital will certainly remain. Consequently, one of the main
tasks that will henceforth confront the trade unions is to
protect in every way the class interests of the proletariat in
its struggle against capital. This task should be openly put
in the forefront, and the machinery of the trade unions
must be reorganised, changed or supplemented accordingly
(conflict commissions, strike funds, mutual aid funds, etc.,
should be formed, or rather, built up).

3. THE STATE ENTERPRISES THAT ARE BEING PUT ON A PROFIT BASIS AND THE TRADE UNIONS

The transfer of state enterprises to the so-called profit
basis is inevitably and inseparably connected with the New
Economic Policy; in the near future this is bound to become
the predominant, if not the sole, form of state enterprise.
In actual fact, this means that with the free market now
permitted and developing the state enterprises will to a
large extent be put on a commercial basis. In view of the

urgent need to increase the productivity of labour and make every state enterprise pay its way and show a profit, and in view of the inevitable rise of narrow departmental interests and excessive departmental zeal, this circumstance is bound to create a certain conflict of interests in matters concerning labour conditions between the masses of workers and the directors and managers of the state enterprises, or the government departments in charge of them. Therefore, as regards the socialised enterprises, it is undoubtedly the duty of the trade unions to protect the interests of the working people, to facilitate as far as possible the improvement of their standard of living, and constantly to correct the blunders and excesses of business organisations resulting from bureaucratic distortions of the state apparatus.

4. THE ESSENTIAL DIFFERENCE BETWEEN THE CLASS STRUGGLE OF THE PROLETARIAT IN A STATE WHICH RECOGNISES PRIVATE OWNERSHIP OF THE LAND, FACTORIES, ETC., AND WHERE POLITICAL POWER IS IN THE HANDS OF THE CAPITALIST CLASS, AND THE ECONOMIC STRUGGLE OF THE PROLETARIAT IN A STATE WHICH DOES NOT RECOGNISE PRIVATE OWNERSHIP OF THE LAND AND THE MAJORITY OF THE LARGE ENTERPRISES AND WHERE POLITICAL POWER IS IN THE HANDS OF THE PROLETARIAT

As long as classes exist, the class struggle is inevitable. In the period of transition from capitalism to socialism the existence of classes is inevitable; and the Programme of the Russian Communist Party definitely states that we are taking only the first steps in the transition from capitalism to socialism. Hence, the Communist Party, the Soviet government and the trade unions must frankly admit the existence of an economic struggle and its inevitability until the electrification of industry and agriculture is completed— at least in the main—and until small production and the supremacy of the market are thereby cut off at the roots.

On the other hand, it is obvious that under capitalism the ultimate object of the strike struggle is to break up the state machine and to overthrow the given class state power.

Under the transitional type of proletarian state such as ours, however, the ultimate object of every action taken by the working class can only be to fortify the proletarian state and the state power of the proletarian class by combating the bureaucratic distortions, mistakes and flaws in this state, and by curbing the class appetites of the capitalists who try to evade its control, etc. Hence, the Communist Party, the Soviet government and the trade unions must never forget and must never conceal from the workers and the mass of the working people that the strike struggle in a state where the proletariat holds political power can be explained and justified only by the bureaucratic distortions of the proletarian state and by all sorts of survivals of the old capitalist system in the government offices on the one hand, and by the political immaturity and cultural backwardness of the mass of the working people on the other.

Hence, when friction and disputes arise between individual contingents of the working class and individual departments and organs of the workers' state, the task of the trade unions is to facilitate the speediest and smoothest settlement of these disputes to the maximum advantage of the groups of workers they represent, taking care, however, not to prejudice the interests of other groups of workers and the development of the workers' state and its economy as a whole; for only this development can lay the foundations for the material and cultural welfare of the working class. The only correct, sound and expedient method of removing friction and of settling disputes between individual contingents of the working class and the organs of the workers' state is for the trade unions to act as mediators, and through their competent bodies either to enter into negotiations with the competent business organisations on the basis of precise demands and proposals formulated by both sides, or appeal to higher state bodies.

In cases where wrong actions of business organisations, the backwardness of certain sections of workers, the provocations of counter-revolutionary elements or, lastly, lack of foresight on the part of the trade union organisations themselves lead to open disputes in the form of strikes in state enterprises, and so forth, the task of the trade unions is to bring about the speediest settlement of a dispute by taking measures in conformity with the general nature of trade union activities, that is, by taking steps to remove the real injustices and irregularities and to satisfy the lawful and practicable demands of the masses, by exercising political influence on the masses, and so forth.

One of the most important and infallible tests of the correctness and success of the activities of the trade unions is the degree to which they succeed in averting mass disputes in state enterprises by pursuing a far-sighted policy with a view to effectively protecting the interests of the masses of the workers in all respects and to removing in time all causes of dispute.

5. REVERSION TO VOLUNTARY TRADE UNION MEMBERSHIP

The formal attitude of the trade unions to the automatic enrolment of all wage-workers as union members has introduced a certain degree of bureaucratic distortion in the trade unions and has caused the latter to lose touch with the broad mass of their membership. Hence, it is necessary most resolutely to implement voluntary enrolment both of individuals and of groups into trade unions. Under no circumstances must trade union members be required to subscribe to any specific political views; in this respect, as well as in respect of religion, the trade unions must be non-partisan. All that must be required of trade union members in the proletarian state is that they should understand comradely discipline and the necessity of uniting the workers' forces for the purpose of protecting the interests of the working people and of assisting the working people's government, i. e., the Soviet government. The proletarian state must encourage the workers to organise in trade unions both by juridical and material means; but the trade unions can have no rights without duties.

6. THE TRADE UNIONS
AND THE MANAGEMENT OF INDUSTRY

Following its seizure of political power, the principal and fundamental interest of the proletariat lies in securing an enormous increase in the productive forces of society and in the output of manufactured goods. This task, which is clearly formulated in the Programme of the Russian Communist Party, is particularly urgent in our country today owing to post-war ruin, famine and dislocation. Hence, the speediest and most enduring success in restoring large-scale industry is a condition without which no success can be achieved in the general cause of emancipating labour from the yoke of capital and securing the victory of socialism. To achieve this success in Russia, in her present state, it is absolutely essential that all authority in the factories should be concentrated in the hands of the management. The factory management, usually built up on the principle of one-man responsibility, must have authority independently to fix and pay out wages, and also distribute rations, working clothes, and all other supplies on the basis and within the limits of collective agreements concluded with the trade unions; it must enjoy the utmost freedom to manoeuvre, exercise strict control of the actual successes achieved in increasing production, in making the factory pay its way and in increasing profits, and carefully select the most talented and capable administrative personnel, etc.

Under these circumstances, all direct interference by the trade unions in the management of factories must be regarded as positively harmful and impermissible.

It would be absolutely wrong, however, to interpret this indisputable axiom to mean that the trade unions must play no part in the socialist organisation of industry and in the management of state industry. Their participation in this is necessary in the following strictly defined forms.

7. THE ROLE AND FUNCTIONS OF THE TRADE UNIONS IN THE BUSINESS AND ADMINISTRATIVE ORGANISATIONS OF THE PROLETARIAN STATE

The proletariat is the class foundation of the state accomplishing the transition from capitalism to socialism. In a country where the small peasantry is overwhelmingly predominant the proletariat can successfully fulfil this function only if it very skilfully, cautiously and gradually establishes an alliance with the vast majority of the peasantry. The trade unions must collaborate closely and constantly with the government, all the political and economic activities of which are guided by the class-conscious vanguard of the working class—the Communist Party. Being a school of communism in general, the trade unions must, in particular, be a school for training the whole mass of workers, and eventually all working people, in the art of managing socialist industry (and gradually also agriculture).

Proceeding from these principles, the trade unions' part in the activities of the business and administrative organisations of the proletarian state should, in the immediate period, take the following main forms:

1. The trade unions should help to staff all the state business and administrative bodies connected with economics: nominate their candidates for them, stating their length of service, experience, and so forth. Right of decision lies solely with the business organisations, which also bear full responsibility for the activities of the respective organisations. The business organisations, however, must give careful consideration to the views on all candidates expressed by the trade unions concerned.

2. One of the most important functions of the trade unions is to promote and train factory managers from among the workers and the masses of the working people generally. At the present time we have scores of such factory managers who are quite satisfactory, and hundreds who are more or less satisfactory, but very soon, however, we must have hundreds of the former and thousands of the latter. The trade unions must much more carefully and regularly than hitherto keep a systematic register of all workers and peasants capable of holding posts of this kind, and thoroughly, efficiently and from every aspect verify the progress they make in learning the art of management.

3. The trade unions must take a far greater part in the activities of all the planning bodies of the proletarian state, in drawing up economic plans and also programmes of production and expenditure of stocks of material supplies for the workers, in selecting the factories that are to continue to receive state supplies, to be leased, or to be given out as concessions, etc. The trade unions should undertake no

direct functions of controlling production in private and leased enterprises, but participate in the regulation of private capitalist production exclusively by sharing in the activities of the competent state bodies. In addition to participating in all cultural and educational activities and in production propaganda, the trade unions must also, on an increasing scale, enlist the working class and the masses of the working people generally for all branches of the work of building up the state economy; they must make them familiar with all aspects of economic life and with all details of industrial operations—from the procurement of raw materials to the marketing of the product; give them a more and more concrete understanding of the single state plan of socialist economy and the worker's and peasant's practical interest in its implementation.

4. The drawing up of scales of wages and supplies, etc., is one of the essential functions of the trade unions in the building of socialism and in their participation in the management of industry. In particular, disciplinary courts should steadily improve labour discipline and proper ways of promoting it and achieving increased productivity; but they must not interfere with the functions of the People's Courts in general or with the functions of factory managements.

This list of the major functions of the trade unions in the work of building up socialist economy should, of course, be drawn up in greater detail by the competent trade union and government bodies. Taking into account the experience of the enormous work accomplished by the unions in organising the economy and its management, and also the mistakes which have caused no little harm and which resulted from direct, unqualified, incompetent and irresponsible interference in administrative matters, it is most important, in order to restore the economy and strengthen the Soviet system, deliberately and resolutely to start persevering practical activities calculated to extend over a long period of years and designed to give the workers and all working people generally practical training in the art of managing the economy of the whole country.

8. CONTACT WITH THE MASSES—THE FUNDAMENTAL
CONDITION FOR ALL TRADE UNION ACTIVITY

Contact with the masses, i. e., with the overwhelming majority of the workers (and eventually of all the working people), is the most important and most fundamental condition for the success of all trade union activity. In all the trade union organisations and their machinery, from bottom up, there should be instituted, and tested in practice over a period of many years, a system of responsible comrades—who must not all be Communists—who should live right among the workers, study their lives in every detail, and be able unerringly, on any question, and at any time, to judge the mood, the real aspirations, needs and thoughts of the masses. They must be able without a shadow of false idealisation to define the degree of their class-consciousness and the extent to which they are influenced by various prejudices and survivals of the past; and they must be able to win the boundless confidence of the masses by comradeship and concern for their needs. One of the greatest and most serious dangers that confront the numerically small Communist Party which, as the vanguard of the working class, is guiding a vast country in the process of transition to socialism (for the time being without the direct support of the more advanced countries), is isolation from the masses, the danger that the vanguard may run too far ahead and fail to "straighten out the line", fail to maintain firm contact with the whole army of labour, i. e., with the overwhelming majority of workers and peasants. Just as the very best factory, with the very best motors and first-class machines, will be forced to remain idle if the transmission belts from the motors to the machines are damaged, so our work of socialist construction must meet with inevitable disaster if the trade unions—the transmission belts from the Communist Party to the masses—are badly fitted or function badly. It is not sufficient to explain, to reiterate and corroborate this truth; it must be backed up organisationally by the whole structure of the trade unions and by their everyday activities.

9. THE CONTRADICTIONS IN THE STATUS
OF THE TRADE UNIONS UNDER THE DICTATORSHIP
OF THE PROLETARIAT

From all the foregoing it is evident that there are a number of contradictions in the various functions of the trade unions. On the one hand, their principal method of operation is that of persuasion and education; on the other hand, as participants in the exercise of state power they cannot refuse to share in coercion. On the one hand, their main function is to protect the interests of the masses of the working people in the most direct and immediate sense of the term; on the other hand, as participants in the exercise of state power and builders of the economy as a whole they cannot refuse to resort to pressure. On the one hand, they must operate in military fashion, for the dictatorship of the proletariat is the fiercest, most dogged and most desperate class war; on the other hand, specifically military methods of operation are least of all applicable to the trade unions. On the one hand, they must be able to adapt themselves to the masses, to their level; on the other hand, they must never pander to the prejudices and backwardness of the masses, but steadily raise them to a higher and higher level, etc., etc. These contradictions are no accident, and they will persist for several decades; for as long as survivals of capitalism and small production remain, contradictions between them and the young shoots of socialism are inevitable throughout the social system.

Two practical conclusions must be drawn from this. First, for the successful conduct of trade union activities it is not enough to understand their functions correctly, it is not enough to organise them properly. In addition, special tact is required, ability to approach the masses in a special way in each individual case for the purpose of raising these masses to a higher cultural, economic and political stage with the minimum of friction.

Second, the afore-mentioned contradictions will inevitably give rise to disputes, disagreements, friction, etc. A higher body is required with sufficient authority to settle these at once. This higher body is the Communist Party and the international federation of the Communist Parties of all countries—the Communist International.

10. THE TRADE UNIONS AND THE SPECIALISTS

The main principles of this question are set forth in the Programme of the Russian Communist Party; but these will remain paper principles if constant attention is not paid to the facts which indicate the degree to which they are put into practice. Recent facts of this kind are: first, cases of the murder of engineers by workers in socialised mines not only in the Urals, but also in the Donets Basin; second, the suicide of V. V. Oldenborger, Chief Engineer of the Moscow Waterworks, because of the intolerable working conditions due to the incompetent and impermissible conduct of the members of the Communist group, as well as of organs of the Soviet government, which prompted the All-Russia Central Executive Committee to turn the whole matter over to the judicial authorities.

The Communist Party and the Soviet government as a whole bear a far greater share of the blame for cases of this kind than the trade unions. But the present issue is not one of establishing the degree of political guilt, but of drawing certain political conclusions. Unless our leading bodies, i. e., the Communist Party, the Soviet government and the trade unions, guard as the apple of their eye every specialist who does his work conscientiously and knows and loves it—even though the ideas of communism are totally alien to him—it will be useless to expect any serious progress in socialist construction. We may not be able to achieve it soon, but we must at all costs achieve a situation in which specialists—as a separate social stratum, which will persist until we have reached the highest stage of development of communist society—can enjoy better conditions of life under socialism than they enjoyed under capitalism insofar as concerns their material and legal status, comradely collaboration with the workers and peasants, and in the mental plane, i. e., finding satisfaction in their work, realising that it is socially useful and independent of the sordid interests of the capitalist class. Nobody will regard a government department as being tolerably well organised if it does not take systematic measures to provide for all the needs of the specialists, to reward the best of them, to safeguard and protect their interests, etc., and does not secure practical results in this.

The trade unions must conduct all the activities of the
type indicated (or systematically collaborate in the activities of all the government departments concerned) not from
the point of view of the interests of the given department,
but from the point of view of the interests of labour and of
the economy as a whole. With regard to the specialists, on
the trade unions devolves the very arduous duty of daily
exercising influence on the broad masses of the working
people in order to create proper relations between them and
the specialists. Only such activities can produce really
important practical results.

11. THE TRADE UNIONS AND PETTY-BOURGEOIS INFLUENCE ON THE WORKING CLASS

Trade unions are really effective only when they unite
very broad strata of the non-Party workers. This must give
rise—particularly in a country in which the peasantry greatly predominates—to relative stability, specifically among
the trade unions, of those political influences that serve as
the superstructure over the remnants of capitalism and over
small production. These influences are petty-bourgeois, i. e.,
Socialist-Revolutionary and Menshevik (the Russian variety of the parties of the Second and Two-and-a-Half Internationals) on the one hand, and anarchist on the other. Only
among these trends has any considerable number of people
remained who defend capitalism ideologically and not from
selfish class motives, and continue to believe in the non-class
nature of the "democracy", "equality", and "liberty" in
general that they preach.

It is to this socio-economic cause and not to the role
of individual groups, still less of individual persons, that
we must attribute the survivals (sometimes even the revival) in our country of such petty-bourgeois ideas among
the trade unions. The Communist Party, the Soviet bodies
that conduct cultural and educational activities and all
Communist members of trade unions must therefore devote
far more attention to the ideological struggle against petty-
bourgeois influences, trends and deviations among the
trade unions, especially because the New Economic Policy

is bound to lead to a certain strengthening of capitalism. It is urgently necessary to counteract this by intensifying the struggle against petty-bourgeois influences upon the working class.

Central Committee,
Russian Communist Party (Bolsheviks)

Written December 30,
1921-January 4, 1922

Published in *Pravda* No. 12,
January 17, 1922

Published according to
the newspaper text
checked with
the manuscript

DRAFT DIRECTIVE OF THE POLITICAL BUREAU ON THE NEW ECONOMIC POLICY[48]

Draft

The Political Bureau brings to the notice of all economic bodies that now, after the Party Conference in December 1921 and the Ninth Congress of Soviets, the New Economic Policy has been quite firmly and clearly established.

The maximum effort must therefore be made to test it in practice as quickly and as widely as possible. All general arguments, theoretical arguments and debates on the subject of the New Economic Policy must be relegated to debating clubs, partly to the press. They must be rooted out relentlessly from the Council of People's Commissars, the Council of Labour and Defence and all economic bodies. All sorts of commissions must be reduced to the absolute minimum and commission conferences replaced by the demand for written amendments or counter-drafts from all interested departments within the shortest period (one or two days). The Higher Economic Commission should be turned into a body engaged solely in classifying and pooling the economic acts promulgated by the state, and all sorts of so-called commission discussion should, if possible, be ruled out. The Higher Economic Commission must accelerate and not slow down the general course of the work.

The Political Bureau requires the People's Commissariat of Finance to concentrate all its efforts on achieving the speediest possible increase of the number of taxes and increasing the revenues from them, and also on business-like amendments to the general budget. All arguments about the money policy, the replacement of the tax in kind by cash taxes, etc., should be taken partly to debating clubs and partly to the press.

The Political Bureau requires all People's Commissars to display the utmost speed and energy in eliminating bureaucracy and red tape in the testing of the New Economic Policy in practice; the Political Bureau requires that bonuses be instituted for the largest possible number of persons holding responsible positions for speedily increasing output and expanding both home and foreign trade. This requirement concerns, first and foremost, the People's Commissariat of Foreign Trade, then the State Bank (particularly its trade department), the Central Council of Co-operative Societies and the Supreme Economic Council.

After this draft has been endorsed in the Political Bureau, have it read to and signed by all members of the collegiums of all People's Commissariats and all members of the Presidium of the All-Russia Central Executive Committee.

Written between
January 9 and 12, 1922

First published in 1942
in *Lenin Miscellany XXXIV*

Published according to
the manuscript and a
typewritten copy

TO THE WORKING PEOPLE OF DAGHESTAN[49]

I gratefully accept your gift, which is the result of the creative initiative of the working people of Daghestan.

I wish you success in the difficult work of reviving the economy of Daghestan.

Lenin,

Chairman of the Council
of People's Commissars
of the R.S.F.S.R.

January 12, 1922

Izvestia No. 10,
January 14, 1922

Dictated by telephone
Published according to
a typewritten copy

LETTER TO G. K. ORJONIKIDZE
ON THE STRENGTHENING
OF THE GEORGIAN RED ARMY[50]

Comrade Sergo,

It is absolutely essential that the Congress of Soviets of Georgia should adopt a decision to strengthen the *Georgian* Red Army without fail, and that the decision is *really* carried out.

In the last resort, if the peasants are opposed to this, a decision, couched in the most general terms, should be adopted, such as it is deemed essential "without fail to strengthen the Georgian Red Army and to call upon all government bodies and all the working people to work to secure this", etc.

Actually, however, it is necessary, at all costs, and *immediately*, to develop and strengthen the Georgian Red Army. As a beginning let it consist only of one brigade or even less; two or three thousand Red cadets—of whom 1,500 should be Communists—who (as cadres) could serve as the nucleus of an army *when the contingency arises*. This is absolutely essential.

Perhaps Stalin will enlarge on the military and technical methods of carrying this out.

I am confining myself to the political aspect of the matter: those who fail to carry this out will be expelled from the Party *without compunction*. This is not a matter to be trifled with. It is absolutely essential politically; and you personally, and the entire Georgian Central Committee, will be held responsible to the whole Party for this.

I await your reply.

Yours,
Lenin

February 13

This is for Comrade Sergo and for all the members of the Central Committee of the Georgian Communist Party.

Written on February 13, 1922

First published in 1925 in M. D. Orakhelashvili, *Lenin i Z.S.F.S.R.* (*Materialy*) (Lenin and the Transcaucasian Soviet Federative Socialist Republic [Documents]), Tiflis, Sovetsky Kavkaz Publishing House

Published according to a typewritten copy supplemented and signed by Lenin

LETTER TO D. I. KURSKY WITH NOTES
ON THE DRAFT CIVIL CODE

February 28, 1922

Comrade Kursky,

Re your letter of February 23 (No. 255) in reply to my letter.

I shall try to see you personally, but I cannot promise it because I am not feeling well.

I hope that *after* the meeting of executives in connection with my letter, you will write to me about its practical results. It is particularly important to organise a real check of what is *actually* being done, what is actually being accomplished, what the People's Courts and the Revolutionary Tribunals have achieved and how this can be assessed and verified.

How many cases of abuses of the *New Economic Policy* have been tried?

How many sentenced, and what punishments (as a whole and not in individual cases)?

etc.

With communist greetings,

Lenin

Especially urgent and important:

P. S. *Re the Civil Code*[51] : I am unable to go into the wording of individual articles. My health does not permit me to do so.

I must confine myself to the following points:

1) The People's Commissar of Justice must find out and *personally* check who precisely is responsible for each major section of the Civil Code.

2) Everything that the literature and experience of the West-European countries contain on the *protection* of the working people must be used.

3) Do not limit yourself to that (this is most important). Do not follow the People's Commissariat of Foreign Affairs blindly. *We must not play up to "Europe"* but MOVE FARTHER *in intensifying state interference in "private legal relations", in civil affairs.* I cannot say exactly how that ought to be done because I am in no condition either to study the question or to go into even an individual code. But that that must be done is clear to me. The danger threatening us in this field is that of *underdoing* it (and not that of overdoing it); that, too, is perfectly clear to me. On the eve of Genoa [52] we must not make a false move, show a lack of spirit, let slip out of our hands the slightest possibility of *extending* state interference in "civil" relations.

Lenin

First published in 1945
in *Lenin Miscellany XXXV*

Published according to
the manuscript

NOTES OF A PUBLICIST

ON ASCENDING A HIGH MOUNTAIN; THE HARM OF DESPONDENCY;
THE UTILITY OF TRADE; ATTITUDE TOWARDS
THE MENSHEVIKS, ETC.[13]

I

BY WAY OF EXAMPLE

Let us picture to ourselves a man ascending a very high, steep and hitherto unexplored mountain. Let us assume that he has overcome unprecedented difficulties and dangers and has succeeded in reaching a much higher point than any of his predecessors, but still has not reached the summit. He finds himself in a position where it is not only difficult and dangerous to proceed in the direction and along the path he has chosen, but positively impossible. He is forced to turn back, descend, seek another path, longer, perhaps, but one that will enable him to reach the summit. The descent from the height that no one before him has reached proves, perhaps, to be more dangerous and difficult for our imaginary traveller than the ascent—it is easier to slip; it is not so easy to choose a foothold; there is not that exhilaration that one feels in going upwards, straight to the goal, etc. One has to tie a rope round oneself, spend hours with an alpenstock to cut footholds or a projection to which the rope could be tied firmly; one has to move at a snail's pace, and move downwards, descend, away from the goal; and one does not know where this extremely dangerous and painful descent will end, or whether there is a fairly safe detour by which one can ascend more boldly, more quickly and more directly to the summit.

It would hardly be natural to suppose that a man who had climbed to such an unprecedented height but found himself in such a position did not have his moments of despondency. In all probability these moments would be more numerous, more frequent and harder to bear if he heard the voices of those below, who, through a telescope and from a safe distance, are watching his dangerous descent, which cannot even be described as what the *Smena Vekh* [54] people call "descending with the brakes on"; brakes presuppose a well-designed and tested vehicle, a well-prepared road and previously tested appliances. In this case, however, there is no vehicle, no road, absolutely nothing that had been tested beforehand.

The voices from below ring with malicious joy. They do not conceal it; they chuckle gleefully and shout: "He'll fall in a minute! Serve him right, the lunatic!" Others try to conceal their malicious glee and behave mostly like Judas Golovlyov. [55] They moan and raise their eyes to heaven in sorrow, as if to say: "It grieves us sorely to see our fears justified! But did not we, who have spent all our lives working out a judicious plan for scaling this mountain, demand that the ascent be postponed until our plan was complete? And if we so vehemently protested against taking this path, which this lunatic is now abandoning (look, look, he has turned back! He is descending! A single step is taking him hours of preparation! And yet we were roundly abused when time and again we demanded moderation and caution!), if we so fervently censured this lunatic and warned everybody against imitating and helping him, we did so entirely because of our devotion to the great plan to scale this mountain, and in order to prevent this great plan from being generally discredited!"

Happily, in the circumstances we have described, our imaginary traveller cannot hear the voices of these people who are "true friends" of the idea of ascent; if he did, they would probably nauseate him. And nausea, it is said, does not help one to keep a clear head and a firm step, particularly at high altitudes.

II

WITHOUT METAPHORS

An analogy is not proof. Every analogy is lame. These are incontrovertible and common truths; but it would do no harm to recall them in order to see the limits of every analogy more clearly.

Russia's proletariat rose to a gigantic height in its revolution, not only when it is compared with 1789 and 1793, but also when compared with 1871. We must take stock of what we have done and what we have not as dispassionately, as clearly and as concretely as possible. If we do that we shall be able to keep clear heads. We shall not suffer from nausea, illusions, or despondency.

We wound up the bourgeois-democratic revolution more thoroughly than had ever been done before anywhere in the world. That is a great gain, and no power on earth can deprive us of it.

We accomplished the task of getting out of the most reactionary imperialist war in a revolutionary way. That, too, is a gain no power on earth can deprive us of; it is a gain which is all the more valuable for the reason that reactionary imperialist massacres are inevitable in the not distant future if capitalism continues to exist; and the people of the twentieth century will not be so easily satisfied with a second edition of the "Basle Manifesto", with which the renegades, the heroes of the Second and the Two-and-a-Half Internationals, fooled themselves and the workers in 1912 and 1914-18.

We have created a Soviet type of state and by that we have ushered in a new era in world history, the era of the political rule of the proletariat, which is to supersede the era of bourgeois rule. Nobody can deprive us of this, either, although the Soviet type of state will have the finishing touches put to it only with the aid of the practical experience of the working class of several countries.

But we have not finished building even the foundations of socialist economy and the hostile powers of moribund capitalism can still deprive us of that. We must clearly appreciate this and frankly admit it; for there is nothing more dangerous than illusions (and vertigo, particularly at high altitudes). And there is absolutely nothing terrible, nothing that should give legitimate grounds for the slightest despondency, in admitting this bitter truth; for we have always urged and reiterated the elementary truth of Marxism—that the joint efforts of the workers of several advanced countries are needed for the victory of socialism. We are still alone and in a backward country, a country that was ruined more than others, but we have accomplished a great deal. More than that—we have preserved intact the army of the revolutionary proletarian forces; we have preserved its manoeuvring ability; we have kept clear heads and can sober-ly calculate where, when and how far to retreat (in order to leap further forward); where, when and how to set to work to alter what has remained unfinished. Those Communists are doomed who imagine that it is possible to finish such an epoch-making undertaking as completing the foundations of socialist economy (particularly in a small-peasant country) without making mistakes, without retreats, without numer-ous alterations to what is unfinished or wrongly done. Com-munists who have no illusions, who do not give way to despondency, and who preserve their strength and flexibility "to begin from the beginning" over and over again in approaching an extremely difficult task, are not doomed (and in all probability will not perish).

And still less permissible is it for us to give way to the slightest degree of despondency; we have still less grounds for doing so because, notwithstanding the ruin, poverty, backwardness and starvation prevailing in our country, in the *economics* that prepare the way for socialism we have *begun to make progress*, while side by side with us, all over the world, countries which are more advanced, and a thou-sand times wealthier and militarily stronger than we are, *are still retrogressing* in *their* own vaunted, familiar, capi-talist economic field, in which they have worked for centu-ries.

III

CATCHING FOXES; LEVI AND SERRATI

The following is said to be the most reliable method of catching foxes. The fox that is being tracked is surrounded at a certain distance with a rope which is set at a little height from the snow-covered ground and to which are attached little red flags. Fearing this obviously artificial human device, the fox will emerge only if and where an opening is allowed in this fence of flags; and the hunter waits for it at this opening. One would think that caution would be the most marked trait of an animal that is hunted by everybody.

But it turns out that in this case, too, "virtue unduly prolonged" is a fault. The fox is caught precisely because it is over-cautious.

I must confess to a mistake I made at the Third Congress of the Communist International also as a result of over-caution. At that Congress I was on the extreme Right flank. I am convinced that it was the only correct stand to take, for a very large (and influential) group of delegates, headed by many German, Hungarian and Italian comrades, occupied an inordinately "Left" and incorrectly Left position, and far too often, instead of soberly weighing up the situation that was not very favourable for immediate and direct revolutionary action, they vigorously indulged in the waving of little red flags. Out of caution and a desire to prevent this undoubtedly wrong deviation towards Leftism from giving a false direction to the whole tactics of the Communist International, I did all I could to defend Levi. I suggested that perhaps he had lost his head (I did not deny that he had lost his head) because he had been very frightened by the mistakes of the Lefts; and I argued that there had been cases of Communists who had lost their heads "finding" them again afterwards. Even while admitting, under pressure of the Lefts, that Levi was a Menshevik, I said that such an admission did not settle the question. For example, the whole history of the fifteen years of struggle between the Mensheviks and the Bolsheviks in Russia (1903-17) proves, as the three Russian revolutions also prove, that, in general, the Mensheviks were absolutely wrong and that they were, in fact, agents of the bourgeoisie in the working-class movement. This fact is incontrovertible. But this incontrovertible fact does not eliminate the other fact that in *individual* cases the Mensheviks were right and the Bolsheviks wrong, as, for example, on the question of boycotting the Stolypin Duma in 1907.

Eight months have elapsed since the Third Congress of the Communist International. Obviously, our controversy with the Lefts is now outdated; events have settled it. It has been proved that I was wrong about Levi, because he has definitely shown that he took the Menshevik path not accidentally, not temporarily, not by "going too far" in combating the very dangerous mistakes of the Lefts, but deliberately and permanently, because of his very nature.

Instead of honestly admitting that it was necessary for him to appeal for readmission to the party after the Third Congress of the Communist International, as every person who had temporarily lost his head when irritated by some mistakes committed by the Lefts should have done, Levi began to play sly tricks on the party, to try to put a spoke in its wheel, i. e., actually he began to serve those agents of the bourgeoisie, the Second and the Two-and-a-Half Internationals. Of course, the German Communists were quite right when they retaliated to this recently by expelling several more gentlemen from their party, those who were found to be secretly helping Paul Levi in this noble occupation.

The development of the German and Italian Communist Parties since the Third Congress of the Comintern has shown that the mistakes committed by the Lefts at that Congress have been noted and are being rectified—little by little, slowly, but steadily; the decisions of the Third Congress of the Communist International are being loyally carried out. The process of transforming the old type of European parliamentary party—which in fact is reformist and only slightly tinted with revolutionary colours—into a *new type* of party, into a genuinely revolutionary, genuinely Communist Party, is an extremely arduous one. This is demonstrated most clearly, perhaps, by the example of France. The process of changing the *type* of Party work in everyday life, of getting it out of the humdrum channel; the process of converting the Party into the vanguard of the revolutionary proletariat without permitting it to become divorced from the masses, but, on the contrary, by linking it more and more closely with them, imbuing them with revolutionary consciousness and rousing them for the revolutionary struggle, is a very difficult, but most important one. If the European Communists do not take advantage of the intervals (probably very short) between the periods of particularly acute revolutionary battles—such as took place in many capitalist countries of Europe and America in 1921 and the beginning of 1922—for the purpose of bringing about this fundamental, internal, profound reorganisation of the whole structure of their Parties and of their work, they will be committing the gravest of crimes. Fortunately, there is no reason to fear this. The quiet, steady, calm, not very rapid, but profound work

of creating genuine Communist Parties, genuine revolutionary vanguards of the proletariat, has begun and is proceeding in Europe and America.

Political lessons taken even from the observation of such
a trivial thing as catching foxes prove to be useful. On the
one hand, excessive caution leads to mistakes. On the other
hand, it must not be forgotten that if we give way to mere
"sentiment" or indulge in the waving of little red flags
instead of soberly weighing up the situation, we may commit
irreparable mistakes; we may perish where there is absolutely no need to, although the difficulties are great.

Paul Levi now wants to get into the good graces of the
bourgeoisie—and, *consequently*, of its agents, the Second and
the Two-and-a-Half Internationals—by republishing precisely those writings of Rosa Luxemburg in which she was
wrong. We shall reply to this by quoting two lines from a
good old Russian fable [56]: "Eagles may at times fly lower
than hens, but hens can never rise to the height of eagles."
Rosa Luxemburg was mistaken on the question of the independence of Poland; she was mistaken in 1903 in her appraisal of Menshevism; she was mistaken on the theory of the
accumulation of capital; she was mistaken in July 1914,
when, together with Plekhanov, Vandervelde, Kautsky and
others, she advocated unity between the Bolsheviks and
Mensheviks; she was mistaken in what she wrote in prison
in 1918 (she corrected most of these mistakes at the end of
1918 and the beginning of 1919 after she was released).
But in spite of her mistakes she was—and remains for us—
an eagle. And not only will Communists all over the world
cherish her memory, but her biography and her *complete*
works (the publication of which the German Communists
are inordinately delaying, which can only be partly excused
by the tremendous losses they are suffering in their severe
struggle) will serve as useful manuals for training many
generations of Communists all over the world. "Since
August 4, 1914,[57] German Social-Democracy has been a stinking corpse"—this statement will make Rosa Luxemburg's
name famous in the history of the international working-
class movement. And, of course, in the backyard of the working-class movement, among the dung heaps, hens like Paul
Levi, Scheidemann, Kautsky and all that fraternity will

cackle over the mistakes committed by the great Communist. To every man his own.

As for Serrati, he is like a bad egg, which bursts with a loud noise and with an exceptionally—pungent smell. Is it not too rich to get carried at "his" congress a resolution that declares readiness to submit to the decision of the Congress of the Communist International, then to send old Lazzari to the Congress, and finally, to cheat the workers as brazenly as a horse-coper? The Italian Communists who are training a real party of the revolutionary proletariat in Italy will now be able to give the working masses an object lesson in political chicanery and Menshevism. The useful, *repelling* effect of this will not be felt immediately, not without many repeated object lessons, but it will be felt. The victory of the Italian Communists is assured if they do not isolate themselves from the masses, if they do not lose patience in the hard work of exposing all of Serrati's chicanery to rank-and-file workers in a practical way, if they do not yield to the very easy and very dangerous temptation to say "minus *a*" whenever Serrati says "a", if they steadily train the masses to adopt a revolutionary world outlook and prepare them for revolutionary action, if they also take practical advantage of the practical and magnificent (although costly) object lessons of fascism.

Levi and Serrati are not characteristic in themselves; they are characteristic of the modern type of the extreme Left wing of petty-bourgeois democracy, of the camp of the "other side", the camp of the international capitalists, the camp that is against us. The whole of "their" camp, from Gompers to Serrati, are gloating, exulting, or else shedding crocodile tears over our retreat, our "descent", our New Economic Policy. Let them gloat, let them perform their clownish antics. To every man his own. But we shall not harbour any illusions or give way to despondency. If we are not afraid of admitting our mistakes, not afraid of making repeated efforts to rectify them—we shall reach the very summit. The cause of the international bloc from Gompers to Serrati is doomed.

Written at the end
of February 1922
First published in *Pravda*
No. 87, April 16, 1924

Published according
to the manuscript

THE INTERNATIONAL AND DOMESTIC SITUATION OF THE SOVIET REPUBLIC

SPEECH DELIVERED TO A MEETING OF THE COMMUNIST GROUP AT THE ALL-RUSSIA CONGRESS OF METALWORKERS, MARCH 6, 1922[58]

(*Stormy applause.*) Comrades, permit me to depart somewhat from your usual procedure and speak today not of the subjects on the agenda of your meeting and Congress, but of my conclusions and opinions on the principal political problems. It has now become the custom to address those who, while not being official representatives of state departments, actually perform an enormous part of the work of the state. You all know that really business-like work is being done in most of our state departments by representatives of the working class, and this, of course, includes the metalworkers, who are in the front ranks.

That is why I think in this case it will not be out of place to depart from the usual procedure and to speak not so much on trade union and Party issues as on political issues, on our international and domestic situation. In my opinion there is something in our international and domestic situation that resembles some change of policy to which every Party member, and, of course, every class-conscious worker, should pay special attention in order that he may fully understand the significance of this change of policy, and be able properly to assimilate it and apply it in his Soviet, Party, trade union or other work.

Of course, comrades, you all know that Genoa remains in the forefront of the problems of our international politics. I am not very sure that it does so legitimately, for when we say "Genoa" we mean the Conference that everybody long ago heard about, the Conference that was to have taken place in Genoa, Italy. The preparations for it had been almost completed; but now, unfortunately, the situation is so indefinite that nobody knows (and I am afraid that even the initiators and organisers themselves do not know) whether there is much chance of its taking place or not. At all events, we must say to ourselves, and to all those who have any interest in the destiny of the workers' and peasants' republic, that our position on this question, that is, on the question of the Genoa Conference, has been absolutely firm from the very beginning, and remains so. It is not our fault if certain people lack not only firmness but even the most elementary determination, the most elementary ability to carry out their own plans. From the very beginning we declared that *we welcomed Genoa and would attend it.* We understood perfectly well and did not in the least conceal the fact that we were going there as merchants, because trade with capitalist countries (as long as they have not entirely collapsed) is absolutely essential to us; we realised that we were going to Genoa to bargain for the most proper and most advantageous and politically suitable terms for this trade, and nothing more. This is by no means a secret to those capitalist countries whose governments drew up the first plan for the Genoa Conference and got it going. Those countries know perfectly well that the list of commercial agreements linking us with different capitalist states is growing longer and longer, that the number of practical transactions is increasing, and that we are now discussing in the greatest detail a huge number of joint Russian and foreign commercial projects between the most diverse combinations of foreign countries and various branches of our industry. Thus, the capitalist states are well aware of the practical basis of what is mainly to be discussed at Genoa. And this basis has a superstructure consisting of all sorts of political talk, assumptions and projects, but we must realise that it is only a little one, largely artificial, designed and erected by those who are interested in it.

It goes without saying that during the more than four years' existence of Soviet power we have acquired sufficient practical experience (apart from the fact that we are already quite familiar with it in theory) to enable us to appraise correctly the diplomatic game the gentlemen who

represent the bourgeois countries are today playing according
to all the rules of the obsolete art of bourgeois diplomacy.
We know perfectly well what lies at the bottom of this
game; we know that it is trade. *The bourgeois countries must
trade with Russia*; they know that unless they establish some
form of economic relations their disintegration will continue
in the way it has done up to now. Notwithstanding all their
magnificent victories, notwithstanding the endless boasting
with which they fill the newspapers and telegraph services
of the whole world, their economy is falling to pieces. And
after more than three years of effort, after their great victories, they cannot cope with the very simple task of restoring
the old, let alone building anything new, and are still rack-
ing their brains over the problem of how to get together and
form some combination of three, four, or five (the number
is so large, you see, that it is frightfully difficult to reach an
agreement) so as to be able to trade.

I can understand that Communists need time to learn to
trade, and I know that those who are learning will be making
the crudest of mistakes for several years; but history will
forgive them because they are entirely new to the business.
For this purpose we must make our thinking more flexible,
and must discard all communist, or rather Russian, Oblomovism,[59] and much more besides. But it is strange for
representatives of bourgeois countries to have to learn the
trading business all over again, after they have been engaged
in it for hundreds of years, and when the whole of their
social life is based upon it. Incidentally, it should not seem
so strange to us. For a long time we have been saying, and we
always knew, that their appraisal of the imperialist war was
less correct than ours. They appraised it from what they
could see directly in front of them, and three years after their
tremendous victories they still cannot find a way out of the
situation.

We Communists said that our appraisal of the war was
more profound and correct; that its contradictions and its
disasters would have a far broader impact than the capitalist countries imagined. And, looking at the bourgeois victor
countries from outside, we said: they will recall our forecast and our appraisal of the war and its consequences more
than once. The fact that they do not understand the simplest

things does not surprise us. But we nevertheless say,   "We must trade with the capitalist countries as long as they exist." We shall negotiate with them as merchants; and the fact we can do so is proved by the increasing number of trade agreements we are signing and negotiating with them. But we cannot publish them until they are signed. From the commercial point of view we, of course, have to agree when a capitalist merchant comes to us and says, "This deal must remain between ourselves until the negotiations are completed." We, however, know how many agreements are in course of preparation—the list alone fills several pages, and it includes scores of practical proposals that have been discussed in detail with important financial groups. Of course, the gentlemen representing the bourgeois countries gathering at Genoa are as well aware of this as we are; whatever the position may be as regards other matters, contacts between these governments and their capitalist firms have, of course, been maintained. Even they are not so terribly lax as not to know of this.

Since in foreign telegrams we are continually reading statements which create the impression that they do not know exactly what will take place at Genoa, that they have something new up their sleeve, that they want to astonish the world by submitting new terms to Russia, permit me to say to them (and I hope I shall have the opportunity of saying it to Lloyd George personally, at Genoa): "You will not surprise anyone by this, gentlemen. You are businessmen, and you know your job well. We are only just learning to trade and are still clumsy at it. But we have tens and hundreds of agreements and draft agreements, which show how we trade and what transactions we conduct or shall conduct, and on what terms." And we smile quietly to ourselves when we read in the newspapers all sorts of reports—published for the purpose of scaring someone—to the effect that they intend to put us to some sort of test. We have been threatened often enough, and with much more serious threats than those uttered by the merchant who intends to slam the door after making his last offer. We have been threatened with the guns of the Allied powers that rule almost the whole world. *We were not frightened by those threats. Please, gentlemen, European diplomats, do not forget that.*

We are not in the least concerned about maintaining our diplomatic prestige, the good name to which the bourgeois states attach so much importance. Officially, we shall not even talk about it. But we have not forgotten it. Not one of our workers, not one of our peasants has forgotten, can forget, or ever will forget that he fought in defence of the workers' and peasants' government against the alliance of all those very powerful states that supported the intervention. We have a whole collection of treaties which those countries concluded with Kolchak and Denikin over a number of years. They have been published; we are familiar with them and the whole world is familiar with them. What is the use of playing hide-and-seek and pretending that we have all become Simple Simons? Every peasant and every worker knows that he fought against those countries, and that they failed to vanquish him. And if you gentlemen, who represent the bourgeois governments, care to amuse yourselves, to waste your paper (of which you have ever so much more than you need) and your ink, and to overload your cables and radio stations with messages announcing to the whole world: "We shall put Russia to the test", we shall see who comes off best. We have already been put to the test, not the test of words, not the test of trade, not the test of money, but the test of the bludgeon. And in view of the severe, bleeding and painful wounds inflicted on us, we have earned that it be said of us—not by ourselves, but by our enemies— "A man who has been beaten is worth two who have not."

We have earned this on the field of battle. As far as trade is concerned, it is a pity that we Communists are not being thrashed enough, but I trust that this defect will be made good in the near future with equal success.

I said that I hope to discuss these subjects with Lloyd George personally, in Genoa, and to tell him that *it is no use trying to frighten us with such trivialities* because it will only damage the prestige of those who try it. I hope that I shall not be prevented from doing this by ill health, which during the past few months has prevented me from taking a direct part in political affairs, and which totally incapacitates me for the Soviet duties which I have been appointed to perform. I have reason to believe that I shall be able to return to my duties within a few weeks. *But will three or four of them succeed within the next few weeks in reaching an agreement on what they have informed the world they are already agreed upon? I am not sure about that.* I even dare assert that nobody in the world is sure about it, and what is more, that they themselves are not sure, because when these victorious powers, which rule the whole world, gathered at Cannes after numerous preliminary conferences—the number of these conferences is infinite, and even the European bourgeois press is jeering—they could not say definitely what they wanted.

From the point of view of practical tasks and not that of a game of diplomatic leap-frog, therefore, Comrade Trotsky has defined the position more correctly than anybody else. The day after the news was received that all the arrangements for Genoa had been made, that everything had been settled, that complete agreement had been reached about Genoa and that it was only the instability of one of the bourgeois governments (they seem to have become suspiciously unstable these days) that necessitated the temporary postponement of the Conference, he issued the following order: "Let every man of the Red Army get a clear understanding of the international situation. We know definitely that there is a permanent group over there who want to try their hand at intervention. We shall be on the alert. Let every man of the Red Army know all about the diplomatic game and what is meant by force of arms, which, up to now, has decided all class conflicts."

Let every man of the Red Army know all about this game and what is meant by force of arms, and then we shall see what happens. No matter how shaky capitalism may have become in all capitalist countries, many quite influential parties may still try their hand at this game. And if the governments are so unstable that they cannot convene a conference at the date set for it, who knows whose hands they will fall into? We know that in those countries there are influential parties and influential persons and business magnates who want war. We are perfectly well aware of this, and we are well informed of what really lies at the bottom of economic treaties. We have endured exceptional hardship, and we know what misfortune and suffering a fresh attempt at war must entail for us. But we say we *shall be able to stand it again—just try and do it!* When Comrade Trotsky issued his definite order instead of publishing opinions about the game of diplomatic leap-frog, he had drawn the conclusion that we must again explain the international situation to every man of the Red Army, and tell him that the postponement of the Genoa Conference, owing to the instability of the Italian Cabinet, is a danger signal of war. *We shall see to it that every man of the Red Army understands this.* It will be easy for us to do this because there is hardly a family, hardly a man of the Red Army in Russia who does not know this, not only from newspapers, circulars and orders, but from his own village, where he has seen cripples, and knows families that have gone through this war, where he sees crop failures, appalling hunger and ruin, hellish poverty, and knows what causes them—even though he does not read the Paris publications of the Mensheviks and Socialist-Revolutionaries which attribute all this to the malignant nature of the Bolsheviks. There can scarcely be a desire so deeply ingrained in him as the desire to repel (to say the least) those who forced upon us the war waged by Kolchak and Denikin and supported it. There is no need for us to appoint new agitation and propaganda commissions for this purpose.

In respect of the Genoa Conference we must distinguish exactly between its real nature and the newspaper canards circulated by the bourgeoisie. They think that these canards are frightful bombs, but they do not frighten us, because we have seen so many of them; and sometimes they do not deserve answering even with a smile. Every attempt to impose terms upon us as if we were vanquished is so very foolish that it is not worthy of a reply. *We are establishing relations as merchants; we know what you owe us and what we owe you; and we know what your legitimate profit and even your super-profit may be.* We get many proposals, and the number of agreements we are concluding is growing and will continue to grow, no matter how three or four of the victor powers combine. You will lose by this postponement of the Conference, because you will show your own people that you do not know what you want, and that the disease you are suffering from is lack of will power, and a failure to understand economics and politics, which we have appraised more profoundly than you. It will soon be ten years since we made this appraisal, and all the ruin and disorder that has occurred since then is still not understood by the bourgeois countries.

We already see clearly the position that has taken shape in our country, and we can say with full conviction that *we can now stop the retreat we began, we are already stopping it. Enough!* We clearly realise that the New Economic Policy is a retreat, and we do not conceal it. We grasped more than we could hold, but such is the logic of the struggle. Those of you who remember what the position was in October 1917, or those of you who were politically immature at the time and have learned since what the position was in 1917, know what a large number of compromise proposals we Bolsheviks made to the bourgeoisie at that time. "Gentlemen, your affairs are in a bad way," we said, "we shall be in power, however, and will remain in power. Wouldn't you like to consider how you could settle things without a rumpus, as the muzhik would say?" We know that there was not only a rumpus, but attempts at rebellion, which the Mensheviks and Socialist-Revolutionaries instigated and supported. Formerly they said: "We are prepared to surrender power to the Soviets right now." A few days ago I read an article by Kerensky, who opposed Chernov in a Paris journal (there's lots of that stuff there). "Did we cling to power?" asked Kerensky. "Even at the time of the Democratic Conference[60] I said that if anyone could be found to form a homogeneous government, power would be transferred to the new government without the slightest upheaval."

We have never refused to take power alone. We said that as early as June 1917,[61] and took power at the Congress of Soviets in October 1917. We Bolsheviks obtained a majority at that Congress of Soviets. Then Kerensky appealed to the officer cadets,[62] rushed off to Krasnov and wanted to muster an army to march on Petrograd. We knocked them about a bit, and now they say in an offended tone, "You are insolent, you are usurpers, butchers!" And we say in reply, "You have only yourselves to blame, friends! Do not imagine that the Russian peasants and workers have forgotten what you did. In October you challenged us to the most desperate fight, and we retaliated with terror and redoubled terror;

*and we shall adopt terror again if necessary, if you try it
again."* Not a single worker, not a single peasant doubts the
need for it. No one doubts it but whimpering intellectuals.

Under conditions of unheard-of economic hardship we
were compelled to wage war against an enemy whose forces
were a hundred times superior to ours. It goes without saying that under these circumstances we were obliged to go
to greater lengths in our urgent communist measures than
would otherwise have been the case; we were forced to do it.
Our enemies thought they could finish us off; they thought
they could bring us to our knees, not in words, but in deeds.
They said they would not make any concessions. We
replied that if they thought we dared not resort to the most
extreme communist measures they were mistaken. And we
did dare; we did it, and we won. Now we say we cannot hold
these positions, we are retreating, because we have won enough
to be able to hold essential positions. All the whiteguards,
headed by the Mensheviks and Socialist-Revolutionaries,
wax jubilant and say, "Aha, you are retreating!" We say,
"Rejoice, since it puts you in good humour." We stand
to gain if our enemy pats himself on the back instead of
engaging in practical work. Rejoice, you are only putting us in
a more favourable position by deceiving yourselves with
illusions. We have captured vast positions, and had we not
captured them in the period from 1917 to 1921 we would have
had no room to retreat, geographically, economically or
politically. We are maintaining power in alliance with the
peasantry, and if you reject terms offered you before a war,
you get worse terms after the war. This is definitely recorded
in the diplomatic, economic and political history of the
period 1917-21, so that we are not boasting at all. It is a plain
statement of fact, a simple reminder. Had the capitalist gentlemen accepted the proposals we made to them in October
1917, they would have had five times as much as they have
now. You fought for three years. What have you gained by
it? Do you want to fight again? We know perfectly well that
by no means all of you want to fight. On the other hand,
we know that in view of the desperate famine and the present state of industry, we cannot hold all the positions we
won in the period 1917-21. We have surrendered a number
of them. But we can now say that, *so far as making con-*

cessions to the capitalists is concerned, the retreat is at an end. We have weighed up our own forces and those of the capitalists. We have done some reconnoitring by way of concluding agreements with Russian and foreign capitalists, and we say—and I hope, I am sure, that the Party Congress will say the same, officially, on behalf of the ruling party of Russia—*"We can now stop our economic retreat. Enough! We shall not retreat any further*; we shall set about deploying and regrouping our forces properly."

When I say that we are halting our economic retreat I do not want to suggest that I have for a moment forgotten the hellishly difficult conditions in which we find ourselves; nor do I want to soothe or console you on that score. The question of the limits of the retreat, and of whether we are stopping the retreat or not, is not one of the difficulties that confront us. We are aware of these difficulties. We know what famine in a peasant country like Russia means. We know that we have not yet succeeded in alleviating the sufferings caused by the famine. We know what a financial crisis means in a country which is compelled to trade and where paper currency has been issued on a scale such as the world has never seen before. We are well aware of these difficulties and fully appreciate their immensity. I am not afraid to say that they are tremendous. This does not frighten us in the least. On the contrary, we gain strength from saying openly to the workers and peasants that these are the difficulties that confront us; this is the danger with which the Western powers threaten us. Let us work and weigh up our tasks soberly. The fact that we are stopping our retreat does not mean that we are not aware of the dangers. We look them straight in the face. "This," we say, "is where the main danger lies; we must alleviate the sufferings caused by the famine. We have not done so yet. We have not yet overcome the financial crisis." Hence, you must not interpret what I say about halting the retreat to mean that we think that we have already laid the foundation (of our new economy) and that we can now calmly advance. No, the foundation has not yet been laid. We still cannot look calmly to the future. We are surrounded by threats of war, about which I have said enough, and by still greater internal dangers, economic dangers within the country; these are the frightful state of ruin of the peasantry, the famine, and our disrupted finances. These dangers are very great. They call for tremendous effort on our part. But if we are forced to go to war, we shall be able to fight. It will not be easy for them to fight, either. It was easy for them to start war in 1918 and as easy to continue it in 1919. But much water, and blood, and many other things have flowed under the bridge since then. The Western workers and peasants have changed since 1919. And it is impossible to fool them by saying, "We are fighting the Germans; the Bolsheviks are nothing more than German agents." We do not become panic-stricken over our economic situation. Today we have scores of agreements concluded with Russian and foreign capitalists. We know what difficulties lay and still lie before us. We know why the Russian capitalists consented to conclude these agreements. We know on what terms these agreements were concluded. The majority of the capitalists concluded the agreements as practical men, as merchants. We, too, are acting as merchants. But every merchant takes some account of politics. If he is a merchant from a not altogether barbarous country, he will not enter into transactions with a government unless it shows considerable signs of stability, unless it is very reliable. The merchant who did such a thing would not be a merchant, but a fool. Most merchants are not fools, for the logic of the commercial struggle eliminates the fools. If, formerly, the test was, "Denikin has beaten you, now show that you can beat Denikin", today the test is, "If the merchant has beaten you, prove that you can compel him to do business". We have proved it. We have already concluded a number of agreements with very big capitalist firms, both Russian and West-European. We know what they are after, they know what we are after.

Today the object of our activities has changed somewhat. That is exactly what I want to say a few words about, to supplement my already somewhat lengthy report.

In view of the fact that the Genoa situation is precarious and the end of the wavering is not in sight, and because we have made so many concessions in our domestic policy, we must now say: *"Enough! No more concessions!"* The capitalist gentlemen think that they can dally, and the longer they dally the more concessions they will get, but we must say,

"Enough! Tomorrow you will get nothing." If they have not learned anything from the history of Soviet power and its victories, they can do as they please. For our part we have done all we could and have informed the whole world about it. I hope the Congress will confirm the fact that we shall not retreat any further. *The retreat has come to an end*, and, in consequence of that, the nature of our work is changing.

It must be stated that considerable nervousness, almost morbidness, is still observed in our ranks when this question is discussed. All sorts of plans are drawn up, and all sorts of decisions are adopted. In this connection I want to mention the following. Yesterday I happened to read in *Izvestia* a political poem by Mayakovsky.[63] I am not an admirer of his poetical talent, although I admit that I am not a competent judge. But I have not for a long time read anything on politics and administration with so much pleasure as I read this. In his poem he derides this meeting habit, and taunts the Communists with incessantly sitting at meetings. I am not sure about the poetry; but as for the politics, I vouch for their absolute correctness. We are indeed in the position, and it must be said that it is a very absurd position, of people sitting endlessly at meetings, setting up commissions and drawing up plans without end. There was a character who typified Russian life—Oblomov. He was always lolling on his bed and mentally drawing up schemes. That was a long time ago. Russia has experienced three revolutions, but the Oblomovs have survived, for there were Oblomovs not only among the landowners but also among the peasants; not only among the peasants, but among the intellectuals too; and not only among the intellectuals, but also among the workers and Communists. It is enough to watch us at our meetings, at our work on commissions, to be able to say that *old Oblomov still lives; and it will be necessary to give him a good washing and cleaning, a good rubbing and scouring to make a man of him.* In this respect we must have no illusions about our position. We have not imitated any of those who write the word "revolution" with a capital R, as the Socialist-Revolutionaries do. But we can quote the words of Marx that many foolish things are done during a revolution, perhaps more than at any other time.[64] We revolutionaries must learn to regard these foolish acts dispassionately and fearlessly.

In this revolution we have done so much that is ineradicable, that we have finally won; the whole world knows about it and we have no reason whatever to be embarrassed or nervous. On the basis of our reconnaissance we are now checking up on what we have done. This check is very important and should serve as the starting point for our further progress. And since we have to hold out in the struggle against the capitalists, we must pursue our new line with determination. *We must build up our whole organisation in such a way that our commercial enterprises are not headed by people who lack experience in that field.* Very often we find a Communist at the head of a government office who is admittedly a conscientious comrade, tried and tested in the struggle for communism, who suffered imprisonment for the cause, and for that reason has been put at the head of a state trust. But he does not know how to trade. He has all the undoubted qualities of a Communist, but the merchant cheats him, and is quite right in doing so; it is a mistake to put a very worthy, excellent Communist, whose loyalty no one but a madman would doubt, in a place that should be occupied by a shrewd, conscientious salesman who could cope with his work ever so much better than the most devoted Communist. This is just where our Oblomovism makes itself felt.

We have given Communists, with all their splendid qualities, practical executive jobs for which they are totally unfitted. How many Communists are there in government offices? We have huge quantities of material, bulky works, that would cause the heart of the most methodical German scientist to rejoice; we have mountains of paper, and it would take Istpart [65] fifty times fifty years to go through it all; but if you tried to find anything practical in a state trust, you would fail; and you would never know who was responsible for what. The practical fulfilment of decrees—of which we have more than enough, and which we bake as fast as Mayakovsky describes—is never checked. Are the orders of the responsible Communist officials carried out? Can they get this done? No. They cannot; and that is why we are changing our domestic policy to the very core. Of what value are our meetings and commissions? Very often they are just make-

believe. After we began to purge our Party and said to ourselves: "Out with the self-seekers who have crept into the
Party, out with the thieves!" things improved. We have
expelled about a hundred thousand; that is splendid, but it
is only a beginning. We shall discuss this question thoroughly at the Party Congress. And then, I think, the tens of thousands who now only organise commissions, and do not, and
cannot, carry on practical work, will meet with the same
fate. And after we have completed the purge in this way, our
Party will get down to real work and learn to understand
it as it learnt to understand war work. This, of course, is
not a matter of several months, or even a year. We must
display rock-like firmness in this question. We are not afraid
to say that the nature of our work has changed. Our worst
internal enemy is the bureaucrat—the Communist who
occupies a responsible (or not responsible) Soviet post and
enjoys universal respect as a conscientious man. As the Russian
saying goes, "Although he never touches a drop, he sings
false". He is very conscientious, but he has not learnt to combat red tape, he is unable to combat it, he condones it. *We
must rid ourselves of this enemy, and with the aid of all
class-conscious workers and peasants we shall get at him. The
whole mass of non-Party workers and peasants will follow
the lead of the vanguard of the Communist Party in the
fight against this enemy and this inefficiency and Oblomovism.
There must be no hesitation whatever in this matter.*

In conclusion, I will sum up briefly. The Genoa game,
the game of leap-frog that is going on around it, will not
compel us to waver in the least. They cannot catch us now.
*We shall go to the merchants and agree to do business, contin-
uing our policy of concessions; but the limits of these concessions are already defined.* What we have given the merchants
in our agreements up to now has been a step backward in
our legislation; but we shall not retreat any further.

In connection with this, our main tasks in our internal
and, particularly, our economic policy are undergoing
a change. We do not need new decrees, new institutions
or new methods of struggle, *What we need is the testing
of the fitness of our officials; we need executive control.*
The next purge will affect the Communists who *imagine*
that they are administrators. All those who run all these

commissions and conferences and talk but do no practical
work would do better to go into the field of propaganda,
agitation and other useful work of that kind. All sorts
of extraordinary and intricate things are invented on the
plea that the New Economic Policy requires something
new; but they do not do the work they are instructed to
do. They make no effort to look after the kopeks entrusted
to them; they make no effort to make one kopek grow into
two; but they draw up plans affecting billions and even
trillions of Soviet rubles. It is this evil that we shall combat. *To test men and verify what has actually been done—*
this, this again, this alone is now the main feature of all
our activities, of our whole policy. This is not a matter
of a few months or of a year, but of several years. We must
say officially, on behalf of the Party, what the main feature of our activities is at the present time, and reorganise
our ranks accordingly. If we do that we shall be as victorious in this new field as we have been up to now in all the
fields of activity engaged in by Bolshevik, proletarian
power, supported by the peasant masses. (*Applause.*)

Pravda No. 54,   Published according to
March 8, 1922   the *Pravda* text

ON THE SIGNIFICANCE OF MILITANT MATERIALISM

Comrade Trotsky has already said everything necessary, and said it very well, about the general purposes of *Pod Znamenem Marksizma*[66] in issue No. 1-2 of that journal. I should like to deal with certain questions that more closely define the content and programme of the work which its editors have set forth in the introductory statement in this issue.

This statement says that not all those gathered round the journal *Pod Znamenem Marksizma* are Communists but that they are all consistent materialists. I think that this alliance of Communists and non-Communists is absolutely essential and correctly defines the purposes of the journal. One of the biggest and most dangerous mistakes made by Communists (as generally by revolutionaries who have successfully accomplished the beginning of a great revolution) is the idea that a revolution can be made by revolutionaries alone. On the contrary, to be successful, all serious revolutionary work requires that the idea that revolutionaries are capable of playing the part only of the vanguard of the truly virile and advanced class must be understood and translated into action. A vanguard performs its task as vanguard only when it is able to avoid being isolated from the mass of the people it leads and is able really to lead the whole mass forward. Without an alliance with non-Communists in the most diverse spheres of activity there can be no question of any successful communist construction.

This also applies to the defence of materialism and Marxism, which has been undertaken by *Pod Znamenem Marksizma*. Fortunately, the main trends of advanced

8*

social thinking in Russia have a solid materialist tradition. Apart from G. V. Plekhanov, it will be enough to mention Chernyshevsky,[67] from whom the modern Narodniks (the Popular Socialists,[68] Socialist-Revolutionaries, etc.) have frequently retreated in quest of fashionable reactionary philosophical doctrines, captivated by the tinsel of the so-called last word in European science, and unable to discern beneath this tinsel some variety of servility to the bourgeoisie, to bourgeois prejudice and bourgeois reaction.

At any rate, in Russia we still have—and shall undoubtedly have for a fairly long time to come—materialists from the non-communist camp, and it is our absolute duty to enlist all adherents of consistent and militant materialism in the joint work of combating philosophical reaction and the philosophical prejudices of so-called educated society. Dietzgen senior[69]—not to be confused with his writer son, who was as pretentious as he was unsuccessful— correctly, aptly and clearly expressed the fundamental Marxist view of the philosophical trends which prevail in bourgeois countries and enjoy the regard of their scientists and publicists, when he said that in effect the professors of philosophy in modern society are in the majority of cases nothing but "graduated flunkeys of clericalism".

Our Russian intellectuals, who, like their brethren in all other countries, are fond of thinking themselves advanced, are very much averse to shifting the question to the level of the opinion expressed in Dietzgen's words. But they are averse to it because they cannot look the truth in the face. One has only to give a little thought to the governmental and also the general economic, social and every other kind of dependence of modern educated people on the ruling bourgeoisie to realise that Dietzgen's scathing description was absolutely true. One has only to recall the vast majority of the fashionable philosophical trends that arise so frequently in European countries, beginning for example with those connected with the discovery of radium and ending with those which are now seeking to clutch at the skirts of Einstein, to gain an idea of the connection between the class interests and the class position of the bourgeoisie and its support of all forms of religion on the one hand, and the ideological content of the fashionable philosophical trends on the other.

It will be seen from the above that a journal that sets out to be a militant materialist organ must be primarily a militant organ, in the sense of unflinchingly exposing and indicting all modern "graduated flunkeys of clericalism", irrespective of whether they act as representatives of official science or as free lances calling themselves "democratic Left or ideologically socialist" publicists.

In the second place, such a journal must be a militant atheist organ. We have departments, or at least state institutions, which are in charge of this work. But the work is being carried on with extreme apathy and very unsatisfactorily, and is apparently suffering from the general conditions of our truly Russian (even though Soviet) bureaucratic ways. It is therefore highly essential that in addition to the work of these state institutions, and in order to improve and infuse life into that work, a journal which sets out to propagandise militant materialism must carry on untiring atheist propaganda and an untiring atheist fight. The literature on the subject in all languages should be carefully followed and everything at all valuable in this sphere should be translated, or at least reviewed.

Engels long ago advised the contemporary leaders of the proletariat to translate the militant atheist literature of the late eighteenth century[70] for mass distribution among the people. We have not done this up to the present, to our shame be it said (this is one of the numerous proofs that it is much easier to seize power in a revolutionary epoch than to know how to use this power properly). Our apathy, inactivity and incompetence are sometimes excused on all sorts of "lofty" grounds, as, for example, that the old atheist literature of the eighteenth century is antiquated, unscientific, naïve, etc. There is nothing worse than such pseudo-scientific sophistry, which serves as a screen either for pedantry or for a complete misunderstanding of Marxism. There is, of course, much that is unscientific and naïve in the atheist writings of the eighteenth-century revolutionaries. But nobody prevents the publishers of these writings from abridging them and providing them with brief postscripts pointing out the progress made by mankind in the scientific criticism of religions since the end of the eighteenth century, mentioning the latest writings on the subject, and so forth. It would be the biggest and most grievous mistake a Marxist could make to think that the millions of the people (especially the peasants and artisans), who have been condemned by all modern society to darkness, ignorance and superstition, can extricate themselves from this darkness only along the straight line of a purely Marxist education. These masses should be supplied with the most varied atheist propaganda material, they should be made familiar with facts from the most diverse spheres of life, they should be approached in every possible way, so as to interest them, rouse them from their religious torpor, stir them from the most varied angles and by the most varied methods, and so forth.

The keen, vivacious and talented writings of the old eighteenth-century atheists wittily and openly attacked the prevailing clericalism and will very often prove a thousand times more suitable for arousing people from their religious torpor than the dull and dry paraphrases of Marxism, almost completely unillustrated by skilfully selected facts, which predominate in our literature and which (it is no use hiding the fact) frequently distort Marxism. We have translations of all the major works of Marx and Engels. There are absolutely no grounds for fearing that the old atheism and old materialism will remain unsupplemented by the corrections introduced by Marx and Engels. The most important thing—and it is this that is most frequently overlooked by those of our Communists who are supposedly Marxists, but who in fact mutilate Marxism—is to know how to awaken in the still undeveloped masses an intelligent attitude towards religious questions and an intelligent criticism of religions.

On the other hand, take a glance at modern scientific critics of religion. These educated bourgeois writers almost invariably "supplement" their own refutations of religious superstitions with arguments which immediately expose them as ideological slaves of the bourgeoisie, as "graduated flunkeys of clericalism".

Two examples. Professor R. Y. Wipper published in 1918 a little book entitled *Vozniknovenie Khristianstva* (The Origin of Christianity—Pharos Publishing House, Moscow). In his account of the principal results of modern science, the author not only refrains from combating the superstitions and deception which are the weapons of the church as a political organisation, not only evades these questions, but makes the simply ridiculous and most reactionary claim that he is above both "extremes"—the idealist and the materialist. This is toadying to the ruling bourgeoisie, which all over the world devotes to the support of religion hundreds of millions of rubles from the profits squeezed out of the working people.

The well-known German scientist, Arthur Drews, while refuting religious superstitions and fables in his book, *Die Christusmythe* (The Christ Myth), and while showing that Christ never existed, at the end of the book declares in favour of religion, albeit a renovated, purified and more subtle religion, one that would be capable of withstanding "the daily growing naturalist torrent" (fourth German edition, 1910, p. 238). Here we have an outspoken and deliberate reactionary, who is openly helping the exploiters to replace the old, decayed religious superstitions by new, more odious and vile superstitions.

This does not mean that Drews should not be translated. It means that while in a certain measure effecting an alliance with the progressive section of the bourgeoisie, Communists and all consistent materialists should unflinchingly expose that section when it is guilty of reaction. It means that to shun an alliance with the representatives of the bourgeoisie of the eighteenth century, i.e., the period when it was revolutionary, would be to betray Marxism and materialism; for an "alliance" with the Drewses, in one form or another and in one degree or another, is essential for our struggle against the predominating religious obscurantists.

Pod Znamenem Marksizma, which sets out to be an organ of militant materialism, should devote much of its space to atheist propaganda, to reviews of the literature on the subject and to correcting the immense shortcomings of our governmental work in this field. It is particularly important to utilise books and pamphlets which contain many concrete facts and comparisons showing how the class interests and class organisations of the modern bourgeoisie are connected with the organisations of religious institutions and religious propaganda.

All material relating to the United States of America, where the official, state connection between religion and capital is less manifest, is extremely important. But, on the other hand, it becomes all the clearer to us that so-called modern democracy (which the Mensheviks, the Socialist-Revolutionaries, partly also the anarchists, etc., so unreasonably worship) is nothing but the freedom to preach whatever is to the advantage of the bourgeoisie, to preach, namely, the most reactionary ideas, religion, obscurantism, defence of the exploiters, etc.

One would like to hope that a journal which sets out to be a militant materialist organ will provide our reading public with reviews of atheist literature, showing for which circle of readers any particular writing might be suitable and in what respect, and mentioning what literature has been published in our country (only decent translations should be given notice, and they are not so many), and what is still to be published.

In addition to the alliance with consistent materialists who do not belong to the Communist Party, of no less and perhaps even of more importance for the work which militant materialism should perform is an alliance with those modern natural scientists who incline towards materialism and are not afraid to defend and preach it as against the modish philosophical wanderings into idealism and scepticism which are prevalent in so-called educated society.

The article by A. Timiryazev on Einstein's theory of relativity published in *Pod Znamenem Marksizma* No. 1-2 permits us to hope that the journal will succeed in effecting this second alliance too. Greater attention should be paid to it. It should be remembered that the sharp upheaval which modern natural science is undergoing very often gives rise to reactionary philosophical schools and minor schools, trends and minor trends. Unless, therefore, the problems raised by the recent revolution in natural science are followed, and unless natural scientists are enlisted in the work of a philosophical journal, militant materialism can be neither militant nor materialism. Timiryazev was obliged to observe in the first issue of the journal that the theory of Einstein, who, according to Timiryazev, is himself not making any active attack on the foundations of materialism, has already been seized upon by a vast number of bourgeois intellectuals of all countries; it should be noted that this applies not only to Einstein, but to a number, if not to the majority, of the great reformers of natural science since the end of the nineteenth century.

For our attitude towards this phenomenon to be a politically conscious one, it must be realised that no natural science and no materialism can hold its own in the struggle against the onslaught of bourgeois ideas and the restoration of the bourgeois world outlook unless it stands on solid philosophical ground. In order to hold his own in this struggle and carry it to a victorious finish, the natural scientist must be a modern materialist, a conscious adherent of the materialism represented by Marx, i.e., he must be a dialectical materialist. In order to attain this aim, the contributors to *Pod Znamenem Marksizma* must arrange for the systematic study of Hegelian dialectics from a materialist standpoint, i.e., the dialectics which Marx applied practically in his *Capital* and in his historical and political works, and applied so successfully that now every day of the awakening to life and struggle of new classes in the East (Japan, India, and China)—i.e., the hundreds of millions of human beings who form the greater part of the world population and whose historical passivity and historical torpor have hitherto conditioned the stagnation and decay of many advanced European countries—every day of the awakening to life of new peoples and new classes serves as a fresh confirmation of Marxism.

Of course, this study, this interpretation, this propaganda of Hegelian dialectics is extremely difficult, and the first experiments in this direction will undoubtedly be accompanied by errors. But only he who never does anything never makes mistakes. Taking as our basis Marx's

method of applying materialistically conceived Hegelian
dialectics, we can and should elaborate this dialectics
from all aspects, print in the journal excerpts from Hegel's
principal works, interpret them materialistically and
comment on them with the help of examples of the way
Marx applied dialectics, as well as of examples of dialectics in the sphere of economic and political relations,
which recent history, especially modern imperialist war
and revolution, provides in unusual abundance. In my
opinion, the editors and contributors of *Pod Znamenem
Marksizma* should be a kind of "Society of Materialist
Friends of Hegelian Dialectics". Modern natural scientists (if they know how to seek, and if we learn to help
them) will find in the Hegelian dialectics, materialistically interpreted, a series of answers to the philosophical
problems which are being raised by the revolution in natural
science and which make the intellectual admirers of bourgeois fashion "stumble" into reaction.

Unless it sets itself such a task and systematically ful-
fils it, materialism cannot be militant materialism. It will
be not so much the fighter as the fought,[71] to use an expression of Shchedrin's. Without this, eminent natural scientists will as often as hitherto be helpless in making their
philosophical deductions and generalisations. For natural
science is progressing so fast and is undergoing such a
profound revolutionary upheaval in all spheres that it
cannot possibly dispense with philosophical deductions.

In conclusion, I will cite an example which has nothing
to do with philosophy, but does at any rate concern social
questions, to which *Pod Znamenem Marksizma* also desires
to devote attention.

It is an example of the way in which modern pseudo-
science actually serves as a vehicle for the grossest and
most infamous reactionary views.

I was recently sent a copy of *Ekonomist* No. 1 (1922),
published by the Eleventh Department of the Russian
Technical Society.[72] The young Communist who sent me
this journal (he probably had no time to read it) rashly
expressed considerable agreement with it. In reality the
journal is—I do not know to what extent deliberately—

an organ of the modern feudalists, disguised of course under a cloak of science, democracy and so forth.

A certain Mr. P. A. Sorokin publishes in this journal an extensive, so-called "sociological", inquiry on "The Influence of the War". This learned article abounds in learned references to the "sociological" works of the author and his numerous teachers and colleagues abroad. Here is an example of his learning.

On page 83, I read:

"For every 10,000 marriages in Petrograd there are now 92.2 divorces—a fantastic figure. Of every 100 annulled marriages, 51.1 had lasted less than one year, 11 per cent less than one month, 22 per cent less than two months, 41 per cent less than three to six months and only 26 per cent over six months. These figures show that modern legal marriage is a form which conceals what is in effect extra-marital sexual intercourse, enabling lovers of 'strawberries' to satisfy their appetites in a 'legal' way" (*Ekonomist* No. 1, p. 83)

Both this gentleman and the Russian Technical Society, which publishes this journal and gives space to this kind of talk, no doubt regard themselves as adherents of democracy and would consider it a great insult to be called what they are in fact, namely, feudalists, reactionaries, "graduated flunkeys of clericalism".

Even the slightest acquaintance with the legislation of bourgeois countries on marriage, divorce and illegitimate children, and with the actual state of affairs in this field, is enough to show anyone interested in the subject that modern bourgeois democracy, even in all the most democratic bourgeois republics, exhibits a truly feudal attitude in this respect towards women and towards children born out of wedlock.

This, of course, does not prevent the Mensheviks, the Socialist-Revolutionaries, a part of the anarchists and all the corresponding parties in the West from shouting about democracy and how it is being violated by the Bolsheviks. But as a matter of fact the Bolshevik revolution is the only consistently democratic revolution in respect to such questions as marriage, divorce and the position of children born out of wedlock. And this is a question which most directly affects the interests of more than half the population of any country. Although a large number of bourgeois revolutions preceded it and called themselves democratic, the Bolshevik revolution was the first and only revolution to wage a resolute struggle in this respect both against reaction and feudalism and against the usual hypocrisy of the ruling and propertied classes.

If 92 divorces for every 10,000 marriages seem to Mr. Sorokin a fantastic figure, one can only suppose that either the author lived and was brought up in a monastery so entirely walled off from life that hardly anyone will believe such a monastery ever existed, or that he is distorting the truth in the interest of reaction and the bourgeoisie. Anybody in the least acquainted with social conditions in bourgeois countries knows that the real number of actual divorces (of course, not sanctioned by church and law) is everywhere immeasurably greater. The only difference between Russia and other countries in this respect is that our laws do not sanctify hypocrisy and the debasement of the woman and her child, but openly and in the name of the government declare systematic war on all hypocrisy and all debasement.

The Marxist journal will have to wage war also on these modern "educated" feudalists. Not a few of them, very likely, are in receipt of government money and are employed by our government to educate our youth, although they are no more fitted for this than notorious perverts are fitted for the post of superintendents of educational establishments for the young.

The working class of Russia proved able to win power; but it has not yet learned to utilise it, for otherwise it would have long ago very politely dispatched such teachers and members of learned societies to countries with a bourgeois "democracy". That is the proper place for such feudalists.

But it will learn, given the will to learn.

March 12, 1922

Pod Znamenem Marksizma No. 3,
March 1922
Signed: *N Lenin**Pod Znamenem Marksizma* No. 3,
March 1922
Signed: *N Lenin*

Published according to
the *Pod Znamenem
Marksizma* text

TO COMRADE MOLOTOV
FOR THE MEMBERS OF THE POLITICAL BUREAU
RE COMRADE PREOBRAZHENSKY'S THESES[*]

1. The heading will not do. These are not "fundamental principles", which have already been laid down by our Programme, but theses on "The Organisation of the Russian Communist Party's Work in the Rural Districts Under Present Conditions".

I propose that the author be instructed to *shorten* and partly alter the theses in conformity with this new subject. In particular, he should shorten the recapitulation of general principles (these should be given in a leaflet explaining and commenting on the decision to be adopted by the Congress) and enlarge in greater detail on the *practical* and, particularly, the *organisational* conclusions.

2. In the heading of § I: "social relations" instead of the singular.

(The typing is careless: "obyedineniya" instead of "*obedneniya*",

"besploshchadnykh" instead of "bezloshadnykh"....)[*]

3. In § I, particularly, many of the passages are far too long; much of this should be transferred to a pamphlet.

4. Statements about "co-operation" in § I, and in other places, are bare and abstract. Too much has been said about this, and we are sick of it. It must be formulated quite differently, without repeating the bare slogan: "Co-operate!" but *showing concretely* what *practical experience*

---

[*] i.e., "amalgamation" instead of "impoverishment"; "plotless" instead of "horseless".—*Ed.*

has already been acquired in the field of co-operation, and *how* it can be promoted. If the author lacks this material, then the decision of the Congress must contain a *demand* that it be collected and analysed not academically, but practically. (All Comrade Preobrazhensky's theses are ultra- and super-academic; they smack of the intelligentsia, the study circle and the littérateur, and not of practical state and economic activity.)

5. "With the exception of collective farms" we have no development, but a "tendency to decline" (among the poor peasants). This will not do. In the first place, there is no proof that the "collectives" are, in general, better We must not irritate the peasants with false communist self-adulation. In the second place, not "tendency to decline" but retarded development *everywhere*; decline—*often*.

6. The "good husbandmen" are *"carried away"* by "the task of improving farming methods". This is a clumsy expression and, unfortunately, is also a piece of "communist self-adulation". It should read: "are beginning, although slowly" (§ I).

7. "Peasant (?) equality is dissolving" (?). You cannot say a thing like that.

The end of § I is no good at all; it is an article, not a thesis; an assumption unsupported by facts.

8. The beginning of § II is far too abstruse. Properly speaking, it has no business to be in these theses. It is quite out of context.

9. The second sentence in § II (levelled against the "methods of the Poor Peasants' Committees"[74]) is pernicious and wrong, because war, for example, may compel us to resort to the methods of the Poor Peasants' Committees.

This must be said quite differently; in this way, for example: in view of the supreme importance of reviving agriculture and increasing the output of farm produce, the proletariat's policy towards the kulaks and well-to-do peasantry must, at present, mainly pursue the object of *curbing* their exploiting appetites, etc.

The whole point is: How can and should our state curb these appetites and protect the poor peasants? This must be studied, and we must compel people to study it practically; general phrases are *useless*.

10. The last words in § II are correct, but they are abstruse and insufficiently enlarged upon. This must be explained in greater detail.

11. In § III the sentence starting with "The divorcement" is badly distorted.

12. Strictly speaking, the whole of § III teems with commonplaces. This is no use. To repeat them so emptily is harmful; it causes nausea, ennui and irritation at the useless chewing over of phrases.

Instead of irritating the peasants by this *foolish communistic playing at co-operation* it would be far better to take at least one *uyezd* and show by a *practical* analysis how "co-operation" can be promoted; to show how we have *actually* helped to improve farming methods, etc., how we ought to help, etc.

This is not the right approach to the subject. It is a harmful approach. The general phrases are nauseating. They *breed* bureaucracy and encourage it.

13. The beginning of § IV is particularly unhappy. It is an abstruse article and not a thesis for a congress.

Further. "Instructions in the form of decrees" is what the author proposes. It is radically wrong. Bureaucracy is throttling us precisely because we are still playing with "instructions in the form of decrees". The author could not have invented anything worse or more pernicious than this.

Further. To say at a congress of the Russian Communist Party that "we must put into effect the decisions of the Ninth Congress of Soviets" is positively scandalous. To write theses for that!

This whole section is bad. Commonplaces. Phrases. Pious wishes that everybody is sick of. It is typical of *contemporary* "communist bureaucracy".

Instead of that it would be far better to take the *practical* experience even of one uyezd—even of one volost—and examine the facts not academically, but in a *practical* way and say: Learn, dear communist bureaucrats, *not to do things like this* (give concrete examples, the names of places and definite facts) but *like that* (also giving the concrete facts).

As regards "co-operation", this defect in the theses is particularly striking and particularly harmful in § IV.

14. In § V the "workers employed on the state farms" are declared to be the "cadres of the agricultural proletariat". That is wrong. It is an example of "communist conceit". Far more often they are *not* proletarians but "paupers", petty bourgeois, or what you will. We must not delude ourselves with lies. That is harmful. It is the main source of our bureaucracy. And it *quite unnecessarily* irritates and offends the peasants. It would be far wiser for the time being to keep silent about the "cadres of the agricultural proletariat" employed on our state farms.

Further on it is quite rightly stated that it is "very difficult" to organise this "proletariat" ("which is of a very heterogeneous composition": quite right! And therefore more like ... something indecent, but not "cadres").

Quite true! And therefore one should not say such things as "the staffs of the state farms must be purged of the petty proprietor elements", for this will only excite *ridicule* and legitimately so (it sounds like: purging the peasants' huts of bad air).

Far better say nothing about it.

15. § VI begins (at last!) to approach practical tasks. But this approach is so feeble and backed by so little practical experience that one is inevitably driven to the conclusion that (in place of the proposal made above, in § I):

the theses are unsuitable;

the author plus Osinsky plus Teodorovich plus Yakovenko should be instructed to make arrangements at the Congress for a conference of delegates who are working in the rural districts;

the object of this conference should not be to discuss "principles", etc., but solely to *study and appraise practical experience of*:

how to organise co-operatives?

how to combat the bad organisation of state farms? the bad organisation of co-operatives and collective farms?

how to strengthen the All-Russia Trade

Union of Land and Forestry Workers? (send the author to work there for a *long* period).

The Central Committee should instruct this conference not to repeat generalities, but solely to study in detail local (uyezd, volost, village) *practical* experience. If there is not enough information about this experience (as is probably the case, because nobody has taken the trouble to collect it; but there is a lot of uncollected information), then it would be better for the Congress:

(a) to elect a commission to study this practical experience;

(b) the commission to be subordinate to the Central Committee;

(c) to include Comrade Preobrazhensky in this commission;

(d) to include him also in the All-Russia Trade Union of Land and Forestry Workers....

(e) to instruct the commission to collect information on the experience acquired, to study it and draft (after publishing a series of articles)

a *letter on behalf of the* (new) *Central Committee* on the organisation of work in the rural districts in which the most concrete directions must be given on *how* to organise co-operatives, *how* to "curb" the kulaks, while not checking the growth of the productive forces, *how* to run the All-Russia Trade Union of Land and Forestry Workers, *how* to strengthen it, etc., etc.

The Central Committee's resolution for the Congress should be drafted on the following lines (approximately):

The facts show, and the special commission of the Congress confirms it, that the main defect in the Party's work in the rural districts is the failure to study practical experience. This is the root of all evil, and the root of bureaucracy. The Congress instructs the Central Committee, first and foremost, to combat this—among other things, with the aid of such-and-such a commission, one (or two, or three) of the members of which should be sent for *permanent* work in the All-Russia Trade Union of Land and Forestry Workers.

The commission should publish leaflets and pamphlets, and systematically study experience so as to be able to advise and to order how the work should and should not be done.

Lenin

March 16, 1922

First published in 1925

Published according to
the manuscript

243

MEMO TO G. Y. ZINOVIEV WITH THE DRAFT OF
THE SOVIET GOVERNMENT'S REPLY
TO E. VANDERVELDE[75]

To Comrade Zinoviev
Copy to Comrade Kamenev
to Comrade Molotov

I have just spoken to Kamenev and we have arranged
that late tonight you will reply to Vandervelde that you
have delivered his telegram to the Soviet Government.
Comrade Kursky, the People's Commissar of Justice, will
send him a reply tomorrow on behalf of the Soviet Government.

I propose that the text of the reply be discussed in the
Political Bureau and, for my part, suggest the following
text:

"No member of the Soviet Government in Russia has
ever doubted that representatives of the Second International always steadfastly pursued the policy likewise followed with some vacillation by representatives of the
Viennese Socialist Association.[76] They were the ones who
pursued the policy of forming a direct and indirect alliance
with those exploiter classes that have in all countries
persecuted and killed Communists, examples of which are
particularly numerous and striking in the democratic
republic of Germany. The confidence in the Socialist-
Revolutionaries and Mensheviks that certain political
circles in Western Europe are showing may be explained
only by this alliance and political closeness of the Socialist-
Revolutionaries and Mensheviks, who, in effect, supported the invasion of Russia by Kolchak, Denikin and

others As a matter of fact, far from a sentence having been passed in the case of the Socialist-Revolutionaries you write about, there has not even been a trial and they have not yet been indicted. In any case, I consider it my duty to add that the Soviet Government did not turn down practical proposals like the proposal to exchange prisoners of war or to free various categories of war prisoners, when proposals of that kind came from Denikin's government during his direct invasion of Soviet Russia with the objective of restoring the rule of the landowners.

"Kursky,
"People's Commissar of Justice."
V. Ulyanov (Lenin),
Chairman of the Council
of People's Commissars

Dictated by telephone
on March 17, 1922

Published in full for the first time, according to the stenographer's notes (typewritten copy)

PREFACE TO I. I. STEPANOV'S
THE ELECTRIFICATION OF THE R.S.F.S.R. AND THE TRANSITIONAL PHASE OF WORLD ECONOMY

I heartily recommend this book by Comrade Stepanov to all Communists.

The author has succeeded in giving a very able exposition of exceedingly difficult and important problems. He did very well in not writing a book for intellectuals (as is the practice among many of us who copy the worst manners of bourgeois writers), but for the working people, for the masses, for rank-and-file workers and peasants. To his book the author has appended a list of references for supplementary reading for the benefit of those who may find it difficult to understand some parts of it without further explanation, as well as for the benefit of those who would like to consult the principal works on this subject published in Russia and abroad. Special reference must be made to the beginning of Chapter VI, where the author splendidly outlines the significance of the New Economic Policy, and magnificently answers the "airy" scepticism that is displayed in some quarters about the possibility of electrification This scepticism is usually a cloak to conceal the absence of serious thought on the subject (that is, if it is not a cloak to conceal whiteguard, Socialist-Revolutionary and Menshevik hostility to all Soviet construction, which, in fact, is sometimes the case).

What we lack most for genuine (and not idle-bureaucratic) popular education is precisely "school manuals" (for absolutely all schools) like this one. If all our Marxist writers sat down to write such manuals, or textbooks, on all social questions without exception, instead of wasting their efforts on newspaper and magazine political fireworks, which everybody is sick and tired of, we should not have the present disgraceful situation where, nearly five years after the proletariat captured political power, the young people in the *proletariat's* state schools and universities are taught (or rather, corrupted) by the old bourgeois scientists using the old bourgeois junk.

The Eighth Congress of Soviets decreed that instruction on the Plan for Electrification should be compulsory in all educational establishments in the R.S.F.S.R.[77] without exception. This decree, like many others, has remained a dead letter because of our (Bolsheviks') lack of culture. Now that Comrade Stepanov's "manual for schools" has been published we must see to it—and we shall see to it!— that every uyezd library (and later every volost library) obtains several copies of it and that every electric power station in Russia (there are over 800 of them) not only has copies of this book but also arranges popular lectures on electricity, on the electrification of the R.S.F.S.R. and on engineering in general. We must see to it that every village schoolteacher reads and assimilates this manual (to help him in this a circle or group of engineers and teachers of physics should be organised in every uyezd), and not only reads, understands and assimilates it himself but is able to relate what is in it in a plain and intelligible way to his pupils, and to young peasants in general.

It will require no little effort to do this. We are poor and uneducated. But that does not matter so long as our people realise that they must learn, and so long as they are willing to learn; so long as the workers and peasants clearly understand that they must now learn not to "benefit" and produce profits for the landowners and capitalists, but to improve *their own* conditions of life.

This knowledge and desire exist. And so we definitely shall start learning, and shall certainly learn something.

N. Lenin

March 18, 1922

Pravda No. 64,
March 21, 1922

Published according to the text in I. Stepanov's *The Electrification of the R.S.F.S.R. and the Transitional Phase of World Economy*, Moscow, 1922, checked with the manuscript

LETTER TO J. V. STALIN ON THE FUNCTIONS OF THE DEPUTY CHAIRMEN OF THE COUNCIL OF PEOPLE'S COMMISSARS AND OF THE COUNCIL OF LABOUR AND DEFENCE

March 21, 1922

I have had a talk with Tsyurupa and Rykov. I hope the work will proceed smoothly. Incidentally, one of the questions concerns your Commissariat.[78] Tsyurupa's and Rykov's main job is (must be now) to verify fulfilment and select personnel.

Assistants are needed. The Executive Secretary's staff at the Council of People's Commissars is much too small to handle the work, but it would be irrational to enlarge it. I expressed the idea that the Workers' and Peasants' Inspection should be used for the purpose (of directly helping Tsyurupa and Rykov verify fulfilment and supervise the *lower echelons* of the People's Commissariats). I should like to know if you approve of this; if you do, a written agreement is necessary between you and the deputies, and I should like to participate in drawing up that agreement.

The purpose is to train (by having them tested by you and the two deputies on *practical* assignments) specially and unquestionably reliable people, from among the best workers of the Workers' and Peasants' Inspection, whom Tsyurupa and Rykov select by agreement with you, who would be able quickly and unconditionally a) to *secure* fulfilment; b) to verify fulfilment; c) to check the correctness of the *apparatus* in the various People's Commissariats, departments, the Moscow Soviet or the Petrograd Soviet, etc.; d) to issue instructions on *how* the work should be organised.

These people are to carry on their work in such a way as to *personally* report on the course and results of it to the deputies and you They must be selected *very* gradually so that only after repeated tests they are made, so to say, inspectors and instructors "with special authority"; their number must be *gradually* brought up to several dozen. In their turn, they will (*actually*) enlist non-Party workers and peasants into the work of the Workers' and Peasants' Inspection.

If you approve of the above, send a copy of this to Tsyurupa and Rykov with your postscript. If you have objections, write me a note (and telephone) immediately. I should like to speak of this in the report to the Congress.

Lenin

First published
in *Pravda* No. 21.
January 21, 1930

Published according to
a typewritten copy

FOURTH ANNIVERSARY OF *BEDNOTA*[79]

My congratulations to the Editorial Board of *Bednota* on the occasion of the fourth anniversary of their newspaper.

For four years the paper has worked honourably and successfully to serve the interests of the working peasantry. The war that was forced upon the people by the capitalists and landowners ruined Russia to such an extent that our working peasantry still remain poor. The working people of Russia have still a lot of real hard work to do to overcome the starvation and poverty, the want and ruin that prevail as a consequence of the war.

But the peasants and workers of Russia will get down to this hard work and finish it, come what may. In this effort the workers and peasants will be inspired by the knowledge that they will be working for their own benefit, to improve their own conditions of life, and not for the enrichment of landowners and capitalists

Soviet power has given us the alliance of workers and peasants. Therein lies its strength. Therein lies the guarantee of our successes and of our ultimate victory

This alliance gave us victory over Kolchak and Denikin, who, with the aid of foreign troops sent here by the capitalists, had tried to restore the rule of the landowners in Russia.

Now the foreign capitalists are compelled to conclude trade agreements with Soviet Russia. These agreements will help us to get the agricultural implements, machines and other goods that we need for the restoration of our ruined peasant farms.

We are now experiencing a most difficult spring following a year of famine. But we shall not be downhearted.

Great as the hardships of the workers and peasants may be, we have now won the right and the opportunity to work for our own benefit and not for the benefit of the landowners. And we shall restore and improve our ruined economy.

N. Lenin

March 23, 1922

Bednota No. 1183,
March 26, 1922

Published according to
the manuscript

LETTER TO V. M. MOLOTOV
FOR THE PLENARY MEETING
OF THE C.C., R.C.P.(B.)
WITH THE PLAN OF THE POLITICAL REPORT
FOR THE ELEVENTH PARTY CONGRESS[80]

March 23, 1922

Comrade Molotov,

Please will you convey to the Plenary Meeting of the Central Committee:

1. My request to be excused from attending the Plenary Meeting on account of ill health (I shall not be able to manage both the sittings of the Plenary Meeting and the report at the Congress).

2. If my presence at the Plenary Meeting is necessary to explain the following plan of the report, I shall certainly come, and could arrive within two or three hours of being summoned.

3. Plan of the Political Report of the Central Committee that I propose to deliver at the Congress:

In the main repeat and in several points enlarge on what I said in my speech at the Metalworkers' Congress on March 6, 1922. Very briefly about Genoa. At somewhat greater length about *NEP* and the concept of "state capitalism".

Checking the (economic) retreat and the task of regrouping our forces. The warning given us by the bourgeoisie as expressed by the *Smena Vekh* writer Ustryalov, who said that *NEP* was not the "tactics" but the "evolution" of Bolshevism.

What we lack most is culture, administrative
ability Illustrate this by a few examples.
Economically and politically *NEP* makes it
fully possible for us to lay the foundations of
socialist economy It is "only" a matter of the
cultural forces of the proletariat and of its
vanguard

What our revolution has won irrevocably
and what still remains undone.

The possibility of intervention. The danger
of a financial crisis, Take advantage of the
"respite"· concentrate on choosing men and on
executive control

The gulf between the magnitude of the tasks
already undertaken and our material and cultural poverty

Supplementary to the report, deal with the
functions of the two Deputy Chairmen of the
Council of People's Commissars and of the
Council of Labour and Defence; refer to my
correspondence on this subject with A. D. Tsyurupa beginning from the end of January 1922;
to the regulations we three (plus Rykov) are
now drafting on the reorganisation of this work
and the need for the maximum verification of
fulfilment

Relieve the Council of People's Commissars
of minor matters; demarcate its functions more
precisely from those of the Council of Labour
and Defence and of the Narrow Council of People's Commissars.[81] Enhance the prestige of the
Council of People's Commissars by enlisting
the co-operation of leading comrades, the People's
Commissars, and not only the Deputy Commissars

In this connection and in conformity with
Comrade Kalinin's repeated verbal statements
and Comrade Yenukidze's written communication enclosed herewith, the Central Committee
should recommend that the Congress approve
the plan outlined above and the convocation of

the All-Russia Central Executive Committee for longer sessions than usual for the purpose of discussing the main questions of legislation and for a systematic review of the work of the People's Commissariats and of the Council of People's Commissars.

Lastly, it is necessary to delimit much more precisely the functions of the Party (and of its Central Committee) from those of the Soviet government; to increase the responsibility and independence of Soviet officials and of Soviet government institutions, leaving to the Party the general guidance of the activities of all state bodies, without the present, too frequent, irregular and often petty interference.

Draw up an appropriate resolution for endorsement by the Party Congress.

4. I request that the Central Committee Plenary Meeting appoint a supplementary rapporteur on behalf of the C.C., for my report will be too general. Moreover, I am not quite certain that I shall be able to deliver it. But the main thing is that I am months behind the current work of the Political Bureau.

With communist greetings,
Lenin

First published
in *Pravda* No. 201,
August 30, 1928

Published according to
the manuscript

THE CONDITIONS FOR ADMITTING NEW MEMBERS TO THE PARTY

LETTERS TO V M. MOLOTOV

1

Comrade Molotov,

I request that the following proposal be submitted to the Plenary Meeting of the Central Committee.

I consider it extremely important to lengthen the probation period for new members of the Party. Zinoviev proposes that the probation period should be six months for workers and twelve months for other categories. I propose a period of six months only for those workers who have actually been employed in large industrial enterprises for not less than ten years. A probation period of eighteen months should be established for all other workers, two years for peasants and Red Army men, and three years for other categories. Exceptions are to be permitted in special cases with the joint consent of the Central Committee and the Central Control Commission.

I think it will be extremely dangerous to accept the short periods of probation proposed by Zinoviev. There is no doubt that we constantly regard as workers people who have not had the slightest real experience of large-scale industry. There has been case after case of petty bourgeois, who have become workers by chance and only for a very short time, being classed as workers. All shrewd whiteguards are very definitely banking on the fact that the alleged proletarian character of our Party does not in the least safeguard it against the small-proprietor elements gaining predominance in it, and very rapidly, too. In view of the lackadaisical and unsystematic methods that prevail in our ranks, short probation periods will actually mean that no real test will be made to ascertain whether the applicants are really more or less tried Communists. If we have 300,000 to 400,000 members in the Party, even that number is excessive, for literally everything goes to show that the level of training of the present Party membership is inadequate. That is why I strongly insist on longer probation periods, and on instructing the Organising Bureau to draw up and strictly apply rules that will really make the period of probation a serious test and not an empty formality.

I think that this question should be discussed at the Congress with special care.

Lenin

March 24, 1922

2

Comrade Molotov,

Please give this to be read to all the members of the Central Committee before the question of the conditions for admitting new members to the Party is brought up at the Congress

Having read the decision of the Plenary Meeting of March 25 on the question of the probation periods for new Party members, I should like to challenge this decision at the Congress. I am afraid, however, that I shall not be able to speak at the Congress, and so I request that my opinion be read.

There is no doubt that judged by the bulk of its present membership our Party is not proletarian enough I do not think anybody can challenge this, and a mere glance at the statistics will bear it out. Since the war, the industrial workers of Russia have become much less proletarian than they were before, because during the war all those who desired to evade military service went into the factories. This is common knowledge. On the other hand, it is equally undoubted that, taken as a whole (if we take the level of the overwhelming majority of Party members), our Party is less politically trained than is necessary for real proletarian leadership in the present difficult situation, especially in view of the tremendous preponderance of the peasantry, which is rapidly awakening to independent class politics. Further, it must be borne in mind that the temptation to join the ruling party at the present time is very great. It is sufficient to recall all the literary productions of the *Smena Vekh* writers to see that the types who have been carried away by the political successes of the Bolsheviks are very remote from everything proletarian

If the Genoa Conference results in further political successes for us, there will be a big increase in the efforts of petty-bourgeois elements, and of elements positively hostile to all that is proletarian, to penetrate into the Party. Six months' probation for workers will not diminish this pressure in the least, for it is the easiest thing in the world for anyone to qualify for this short probation period by fraudulent means, the more so that it is not in the least difficult under present conditions for very many intellectual and semi-intellectual elements to join the ranks of the workers. From all this I draw the conclusion that we must establish much longer probation periods and this opinion is strengthened by the fact that the whiteguards are definitely banking on the non-proletarian composition of our Party membership. If we agree to a six months' period for workers, we must without fail, in order not to deceive ourselves and others, define the term "worker" in such a way as to include only those who have acquired a proletarian mentality from their very conditions of life. But this is impossible unless the persons concerned have worked in a factory for many years—not from ulterior motives, but because of the general conditions of their economic and social life.

If we do not close our eyes to reality we must admit that at the present time the proletarian policy of the Party is not determined by the character of its membership, but by the enormous undivided prestige enjoyed by the small group which might be called the Old Guard of the Party. A slight conflict within this group will be enough, if not to destroy this prestige, at all events to weaken the group to such a degree as to rob it of its power to determine policy.

Hence, it is necessary: 1) to lengthen the probation period for all categories; 2) to define in great detail how the applicant is to pass the probation period; what concrete and practical tests should be applied to determine whether the probation period is really a period of probation and not a mere formality; 3) to create a qualified majority on the bodies which decide on the applications of new members; 4) to make it a rule that the decision to admit new members be endorsed, not only by the Gubernia Party Committees, but also by the Control Commissions; 5) to

devise other measures for the purpose of helping the Party
to rid itself of those members who are by no means Communists consciously implementing a proletarian policy.
I do not propose that a new general purging of the Party
be undertaken, because I think at the moment it is impracticable; but I do think it is necessary to find some means
of actually purging the Party, i.e., of reducing its membership. I am sure that if the necessary thought is given to
the matter a number of suitable measures can be devised.

I would ask the members of the Central Committee who
will read this to reply to me if possible, if only in a brief
telephone message to one of the secretaries of the Council
of People's Commissars.

Lenin

March 26, 1922

First published
in December 1925

Dictated by telephone
Published according to
a typewritten copy

ELEVENTH CONGRESS
OF THE R.C.P. (B.)[82]

MARCH 27-APRIL 2, 1922

Published in 1922 in *Odinnadtsaty syezd R.K.P.(B.). Stenografichesky otchot* (Eleventh Congress of the Russian Communist Party [Bolsheviks]. Verbatim Report), Moscow, Publishing Department of the Central Committee of the R.C.P.

Published according to the text in the book checked with the verbatim report; speech at the closing session published according to the manuscript

1

SPEECH IN OPENING THE CONGRESS
MARCH 27

Comrades, on behalf of the Central Committee of the Party I declare the Eleventh Congress of the R.C.P. open.

Comrades, you have gathered in congress after a whole year, in the course of which we have, for the first time, been free from the intervention and invasion of capitalist countries, at all events, in their most direct form. This is the first year that we have had the opportunity of devoting our efforts to the real, main and fundamental tasks of socialist construction.

In this field we have undoubtedly taken only the first steps. But I am sure that if we soberly appraise what we have achieved and are not afraid to look facts—which are not always pleasant, and sometimes very unpleasant— straight in the face, we shall certainly overcome all the difficulties that only now are looming ahead of us in all their magnitude.

The disasters that befell us in the past year were, if anything, even more severe than those of the preceding years.

It seemed as if all the consequences of the imperialist war and of the war which the capitalists forced upon us had combined and hurled themselves upon us in the shape of famine and the most desperate ruin. These disasters have as yet been far from overcome; and none of us expects that they can be overcome soon.

But if we maintain and strengthen the unity of our Party, if we emerge from international difficulties as successfully as we have done up to now, if we concentrate all our efforts on the tasks that now necessarily arise from present conditions, there can be no doubt that we shall overcome these difficulties.

All over the world the communist movement is growing, if not as fast as those of us who measured it by wartime and immediate post-war standards expected, at all events it is growing and is becoming sound, solid, broad and deep. And if we, in co-operation with the Communist Parties that now exist in all, or nearly all, countries, soberly assess our position and are not afraid to admit our mistakes, we shall victoriously emerge from all these difficulties.

2

POLITICAL REPORT
OF THE CENTRAL COMMITTEE OF THE R.C.P. (B.)
MARCH 27

(*Applause.*) Comrades, permit me to start the political report of the Central Committee from the end and not from the beginning of the year. The political question most discussed today is Genoa. But since a great deal has already heen said on the subject in our press, and since I have already said what is most essential to it in my speech on March 6, which has been published, I would ask you to permit me to refrain from going into details unless you particularly wish me to do so.

On the whole you know everything about Genoa, because much has been written about it in the newspapers—in my opinion too much, to the detriment of the real, practical and urgent requirements of our work of construction in general, and of our economic development in particular. In Europe, in all bourgeois countries, of course, they like to occupy people's minds, or stuff their heads, with all sorts of trash about Genoa. On this occasion (I would say not only on this occasion) we are copying them, and copying them far too much.

I must say that in the Central Committee we have taken very great pains to appoint a delegation of our best diplomats (we now have a fair number of Soviet diplomats, which was not the case in the early period of the Soviet Republic). The Central Committee has drawn up sufficiently detailed instructions for our diplomats at the Genoa Conference; we spent a long time discussing these instructions and considered and reconsidered them several times. It goes without saying that the question here is, I shall not say of war, because that term is likely to be misunderstood, but at all events one of rivalry. In the bourgeois camp there is a very strong trend, much stronger than any other, that wants to wreck the Genoa Conference. There are trends which greatly favour the Genoa Conference and want it to meet at all costs. The latter have now gained the upper hand. Lastly, in all bourgeois countries there are trends which might be called pacifist trends, among which should be included the entire Second and Two-and-a-Half Internationals. It is this section of the bourgeoisie which is advocating a number of pacifist proposals and is trying to concoct something in the nature of a pacifist policy. As Communists we have definite views about this pacifism which it would be superfluous to expound here. Needless to say, we are going to Genoa not as Communists, but as merchants. We must trade, and they must trade. We want the trade to benefit us; they want it to benefit them. The course of the issue will be determined, if only to a small degree, by the skill of our diplomats.

Insofar as we are going to Genoa as merchants it is obviously by no means a matter of indifference to us whether we shall deal with those people from the bourgeois camp who are inclined to settle the problem by war, or with those who are inclined towards pacifism, even the worst kind of pacifism, which from the communist viewpoint will not stand the slightest criticism. It would be a bad merchant, indeed, if he were unable to appreciate this distinction, and, by shaping his tactics accordingly, achieve practical aims.

We are going to Genoa for the practical purpose of expanding trade and of creating the most favourable conditions for its successful development on the widest scale. But we cannot guarantee the success of the Genoa Conference. It would be ridiculous and absurd to give any guarantees on that score. I must say, however, that, weighing up the present possibilities of Genoa in the most sober and cautious manner, I think that it will not be an exaggeration to say that we shall achieve our object.

Through Genoa, if the other parties in the negotiations

are sufficiently shrewd and not too stubborn; bypassing Genoa if they take it into their heads to be stubborn. But we shall achieve our goal!

The fact of the matter is that the most urgent, pressing and practical interests that have been sharply revealed in all the capitalist countries during the past few years call for the development, regulation and expansion of trade with Russia. Since such interests exist, we may argue, we may quarrel, we may disagree on specific combinations— it is highly probable that we shall have to disagree—this fundamental economic necessity will, nevertheless, after all is said and done, make a way for itself. I think we can rest assured of that. I cannot vouch for the date; I cannot vouch for success; but at this gathering we can say with a fair amount of certainty that regular trade relations between the Soviet Republic and all the capitalist countries in the world are certain to continue developing. When I come to it in another part of my report I shall mention the hitches that may possibly occur; but I think that this is all that need be said on the question of Genoa.

Needless to say, the comrades who desire to study the question in greater detail and who are not content with the list of delegates published in the newspapers may set up a commission, or a section, and acquaint themselves with all the material of the Central Committee, and all the correspondence and instructions. Of course, the details we have outlined are provisional, for no one up to now knows exactly who will sit round the table at Genoa, and what terms, or preliminary terms or provisions will be announced. It would be highly inexpedient, and I think practically impossible, to discuss all this here. I repeat, this Congress, through the medium of a section, or a commission, has every opportunity to collect all the documents on this question—both the published documents and those in the possession of the Central Committee.

I shall not say any more, for I am sure that it is not here that our greatest difficulties lie. This is not the question on which the attention of the whole Party should be focussed. The European bourgeois press is artificially and deliberately inflating and exaggerating the importance of this Conference in order to deceive the masses of the working people (as nine-tenths of the bourgeois press in all these free democratic countries and republics always does). We have succumbed to the influence of this press to some extent. As usual, our press still yields to the old bourgeois habits; it refuses to adopt new, socialist methods, and we have made a greater fuss about this subject than it deserves. In fact, for Communists, especially for those who have lived through such stern years as we have lived through since 1917, and witnessed the formidable political combinations that have appeared in that period, Genoa does not present any great difficulties. I cannot recall any disagreement or controversy on this question either in the Central Committee or in the ranks of the Party. This is natural, for there is nothing controversial here from the point of view of Communists, even bearing in mind the various shades of opinion among them. I repeat: we are going to Genoa as merchants for the purpose of securing the most favourable terms for promoting the trade which has started, which is being carried on, and which, even if someone succeeded in forcibly interrupting it for a time, would inevitably continue to develop after the interruption.

Hence, confining myself to these brief remarks about Genoa, I shall now proceed to deal with the issues which, in my opinion, have been the major political questions of the past year and which will be such in the ensuing year. It seems to me that the political report of the Central Committee should not merely deal with the events of the year under review, but also point out (that, at any rate, is what I usually do) the main, fundamental political lessons of the events of that year, so that we may learn something for the ensuing year and be in a position to correctly determine our policy for that year.

The New Economic Policy is, of course, the major question. This has been the dominant question throughout the year under review. If we have any important, serious and irrevocable gain to record for this year (and I am not so very sure that we have), it is that we have learnt something from the launching of this New Economic Policy. If we have learnt even a little, then, during the past year, we have learnt a great deal in this field. And the test of whether we have really learnt anything, and to what extent, will probably be made by subsequent events of a kind which we ourselves can do little to determine, as for example the impending financial crisis. It seems to me that in connection with the New Economic Policy, the most important things to keep in mind as a basis for all our arguments, as a means of testing our experience during the past year, and of learning practical lessons for the ensuing year are contained in the following three points.

First, the New Economic Policy is important for us primarily as a means of testing whether we are really establishing a link with the peasant economy. In the preceding period of development of our revolution, when all our attention and all our efforts were concentrated mainly on, or almost entirely absorbed by, the task of repelling invasion, we could not devote the necessary attention to this link; we had other things to think about. To some extent we could and had to ignore this bond when we were confronted by the absolutely urgent and overshadowing task of warding off the danger of being immediately crushed by the gigantic forces of world imperialism.

The turn towards the New Economic Policy was decided on at the last Congress with exceptional unanimity, with even greater unanimity than other questions have been decided by our Party (which, it must be admitted, is generally distinguished for its unanimity). This unanimity showed that the need for a new approach to socialist economy had fully matured. People who differed on many questions, and who assessed the situation from different angles, unanimously and very quickly and unhesitantly agreed that we lacked a real approach to socialist economy, to the task of building its foundation; that the only means of finding this approach was the New Economic Policy. Owing to the course taken by the development of war events, by the development of political events, by the development of capitalism in the old, civilised West, and owing also to the social and political conditions that developed in the colonies, we were the first to make a breach in the old bourgeois world at a time when our country was economically, if not the most backward, at any rate one of the most backward countries in the world. The vast majority of the peasants in our country are engaged in small individual farming. The items of our programme of building a communist society, that we could apply immediately, were to some extent outside the sphere of activity of the broad mass of the peasantry, upon whom we imposed very heavy obligations, which we justified on the grounds that war permitted no wavering in this matter. Taken as a whole, this was accepted as justification by the peasantry, notwithstanding the mistakes we could not avoid. On the whole, the mass of the peasantry realised and understood that the enormous burdens imposed upon them were necessary in order to save the workers' and peasants rule from the landowners and prevent it from being strangled by capitalist invasion, which threatened to wrest away all the gains of the revolution. But there was no link between the peasant economy and the economy that was being built up in the nationalised, socialised factories and on state farms.

We saw this clearly at the last Party Congress. We saw it so clearly that there was no hesitation whatever in the Party on the question as to whether the New Economic Policy was inevitable or not.

It is amusing to read what is said about our decision in the numerous publications of the various Russian parties abroad. There are only trifling differences in the opinions they express. Living with memories of the past, they still continue to reiterate that to this day the Left Communists are opposed to the New Economic Policy. In 1921 they remembered what had occurred in 1918 and what our Left Communists themselves have forgotten; and they go on chewing this over and over again, assuring the world that these Bolsheviks are a sly and false lot, and that they are concealing from Europe that they have disagreements in their ranks. Reading this, one says to oneself, "Let them go on fooling themselves." If this is what they imagine is going on in this country, we can judge the degree of intelligence of these allegedly highly educated old fogies who have fled abroad. We know that there have been no disagreements in our ranks, and the reason for this is that the practical necessity of a different approach to the task of building the foundation of socialist economy was clear to all.

There was no link between the peasant economy and the new economy we tried to create. Does it exist now? Not yet. We are only approaching it. The whole significance of the New Economic Policy—which our press still often searches for everywhere except where it should search— the whole purpose of this policy is to find a way of establishing a link between the new economy, which we are creating with such enormous effort, and the peasant economy. That is what stands to our credit; without it we would not be communist revolutionaries.

We began to develop the new economy in an entirely new way, brushing aside everything old. Had we not begun to develop it we would have been utterly defeated in the very first months, in the very first years. But the fact that we began to develop this new economy with such splendid audacity does not mean that we must necessarily continue in the same way. Why should we? There is no reason.

From the very beginning we said that we had to undertake an entirely new task, and that unless we received speedy assistance from our comrades, the workers in the capitalistically more developed countries, we should encounter incredible difficulties and certainly make a number of mistakes. The main thing is to be able dispassionately to examine where such mistakes have been made and to start again from the beginning. If we begin from the beginning, not twice, but many times, it will show that we are not bound by prejudice, and that we are approaching our task, which is the greatest the world has ever seen, with a sober outlook.

Today, as far as the New Economic Policy is concerned the main thing is to assimilate the experience of the past year correctly. That must be done, and we want to do it. And if we want to do it, come what may (and we do want to do it, and shall do it!), we must know that the problem of the New Economic Policy, the fundamental, decisive and overriding problem, is to establish a link between the new economy that we have begun to create (very badly, very clumsily, but have nevertheless begun to create, on the basis of an entirely new, socialist economy, of a new system of production and distribution) and the peasant economy, by which millions and millions of peasants obtain their livelihood.

This link has been lacking, and we must create it before anything else. Everything else must be subordinated to this. We have still to ascertain the extent to which the New Economic Policy has succeeded in creating this link without destroying what we have begun so clumsily to build.

We are developing our economy together with the peasantry. We shall have to alter it many times and organise it in such a way that it will provide a link between our socialist work on large-scale industry and agriculture and the work every peasant is doing as best he can, struggling out of poverty, without philosophising (for how can philosophising help him to extricate himself from his position and save him from the very real danger of a painful death from starvation?).

We must reveal this link so that we may see it clearly, so that all the people may see it, and so that the whole mass of the peasantry may see that there is a connection between their present severe, incredibly ruined, incredibly impoverished and painful existence and the work which is being done for the sake of remote socialist ideals. We must bring about a situation where the ordinary, rank-and-file working man realises that he has obtained some improvement, and that he has obtained it not in the way a few peasants obtained improvements under the rule of landowners and capitalists, when every improvement (undoubtedly there were improvements and very big ones) was accompanied by insult, derision and humiliation for the muzhik, by violence against the masses, which not a single peasant has forgotten, and which will not be forgotten in Russia for decades. Our aim is to restore the link, to prove to the peasant by deeds that we are beginning with what is intelligible, familiar and immediately accessible to him, in spite of his poverty, and not with something remote and fantastic from the peasant's point of view. We must prove that we can help him and that in this period, when the small peasant is in a state of appalling ruin, impoverishment and starvation, the Communists are really helping him. Either we prove that, or he will send us to the devil. That is absolutely inevitable.

Such is the significance of the New Economic Policy; it is the basis of our entire policy; it is the major lesson taught by the whole of the past year's experience in applying the New Economic Policy, and, so to speak, our main political rule for the coming year. The peasant is allowing us credit, and, of course, after what he has lived through, he cannot do otherwise. Taken in the mass, the peasants go on saying: "Well, if you are not able to do it yet, we shall wait; perhaps you will learn." But this credit cannot go on for ever.

This we must know; and having obtained credit we must hurry. We must know that the time is approaching when this peasant country will no longer give us credit, when it will demand cash, to use a commercial term. It will say: "You have postponed payment for so many months, so many years. But by this time, dear rulers, you must have learnt the most sound and reliable method of helping us free ourselves from poverty, want, starvation and ruin. You can do it, you have proved it." This is the test that we shall inevitably have to face; and, in the last analysis, this test will decide everything: the fate of NEP and the fate of communist rule in Russia.

Shall we accomplish our immediate task or not? Is this NEP fit for anything or not? If the retreat turns out to be correct tactics, we must link up with the peasant masses while we are in retreat, and subsequently march forward with them a hundred times more slowly, but firmly and unswervingly, in a way that will always make it apparent to them that we are really marching forward. Then our cause will be absolutely invincible, and no power on earth can vanquish us. We did not accomplish this in the first year. We must say this frankly. And I am profoundly convinced (and our New Economic Policy enables us to draw this conclusion quite definitely and firmly) that if we appreciate the enormous danger harboured by NEP and concentrate all our forces on its weak points, we shall solve this problem.

Link up with the peasant masses, with the rank-and-file working peasants, and begin to move forward immeasurably, infinitely more slowly than we expected, but in such a way that the entire mass will actually move forward with us. If we do that we shall in time progress much more quickly than we even dream of today. This, in my opinion, is the first fundamental political lesson of the New Economic Policy.

The second, more specific lesson is the test through competition between state and capitalist enterprises. We are now forming mixed companies—I shall have something to say about these later on—which, like our state trade and our New Economic Policy as a whole, mean that we Communists are resorting to commercial, capitalist methods. These mixed companies are also important because through them practical competition is created between capitalist methods and our methods. Consider it practically. Up to now we have been writing a programme and making promises. In its time this was absolutely necessary. It is impossible to launch on a world revolution without a programme and without promises. If the whiteguards, including the Mensheviks, jeer at us for this, it only shows that the Mensheviks and the socialists of the Second and Two-and-a-Half Internationals have no idea, in general, of the way a revolution develops. We could proceed in no other way.

Now, however, the position is that we must put our work to a serious test, and not the sort of test that is made by control institutions set up by the Communists themselves, even though these control institutions are magnificent, even though they are almost the ideal control institutions in the Soviet system and the Party; such a test may be mockery from the point of view of the actual requirements of the peasant economy, but it is certainly no mockery from the standpoint of our construction. We are now setting up these control institutions but I am referring not to this test but to the test from the point of view of the entire economy.

The capitalist was able to supply things. He did it inefficiently, charged exorbitant prices, insulted and robbed us. The ordinary workers and peasants, who do not argue about communism because they do not know what it is, are well aware of this.

"But the capitalists were, after all, able to supply things—are you? You are not able to do it." That is what we heard last spring; though not always clearly audible, it was the undertone of the whole of last spring's crisis. "As people you are splendid, but you cannot cope with the economic task you have undertaken." This is the simple and withering criticism which the peasantry—and through the peasantry, some sections of workers—levelled at the Communist Party last year. That is why in the NEP question, this old point acquires such significance.

We need a real test. The capitalists are operating alongside us. They are operating like robbers; they make profit; but they know how to do things. But you—you are trying to do it in a new way: you make no profit, your principles are communist, your ideals are splendid; they are written out so beautifully that you seem to be saints, that you should go to heaven while you are still alive. But can you get things done? We need a test, a real test, not the kind the Central Control Commission makes when it censures somebody and the All-Russia Central Executive Committee imposes some penalty. Yes, we want a real test from the viewpoint of the national economy.

We Communists have received numerous deferments, and more credit has been allowed us than any other government has ever been given. Of course, we Communists helped to get rid of the capitalists and landowners. The peasants appreciate this and have given us an extension of time, longer credit, but only for a certain period. After that comes the test: can you run the economy as well as the others? The old capitalist can; you cannot.

That is the first lesson, the first main part of the political report of the Central Committee. We cannot run the economy. This has been proved in the past year. I would like very much to quote the example of several Gos-trests (if I may express myself in the beautiful Russian language that Turgenev praised so highly)* to show how we run the economy.

Unfortunately, for a number of reasons, and largely owing to ill health, I have been unable to elaborate this part of my report and so I must confine myself to express-

---

* An ironical reference to the habit, then emerging, of abbreviating the names of various institutions. Here the abbreviation stands for *state trusts.—Ed.*

ing my conviction, which is based on my observations of
what is going on. During the past year we showed quite
clearly that we cannot run the economy. That is the fundamental lesson. Either we prove the opposite in the coming
year, or Soviet power will not be able to exist. And the
greatest danger is that not everybody realises this. If all
of us Communists, the responsible officials, clearly realise
that we lack the ability to run the economy, that we must
learn from the very beginning, then we shall win—that,
in my opinion, is the fundamental conclusion that should
be drawn. But many of us do not appreciate this and believe
that if there are people who do think that way, it can only
be the ignorant, who have not studied communism; perhaps
they will some day learn and understand. No, excuse me,
the point is not that the peasant or the non-Party worker
has not studied communism, but that the time has passed
when the job was to draft a programme and call upon
the people to carry out this great programme. That time
has passed. Today you must prove that you can give
practical economic assistance to the workers and to the
peasants under the present difficult conditions, and thus
demonstrate to them that you have stood the test of
competition.

The mixed companies that we have begun to form, in
which private capitalists, Russian and foreign, and Communists participate, provide one of the means by which
we can learn to organise competition properly and show
that we are no less able to establish a link with the peasant
economy than the capitalists; that we can meet its requirements; that we can help the peasant make progress even
at his present level, in spite of his backwardness; for it
is impossible to change him in a brief span of time.

That is the sort of competition confronting us as an absolutely urgent task. It is the pivot of the New Economic
Policy and, in my opinion, the quintessence of the Party's
policy. We are faced with any number of purely political
problems and difficulties. You know what they are: Genoa,
the danger of intervention. The difficulties are enormous
but they are nothing compared with this economic difficulty. We know how things are done in the political field;
we have gained considerable experience; we have learned

a lot about bourgeois diplomacy. It is the sort of thing the Mensheviks taught us for fifteen years, and we got something useful out of it. This is not new.

But here is something we must do now in the economic field. We must win the competition against the ordinary shop assistant, the ordinary capitalist, the merchant, who will go to the peasant without arguing about communism. Just imagine, he will not begin to argue about communism, but will argue in this way—if you want to obtain something, or carry on trade properly, or if you want to build, I will do the building at a high price; the Communists will, perhaps, build at a higher price, perhaps even ten times higher. It is this kind of agitation that is now the crux of the matter; herein lies the root of economics.

I repeat, thanks to our correct policy, the people allowed us a deferment of payment and credit, and this, to put it in terms of NEP, is a promissory note. But this promissory note is undated, and you cannot learn from the wording when it will be presented for redemption. Therein lies the danger; this is the specific feature that distinguishes these political promissory notes from ordinary, commercial promissory notes. We must concentrate all our attention on this, and not rest content with the fact that there are responsible and good Communists in all the state trusts and mixed companies. That is of no use, because these Communists do not know how to run the economy and, in that respect, are inferior to the ordinary capitalist salesmen, who have received their training in big factories and big firms. But we refuse to admit this; in this field communist conceit—komchvanstvo,* to use the great Russian language again—still persists. The whole point is that the responsible Communists, even the best of them, who are unquestionably honest and loyal, who in the old days suffered penal servitude and did not fear death, do not know how to trade, because they are not businessmen, they have not learnt to trade, do not want to learn and do not understand that they must start learning from the beginning, Communists, revolutionaries who have accomplished the greatest revolution in the world, on whom the

---

* Literally, "comconceit".—*Ed.*

eyes of, if not forty pyramids, then, at all events, forty
European countries are turned in the hope of emancipation from capitalism, must learn from ordinary salesmen.
But these ordinary salesmen have had ten years' ware-
house experience and know the business, whereas the responsible Communists and devoted revolutionaries do not
know the business, and do not even realise that they do
not know it.

And so, comrades, if we do away with at least this elementary ignorance we shall achieve a tremendous victory.
We must leave this Congress with the conviction that we
are ignorant of this business and with the resolve to start
learning it from the bottom. After all, we have not ceased
to be revolutionaries (although many say, and not altogether without foundation, that we have become bureaucrats) and can understand this simple thing, that in a new
and unusually difficult undertaking we must be prepared
to start from the beginning over and over again. If after
starting you find yourselves at a dead end, start again,
and go on doing it ten times if necessary, until you attain
your object. Do not put on airs, do not be conceited because
you are a Communist while there is some non-Party salesman, perhaps a whiteguard—and very likely he is a whiteguard—who can do things which economically must be
done at all costs, but which you cannot do. If you, responsible Communists, who have hundreds of ranks and titles
and wear communist and Soviet Orders, realise this, you
will attain your object, because this is something that
can be learned.

We have some successes, even if only very tiny ones, to
record for the past year, but they are insignificant. The
main thing is that there is no realisation nor widespread
conviction among all Communists that at the present
time the responsible and most devoted Russian Communist
is less able to perform these functions than any salesman
of the old school. I repeat, we must start learning from
the very beginning. If we realise this, we shall pass our
test; and the test is a serious one which the impending
financial crisis will set—the test set by the Russian and
international market to which we are subordinated, with
which we are connected, and from which we cannot isolate

ourselves. The test is a crucial one, for here we may be beaten economically and politically.

That is how the question stands and it cannot be otherwise, for the competition will be very severe, and it will be decisive. We had many outlets and loopholes that enabled us to escape from our political and economic difficulties. We can proudly say that up to now we have been able to utilise these outlets and loopholes in various combinations corresponding to the varying circumstances. But now we have no other outlets. Permit me to say this to you without exaggeration, because in this respect it is really "the last and decisive battle", not against international capitalism—against that we shall yet have many "last and decisive battles"—but against Russian capitalism, against the capitalism that is growing out of the small-peasant economy, the capitalism that is fostered by the latter. Here we shall have a fight on our hands in the immediate future, and the date of it cannot be fixed exactly. Here the "last and decisive battle" is impending; here there are no political or any other flanking movements that we can undertake, because this is a test in competition with private capital. Either we pass this test in competition with private capital, or we fail completely. To help us pass it we have political power and a host of economic and other resources; we have everything you want except ability. We lack ability. And if we learn this simple lesson from the experience of last year and take it as our guiding line for the whole of 1922, we shall conquer this difficulty, too, in spite of the fact that it is much greater than the previous difficulty, for it rests upon ourselves. It is not like some external enemy. The difficulty is that we ourselves refuse to admit the unpleasant truth forced upon us; we refuse to undertake the unpleasant duty that the situation demands of us, namely, to start learning from the beginning. That, in my opinion, is the second lesson that we must learn from the New Economic Policy.

The third, supplementary lesson is on the question of state capitalism. It is a pity Comrade Bukharin is not present at the Congress. I should have liked to argue with him a little, but that had better be postponed to the next Congress. On the question of state capitalism, I think that generally our press and our Party make the mistake of dropping into intellectualism, into liberalism; we philosophise about how state capitalism is to be interpreted, and look into old books. But in those old books you will not find what we are discussing; they deal with the state capitalism that exists under capitalism. Not a single book has been written about state capitalism under communism. It did not occur even to Marx to write a word on this subject; and he died without leaving a single precise statement or definite instruction on it. That is why we must overcome the difficulty entirely by ourselves. And if we make a general mental survey of our press and see what has been written about state capitalism, as I tried to do when I was preparing this report, we shall be convinced that it is missing the target, that it is looking in an entirely wrong direction.

The state capitalism discussed in all books on economics is that which exists under the capitalist system, where the state brings under its direct control certain capitalist enterprises. But ours is a proletarian state; it rests on the proletariat; it gives the proletariat all political privileges; and through the medium of the proletariat it attracts to itself the lower ranks of the peasantry (you remember that we began this work through the Poor Peasants' Committees). That is why very many people are misled by the term state capitalism. To avoid this we must remember the fundamental thing that state capitalism in the form we have here is not dealt with in any theory, or in any books, for the simple reason that all the usual concepts connected with this term are associated with bourgeois rule in capitalist society. Our society is one which has left the rails of capitalism, but has not yet got on to new rails. The state in this society is not ruled by the bourgeoisie, but by the proletariat. We refuse to understand that when we say "state" we mean ourselves, the proletariat, the vanguard of the working class. State capitalism is capitalism which we shall be able to restrain, and the limits of which we shall be able to fix. This state capitalism is connected with the state, and the state is the workers, the advanced section of the workers, the vanguard. We are the state.

State capitalism is capitalism that we must confine within certain bounds; but we have not yet learned to confine it within those bounds. That is the whole point. And it rests with us to determine what this state capitalism is to be. We have sufficient, quite sufficient political power; we also have sufficient economic resources at our command, but the vanguard of the working class which has been brought to the forefront to directly supervise, to determine the boundaries, to demarcate, to subordinate and not be subordinated itself, lacks sufficient ability for it. All that is needed here is ability, and that is what we do not have.

Never before in history has there been a situation in which the proletariat, the revolutionary vanguard, possessed sufficient political power and had state capitalism existing alongside it. The whole question turns on our understanding that this is the capitalism that we can and must permit, that we can and must confine within certain bounds; for this capitalism is essential for the broad masses of the peasantry and for private capital, which must trade in such a way as to satisfy the needs of the peasantry. We must organise things in such a way as to make possible the customary operation of capitalist economy and capitalist exchange, because this is essential for the people. Without it, existence is impossible. All the rest is not an absolutely vital matter to this camp. They can resign themselves to all that. You Communists, you workers, you, the politically enlightened section of the proletariat, which under took to administer the state, must be able to arrange it so that the state, which you have taken into your hands, shall function the way you want it to. Well, we have lived through a year, the state is in our hands; but has it operated the New Economic Policy in the way we wanted in this past year? No. But we refuse to admit that it did not operate in the way we wanted. How did it operate? The machine refused to obey the hand that guided it. It was like a car that was going not in the direction the driver desired, but in the direction someone else desired; as if it were being driven by some mysterious, lawless hand, God knows whose, perhaps of a profiteer, or of a private capitalist, or of both. Be that as it may, the car is not going quite in the direction the man at the wheel imagines, and often it goes in an altogether different direction.

This is the main thing that must be remembered in regard to
state capitalism. In this main field we must start learning
from the very beginning, and only when we have thoroughly understood and appreciated this can we be sure that
we shall learn.

Now I come to the question of halting the retreat, a question I dealt with in my speech at the Congress of Metalworkers. Since then I have not heard any objection, either
in the Party press, or in private letters from comrades, or in
the Central Committee. The Central Committee approved my
plan, which was, that in the report of the Central Committee
to the present Congress strong emphasis should be laid on
calling a halt to this retreat and that the Congress should
give binding instructions on behalf of the whole Party
accordingly. For a year we have been retreating. On behalf
of the Party we must now call a halt. The purpose pursued
by the retreat has been achieved. This period is drawing, or
has drawn, to a close. We now have a different objective,
that of regrouping our forces. We have reached a new line;
on the whole, we have conducted the retreat in fairly good
order. True, not a few voices were heard from various sides
which tried to convert this retreat into a stampede. Some—
for example, several members of the group which bore the
name of Workers' Opposition (I don't think they had any
right to that name)—argued that we were not retreating
properly in some sector or other. Owing to their excessive
zeal they found themselves at the wrong door, and now they
realise it. At that time they did not see that their activities
did not help us to correct our movement, but merely had
the effect of spreading panic and hindering our effort to beat
a disciplined retreat.

Retreat is a difficult matter, especially for revolutionaries
who are accustomed to advance; especially when they have
been accustomed to advance with enormous success for several years; especially if they are surrounded by revolutionaries in other countries who are longing for the time when
they can launch an offensive. Seeing that we were retreating,
several of them burst into tears in a disgraceful and childish manner, as was the case at the last extended Plenary
Meeting of the Executive Committee of the Communist
International. Moved by the best communist sentiments

and communist aspirations, several of the comrades burst
into tears because—oh horror!—the good Russian Communists were retreating. Perhaps it is now difficult for me to understand this West-European mentality, although I lived for
quite a number of years in those marvellous democratic countries as an exile. Perhaps from their point of view this is
such a difficult matter to understand that it is enough to
make one weep. We, at any rate, have no time for sentiment.
It was clear to us that because we had advanced so successfully for many years and had achieved so many extraordinary
victories (and all this in a country that was in an appalling
state of ruin and lacked the material resources!), to consolidate that advance, since we had gained so much, it was
absolutely essential for us to retreat. We could not hold
all the positions we had captured in the first onslaught.
On the other hand, it was because we had captured so much in
the first onslaught, on the crest of the wave of enthusiasm
displayed by the workers and peasants, that we had room
enough to retreat a long distance, and can retreat still further now, without losing our main and fundamental positions. On the whole, the retreat was fairly orderly, although
certain panic-stricken voices, among them that of the Workers' Opposition (this was the tremendous harm it did!),
caused losses in our ranks, caused a relaxation of discipline,
and disturbed the proper order of retreat. The most dangerous thing during a retreat is panic. When a whole army (I
speak in the figurative sense) is in retreat, it cannot have the
same morale as when it is advancing. At every step you find
a certain mood of depression. We even had poets who wrote
that people were cold and starving in Moscow, that "everything before was bright and beautiful, but now trade and
profiteering abound". We have had quite a number of
poetic effusions of this sort.

Of course, retreat breeds all this. That is where the serious danger lies; it is terribly difficult to retreat after a great
victorious advance, for the relations are entirely different.
During a victorious advance, even if discipline is relaxed,
everybody presses forward on his own accord. During a retreat, however, discipline must be more conscious and is a
hundred times more necessary, because, when the entire
army is in retreat, it does not know or see where it should halt.

It sees only retreat; under such circumstances a few panic-stricken voices are, at times, enough to cause a stampede. The danger here is enormous. When a real army is in retreat, machine-guns are kept ready, and when an orderly retreat degenerates into a disorderly one, the command to fire is given, and quite rightly, too.

If, during an incredibly difficult retreat, when everything depends on preserving proper order, anyone spreads panic— even from the best of motives—the slightest breach of discipline must be punished severely, sternly, ruthlessly; and this applies not only to certain of our internal Party affairs, but also, and to a greater extent, to such gentry as the Mensheviks, and to all the gentry of the Two-and-a-Half International.

The other day I read an article by Comrade Rakosi in No. 20 of *The Communist International* on a new book by Otto Bauer, from whom at one time we all learned, but who, like Kautsky, became a miserable petty bourgeois after the war.[83] Bauer now writes: "There, they are now retreating to capitalism! We have always said that it was a bourgeois revolution."

And the Mensheviks and Socialist-Revolutionaries, all of whom preach this sort of thing, are astonished when we declare that we shall shoot people for such things. They are amazed; but surely it is clear. When an army is in retreat a hundred times more discipline is required than when it is advancing, because during an advance everybody presses forward. If everybody started rushing back now, it would spell immediate and inevitable disaster.

The most important thing at such a moment is to retreat in good order, to fix the precise limits of the retreat, and not to give way to panic. And when a Menshevik says, "You are now retreating; I have been advocating retreat all the time, I agree with you, I am your man, let us retreat together," we say in reply, "For the public manifestations of Menshevism our revolutionary courts must pass the death sentence, otherwise they are not our courts, but God knows what."

They cannot understand this and exclaim: "What dictatorial manners these people have!" They still think we are persecuting the Mensheviks because they fought us in Geneva.[84] But had we done that we should have been unable to hold power even for two months. Indeed, the sermons which Otto Bauer, the leaders of the Second and Two-and-a-Half Internationals, the Mensheviks and Socialist-Revolutionaries preach express their true nature—"The revolution has gone too far. What you are saying now we have been saying all the time, permit us to say it again." But we say in reply: "Permit us to put you before a firing squad for saying that. Either you refrain from expressing your views, or, if you insist on expressing your political views publicly in the present circumstances, when our position is far more difficult than it was when the whiteguards were directly attacking us, then you will have only yourselves to blame if we treat you as the worst and most pernicious whiteguard elements." We must never forget this.

When I speak about halting the retreat I do not mean that we have learned to trade. On the contrary, I am of the opposite opinion; and if my speech were to create that impression it would show that I had been misunderstood and that I am unable to express my thoughts properly.

The point, however, is that we must put a stop to the nervousness and fuss that have arisen with the introduction of NEP—the desire to do everything in a new way and to adapt everything. We now have a number of mixed companies. True, we have only very few. There are nine companies formed in conjunction with foreign capitalists and sanctioned by the Commissariat of Foreign Trade. The Sokolnikov Commission[85] has sanctioned six and the Northern Timber Trust[86] has sanctioned two. Thus we now have seventeen companies with an aggregate capital amounting to many millions, sanctioned by several government departments (of course, there is plenty of confusion with all these departments, so that some slip here is also possible). At any rate, we have formed companies jointly with Russian and foreign capitalists. There are only a few of them. But this small but practical start shows that the Communists have been judged by what they do. They have not been judged by such high institutions as the Central Control Commission and the All-Russia Central Executive Committee. The Central Control Commission is a splendid institution, of course, and we shall now give it more power. For all that, the judgement these institutions pass on Communists is not—just imagine—recognised on the international market. (*Laughter*.) But now that ordinary Russian and foreign capitalists are joining the Communists in forming mixed companies, we say, "We can do things after all; bad as it is, meagre as it is, we have got something for a start." True, it is not very much. Just think of it: a year has passed since we declared that we would devote all our energy (and it is said that we have a great deal of energy) to this matter, and in this year we have managed to form only seventeen companies.

This shows how devilishly clumsy and inept we are; how much Oblomovism still remains, for which we shall inevitably get a good thrashing. For all that, I repeat, a start, a reconnaissance has been made. The capitalists would not agree to have dealings with us if the elementary conditions for their operations did not exist. Even if only a very small section of them has agreed to this, it shows that we have scored a partial victory.

Of course, they will cheat us in these companies, cheat us so that it will take several years before matters are straightened out. But that does not matter. I do not say that that is a victory; it is a reconnaissance, which shows that we have an arena, we have a terrain, and can now stop the retreat.

The reconnaissance has revealed that we have concluded an insignificant number of agreements with capitalists; but we have concluded them for all that. We must learn from that and continue our operations. In this sense we must put a stop to nervousness, screaming and fuss. We received notes and telephone messages, one after another asking, "Now that we have NEP, may we be reorganised too?" Everybody is bustling, and we get utter confusion; nobody is doing any practical work; everybody is continuously arguing about how to adapt oneself to NEP, but no practical results are forthcoming.

The merchants are laughing at us Communists, and in all probability are saying, "Formerly there were Persuaders-in-Chief,[87] now we have Talkers-in-Chief." That the capitalists gloated over the fact that we started late, that we were not sharp enough—of that there need not be the slightest doubt. In this sense, I say, these instructions must be endorsed in the name of the Congress.

The retreat is at an end. The principal methods of operation, of how we are to work with the capitalists, are outlined. We have examples, even if an insignificant number.

Stop philosophising and arguing about NEP. Let the poets write verses, that is what they are poets for. But you economists, you stop arguing about NEP and get more companies formed; check up on how many Communists we have who can organise successful competition with the capitalists.

The retreat has come to an end; it is now a matter of regrouping our forces. These are the instructions that the Congress must pass so as to put an end to fuss and bustle. Calm down, do not philosophise; if you do, it will be counted as a black mark against you. Show by your practical efforts that you can work no less efficiently than the capitalists. The capitalists create an economic link with the peasants in order to amass wealth; you must create a link with peasant economy in order to strengthen the economic power of our proletarian state. You have the advantage over the capitalists in that political power is in your hands; you have a number of economic weapons at your command; the only trouble is that you cannot make proper use of them. Look at things more soberly. Cast off the tinsel, the festive communist garments, learn a simple thing simply, and we shall beat the private capitalist. We possess political power; we possess a host of economic weapons. If we beat capitalism and create a link with peasant farming we shall become an absolutely invincible power. Then the building of socialism will not be the task of that drop in the ocean, called the Communist Party, but the task of the entire mass of the working people. Then the rank-and-file peasants will see that we are helping them and they will follow our lead. Consequently, even if the pace is a hundred times slower, it will be a million times more certain and more sure.

It is in this sense that we must speak of halting the retreat; and the proper thing to do is, in one way or another, to make this slogan a Congress decision.

In this connection, I should like to deal with the question: what is the Bolsheviks' New Economic Policy—evolution or tactics? This question has been raised by the *Smena Vekh* people, who, as you know, are a trend which has arisen among Russian émigrés; it is a socio-political trend led by some

of the most prominent Constitutional-Democrats, several
Ministers of the former Kolchak government, people who
have come to the conclusion that the Soviet government is
building up the Russian state and therefore should be supported. They argue as follows: "What sort of state is the
Soviet government building? The Communists say they are
building a communist state and assure us that the new policy
is a matter of tactics: the Bolsheviks are making use of the
private capitalists in a difficult situation, but later they
will get the upper hand. The Bolsheviks can say what they
like; as a matter of fact it is not tactics but evolution,
internal regeneration; they will arrive at the ordinary bourgeois state, and we must support them. History proceeds
in devious ways."

Some of them pretend to be Communists; but there are
others who are more straightforward, one of these is Ustryalov. I think he was a Minister in Kolchak's government.
He does not agree with his colleagues and says: "You can
think what you like about communism, but I maintain that
it is not a matter of tactics, but of evolution." I think that
by being straightforward like this, Ustryalov is rendering
us a great service. We, and I particularly, because of my
position, hear a lot of sentimental communist lies, "communist fibbing", every day, and sometimes we get sick to death
of them. But now instead of these "communist fibs" I get a
copy of *Smena Vekh*, which says quite plainly: "Things are
by no means what you imagine them to be. As a matter of
fact, you are slipping into the ordinary bourgeois morass
with communist flags inscribed with catchwords stuck all
over the place." This is very useful. It is not a repetition of
what we are constantly hearing around us, but the plain class
truth uttered by the class enemy. It is very useful to read
this sort of thing; and it was written not because the communist state allows you to write some things and not others,
but because it really is the class truth, bluntly and frankly
uttered by the class enemy. "I am in favour of supporting
the Soviet government," says Ustryalov, although he was a
Constitutional-Democrat, a bourgeois, and supported intervention. "I am in favour of supporting Soviet power because
it has taken the road that will lead it to the ordinary bourgeois state."

This is very useful, and I think that we must keep it in mind. It is much better for us if the *Smena Vekh* people write in that strain than if some of them pretend to be almost Communists, so that from a distance one cannot tell whether they believe in God or in the communist revolution. We must say frankly that such candid enemies are useful. We must say frankly that the things Ustryalov speaks about are possible. History knows all sorts of metamorphoses. Relying on firmness of convictions, loyalty, and other splendid moral qualities is anything but a serious attitude in politics. A few people may be endowed with splendid moral qualities, but historical issues are decided by vast masses, which, if the few do not suit them, may at times treat them none too politely.

There have been many cases of this kind; that is why we must welcome this frank utterance of the *Smena Vekh* people. The enemy is speaking the class truth and is pointing to the danger that confronts us, and which the enemy is striving to make inevitable. *Smena Vekh* adherents express the sentiments of thousands and tens of thousands of bourgeois, or of Soviet employees whose function it is to operate our New Economic Policy. This is the real and main danger. And that is why attention must be concentrated mainly on the question: "Who will win?" I have spoken about competition. No direct onslaught is being made on us now; nobody is clutching us by the throat. True, we have yet to see what will happen tomorrow; but today we are not being subjected to armed attack. Nevertheless, the fight against capitalist society has become a hundred times more fierce and perilous, because we are not always able to tell enemies from friends.

When I spoke about communist competition, what I had in mind were not communist sympathies but the development of economic forms and social systems. This is not competition but, if not the last, then nearly the last, desperate, furious, life-and-death struggle between capitalism and communism.

And here we must squarely put the question: Wherein lies our strength and what do we lack? We have quite enough political power. I hardly think there is anyone here who will assert that on such-and-such a practical question, in such-and-such a business institution, the Communists, the

Communist Party, lack sufficient power. There are people who
think only of this, but these people are hopelessly looking
backward and cannot understand that one must look ahead.
The main economic power is in our hands. All the vital
large enterprises, the railways, etc., are in our hands. The
number of leased enterprises, although considerable in
places, is on the whole insignificant; altogether it is infinitesimal compared with the rest. The economic power in the
hands of the proletarian state of Russia is quite adequate
to ensure the transition to communism. What then is
lacking? Obviously, what is lacking is culture among the
stratum of the Communists who perform administrative
functions. If we take Moscow with its 4,700 Communists in
responsible positions, and if we take that huge bureaucratic
machine, that gigantic heap, we must ask: who is directing
whom? I doubt very much whether it can truthfully be said
that the Communists are directing that heap. To tell the truth,
they are not directing, they are being directed. Something analogous happened here to what we were told in our
history lessons when we were children: sometimes one nation conquers another, the nation that conquers is the conqueror and the nation that is vanquished is the conquered
nation. This is simple and intelligible to all. But what happens to the culture of these nations? Here things are not so
simple. If the conquering nation is more cultured than the
vanquished nation, the former imposes its culture upon the
latter; but if the opposite is the case, the vanquished nation
imposes its culture upon the conqueror. Has not something
like this happened in the capital of the R.S.F.S.R.? Have the
4,700 Communists (nearly a whole army division, and all of
them the very best) come under the influence of an alien
culture? True, there may be the impression that the vanquished have a high level of culture. But that is not the case at
all. Their culture is miserable, insignificant, but it is still
at a higher level than ours. Miserable and low as it is, it is
higher than that of our responsible Communist administrators, for the latter lack administrative ability. Communists
who are put at the head of departments—and sometimes
artful saboteurs deliberately put them in these positions
in order to use them as a shield—are often fooled. This is a
very unpleasant admission to make, or, at any rate, not a

very pleasant one; but I think we must admit it, for at present this is the salient problem. I think that this is the political lesson of the past year; and it is around this that the struggle will rage in 1922.

Will the responsible Communists of the R.S.F.S.R. and of the Russian Communist Party realise that they cannot administer; that they only imagine they are directing, but are, actually, being directed? If they realise this they will learn, of course; for this business can be learnt. But one must study hard to learn it, and our people are not doing this. They scatter orders and decrees right and left, but the result is quite different from what they want.

The competition and rivalry that we have placed on the order of the day by proclaiming NEP is a serious business. It appears to be going on in all government offices; but as a matter of fact it is one more form of the struggle between two irreconcilably hostile classes. It is another form of the struggle between the bourgeoisie and the proletariat. It is a struggle that has not yet been brought to a head, and culturally it has not yet been resolved even in the central government departments in Moscow. Very often the bourgeois officials know the business better than our best Communists, who are invested with authority and have every opportunity, but who cannot make the slightest use of their rights and authority.

I should like to quote a passage from a pamphlet by Alexander Todorsky.[88] It was published in Vesyegonsk (there is an uyezd town of that name in Tver Gubernia) on the first anniversary of the Soviet revolution in Russia, on November 7, 1918, a long, long time ago. Evidently this Vesyegonsk comrade is a member of the Party—I read the pamphlet a long time ago and cannot say for certain. He describes how he set to work to equip two Soviet factories, and for this purpose enlisted the services of two bourgeois. He did this in the way these things were done at that time—threatened to imprison them and to confiscate all their property. They were enlisted for the task of restoring the factories. We know how the services of the bourgeoisie were enlisted in 1918 (*laughter*); so there is no need for me to go into details. The methods we are now using to enlist the bourgeoisie are different. But here is the conclusion he arrived at: "This is only half the job. It is not enough to defeat the bourgeoisie, to overpower them; they must be compelled to work for us."

Now these are remarkable words. They are remarkable for they show that even in the town of Vesyegonsk, even in 1918, there were people who had a correct understanding of the relationship between the victorious proletariat and the vanquished bourgeoisie.

When we rap the exploiters' knuckles, render them innocuous, overpower them, it is only half the job. In Moscow, however, ninety out of a hundred responsible officials imagine that all we have to do is to overpower, render innocuous and rap knuckles. What I have said about the Mensheviks, Socialist-Revolutionaries and whiteguards is very often interpreted solely as rendering innocuous, rapping knuckles (and, perhaps, not only the knuckles, but some other place) and overpowering. But that is only half the job. It was only half the job even in 1918, when this was written by the Vesyegonsk comrade; now it is even less than one-fourth. We must make these hands work for us, and not have responsible Communists at the head of departments, enjoying rank and title, but actually swimming with the stream together with the bourgeoisie. That is the whole point.

The idea of building communist society exclusively with the hands of the Communists is childish, absolutely childish. We Communists are but a drop in the ocean, a drop in the ocean of the people. We shall be able to lead the people along the road we have chosen only if we correctly determine it not only from the standpoint of its direction in world history. From that point of view we have determined the road quite correctly, and this is corroborated by the situation in every country. We must also determine it correctly for our own native land, for our country. But the direction in world history is not the only factor. Other factors are whether there will be intervention or not, and whether we shall be able to supply the peasants with goods in exchange for their grain. The peasants will say: "You are splendid fellows; you defended our country. That is why we obeyed you. But if you cannot run the show, get out!" Yes, that is what the peasants will say.

We Communists shall be able to direct our economy if we succeed in utilising the hands of the bourgeoisie in building up this economy of ours and in the meantime learn from these bourgeoisie and guide them along the road we want them to travel. But when a Communist imagines that he knows everything, when he says: "I am a responsible Communist, I have beaten enemies far more formidable than any salesman. We have fought at the front and have beaten far more formidable enemies"—it is this prevailing mood that is doing us great harm.

Rendering the exploiters innocuous, rapping them over the knuckles, clipping their wings is the least important part of the job. That must be done; and our State Political Administration and our courts must do it more vigorously than they have up to now. They must remember that they are proletarian courts surrounded by enemies the world over. This is not difficult; and in the main we have learned to do it. Here a certain amount of pressure must be exercised; but that is easy.

To win the second part of the victory, i. e., to build communism with the hands of non-Communists, to acquire the practical ability to do what is economically necessary, we must establish a link with peasant farming; we must satisfy the peasant, so that he will say: "Hard, bitter and painful as starvation is, I see a government that is an unusual one, is no ordinary one, but is doing something practically useful, something tangible." We must see to it that the numerous elements with whom we are co-operating, and who far exceed us in number, work in such a way as to enable us to supervise them; we must learn to understand this work, and direct their hands so that they do something useful for communism. This is the key point of the present situation; for although individual Communists have understood and realised that it is necessary to enlist the non-Party people for this work, the rank-and-file of our Party have not. Many circulars have been written, much has been said about this, but has anything been accomplished during the past year? Nothing. Not five Party committees out of a hundred can show practical results. This shows how much we lag behind the requirements of the present time; how much we are still living in the traditions of 1918 and 1919. Those were great years; a great historical task was then accomplished. But if we only look back on those years and do not see the task that now confronts us, we shall be doomed, certainly and absolutely. And the whole point is that we refuse to admit it.

I should now like to give two practical examples to illustrate how we administer. I have said already that it would be more correct to take one of the state trusts as an example, but I must ask you to excuse me for not being able to apply this proper method, for to do so it would have been necessary to study the concrete material concerning at least one state trust. Unfortunately, I have been unable to do that, and so I will take two small examples. One example is the accusation of bureaucracy levelled at the People's Commissariat of Foreign Trade by the Moscow Consumers' Co-operative Society. The other example I will take from the Donets Basin.

The first example is not quite relevant—I am unable to find a better—but it will serve to illustrate my main point. As you know from the newspapers, I have been unable to deal with affairs directly during these past few months. I have not been attending the Council of People's Commissars, or the Central Committee. During the short and rare visits I made to Moscow I was struck by the desperate and terrible complaints levelled at the People's Commissariat of Foreign Trade. I have never doubted for a moment that the People's Commissariat of Foreign Trade functions badly and that it is tied up with red tape. But when the complaints became particularly bitter I tried to investigate the matter, to take a concrete example and for once get to the bottom of it; to ascertain the cause, to ascertain why the machine was not working properly.

The M.C.C.S. wanted to purchase a quantity of canned goods. A French citizen appeared and offered some. I do not know whether he did it in the interests of the international policy and with the knowledge of the leadership of the Entente countries, or with the approval of Poincaré and the other enemies of the Soviet government (I think our historians will investigate and make this clear after the Genoa Conference), but the fact is that the French bourgeoisie took not only a theoretical, but also a practical interest in this business, as a French bourgeois turned up in Moscow with an offer of canned goods. Moscow is starving; in the summer the situation will be worse; no meat has been delivered, and knowing the merits of our People's Commissariat of Railways, probably none will be delivered.

An offer is made to sell canned meat for Soviet currency (whether the meat is entirely bad or not will be established by a future investigation). What could be simpler? But if the matter is approached in the Soviet way, it turns out to be not so simple after all. I was unable to go into the matter personally, but I ordered an investigation and I have before me the report which shows how this celebrated case developed. It started with the decision adopted on February 11 by the Political Bureau of the Central Committee of the Russian Communist Party on the report of Comrade Kamenev concerning the desirability of purchasing food abroad. Of course, how could a Russian citizen decide such a question without the consent of the Political Bureau of the Central Committee of the Russian Communist Party! Think of it! How could 4,700 responsible officials (and this is only according to the census) decide a matter like purchasing food abroad without the consent of the Political Bureau of the Central Committee? This would be something supernatural, of course. Evidently, Comrade Kamenev understands our policy and the realities of our position perfectly well, and therefore, he did not place too much reliance on the numerous responsible officials. He started by taking the bull by the horns—if not the bull, at all events the Political Bureau—and without any difficulty (I did not hear that there was any discussion over the matter) obtained a resolution stating: "To call the attention of the People's Commissariat of Foreign Trade to the desirability of importing food from abroad; the import duties...", etc. The attention of the People's Commissariat of Foreign Trade was drawn to this. Things started moving. This was on February 11. I remember that I had occasion to be in Moscow at the very end of February, or about that time, and what did I find? The complaints, the despairing complaints of the Moscow comrades. "What's the matter?" I ask. "There is no way we can buy these provisions." "Why?" "Because of the red tape of the People's Commissariat of Foreign Trade." I had not been taking part in affairs for a long time and I did not know that the Political Bureau had adopted a decision on the matter. I merely ordered the Executive Secretary of our Council to investigate, procure the relevant documents and show them to me. The matter was settled when Krasin arrived. Kamenev discussed the matter with him; the transaction was arranged, and the canned meat was purchased. All's well that ends well.

I have not the least doubt that Kamenev and Krasin can come to an understanding and correctly determine the political line desired by the Political Bureau of the Central Committee of the Russian Communist Party. If the political line on commercial matters were decided by Kamenev and Krasin, ours would be the best Soviet Republic in the world. But Kamenev, a member of the Political Bureau, and Krasin—the latter is busy with diplomatic affairs connected with Genoa, affairs which have entailed an enormous, an excessive amount of labour—cannot be dragged into every transaction, dragged into the business of buying canned goods from a French citizen. That is not the way to work. This is not new, not economic, and not a policy, but sheer mockery. Now I have the report of the investigation into this matter. In fact, I have two reports: one, the report of the investigation made by Gorbunov, the Executive Secretary of the Council of People's Commissars, and his assistant, Miroshnikov; and the other, the report of the investigation made by the State Political Administration. I do not know why the latter interested itself in the matter, and I am not quite sure whether it was proper for it to do so; but I will not go into that now, because I am afraid this might entail another investigation. The important thing is that material on the matter has been collected and I now have it before me.

On arriving in Moscow at the end of February I heard bitter complaints, "We cannot buy the canned goods", although in Libau there was a ship with a cargo of canned goods, and the owners were prepared to take Soviet currency for real canned goods! (*Laughter.*) If these canned goods are not entirely bad (and I now emphasise the "if", because I am not sure that I shall not call for another investigation, the results of which, however, we shall have to report at the next Congress), if, I say, these goods are not entirely bad and they have been purchased, I ask: why could not

this matter have been settled without Kamenev and Krasin?
From the report I have before me I gather that one responsible Communist sent another responsible Communist to
the devil. I also gather from this report that one responsible
Communist said to another responsible Communist: "From
now on I shall not talk to you except in the presence of a
lawyer." Reading this report I recalled the time when I was
in exile in Siberia, twenty-five years ago, and had occasion
to act in the capacity of a lawyer. I was not a certified
lawyer, because, being summarily exiled, I was not allowed
to practise; but as there was no other lawyer in the region,
people came and confided their troubles to me. But sometimes I had the greatest difficulty in understanding what the
trouble was. A woman would come and, of course, start
telling me a long story about her relatives, and it was incredibly difficult to get from her what she really wanted. I
said to her: "Bring me a copy." She went on with her endless
and pointless story. When I repeated, "Bring me a copy",
she left, complaining: "He won't hear what I have to say
unless I bring a copy." In our colony we had a hearty laugh
over this copy. I was able, however, to make some progress.
People came to me, brought copies of the necessary documents, and I was able to gather what their trouble was,
what they complained of, what ailed them. This was twenty-
five years ago, in Siberia, in a place many hundreds of
versts from the nearest railway station.

But why was it necessary, three years after the revolution,
in the capital of the Soviet Republic, to have two investigations, the intervention of Kamenev and Krasin and the instructions of the Political Bureau to purchase canned goods?
What was lacking? Political power? No. The money was forthcoming, so they had economic as well as political power.
All the necessary institutions were available. What was
lacking, then? Culture. Ninety-nine out of every hundred
officials of the M.C.C.S.—against whom I have no complaint
to make whatever, and whom I regard as excellent Communists—and of the Commissariat of Foreign Trade lack
culture. They were unable to approach the matter in a
cultured manner.

When I first heard of the matter I sent the following
written proposal to the Central Committee: "All the officials

concerned of the Moscow government departments—except the members of the All-Russia Central Executive Committee, who, as you know, enjoy immunity—should be put in the worst prison in Moscow for six hours, and those of the People's Commissariat of Foreign Trade for thirty-six hours." And then it turned out that no one could say who the culprits were (*laughter*), and from what I have told you it is evident that the culprits will never be discovered. It is simply the usual inability of the Russian intellectuals to get things done—inefficiency and slovenliness. First they rush at a job, do a little bit, and then think about it, and when nothing comes of it, they run to complain to Kamenev and want the matter to be brought before the Political Bureau. Of course, all difficult state problems should be brought before the Political Bureau—I shall have to say something about that later on—but one should think first and then act. If you want to bring up a case, submit the appropriate documents. First send a telegram, and in Moscow we also have telephones; send a telephone message to the competent department and a copy to Tsyurupa saying: "I regard the transaction as urgent and will take proceedings against anyone guilty of red tape." One must think of this elementary culture, one must approach things in a thoughtful manner. If the business is not settled in the course of a few minutes, by telephone, collect the documents and say: "If you start any of your red tape I shall have you clapped in gaol." But not a moment's thought is given to the matter, there is no preparation, the usual bustle, several commissions, everybody is tired out, exhausted, run down, and things begin to move only when Kamenev is put in touch with Krasin. All this is typical of what goes on not only in the capital, Moscow, but also in the other capitals, in the capitals of all independent republics and regions. And the same thing, even a hundred times worse, constantly goes on in the provincial towns.

In our struggle we must remember that Communists must be able to reason. They may be perfectly familiar with the revolutionary struggle and with the state of the revolutionary movement all over the world; but if we are to extricate ourselves from desperate poverty and want we need culture, integrity and an ability to reason. Many lack these qualities. It would be unfair to say that the responsible Communists do not fulfil their functions conscientiously. The overwhelming majority of them, ninety-nine out of a hundred, are not only conscientious—they proved their devotion to the revolution under the most difficult conditions before the fall of tsarism and after the revolution; they were ready to lay down their lives. Therefore, it would be radically wrong to attribute the trouble to lack of conscientiousness. We need a cultured approach to the simplest affairs of state. We must all understand that this is a matter of state, a business matter; and if obstacles arise we must be able to overcome them and take proceedings against those who are guilty of red tape. We have proletarian courts in Moscow; they must bring to account the persons who are to blame for the failure to effect the purchase of several tens of thousands of poods of canned food. I think the proletarian courts will be able to punish the guilty; but in order to punish, the culprits must be found. I assure you that in this case no culprits will be found. I want you all to look into this business: no one is guilty; all we see is a lot of fuss and bustle and nonsense. Nobody has the ability to approach the business properly; nobody understands that affairs of state must not be tackled in this way. And all the whiteguards and saboteurs take advantage of this. At one time we waged a fierce struggle against the saboteurs; that struggle confronts us even now. There are saboteurs today, of course, and they must be fought. But can we fight them when the position is as I have just described it? This is worse than any sabotage. The saboteur could wish for nothing better than that two Communists should argue over the question of when to appeal to the Political Bureau for instructions on principles in buying food; and of course he would soon slip in between them and egg them on. If any intelligent saboteur were to stand behind these Communists, or behind each of them in turn, and encourage them, that would be the end. The matter would be doomed for ever. Who is to blame? Nobody, because two responsible Communists, devoted revolutionaries, are arguing over last year's snow; are arguing over the question of when to appeal to the Political Bureau for instructions on principles in buying food.

That is how the matter stands and that is the difficulty

that confronts us. Any salesman trained in a large capitalist enterprise knows how to settle a matter like that; but
ninety-nine responsible Communists out of a hundred do
not. And they refuse to understand that they do not know
how and that they must learn the ABC of this business.
Unless we realise this, unless we sit down in the preparatory
class again, we shall never be able to solve the economic
problem that now lies at the basis of our entire policy.

The other example I wanted to give you is that of the
Donets Basin. You know that this is the centre, the real
basis of our entire economy. It will be utterly impossible
to restore large-scale industry in Russia, to really build
socialism—for it can only be built on the basis of large-
scale industry—unless we restore the Donets Basin and bring
it up to the proper level. The Central Committee is closely
watching developments there.

As regards this region there was no unjustified, ridiculous or absurd raising of minor questions in the Political
Bureau; real, absolutely urgent business was discussed.

The Central Committee ought to see to it that in such real
centres, bases and foundations of our entire economy, work
is carried on in a real business-like manner. At the head of
the Central Coal Industry Board we had not only undoubtedly devoted, but really educated and very capable people.
I should not be wrong even if I said talented people. That is
why the Central Committee has concentrated its attention on
it. The Ukraine is an independent republic. That is quite
all right. But in Party matters it sometimes—what is the
politest way of saying it?—takes a roundabout course, and
we shall have to get at them. For the people in charge there
are sly, and their Central Committee I shall not say deceives us,
but somehow edges away from us. To obtain a general
view of the whole business, we discussed it in the Central
Committee here and discovered that friction and disagreement exist. There is a Commission for the Utilisation of
Small Mines there and, of course, severe friction between it
and the Central Coal Industry Board. Still we, the Central
Committee, have a certain amount of experience and we unanimously decided not to remove the leading people, but if
there was any friction it was to be reported to us, down
to the smallest detail. For since we have not only devoted but

capable people in the region, we must back them up, and enable them to complete their training, assuming that they have not done so. In the end, a Party Congress was held in the Ukraine—I do not know what happened there; all sorts of things happened. I asked for information from the Ukrainian comrades, and I asked Comrade Orjonikidze particularly—and the Central Committee did the same— to go down there and ascertain what had happened. Evidently, there was some intrigue and an awful mess, which the Commission on Party History would not be able to clear up in ten years should it undertake to do so. But the upshot of it all was that contrary to the unanimous instructions of the Central Committee, this group was superseded by another group. What was the matter? In the main, notwithstanding all its good qualities, a section of the group made a mistake. They were overzealous in their methods of administration. There we have to dea with workers. Very often the word "workers" is taken to mean the factory proletariat. But it does not mean that at all. During the war people who were by no means proletarians went into the factories; they went into the factories to dodge the war. Are the social and economic conditions in our country today such as to induce real proletarians to go into the factories? No. It would be true according to Marx; but Marx did not write about Russia; he wrote about capitalism as a whole, beginning with the fifteenth century. It held true over a period of six hundred years, but it is not true for present-day Russia. Very often those who go into the factories are not proletarians; they are casual elements of every description.

The task is to learn to organise the work properly, not to lag behind, to remove friction in time, not to separate administration from politics. For our administration and our politics rest on the ability of the entire vanguard to maintain contact with the entire mass of the proletariat and with the entire mass of the peasantry. If anybody forgets these cogs and becomes wholly absorbed in administration, the result will be a disastrous one. The mistake the Donets Basin officials made is insignificant compared with other mistakes of ours, but this example is a typical one. The Central Committee unanimously ordered: "Allow this group to remain; bring all conflicts, even minor ones, before the

Central Committee, for the Donets Basin is not an ordinary district, but a vital one, without which socialist construction would simply remain a pious wish." But all our political power, all the authority of the Central Committee proved of no avail.

This time there was a mistake in administration, of course; in addition, a host of other mistakes were made.

This instance shows that it is not a matter of possessing political power, but of administrative ability, the ability to put the right man in the right place, the ability to avoid petty conflicts, so that state economic work may be carried on without interruption. This is what we lack; this is the root of the mistake.

I think that in discussing our revolution and weighing up its prospects, we must carefully single out the problems which the revolution has solved completely and which have irrevocably gone down in history as an epoch-making departure from capitalism. Our revolution has such solutions to its credit. Let the Mensheviks and Otto Bauer of the Two-and-a-Half International shout: "Theirs is a bourgeois revolution." We say that our task was to consummate the bourgeois revolution. As a certain whiteguard newspaper expressed it: Dung had accumulated in our state institutions for four hundred years; but we cleaned it all out in four years. This is the great service we rendered. What have the Mensheviks and Socialist-Revolutionaries done? Nothing. The dung of medievalism has not been cleared out either in our country, or even in advanced, enlightened Germany. Yet they reproach us for doing what stands very much to our credit. The fact that we have consummated the revolution is an achievement that can never be expunged from our record.

War is now in the air. The trade unions, for example, the reformist trade unions, are passing resolutions against war and are threatening to call strikes in opposition to war. Recently, if I am not mistaken, I read a report in the newspapers to the effect that a certain very good Communist delivered an anti-war speech in the French Chamber of Deputies in the course of which he stated that the workers would prefer to rise in revolt rather than go to war. This question cannot be formulated in the way we formulated it in 1912, when the Basle Manifesto was issued. The Russian revolution alone has shown how it is possible to emerge from war, and what effort this entails. It showed what emerging from a reactionary war by revolutionary methods means. Reactionary imperialist wars are inevitable in all parts of the world; and in solving problems of this sort mankind cannot and will not forget that tens of millions were slaughtered then, and will be slaughtered again if war breaks out. We are living in the twentieth century, and the only nation that emerged from a reactionary war by revolutionary methods not for the benefit of a particular government, but by overthrowing it, was the Russian nation, and it was the Russian revolution that extricated it. What has been won by the Russian revolution is irrevocable. No power on earth can erase that; nor can any power on earth erase the fact that the Soviet state has been created. This is a historic victory. For hundreds of years states have been built according to the bourgeois model, and for the first time a non-bourgeois form of state has been discovered. Our machinery of government may be faulty, but it is said that the first steam engine that was invented was also faulty. No one even knows whether it worked or not, but that is not the important point; the important point is that it was invented. Even assuming that the first steam engine was of no use, the fact is that we now have steam engines. Even if our machinery of government is very faulty, the fact remains that it has been created; the greatest invention in history has been made; a proletarian type of state has been created. Therefore, let all Europe, let thousands of bourgeois newspapers broadcast news about the horrors and poverty that prevail in our country, about suffering being the sole lot of the working people in our country; the workers all over the world are still drawn towards the Soviet state. These are the great and irrevocable gains that we have achieved. But for us, members of the Communist Party, this meant only opening the door. We are now confronted with the task of laying the foundations of socialist economy. Has this been done? No, it has not. We still lack the socialist foundation. Those Communists who imagine that we have it are greatly mistaken. The whole point is to distinguish firmly, clearly and dispassionately what constitutes the historic service rendered by the Russian revolution from what we do very badly, from what

has not yet been created, and what we shall have to redo
many times yet.

Political events are always very confused and complicated. They can be compared with a chain. To hold the whole
chain you must grasp the main link. Not a link chosen at ran-
dom. What was the central event in 1917? Withdrawal
from the war. The entire nation demanded this, and it over-
shadowed everything. Revolutionary Russia accomplished
this withdrawal from the war. It cost tremendous effort;
but the major demand of the people was satisfied, and that
brought us victory for many years. The people realised, the
peasants saw, every soldier returning from the front understood perfectly well that the Soviet government was a more
democratic government, one that stood closer to the working people. No matter how many outrageous and absurd
things we may have done in other spheres, the fact that we
realised what the main task was proved that everything was
right.

What was the key feature of 1919 and 1920? Military
resistance. The all-powerful Entente was marching against
us, was at our throats. No propaganda was required there.
Every non-Party peasant understood what was going on.
The landowners were coming back. The Communists knew
how to fight them. That is why, taken in the mass, the
peasants followed the lead of the Communists; that is
why we were victorious.

In 1921, the key feature was an orderly retreat. This
required stern discipline. The Workers' Opposition said:
"You are underrating the workers; the workers should
display greater initiative." But initiative had to be displayed then by retreating in good order and by maintaining strict discipline. Anyone who introduced an undertone of panic or insubordination would have doomed the
revolution to defeat; for there is nothing more difficult
than retreating with people who have been accustomed to
victory, who are imbued with revolutionary views and
ideals, and who, in their hearts, regard every retreat as a
disgraceful matter. The greatest danger was the violation of
good order, and the greatest task was to maintain good order.

And what is the key feature now? The key feature now—
and I would like to sum up my report with this—is not that

we have changed our line of policy. An incredible lot of nonsense is being talked about this in connection with NEP. It is all hot air, pernicious twaddle. In connection with NEP some people are beginning to fuss around, proposing to reorganise our government departments and to form new ones. All this is pernicious twaddle. In the present situation the key feature is people, the proper choice of people. A revolutionary who is accustomed to struggle against petty reformists and uplift educators finds it hard to understand this. Soberly weighed up, the political conclusion to be drawn from the present situation is that we have advanced so far that we cannot hold all the positions; and we need not hold them all.

Internationally our position has improved vastly these last few years. The Soviet type of state is our achievement; it is a step forward in human progress; and the information the Communist International receives from every country every day corroborates this. Nobody has the slightest doubt about that. From the point of view of practical work, however, the position is that unless the Communists render the masses of the peasants practical assistance they will lose their support. Passing laws, passing better decrees, etc., is not now the main object of our attention. There was a time when the passing of decrees was a form of propaganda. People used to laugh at us and say that the Bolsheviks do not realise that their decrees are not being carried out; the entire whiteguard press was full of jeers on that score. But at that period this passing of decrees was quite justified. We Bolsheviks had just taken power, and we said to the peasant, to the worker: "Here is a decree; this is how we would like to have the state administered. Try it!" From the very outset we gave the ordinary workers and peasants an idea of our policy in the form of decrees. The result was the enormous confidence we enjoyed and now enjoy among the masses of the people. This was an essential period at the beginning of the revolution; without it we should not have risen on the crest of the revolutionary wave; we should have wallowed in its trough. Without it we should not have won the confidence of all the workers and peasants who wanted to build their lives on new lines. But this period has passed,

and we refuse to understand this. Now the peasants and
workers will laugh at us if we order this or that government department to be formed or reorganised. The ordinary
workers and peasants will display no interest in this now,
and they will be right, because this is not the central task
today. This is not the sort of thing with which we Communists should now go to the people. Although we who
are engaged in government departments are always overwhelmed with so many petty affairs, this is not the link that
we must grasp, this is not the key feature. The key feature
is that we have not got the right men in the right places; that
responsible Communists who acquitted themselves magnificently during the revolution have been given commercial and industrial functions about which they know nothing; and they prevent us from seeing the truth, for rogues
and rascals hide magnificently behind their backs. The
trouble is that we have no such thing as practical control
of how things have been done. This is a prosaic job, a small
job; these are petty affairs. But after the greatest political
change in history, bearing in mind that for a time we shall
have to live in the midst of the capitalist system, the key
feature now is not politics in the narrow sense of the word
(what we read in the newspapers is just political fireworks;
there is nothing socialist in it at all), the key feature is
not resolutions, not departments and not reorganisation.
As long as these things are necessary we shall do them, but
don't go to the people with them. Choose the proper men
and introduce practical control. That is what the people
will appreciate.

In the sea of people we are after all but a drop in the
ocean, and we can administer only when we express correctly what the people are conscious of. Unless we do this
the Communist Party will not lead the proletariat, the
proletariat will not lead the masses, and the whole machine
will collapse. The chief thing the people, all the working
people, want today is nothing but help in their desperate
hunger and need; they want to be shown that the improvement needed by the peasants is really taking place in the
form they are accustomed to. The peasant knows and is
accustomed to the market and trade. We were unable to
introduce direct communist distribution. We lacked the

factories and their equipment for this. That being the case, we must provide the peasants with what they need through the medium of trade, and provide it as well as the capitalist did, otherwise the people will not tolerate such an administration. This is the key to the situation; and unless something unexpected arises, this, given three conditions, should be the central feature of our activities in 1922.

The first condition is that there shall be no intervention. We are doing all we can in the diplomatic field to avoid it; nevertheless, it may occur any day. We must really be on the alert, and we must agree to make certain big sacrifices for the sake of the Red Army, within definite limits, of course. We are confronted by the entire bourgeois world, which is only seeking a way in which to strangle us. Our Mensheviks and Socialist-Revolutionaries are nothing more nor less than the agents of this bourgeoisie. Such is their political status.

The second condition is that the financial crisis shall not be too severe. The crisis is approaching. You will hear about that when we discuss financial policy. If it is too severe and rigorous we shall have to revise many things again and concentrate all efforts on one thing. If it is not too severe it may even be useful; it will give the Communists in all the state trusts a good shaking; only we must not forget to do it. The financial crisis will shake up government departments and industrial enterprises, and those that are not equal to their task will be the first to burst; only we must take care that all the blame for this is not thrown on the specialists while the responsible Communists are praised for being very good fellows who have fought at the fronts and have always worked well. Thus, if the financial crisis is not too severe we can derive some benefit from it and comb the ranks of the responsible Communists engaged in the business departments not in the way the Central Control Commission and the Central Verification Commission[89] comb them, but very thoroughly.

The third condition is that we shall make no political mistakes in this period. Of course, if we do make political mistakes all our work of economic construction will be disrupted and we shall land ourselves in controversies about how to rectify them and what direction to pursue. But if we make no sad mistakes, the key feature in the near future will be not decrees and politics in the narrow sense of the word, not departments and their organisation—the responsible Communists and the Soviet institutions will deal with these things whenever necessary—the main thing in all our activities will be choosing the right people and making sure that decisions are carried out. If, in this respect, we learn something practical, if we do something practically useful, we shall again overcome all difficulties.

In conclusion I must mention the practical side of the question of our Soviet institutions, the higher government bodies and the Party's relation to them. The relations between the Party and the Soviet government bodies are not what they ought to be. On this point we are quite unanimous. I have given one example of how minor matters are dragged before the Political Bureau. It is extremely difficult to get out of this by formal means, for there is only one governing party in our country; and a member of the Party cannot be prohibited from lodging complaints. That is why everything that comes up on the Council of People's Commissars is dragged before the Political Bureau. I, too, am greatly to blame for this, for to a large extent contact between the Council of People's Commissars and the Political Bureau was maintained through me. When I was obliged to retire from work it was found that the two wheels were not working in unison and Kamenev had to bear a treble load to maintain this contact. Inasmuch as it is barely probable that I shall return to work in the near future, all hope devolves on the fact that there are two other deputies—Comrade Tsyurupa, who has been cleansed by the Germans, and Comrade Rykov, whom they have splendidly cleansed. It seems that even Wilhelm, the German Emperor, has stood us in good stead—I never expected it. He had a surgeon, who happened to be the doctor treating Comrade Rykov, and he removed his worst part, keeping it in Germany, and left the best part intact, sending that part of Comrade Rykov thoroughly cleansed to us. If that method continues to be used it will be a really good thing.

Joking aside, a word or two about the main instructions. On this point there is complete unanimity on the Central Committee, and I hope that the Congress will pay the closest attention to it and endorse the instructions that the Political Bureau and the Central Committee be relieved of minor matters, and that more should be shifted to the responsible officials. The People's Commissars must be responsible for their work and should not bring these matters up first on the Council of People's Commissars and then on the Political Bureau. Formally, we cannot abolish the right to lodge complaints with the Central Committee, for our Party is the only governing party in the country. But we must put a stop to the habit of bringing every petty matter before the Central Committee; we must raise the prestige of the Council of People's Commissars. The Commissars and not the Deputy Commissars must mainly attend the meetings of the Council. The functions of the Council must be changed in the direction in which I have not succeeded in changing them during the past year, that is, it must pay much more attention to executive control. We shall have two more deputies—Rykov and Tsyurupa. When Rykov was in the Extraordinary Authorised Council of Workers' and Peasants' Defence for the Supply of the Red Army and Navy he tightened things up and the work went well. Tsyurupa organised one of the most efficient People's Commissariats. If together they make the maximum effort to improve the People's Commissariats in the sense of efficiency and responsibility, we shall make some, even if a little, progress here. We have eighteen People's Commissariats of which not less than fifteen are of no use at all—efficient People's Commissars cannot be found everywhere, and I certainly hope that people give this more of their attention. Comrade Rykov must be a member of the Central Committee Bureau and of the Presidium of the All-Russia Central Executive Committee because there must be a tie-up between these two bodies, for without this tie-up the main wheels sometimes spin in the air.

In this connection, we must see to it that the number of commissions of the Council of People's Commissars and of the Council of Labour and Defence is reduced. These bodies must know and settle their own affairs and not split up into an infinite number of commissions. A few days ago the commissions were overhauled. It was found that there were one hundred and twenty of them. How many were necessary? Sixteen. And this is not the first cut. Instead of accepting responsibility for their work, preparing a decision for the Council of People's Commissars and knowing that they bear responsibility for this decision, there is a tendency to take shelter behind commissions. The devil himself would lose his way in this maze of commissions. Nobody knows what is going on, who is responsible; everything is mixed up, and finally a decision is passed for which everybody is held responsible.

In this connection, reference must be made to the need for extending and developing the autonomy and activities of the regional economic conferences. The administrative division of Russia has now been drawn up on scientific lines; the economic and climatic conditions, the way of life, the conditions of obtaining fuel, of local industry, etc., have all been taken into account. On the basis of this division, district and regional economic conferences have been instituted. Changes may be made here and there, of course, but the prestige of these economic conferences must be enhanced.

Then we must see to it that the All-Russia Central Executive Committee works more energetically, meets in session more regularly, and for longer periods. The sessions of the All-Russia Central Executive Committee should discuss bills which sometimes are hastily brought before the Council of People's Commissars when there is no need to do so. It would be better to postpone such bills and give the local workers an opportunity to study them carefully. Stricter demands should be made upon those who draft the bills. This is not done.

If the sessions of the All-Russia Central Executive Committee last longer, they can split up into sections and subcommissions, and thus will be able to verify the work more strictly and strive to achieve what in my opinion is the key, the quintessence of the present political situation: to concentrate attention on choosing the right people and on verifying how decisions are carried out.

It must be admitted, and we must not be afraid to admit, that in ninety-nine cases out of a hundred the responsible Communists are not in the jobs they are now fit for; that they are unable to perform their duties, and that they must sit down to learn. If this is admitted, and since we have the opportunity to learn—judging by the general international situation we shall have time to do so—we must do it, come what may. (*Stormy applause*.)

3

CLOSING SPEECH ON THE POLITICAL REPORT
OF THE CENTRAL COMMITTEE OF THE R.C.P.(B.)
MARCH 28

(*Applause.*) First of all I shall have to devote a little time to criticising the remarks made here by Comrades Preobrazhensky and Osinsky. I think that on the most important and fundamental question Comrades Preobrazhensky and Osinsky were wide of the mark, and their own statements have proved their line of policy to be wrong.

Comrade Preobrazhensky spoke about capitalism and said that we ought to open a general discussion on our Programme. I think that this would be the most unproductive and unjustified waste of time.

First of all about state capitalism.

"State capitalism is capitalism," said Preobrazhensky, "and that is the only way it can and should be interpreted." I say that that is pure scholasticism. Up to now nobody could have written a book about this sort of capitalism, because this is the first time in human history that we see anything like it. All the more or less intelligible books about state capitalism that have appeared up to now were written under conditions and in a situation where state capitalism was capitalism. Now things are different; and neither Marx nor the Marxists could foresee this. We must not look to the past. When you write history, you will write it magnificently; but when you write a textbook, you will say: State capitalism is the most unexpected and absolutely unforeseen form of capitalism—for nobody could foresee that the proletariat would achieve power in one of the least developed countries, and would first try to organise large-scale production and distribution for the peasantry and then, finding that it could not cope with the task owing to the low standard of culture, would enlist the services of capitalism. Nobody ever foresaw this; but it is an incontrovertible fact.

Comrade Larin, in his speech, revealed that he has a very vague conception of the New Economic Policy and of how it should be handled.

Not a single serious objection has been raised to our adoption of the New Economic Policy. The proletariat is not afraid to admit that certain things in the revolution went off magnificently, and that others went awry. All the revolutionary parties that have perished so far, perished because they became conceited, because they failed to see the source of their strength and feared to discuss their weaknesses. We, however, shall not perish, because we are not afraid to discuss our weaknesses and will learn to overcome them. (*Applause*.) The capitalism that we have permitted is essential. If it is ugly and bad, we shall be able to rectify it, because power is in our hands and we have nothing to fear. Everybody admits this, and so it is ridiculous to confuse this with panic-mongering. If we were afraid to admit this our doom would be sealed. But the fact that we will learn and want to learn this is proved by the experience of the past three, four, five years, during which we learnt more complicated matters in a shorter period. True, then we were driven by necessity. During the war we were driven very hard; I think there was neither a front nor a campaign in which we were not hard pressed. The enemy came within a hundred versts of Moscow; was approaching Orel; was within five versts of Petrograd. That was the time we really woke up and began to learn and to put the lessons we had learnt into practice, and we drove out the enemy.

The position now is that we have to deal with an enemy in mundane economics, and this is a thousand times more difficult. The controversies over state capitalism that have been raging in our literature up to now could at best be included in textbooks on history. I do not in the least deny that textbooks are useful, and recently I wrote that it would be far better if our authors devoted less attention to newspapers and political twaddle and wrote textbooks, as many of them, including Comrade Larin, could do splendidly. His talent would prove most useful on work of this kind and we would solve the problem that Comrade Trotsky emphasised so well when he said that the main task at the present time is to train the younger generation, but we have nothing to train them with. Indeed, from what can the younger generation learn the social sciences? From the old bourgeois junk. This is disgraceful! And this is at a time when we have hundreds of Marxist authors who could write textbooks on all social problems, but do not do so because their minds are taken up with other things.

As regards state capitalism, we ought to know what should be the slogan for agitation and propaganda, what must be explained, what we must get everyone to understand practically. And that is that the state capitalism that we have now is not the state capitalism that the Germans wrote about. It is capitalism that we ourselves have permitted. Is that true or not? Everybody knows that it is true!

At a congress of Communists we passed a decision that state capitalism would be permitted by the proletarian state, and we are the state. If we did wrong we are to blame and it is no use shifting the blame to somebody else! We must learn, we must see to it that in a proletarian country state capitalism cannot and does not go beyond the framework and conditions delineated for it by the proletariat, beyond conditions that benefit the proletariat. It was quite rightly pointed out here that we had to give consideration to the peasants as a mass, and enable them to trade freely. Every intelligent worker appreciates that this is necessary for the proletarian dictatorship, and only Comrade Shlyapnikov can joke about and mock it. This is appreciated by everybody and has been chewed over a thousand times, but you simply refuse to understand it. If under present conditions the peasant must have freedom to trade within certain limits, we must give it to him, but this does not mean that we are permitting trade in raw brandy. We shall punish people for that sort of trade. It does not mean that we are permitting the sale of political literature called Menshevik and Socialist-Revolutionary and financed by the capitalists of the whole world.

That is what I meant when I mentioned machine-guns, and Comrade Shlyapnikov should have understood it. What he says is nonsensical!

You will not frighten anybody and you will not win any sympathy! (*Applause. Laughter.*)

Poor Shlyapnikov! Lenin had planned to use machine-guns against him!

What I had in mind was Party disciplinary measures, and not machine-guns as such. When we talk about machine-guns we have in mind the people in this country whom we call Mensheviks and Socialist-Revolutionaries and who argue as follows: "You say you are retreating towards capitalism, and we say the same thing; we agree with you!" We are constantly hearing this sort of thing; and abroad a gigantic propaganda campaign is being conducted to prove that while we Bolsheviks are keeping the Mensheviks and Socialist-Revolutionaries in prison, we ourselves are permitting capitalism. True, we are permitting capitalism, but within the limits that the peasants need. This is essential! Without it the peasants could not exist and continue with their husbandry. But we maintain that the Russian peasants can do very well without Socialist-Revolutionary and Menshevik propaganda. To those who assert the contrary we say: We would rather perish to the last man than yield to you! And our courts must understand all this. Now that we are passing from the Cheka to state-political courts we must say at this Congress that there is no such thing as above-class courts. Our courts must be elected, proletarian courts; and they must know what it is that we are permitting. They must clearly understand what state capitalism is.

This is the political slogan of the day and not a controversy about what the German professors meant by state capitalism and what we mean by it. We have gone through a great deal since then, and it is altogether unseemly for us to look back.

The degree to which Comrade Preobrazhensky goes off the political track is shown by what he said about an Economic Bureau and about the Programme.[90] What a magnificent thing our Programme is, but how frightfully we garble it! How is that possible? Because some people read it word for word and line by line, and beyond that they will not look. They pick out a passage and say: "There was a controversy over this." Some say that the line of the Workers' Faculties and of the Communist local cells was correct, but the line of those who said: "Go easy, treat those specialists more carefully", was wrong. True, the Communist cells are splendid and so are the Workers' Faculties, but they are not infallible; they are not saints....

Yes, the Communist cells are the representatives of our Party, and the Workers" Faculties are the representatives of our class; but the fact that they make mistakes and that we must correct them is an elementary truism. How they are to be corrected I do not know, because I did not attend the meetings of the Central Committee at which this question was discussed. But I do know that the Workers' Faculties and the Communist cells overdo things in the line they have taken against the professors. After our Central Committee has examined this question in all its aspects and has decided that things have been overdone and that a more cautious line must be adopted towards these professors, who are the representatives of an alien class, Comrade Preobrazhensky comes along, takes out the Programme and says: "No political concessions to this stratum; that would be an infringement of the Programme."

If we start guiding the Party in this way we shall inevitably go under. And this is not because Comrade Preobrazhensky has wrong ideas about politics in general, but because he approaches everything from the angle of what is his strongest point; he is a theoretician whose mind is restricted by what is customary and usual; he is a propagandist whose mind is taken up with measures directed to the purpose of propaganda. Everybody is aware of and appreciates this strong point of his, but when he approaches things from the political and administrative angle the result is simply monstrous. Set up an Economic Bureau?! But everybody has just said, everybody has agreed, and we have complete unanimity on the point (and this is very important, for action depends upon this unity) that the Party machinery must be separated from the Soviet government machinery.

It is terribly difficult to do this; we lack the men! But Preobrazhensky comes along and airily says that Stalin has jobs in two Commissariats.[91] Who among us has not sinned in this way? Who has not undertaken several duties at once? And how can we do otherwise? What can we do to preserve the present situation in the People's Commissariat of Nationalities; to handle all the Turkestan, Caucasian, and other questions? These are all political questions! They have to be settled. These are questions that have engaged the attention of European states for hundreds of years, and only an infinitesimal number of them have been settled in democratic republics. We are settling them; and we need a man to whom the representatives of any of these nations can go and discuss their difficulties in all detail. Where can we find such a man? I don't think Comrade Preobrazhensky could suggest any better candidate than Comrade Stalin.

The same thing applies to the Workers' and Peasants' Inspection. This is a vast business; but to be able to handle investigations we must have at the head of it a man who enjoys high prestige, otherwise we shall become submerged in and overwhelmed by petty intrigue.

Comrade Preobrazhensky proposes that an Economic Bureau should be set up; but if we do that all our talk about separating Party activities from Soviet government activities will be just hot air. Comrade Preobrazhensky proposes what appears to be a splendid scheme: on the one hand the Political Bureau, then the Economic Bureau, and then the Organising Bureau. But all this is very fine only on paper; in actual practice it is ridiculous! I positively cannot understand how, after Soviet power has been in existence for five years, a man who has an intuition for vital politics can make and insist upon such a proposal.

What is the difference between the Organising Bureau and the Political Bureau? You cannot draw a hard and fast line between a political question and an organisation question. Any political question may be an organisation question, and vice versa. Only after established practice had shown that questions could be transferred from the Organising Bureau to the Political Bureau was it possible to organise the work of the Central Committee properly.

Has anybody ever proposed anything different? No,
because no other rational solution can be proposed. Political questions cannot be mechanically separated from
organisation questions. Politics are conducted by definite
people; but if other people are going to draft documents,
nothing will come of it.

You know perfectly well that there have been revolutions in which parliamentary assemblies drafted documents
which were put into effect by people from another class.
This led to friction, and they were kicked out. Organisation
questions cannot be separated from politics. Politics are
concentrated economics.

Comrade Kosior complained about the Central Committee
and mentioned names (I have written them all down).
I am not personally familiar with the subject, and so I cannot answer; but if you, as the Party Congress, are interested,
it is your duty to elect a commission to investigate every
case and subject Kosior and the persons concerned to examination by third degree. The whole point here is that if
the Central Committee is deprived of the right to distribute forces, it will be unable to direct policy. Although
we make mistakes when we transfer people from one place
to another, nevertheless, I take the liberty of asserting
that all the time it has been functioning, the Political
Bureau of the Central Committee has made the minimum
of mistakes. This is not self-praise. The activities of the
Political Bureau are tested not by commissions, not by
people appointed by our Party, but by the whiteguards,
by our enemies; and the proof is the results of its policy,
in which no serious mistakes have been committed.

Comrade Osinsky's strong point is that if he undertakes
anything he pursues it with energy and vigour. We must
do all we can to cultivate this strong point of his and to
curb his weak points (even if Osinsky raises a howl—he is
such a vigorous fellow—this must be done; otherwise, as
a worker, he will be done for). We on the Central Committee
have taken measures which, I think, will combine his
weak points with his strong ones.

If I wanted to polemise with Comrade Osinsky—which
I do not want to do—I would say that the weightiest evidence that could be brought against him is the speech he

delivered here today. I would have it printed and posted up on a board.... There was once a man....

A Deputy People's Commissar and a leading figure in one of the most important People's Commissariats, and foremost among those who can draw up a platform on any question, this man proposes that we should adopt the Cabinet system.[92] I assert that this man is absolutely done for.... I will not go into this in detail, or polemise; what interests me most is that Comrade Osinsky's vast energy should be directed into proper channels. If Comrade Osinsky does not, in a comradely way, heed the advice that has been often given to him by the Central Committee, and for which I have been largely responsible, and if he does not moderate his zeal in this matter, he will inevitably find himself in the mire, as he found himself today.

This is very unpleasant for a man who is fond of displaying his character; and it is quite legitimate for a man gifted with a strong character to want to display it. Would to God that everybody had such a character to display. But the Central Committee must see to it that this character is displayed for a useful purpose. The Central Committee must see to it that this talk about a Cabinet is cut short, even if the man who undergoes this circumcision, so to speak, complains about it. This will be beneficial. He must put a curb on his talents to prevent himself from landing in the mire; and he must consult comrades in the other People's Commissariats and adhere to the general line. Has any one of our Commissariats done anything without controversy? No.

"Improvement of the system of administration and the psychological mobilisation of the masses." This is sheer murder! If the Congress were to adopt this politically reactionary point of view it would be the surest and best method of committing suicide.

"Improvement of the system of administration"?! Pray God that we succeed, at least, in getting out of the muddle that we are in today.

We have no system?! For five years we have been spending our best efforts in the endeavour to create this system! This system is a tremendous step forward.

The machinery of state is faulty! Do we know what the

trouble is? We do not! But Comrade Osinsky talks as if
he does. Why, he can sit down and in ten minutes devise
a whole system of administration. It will be harmful and
a political mistake if his zeal is not curbed. In other channels, however, the zeal he is displaying now will be very
useful.

Well, that's one illustration. And then Comrades Preobrazhensky and Osinsky bore out in their comments what I said
about the most important thing, and Comrade Larin proved it
still more thoroughly. Look what he did. He hurled accusations at me and laughed and jested very merrily.

He does this magnificently; this is his strong point.
If Comrade Larin could display this strong point of his
in some field other than that of state activities he would
be a thousand times more useful for our Republic; for he
is a very capable man and has a vivid imagination. This
quality is extremely valuable; it is wrong to think that
only poets need imagination. That is a silly prejudice!
It is needed even in mathematics; it would have been
impossible to discover the differential and integral calculus
without imagination. Imagination is a very valuable
asset; but Comrade Larin has a little too much of it.
I would say, for example, that if Comrade Larin's stock
of imagination were divided equally among all the members
of the R.C.P., there would be very good results. (*Laughter.
Applause.*) But until we can perform this operation, Comrade Larin must be kept away from state, administrative,
planning, and economic affairs. Otherwise, we shall have
the same thing occurring as did in the old Supreme Economic Council, when Comrade Rykov had not yet recovered,
and affairs were directed and documents signed by
"Y. Larin" on behalf of the entire Supreme Economic
Council. Things were run badly not because Comrade
Larin displayed his worst qualities, but on the contrary;
it was because he displayed his best qualities—and nobody
can have even a shadow of doubt about his devotion
and knowledge of affairs. Nevertheless, things were run
badly.

This is exactly what I said. True, all these are copybook maxims. As for copybook maxims, even Kamkov
poked fun at me for this at the Congress of the Socialist-

Revolutionaries. He said: "Today, Lenin is preaching: 'Thou shalt not steal'; and tomorrow he will add: 'Thou shalt not commit adultery.' This is all that Lenin's wisdom amounts to." I heard this from Kamkov, the Socialist-Revolutionary, as far back as 1918. And if Kamkov, who backed these arguments with artillery, made no impression on anyone, what impression can Comrade Larin's jokes make? Now we must concentrate all our attention on the major problems of our New Economic Policy. Here Comrade Larin tried to divert the Party on to the wrong road. If he were engaged with matters on which he could usefully display his numerous talents, where he could be of great benefit to the younger generation, and where he would not play such a trick as he played in the State Planning Commission, it would be entirely different. If he were engaged in such work he would make an impression on the younger generation—I think I am speaking plainly enough—and we should not have the confusion that he has caused here.[93]

I said that Comrade Kamenev proposed on the Political Bureau that a resolution be adopted to the effect that it would be useful to import food and that canned goods be purchased with Soviet currency. Larin sat here, heard this perfectly well, and remembering it perfectly well, said as soon as he got on to the platform: "Lenin forgot, owing to ill health—we shall forgive him this time—that the permission of the Political Bureau has to be obtained for disbursements from the gold reserve." Had Comrade Kamenev proposed that we should take money out of the gold reserve and give it to French profiteers in exchange for canned goods we would not have listened to him. We did not offer a single gold kopek for the canned goods, we offered Soviet paper currency and—just imagine—it was accepted. Wolfson even assured me yesterday that these canned goods were of good quality (although they have not arrived yet); but I shall not believe him until we have tasted them, because here they may try to cheat us. The point is, however, that Comrade Larin garbled the facts; we did not spend a single gold kopek; we spent 160,000 million Soviet paper rubles.

Of course, it would be ridiculous and absurd to think that Comrade Larin did this with malicious intent. No,

that is not the point. The point is that his imagination
soars a trillion kilometres high and, as a consequence, he
mixes everything up.

Then he went on to say that the State Planning Commission had proposed to lease out three-fourths of our
railways. It is a good thing that he said this at the Party
Congress, where Krzhizhanovsky immediately refuted him.
It does not often happen like that. You think that talk
of this sort is heard only at Party congresses? Inquire at
the Central Control Commission and they will tell you how
they examined the case of the Moscow Debating Club,[94] and
what brought up the case of the Moscow Debating Club,
where Comrades Larin and Ryazanov.... (*Ryazanov from
his seat*: "I said nothing about the gold reserve there;
worse things were said.") I was not in Moscow and took no
part in the investigation of this case, I merely had a brief
report.... (*Ryazanov*: "Don't believe every rumour.")
I learned this from a conversation I had with Comrade
Solts; it is not a rumour, but a conversation I had with
a man whom our supreme body, the Party Congress, had
appointed to the Central Control Commission. It was he
who told me; and what he told me cannot rouse the slightest doubt. One must be very thoughtless to call this a
rumour. The Central Control Commission investigated the
affair of the Debating Club and was obliged to state unanimously that it was not being run properly. What is wrong
is quite clear to me. Today, Larin, in passing, carried
away by his own eloquence, went to the length of saying
that a proposal had been made to lease out three-fourths
of our railways, but that the Central Committee had put
the matter right. Krzhizhanovsky said that nothing of
the kind had happened; the Central Committee had put
nothing right; Larin had simply muddled up his facts.
This is constantly happening.

For four years we have been unable to put a useful worker
like Larin to really useful work and to relieve him of work
where he causes harm, in spite of himself.

The situation is rather unnatural, I think. We have
the dictatorship of the proletariat, a reign of terror, victory
over all the armies in the world, but no victory over Larin's
army! Here we have suffered utter defeat! He is always

doing what he has no business to do. His vast knowledge and his ability to enthuse people would be of real benefit to the younger generation, which is groping in the dark. We are unable to utilise his knowledge, and this gives rise to friction and resistance. Here the Political Bureau, the Organising Bureau of the Central Committee and the Plenary Meetings of the Central Committee, which are accused of enjoying too much authority, turn out to have insufficient authority, or prestige, to distribute all the comrades properly.

We must think this question over and discuss it seriously. This is the pivot of our work, and we must set things right here. If we do, we shall emerge from our difficulties. We shall achieve this by rectifying things, but not by talking about the new tasks of the Agrarian Programme as Osinsky and Larin did. I wrote a review of this programme for the Central Committee.[95] I shall not discuss it now; every member of the Party interested in the subject has a right to go to the Secretariat and read it there. Please do so. If we divert the efforts of Larin and Osinsky into the proper channels and curb their misguided zeal, enormous benefit will accrue.

In conclusion I shall say a few words about Shlyapnikov. I intended to speak about him at greater length, but ninety-nine per cent of this subject has been covered by Trotsky and Zinoviev, who on instructions of the Central Committee replied to the Statement of the Twenty-Two[96] at the meeting of the Communist International.

Firstly, Comrade Shlyapnikov pretended not to understand why I referred to machine-guns and panic-mongers; and he jokingly said that he had been tried lots of times. Of course, comrades, it is not a bad thing to make a joke. One cannot speak at a big meeting without cracking a joke or two, because one's audience gets weary. One must be human. But there are certain things that one must not joke about; there is such a thing as Party unity.

At a time when we are completely surrounded by enemies; when the international bourgeoisie is sufficiently astute to shift Milyukov to the left, to supply the Socialist-Revolutionaries with money for the publication of all sorts of newspapers and to incite Vandervelde and Otto

Bauer to launch a campaign against the trial of the Socialist-Revolutionaries and to howl that the Bolsheviks are brutes; when all these people, who have studied politics for ages and have thousands of millions of gold rubles, francs, etc., at their disposal, are arrayed against us, for Comrade Shlyapnikov to crack jokes and to say: "I have been tried by the Central Committee", and so forth, is a deplorable thing, comrades. The Party Congress must draw definite conclusions. We do not arrange trials at the Central Committee for nothing! Comrade Shlyapnikov was tried by the Central Committee, and we were short of three votes to expel him from the Party.[97] The members of the Party gathered at this Congress should interest themselves in the matter and read the minutes of that meeting of the Central Committee. This is no laughing matter!

You have a legitimate right to appeal to the Communist International. But a long time before that appeal was lodged a large majority of the Central Committee was in favour of expelling Comrade Shlyapnikov; only the necessary two-third vote was lacking. You cannot trifle with a thing like that! It will do you no harm to know that at the meeting of the Communist group at the Metalworkers' Congress Comrade Shlyapnikov openly advocated a split.

Comrade Trotsky has already dealt with the significance of Comrade Kollontai's pamphlet.

If we trifle with things like this it will be utterly hopeless to expect that we shall hold on in the difficult situation in which we now find ourselves. I have indicated the three conditions under which it will be possible for us to hold on: first, that there shall be no intervention; second, that the financial crisis shall not be too severe; and third, that we shall make no political mistakes.

One of the speakers stated that I said political complications. No, I said political mistakes. If we make no political mistakes, I say, 99 per cent of the Party membership will be with us, and so also will the non-Party workers and peasants, who will understand that this is the time to learn.

I remember that in the article he wrote on the anniversary of the Red Army Comrade Trotsky said: "A year of tuition." This slogan applies equally to the Party and to the working class. During this period we have rallied around us a vast number of heroic people who have undoubtedly made the turn in world history permanent. But this does not justify our failure to understand that we now have ahead of us a "year of tuition".

We are standing much more firmly on our feet today than we stood a year ago. Of course, even today the bourgeoisie may attempt another armed intervention, but they will find it much more difficult than before; it is much more difficult today than it was yesterday.

To ensure ourselves the opportunity to learn we must make no political mistakes. We must waste no time playing with the unity of the Party, as Comrade Shlyapnikov is doing. We cannot afford games of that kind! We know that the conflict within the Party is costing us a great deal. Comrades, we must not forget this lesson! Concerning the past year, the Central Committee has every right to say that at the opening of this Congress there was less factional strife in the Party, it was more united than last year. I do not want to boast that all factionalism in the Party has vanished. But it is an incontrovertible fact that there is less factionalism in the Party today. This has been proved.

You know that the present Workers' Opposition is only a wreck of the former Workers' Opposition. Compare the signatures appended to the Statement of the Twenty-Two with those appended to the platform that was issued before the Tenth Congress. You will find that many of those signatures are missing. We must tell those people who legitimately used their right to appeal to the Communist International that they had no right to appeal on behalf of Myasnikov. The Myasnikov case came up last summer [98] I was not in Moscow at the time, but I wrote Myasnikov a long letter,[99] which he inserted in his pamphlet. I saw that he was a capable man and that it was worth while having a talk with him; but this man must be told that if he comes out with criticism of this sort it will not be tolerated.

He writes a letter saying: "Collect all the discontented in the district." Yes, it is not a very difficult matter to collect all the discontented in a district. Take the speeches that Shlyapnikov delivers here, and which Comrade Medvedyev delivers elsewhere. (*Medvedyev from his seat*: "Where did you obtain your information?") I obtained my information from the bodies appointed by the Congress of the R.C.P.: the Organising Bureau of the Central Committee, the Secretariat of the Central Committee, and the Central Control Commission. Make inquiries there, if you like, and you will learn what sort of speeches Comrade Medvedyev delivers. If we do not put a stop to this sort of thing we shall be unable to maintain unity which, perhaps, is our greatest asset. We must ruthlessly expose our mistakes and discuss them. If we clearly understand this— and we are beginning to understand it at this Congress— there is not the slightest doubt that we shall be able to overcome them. (*Stormy applause.*)

4

SPEECH IN CLOSING THE CONGRESS
APRIL 2

Comrades, we have reached the end of our Congress. The first difference that strikes one in comparing this Congress with the preceding one is the greater solidarity, the greater unanimity and greater organisational unity that have been displayed.

Only a small part of one of the sections of the opposition that existed at the last Congress has placed itself outside the Party.

On the trade union question and on the New Economic Policy no disagreements, or hardly any disagreements, have been revealed in our Party.

The radically and fundamentally "new" achievement of this Congress is that it has provided vivid proof that our enemies are wrong in constantly reiterating that our Party is becoming senile and is losing its flexibility of mind and body.

No. We have not lost this flexibility.

When the objective state of affairs in Russia, and all over the world, called for an advance, for a supremely bold, swift and determined onslaught on the enemy, we made that onslaught. If necessary, we shall do it again and again.

By that we raised our revolution to a height hitherto unparalleled in the world. No power on earth, no matter how much evil, hardship and suffering it may yet cause millions and hundreds of millions of people, can annul the major gains of our revolution, for these are no longer our but historic gains.

But when in the spring of 1921 it turned out that the vanguard of the revolution was in danger of becoming isolated from the masses of the people, from the masses of the peasants, whom it must skilfully lead forward, we unanimously and firmly decided to retreat. And on the whole, during the past year we retreated in good revolutionary order.

The proletarian revolutions maturing in all advanced countries of the world will be unable to solve their problems unless they combine the ability to fight heroically and to attack with the ability to retreat in good revolutionary order. The experience of the second period of our struggle, i.e., the experience of retreat, will in the future probably be just as useful to the workers of at least some countries, as the experience of the first period of our revolution, i.e., the experience of bold attack, will undoubtedly prove useful to the workers of all countries.

Now we have decided to halt the retreat.

This means that the entire object of our policy must be formulated in a new way.

The central feature of the situation now is that the vanguard must not shirk the work of educating itself, of remoulding itself, must not be afraid of frankly admitting that it is not sufficiently trained and lacks the necessary skill. The main thing now is to advance as an immeasurably wider and larger mass, and only together with the peasantry, proving to them by deeds, in practice, by experience, that we are learning, and that we shall learn to assist them, to lead them forward. In the present international situation, in the present state of the productive forces of Russia, this problem can be solved only very slowly, cautiously, in a business-like way, and by testing a thousand times in a practical way every step that is taken.

If voices are raised in our Party against this extremely slow and extremely cautious progress, these voices will be isolated ones.

The Party as a whole has understood—and will now prove by deeds that it has understood—that at the present time its work must be organised exactly along these lines, and since we have understood it, we shall achieve our goal!

I declare the Eleventh Congress of the Russian Communist Party closed.

ON THE DRAFT OF THE ELEVENTH PARTY CONGRESS RESOLUTION ON WORK IN THE COUNTRYSIDE[100]

LETTER TO COMRADE OSINSKY

April 1, 1922

Comrade Osinsky,

After thinking over the conversation I had with you about the work of the Agricultural Section of the Party Congress, I have arrived at the conclusion that the most urgent thing at the present time is:

not to tie our (neither the Party's nor the Soviet Government's) hands by any orders, directives or rules until we have collected sufficient facts about economic life in the localities and until we have sufficiently studied the actual conditions and requirements of present-day peasant farming;

under no circumstances to permit what would be most dangerous and harmful at the present time, and what the local authorities may easily slip into—superfluous, clumsy and hasty regulation that has not been tested by experience.

The recent Congress of Soviets laid down the line. The task of the Party Congress, in my opinion, is to discuss in the Agricultural Section the application of this line in the light of *practical experience in the localities*; to instruct the Central Committee of the R.C.P. and the People's Commissariat of Agriculture (the Soviet government bodies in general) more thoroughly to collect detailed facts that can be used as verification material; to order, or rather, to give directions to the Communist group at the next session of the All-Russia Central Executive Committee to the effect that in working out the details of the decision of the Congress of Soviets, i.e., in converting this decision into new and more detailed laws, to be as cautious as possible so as not to hinder the successful development of agricultural production by clumsy interference.

What we must fear most of all, I think, is clumsy interference; for we have not yet made a thorough study of the actual requirements of *local* agricultural life and the actual abilities of the machinery of local administration (the ability not to do evil in the name of doing good).

Hence, it seems to me that it is desirable that something *approximating* the following be included in the resolution of the Party Congress based on the proceedings of the Agricultural Section:

1) The Party Congress, having heard the report of the proceedings of the Agricultural Section, accepts it as information; it finds that the material so far collected on the experience of the localities is inadequate and that the primary task of the Party and of Communist groups in all Soviet bodies is to collect carefully and make a close study of local practical experience.

2) The Congress regards the dissolution (or hasty reorganisation?) of the agricultural co-operative organisations as a mistake, and recommends the greatest caution in this matter.

3) On the question of the conditions on which hired labour may be employed on the farms, and of the terms on which land may be rented, the Party Congress recommends all officials engaged in this field of work not to restrict either of these transactions by unnecessary formalities, but to confine themselves to putting into effect the decisions of the recent Congress of Soviets and to studying the practical measures it would be expedient to adopt to curb all tendencies to go to extremes and harmful excesses in these matters.

4) The Congress considers that the primary and main object of all Party activities among the peasantry is to render practical assistance in immediately extending the area planted to crops, bringing fresh lands under the plough, increasing the output of farm produce and in alleviating the hardships of

the peasantry. All efforts and resources must be devoted to assisting and encouraging the poor section of the peasantry, and every effort must be made to devise measures that in practice will prove suitable for this purpose even under the present difficult conditions.

With communist greetings,

Lenin

First published in 1925

Published according to
the manuscript

WE HAVE PAID TOO MUCH

Imagine that a Communist has to enter premises in which agents of the bourgeoisie are carrying on their propaganda at a fairly large meeting of workers. Imagine also that the bourgeoisie demands from us a high price for admission to these premises. If the price has not been agreed to beforehand we must bargain, of course, in order not to impose too heavy a burden upon our Party funds. If we pay too much for admission to these premises we shall undoubtedly commit an error. But it is better to pay a high price—at all events until we have learned to bargain properly—than to reject an opportunity of speaking to workers who hitherto have been in the exclusive "possession", so to speak, of the reformists, i.e., of the most loyal friends of the bourgeoisie.

This analogy came to my mind when in today's *Pravda* I read a telegram from Berlin stating the terms on which agreement has been reached between the representatives of the three Internationals.

In my opinion our representatives were wrong in agreeing to the following two conditions: first, that the Soviet Government should not apply the death penalty in the case of the forty-seven Socialist-Revolutionaries; second, that the Soviet Government should permit representatives of the three Internationals to be present at the trial.

These two conditions are nothing more nor less than a political concession on the part of the revolutionary proletariat to the reactionary bourgeoisie. If anyone has any doubt about the correctness of this definition, then, to reveal the political naïveté of such a person, it is sufficient to ask him the following questions. Would the

British or any other contemporary government permit representatives of the three Internationals to attend the trial of Irish workers charged with rebellion? Or the trial of the workers implicated in the recent rebellion in South Africa?[101] Would the British or any other government, in such, or similar circumstances, agree to promise that it would not impose the death penalty on its political opponents? A little reflection over these questions will be sufficient to enable one to understand the following simple truth. All over the world a struggle is going on between the reactionary bourgeoisie and the revolutionary proletariat. In the present case the Communist International, which represents one side in this struggle, makes a political concession to the other side, i.e., the reactionary bourgeoisie; for everybody in the world knows (except those who want to conceal the obvious truth) that the Socialist-Revolutionaries have shot at Communists and have organised revolts against them, and that they have done this actually, and sometimes officially, in a united front with the whole of the international reactionary bourgeoisie.

The question is—what concession has the international bourgeoisie made to us in return? There can only be one reply to this question, and it is that no concession has been made to us whatever.

Only arguments which becloud this simple and clear truth of the class struggle, only arguments which throw dust in the eyes of the masses of working people, can obscure this obvious fact. Under the agreement signed in Berlin by the representatives of the Third International we have made two political concessions to the international bourgeoisie. We have obtained no concession in return.

The representatives of the Second and Two-and-a-Half Internationals acted as blackmailers to extort a political concession from the proletariat for the benefit of the bourgeoisie, while emphatically refusing, or at any rate making no attempt, to induce the international bourgeoisie to make some political concession to the revolutionary proletariat. Of course, this incontrovertible political fact was obscured by shrewd bourgeois diplomats (the bourgeoisie has been training members of its class to become good diplomats for many centuries); but the attempt to obscure the fact does not change it in the least. Whether the various representatives of the Second and Two-and-a-Half Internationals are in direct or indirect collusion with the bourgeoisie is a matter of tenth-rate importance in the present case. We do not accuse them of being in direct collusion. The question of whether there has been direct collusion or fairly intricate, indirect connection has nothing to do with the case. The only point that has anything to do with it is that as a result of the pressure of the representatives of the Second and Two-and-a-Half Internationals, the Communist International has made a political concession to the international bourgeoisie and has obtained no concession in return.

What conclusion should be drawn from this?

First, that Comrades Radek, Bukharin and the others who represented the Communist International acted wrongly.

Further. Does it follow from this that we must tear up the agreement that they signed? No. I think it would be wrong to draw such a conclusion. We ought not to tear up the agreement. All we have to do is to realise that on this occasion the bourgeois diplomats proved to be more skilful than ours, and that next time, if the price of admission is not fixed beforehand, we must bargain and manoeuvre more skilfully. We must make it a rule not to make political concessions to the international bourgeoisie (no matter how skilfully these concessions may be concealed by intermediaries, no matter of what sort) unless we receive in return more or less equivalent concessions from the international bourgeoisie to Soviet Russia, or to the other contingents of the international proletariat which is fighting capitalism.

Perhaps the Italian Communists and a section of the French Communists and Syndicalists, who were opposed to united front tactics, will infer from the above argument that united front tactics are wrong. But such an inference will obviously be wrong. If the communist representatives have paid too much for admission to premises in which they have some, even if small, opportunity of addressing workers up to now in the exclusive "possession" of reformists, such a mistake must be rectified next time. But it would be an incomparably greater mistake to reject all terms, or all payment for admission to these fairly well-guarded and barred premises. The mistake that Comrades Radek, Bukharin and the others made is not a grave one, especially as our only risk is that the enemies of Soviet Russia may be encouraged by the result of the Berlin Conference to make two or three perhaps successful attempts on the lives of certain persons; for they know beforehand that they can shoot at Communists in the expectation that conferences like the Berlin Conference will hinder the Communists from shooting at them.

At all events, we have made some breach in the premises that were closed to us. At all events, Comrade Radek has succeeded in exposing, at least to a section of the workers, the fact that the Second International refused to include among the slogans of the demonstration a demand to annul the Treaty of Versailles. The great mistake the Italian Communists and a section of the French Communists and Syndicalists make is in being content with the knowledge they already possess. They are content with knowing well enough that the representatives of the Second and Two-and-a-Half Internationals, and also Paul Levi, Serrati and others, are very shrewd agents of the bourgeoisie and vehicles of their influence. But people, workers, who really know this, and who really understand its significance, are undoubtedly in the minority in Italy, Britain, the U.S.A. and France. Communists must not stew in their own juice, but must learn to penetrate into prohibited premises where the representatives of the bourgeoisie are influencing the workers; and in this they must not shrink from making certain sacrifices and not be afraid of making mistakes, which, at first, are inevitable in every new and difficult undertaking. The Communists who refuse to understand this and who do not want to learn how to do it cannot hope to win over the majority of the workers; at all events, they are hindering and retarding the work of winning this majority. For Communists, and all genuine adherents of the workers' revolution, this is absolutely unpardonable.

Once again, the bourgeoisie, in the persons of their diplomats, have outwitted the representatives of the Communist International. Such is the lesson of the Berlin

Conference. We shall not forget this lesson. We shall draw
all the necessary conclusions from it. The representatives of
the Second and Two-and-a-Half Internationals need a united front, for they hope to weaken us by inducing us to
make exorbitant concessions; they hope to penetrate into
our communist premises without any payment; they hope
to utilise united front tactics for the purpose of convincing
the workers that reformist tactics are correct and that
revolutionary tactics are wrong. We need a united front
because we hope to convince the workers of the opposite.
We shall put the blame for the mistakes on our communist
representatives who committed them, and on those parties
which commit them, while we shall try to learn from these
mistakes and to prevent a repetition of them in the future.
But under no circumstances shall we thrust the blame for
the mistakes of our Communists upon the proletarian
masses, who all over the world are facing the onslaught of
advancing capital. We adopted united front tactics in order
to help these masses to fight capitalism, to help them
understand the "cunning mechanism" of the two fronts in
international economics and in international politics; and
we shall pursue these tactics to the end.

April 9, 1922

Pravda No. 81, April 11, 1922
Signed: *Lenin*

Dictated by telephone
Published according to
the *Pravda* text

DECREE ON THE FUNCTIONS OF THE DEPUTY CHAIRMEN
OF THE COUNCIL OF PEOPLE'S COMMISSARS AND OF THE COUNCIL OF LABOUR AND DEFENCE[102]

I. THE GENERAL AND MAIN FUNCTIONS OF THE DEPUTY CHAIRMEN

1. The main functions of the Deputy Chairmen, for which they are particularly responsible and to which all their other functions must be subordinated, are to exercise executive control over the fulfilment of decrees, laws and decisions; to reduce the staffs of Soviet government offices and supervise the reorganisation of their business on proper and rational lines, and to combat bureaucratic methods and red tape.

The ensuing gives these main functions in detail or supplements them in minor particulars.

It is the duty of the Deputy Chairmen:

2. To ensure that no question concerning Soviet affairs is discussed by other bodies, government or Party (Presidium of the All-Russia Central Executive Committee, Political Bureau and Organising Bureau of the Central Committee of the R.C.P., and so forth, without exception), without the knowledge and participation of the Deputy Chairmen.

3. To relieve the Council of People's Commissars and the Council of Labour and Defence as far as possible of minor matters, part (and most) of which should be settled by the departmental administrations and part (in urgent

and exceptionally important cases) by the Deputy Chairmen themselves.

4. To ensure by strict supervision that the executive sessions of the *Council of Labour and Defence* and particularly of the *Narrow Council of People's Commissars* shall not assume more functions than are absolutely necessary, shall not complicate their duties and functions, nor permit their functions to become bureaucratically inflated and hypertrophied; they must demand more self-reliance and more responsibility from every People's Commissar and every government department.

5. To compel the People's Commissars and independent government departments to administer their affairs on their own responsibility in accordance with their prescribed rights and duties.

6. To see to it that the degree of responsibility, primarily of members of Collegiums and of the most important Soviet officials, and then of all Soviet officials, shall be precisely and individually defined; to combat relentlessly the prevailing haziness and vagueness concerning each individual's duties and the complete lack of responsibility resulting from this.

7. To become personally acquainted with a certain number of Soviet officials not only of the highest rank, but primarily the medium and lower officials, by summoning them to the centre and, wherever possible, by visiting government offices in Moscow and the provinces, so as to test and choose men, and also to really improve the machinery of Soviet government.

8. To give priority to those People's Commissariats, their departments and offices which for a specific period acquire exceptional importance, and to render them the maximum of assistance in the way of personnel, resources, the personal direction of the Deputy Chairmen, etc.

II. SPECIFIC QUESTIONS CONCERNING
THE WORK OF THE DEPUTY CHAIRMEN

9. The Deputy Chairmen should devote about nine-tenths of their efforts to the People's Commissariats concerned with economic affairs and one-tenth to the rest.

10. Financial questions are in the forefront for the immediate future and the Deputy Chairmen should devote most attention to them.

11. A particularly vital matter is the introduction of a system of bonuses to be paid to Soviet employees in proportion to the turnover and profits of the People's Commissariat of Foreign Trade, the co-operative societies and other trading organisations.

Systematic efforts must be made to study the bonus system of payment to all Soviet employees in general and devise measures for applying it.

12. All work now proceeding for the purpose of forming a separate People's Commissariat of Internal Trade, or of turning these functions over to the People's Commissariat of Foreign Trade or the Supreme Economic Council, should be stopped. The *Council of Labour and Defence* should set up a special *Internal Trade Commission* which shall be furnished with the smallest possible secretarial staff, and the only local organs of which shall be the gubernia economic conferences.

13. It is extremely important to supervise the activities of the state trusts with a view to seeking those that are tolerably well organised among the bulk of badly organised ones, and steadily closing down the latter; to investigate the role played (actually) by the Communists on the management boards of the state trusts; to ascertain who is really responsible for the conduct of affairs and for efficiency in conducting affairs.

14. Each Deputy Chairman should undertake to organise one or two exemplary departments, or offices, of any given People's Commissariat to enable him to arrive at a standard size of staffs, verify the correctness of this standard and establish the best methods of conducting and supervising affairs.

The methods of work, methods of improving efficiency, and the methods of supervision employed in these few really exemplary offices should later be gradually introduced into all Soviet offices.

In view of the exceptional importance of this question, and in view of the stubborn resistance of the Soviet bureaucrats, who want to cling to the old bureaucratic methods, there will have to be a persistent struggle to create a few exemplary offices as a means of tightening up and testing the rest. By agreement with the bodies concerned (the Central Committee of the Soviet Office Employees' Union, the All-Russia Central Council of Trade Unions, the Labour Institute, etc., etc.) and under the supervision of the Deputy Chairmen the best of the latest literature on the organisation of labour and on management, especially the American and German, should be translated and published.

15. It is necessary—if at first only in a very few government offices—to supervise the redistribution of Communists in Soviet offices and to see to it that Communists occupy only such posts (at the very top as well as the very bottom of the hierarchy) as enable them really to watch the progress of work, really to combat bureaucracy and red tape, really to secure an immediate amelioration of the conditions and improvement in the lot of those unfortunate citizens who are compelled to have dealings with our utterly inefficient Soviet machinery of administration.

Special attention must be paid to the Communists who occupy posts at the lower levels of the hierarchy, for often they are actually more important than those at the top.

16. The reports of the gubernia economic conferences must be read regularly, firstly, by the members of the State Planning Commission, the officials of the Central Statistical Board and the staff of *Ekonomicheskaya Zhizn*; and every one of these should write a very brief review for the press or for his respective department, and be responsible for giving the necessary timely directions and conclusions. Secondly, they must be read by a group of several dozen Communists (not less), as far as possible not Soviet officials, who can read reports from the *purely* Communist and not from the departmental point of view.

The group headed by Comrade Milyutin in Petrograd should have charge of the distribution of the reports of the gubernia economic conferences for reading, and as material for newspapers, magazines, pamphlets, etc.

Constant efforts must be made gradually to extend the obligatory printing of reports to an ever increasing number of business organisations (uyezd economic conferences, state trusts, "mixed companies", etc., etc.), for unless an increasing number of the population grow accustomed to reading these reports in the libraries, it is useless talking about transforming this semi-barbarous country into a cultured and socialistic one.

17. *Ekonomicheskaya Zhizn* must actually become the organ of the *Council of Labour and Defence, an organ of business administration*. Both Deputy Chairmen should read it regularly and relentlessly combat the prevailing efforts of all writers and of all Soviet officials to reduce this newspaper to the level of an ordinary "semi-independent", intellectualist bourgeois organ of "opinion", views and wrangling and to keep out of its columns summaries of reports, control of regular receipt of these reports, serious analysis of the business operations of *particular organisations*, serious criticism of efficient and inefficient offices, *persons*, methods of work, etc.

It will take years to convert *Ekonomicheskaya Zhizn* into a real *business management* paper, into a real organ of socialist construction; all the more necessary is it, therefore, to strive steadily and systematically to achieve this.

18. The same applies to the Central Statistical Board. It must not be an "academic" and "independent" organisation—as it mostly is today, owing to old bourgeois habits—but an organ of socialist construction, verification, control and of registration of what the socialist state must primarily know now, immediately. Here, too, the tenacity of old habits will inevitably be very great, and all the more strenuous, therefore, must be the efforts to combat them. (I request that the Deputy Chairmen read my correspondence on this subject in the summer of 1921* with the editor of *Ekonomicheskaya Zhizn* and with the Central Statistical Board.)

III. THE DEPUTY CHAIRMEN'S METHODS OF WORK. THEIR STAFFS

19. The Deputy Chairmen must free themselves as much as possible from minor details and from unnecessary interviews with People's Commissars and members of Collegiums, which usually take up a great deal of their time and prevent them from exercising executive control.

---

* See pp. 36-38, 30-35 of this volume.—*Ed.*

20. The Deputy Chairmen must free themselves as much as possible from the need to attend all sorts of commissions.

21. The Deputy Chairmen must make every effort to dissolve existing commissions (nine-tenths of which are superfluous and show a tendency to revive in a slightly different guise very soon after they have been dissolved) and to prevent the formation of new ones.

22. In those cases where commission work is unavoidable, the Deputy Chairmen must do all they can to avoid taking part in it themselves, and should, as far as possible, confine themselves to finally endorsing the decisions of such commissions, or to expediting their proceedings and sending their decisions for endorsement in the prescribed order.

23. The staff of the Deputy Chairmen shall consist of, firstly, the staffs of the Executive Secretary of the *Council of People's Commissars* and of the *Council of Labour and Defence*, their assistants and secretaries. This absolutely necessary minimum staff, whose size (not too large) is such that the Deputy Chairmen can exercise *personal* supervision, must under no circumstances be enlarged. Secondly, the Deputy Chairmen are to entrust individual members of the Narrow Council of People's Commissars with various commissions. Thirdly, the People's Commissariat of the Workers' and Peasants' Inspection must serve as the main staff of the Deputy Chairmen.

The Deputy Chairmen should personally select assistants and executives from the staff of this People's Commissariat, train them and supervise their work, and make special efforts to enlist non-Party workers and peasants for this work (this is an exceptionally difficult matter, but if it is not steadily developed Soviet power will be doomed).

24. The Deputy Chairmen must to a greater extent than hitherto exercise their powers to impose penalties (expedite the drafting of the law on this subject undertaken by Comrade Tsyurupa) for bureaucratic methods, red tape, inefficiency, neglect, etc. The penalties for the worst offences must be dismissal, legal prosecution, and the People's Commissariat of Justice must organise trials of such cases, to which great publicity must be given.

IV. CO-ORDINATING THE WORK OF THE TWO DEPUTY CHAIRMEN

25. To co-ordinate their work, the two Deputy Chairmen should send each other copies of their most important instructions, and make a practice of keeping a verbatim record of the oral instructions, directions and so forth given by them during personal interviews (in the briefest terms and the most important points, of course). The number of stenographers on the Executive Secretary's staff of the Council of People's Commissars should therefore be increased sufficiently to enable the Deputy Chairmen to have two stenographers constantly at their service during business hours. If necessary, a couple of dictaphones of the best type should be ordered from abroad.

26. The same applies to the most important reports, written and oral.

27. In necessary and important cases the Deputy Chairmen should confer in order to reach a common understanding regarding objects and activities and to avoid duplication and running at cross purposes in the course of their work.

In the event of disagreement arising between the Deputy Chairmen the issue should be settled by the Chairman of the Council of People's Commissars, or, if he is absent, by the Political Bureau of the Central Committee, or by a comrade especially appointed by it for the purpose.

V. DISTRIBUTION OF FUNCTIONS BETWEEN THE DEPUTY CHAIRMEN

28. During the next few months, until further notice, the functions of the Deputy Chairmen shall be distributed as follows.

29. Comrade Tsyurupa shall preside at the meetings of the Full Council of People's Commissars (after he has presided for two hours he should be relieved by Comrade Rykov). The presence of the non-presiding Deputy Chairman is obligatory at sessions of the Full Council of People's Commissars and at (plenary) sessions of the Council of Labour and Defence.

Comrade Tsyurupa shall sign for publication in the press the decisions of the Full Council of People's Commissars and its telegraphic orders, and also supervise the work of the commissions of the Full and Narrow Councils of People's Commissars and the work of the Narrow Council of People's Commissars. He shall closely supervise the work of the Executive Secretary and Secretariat of the Full Council of People's Commissars and at the same time be responsible for co-ordinating the activities of this staff with those of the stuff of the Council of Labour and Defence and see that there is complete contact and harmony between them.

30. Comrade Rykov shall preside at the plenary sessions of the Council of Labour and Defence, sign its decisions for publication in the press and also its telegraphic orders, and closely supervise the work of the Executive Secretary and Secretariat of the Council of Labour and Defence (with the aforementioned proviso that there is complete co-ordination between the work of this staff and that of the staff of the Full Council of People's Commissars).

31. For the purpose of executive control, supervising the reduction of staffs and improving the machinery of administration, and also for the settlement of minor current questions that do not need the decision of the Full Council of People's Commissars and the Council of Labour and Defence, the People's Commissariats are to be divided between the two Deputy Chairmen as follows:

Under Comrade Tsyurupa's supervision:
  People's Commissariat of Agriculture
  People's Commissariat of Railways
  Supreme Economic Council
  People's Commissariat of Post and Telegraph
  People's Commissariat of Justice
  People's Commissariat of the Interior
  People's Commissariat of Nationalities
  People's Commissariat of Education.

Under Comrade Rykov's supervision:
  People's Commissariat of Finance
  People's Commissariat of Foreign Trade
  Internal Trade Commission
  Central Council of Co-operative Societies

People's Commissariat of Labour (and in part the
   All-Russia Central Council of Trade Unions)
People's Commissariat of Public Maintenance
People's Commissariat of Food
People's Commissariat of the Army and Navy
People's Commissariat of Foreign Affairs
People's Commissariat of Public Health
Central Statistical Board
Regional Economic Conferences
Concessions Committee
State Planning Commission.

V. Ulyanov (Lenin),
Chairman of the Council of People's
Commissars

April 11, 1922

First published in 1928   Published according to
                                                       the manuscript

LETTER TO J. V. STALIN

To Comrade Stalin (for the Political Bureau)

April 15

I have just received the book *Materialy po istorii franko-russkikh otnosheni za 1910-1914 gody*.[103]

This massive tome of 733 pages has been published with that disgraceful, truly Soviet slovenliness which ought to be punished by imprisonment. The price is not indicated. The responsible person or persons are not named. There is no index!! The simple *list* of names has been compiled *carelessly*. And so on.

I suggest that:

(1) Hanecki and Karakhan be given two days in which to find all the persons responsible for this publication,

(2) hold up the sale of the book,

(3) write a notice to be inserted in the book to indicate what is missing,

(4) and draw up an intelligible index; in short, that by Thursday they should submit a *brief* report to the Central Committee on all these monstrosities—the defects in the publication, and on the ways of correcting them.

Lenin

P.S. M. N. Pokrovsky is named in the "Preface"—which is *unsigned*!! He has worked on *compiling* the material but it is obvious that he is not responsible for the *publication*, for the *way* the book has been put out.

Published for the first time, according to the manuscript

PREFACE TO THE PAMPHLET
OLD ARTICLES ON ALMOST NEW SUBJECTS

PREFACE TO THE 1922 EDITION[104]

This pamphlet has been published on the recommendation of the Communists of Moscow, not on mine. I was, at first, opposed to the republication of this old stuff, as I considered it to be out of date.

After reading the material prepared by the Moscow comrades for publication I found that it was not as obsolete as might have been expected. In fact, most of it is not obsolete at all, in spite of the extremely turbulent and rapid revolutionary development of the past four years.

The situation in the spring of 1922 duplicates on a broad scale the main features of the situation in the spring of 1918. At that time we had a "respite" between two wars— between the imperialist war, which we brought to an end (it would be more correct to say almost brought to an end) in February 1918, and the Civil War, which did not come to an end with our first victory over counter-revolutionaries of the Bogayevsky type, but for which preparations were being made by the Czechoslovaks, Kornilov, Denikin and Co.

Today Genoa represents another "respite" on a very much larger, on a world scale. It is a respite between the war against Soviet Russia, that was fought and lost by the world bourgeoisie, and the new war which this bourgeoisie is preparing, but is not yet ready for (I am writing these lines on April 28, 1922, when the latest news indicates the danger of a rupture).

Now, as then, the "pivot" of Soviet policy is organisation, accounting and control, a slow, cautious and business-like approach to practical tasks, to executive control and

the study of our practical experience. I spoke about this at
the Eleventh Congress of the R.C.P. a few weeks ago. The
Congress accepted this "line", as is evident from the
resolution it passed on the report of the Central Committee,
and from other resolutions. And I tried to sum up that
line in my speech in closing the Eleventh Congress.

The republication of this old pamphlet of 1918 will
be useful because the controversies that raged at that time
will go a long way to explain the problems that face our
Party today. Speeches like those delivered by Comrades
Preobrazhensky, Osinsky and Larin during the debate on
the report of the Central Committee at the Eleventh Party
Congress clearly revealed that very many prominent and
leading Party officials are not concentrating their attention
on what they should. In their speeches they wrongly defined
the "pivot" of the problems that now confront the Party.
I hope to be able to discuss this matter with the reader in
greater detail in the near future. For the time being, I
must limit myself to the remark that the object of the present pamphlet is to explain why the task that was in the
forefront when this pamphlet was first published was (*and
at the present time still is*) "to learn to work efficiently",
to learn how to put the right men in the right place, to
establish individual responsibility for a definite job, carefully to study and test practical experience instead of hank-
ering after "new" plans of new government departments,
or after new methods of organisation, reorganisation, and
so forth.

Just one more absolutely necessary remark in conclusion.
I have deleted from this pamphlet the speech I delivered
in closing the session of the All-Russia Central Executive
Committee in the spring of 1918.[105] This speech was recorded in such a way as to render it absolutely useless. I must
repeat what I once wrote to the Petrograd comrades in
1919, or 1920, in a letter intended for publication in the
press, but which, unfortunately, they did not publish,* viz.,
that I cannot accept responsibility for the reports of my
speeches in the way they are usually printed in the press, and
I earnestly request that they should not be reprinted—except

---

* See pp. 121-23 of this volume. — *Ed*.

in case of extreme necessity, and, in any case, together with my present definite statement. Whether it is due to the fact that I often speak too fast; whether in many cases my style of delivery is faulty, or whether the ordinary records of speeches are made too hurriedly and are very unsatisfactory—for all these reasons, and for certain others all taken together, the fact remains that I cannot accept responsibility for the text of my speeches as recorded, and request that they should not be reproduced. Let those who make these records be responsible. If it is necessary to reprint anything, there are plenty of pamphlets and articles that can be reprinted, and for the text of which I take full and complete responsibility.

April 28, 1922

N. Lenin

Published in the pamphlet
Old Articles on Almost New Subjects, Moscow, 1922

Published according to the manuscript

TELEGRAM TO THE WORKERS AND ENGINEERS
OF THE AZNEFT TRUST

Baku

On the night of April 9 enemies of the working class tried to destroy the Surakhan oilfields at Baku by fire. I have learned of instances of extraordinary heroism and courage displayed by the workers and engineers of the oilfields, who localised the fire at tremendous risk to their own lives, and consider it my duty to thank the workers and engineers of the Surakhan oilfields on behalf of Soviet Russia. These examples of heroism show better than anything else that despite all the difficulties, despite the uninterrupted conspiracies of the whiteguard-Socialist-Revolutionary enemies of the workers' republic, the Soviet Republic will emerge triumphantly from all difficulties.

V. Ulyanov (Lenin),
Chairman of the Council of People's Commissars

Written on April 28, 1922
First published in 1942

Published according to the original signed by Lenin

ON THE TENTH ANNIVERSARY OF *PRAVDA*

It is ten years since *Pravda*, the legal—legal even under *tsarist* law—Bolshevik daily paper, was founded. This decade was preceded by, approximately, another decade: nine years (1903-12) since the emergence of Bolshevism, or thirteen years (1900-12), if we count from the founding in 1900 of the "Bolshevik-oriented" old *Iskra*.[106]

The tenth anniversary of a Bolshevik daily published in Russia.... Only ten years have elapsed! But measured in terms of our struggle and movement they are equal to a hundred years. For the pace of social development in the past five years has been positively staggering if we apply the old yardstick of European philistines like the heroes of the Second and Two-and-a-Half Internationals. These civilised philistines are accustomed to regard as "natural" a situation in which hundreds of millions of people (over a thousand million, to be exact) in the colonies and in semi-dependent and poor countries tolerate the treatment meted out to Indians or Chinese, tolerate incredible exploitation, and outright depredation, and hunger, and violence, and humiliation, all in order that "civilised" men might "freely", "democratically", according to "parliamentary procedure", decide whether the booty should be divided up peacefully, or whether ten million or so must be done to death in this division of the imperialist booty, yesterday between Germany and Britain, tomorrow between Japan and the U.S.A. (with France and Britain participating in one form or another).

The basic reason for this tremendous acceleration of world development is that new hundreds of millions of people have been drawn into it. The old bourgeois and imperialist Europe, which was accustomed to look upon itself as the centre of the universe, rotted and burst like a putrid ulcer in the first imperialist holocaust. No matter how the Spenglers and all the enlightened philistines, who are capable of admiring (or even studying) Spengler, may lament it, this decline of the old Europe is but an episode in the history of the downfall of the world bourgeoisie, oversatiated by imperialist rapine and the oppression of the majority of the world's population.

That majority has now awakened and has begun a movement which even the "mightiest" powers cannot stem. They stand no chance. For the present "victors" in the first imperialist slaughter have not the strength to defeat small— tiny, I might say—Ireland, nor can they emerge victorious from the confusion in currency and finance issues that reigns in their own midst. Meanwhile, India and China are seething. They represent over 700 million people, and together with the neighbouring Asian countries, that are in all ways similar to them, over half of the world's inhabitants. Inexorably and with mounting momentum they are approaching their 1905, with the essential and important difference that in 1905 the revolution in Russia could still proceed (at any rate at the beginning) in isolation, that is, without other countries being immediately drawn in. But the revolutions that are maturing in India and China are being drawn into—have already been drawn into—the revolutionary struggle, the revolutionary movement, the world revolution.

The tenth anniversary of *Pravda*, the legal Bolshevik daily, is a clearly defined marker of this great acceleration of the greatest world revolution. In 1906-07, it seemed that the tsarist government had completely crushed the revolution. A few years later the Bolshevik Party was able—*in a different form, by a different method*—to penetrate into the very citadel of the enemy and daily, "legally", proceed with its work of undermining the accursed tsarist and landowner autocracy from within. A few more years passed, and the proletarian revolution, organised by Bolshevism, triumphed.

Some ten or so revolutionaries shared in the founding of the old *Iskra* in 1900, and only about forty attended the birth of Bolshevism at the illegal congresses in Brussels and London in 1903.[107]

In 1912-13, when the legal Bolshevik *Pravda* came into being it had the support of hundreds of thousands of workers, who by their modest contributions[108] were able to overcome both the oppression of tsarism and the competition of the Mensheviks, those petty-bourgeois traitors to socialism.

In November 1917, nine million electors out of a total of thirty-six million voted for the Bolsheviks in the elections to the Constituent Assembly. But if we take the actual struggle, and not merely the elections, at the close of October and in November 1917, the Bolsheviks had the support of the *majority* of the proletariat and class-conscious peasantry, as represented by the majority of the delegates at the Second All-Russia Congress of Soviets, and by the majority of the most active and politically conscious section of the working people, namely, the twelve-million-strong army of that day.

These few figures illustrating the "acceleration" of the world revolutionary movement in the past twenty years give a very small and very incomplete picture. They afford only a very approximate idea of the history of no more than 150 million people, whereas in these twenty years the revolution has developed into an invincible force in countries with a total population of over a thousand million (the whole of Asia, not to forget South Africa, which recently reminded the world of its claim to *human* and not slavish existence, and by methods which were not altogether "parliamentary").

Some infant Spenglers—I apologise for the expression—may conclude (every variety of nonsense can be expected from the "clever" leaders of the Second and Two-and-a-Half Internationals) that this estimate of the revolutionary forces fails to take into account the European and American proletariat. These "clever" leaders always argue as if the fact that birth comes nine months after conception necessarily means that the exact hour and minute of birth can be defined beforehand, also the position of the infant during delivery, the condition of the mother and the exact degree of pain and danger both will suffer. Very "clever"! These

gentry cannot for the life of them understand that from the
point of view of the development of the international
revolution the transition from Chartism to Henderson's servility to the bourgeoisie, or the transition from Varlin to
Renaudel, from Wilhelm Liebknecht and Bebel to Süde-
kum, Scheidemann and Noske, can only be likened to an
automobile passing *from* a smooth highway stretching for
hundreds of miles *to* a dirty stinking puddle of a few yards
in length on that highway.

Men are the makers of history. But the Chartists, the
Varlins and the Liebknechts applied their minds and hearts
to it. The leaders of the Second and Two-and-a-Half
Internationals apply other parts of the anatomy: they
fertilise the ground for the appearance of new Chartists,
new Varlins and new Liebknechts.

At this *most difficult* moment it would be most harmful
for revolutionaries to indulge in self-deception. Though
Bolshevism *has become* an international force, though in
all the civilised and advanced countries new Chartists,
new Varlins, new Liebknechts have been born, and are
growing up as legal (just as legal as our *Pravda* was under
the tsars ten years ago) Communist Parties, nonetheless, for
the time being, the international bourgeoisie still remains
incomparably stronger than its class enemy. This bourgeoisie, which has done everything in its power to hamper the
birth of proletarian power in Russia and to multiply tenfold the dangers and suffering attending its birth, is still
in a position to condemn millions and tens of millions to
torment and death through its whiteguard and imperialist
wars, etc. That is something we must not forget. And we
must skilfully adapt our tactics to this specific situation.
The bourgeoisie is still able freely to torment, torture and
kill. But it cannot halt the inevitable and—from the standpoint of world history—not far distant triumph of the
revolutionary proletariat.

May 2, 1922

Pravda No. 98,
May 5, 1922
Signed: *N. Lenin*
Published according to
the *Pravda* text

REPLY TO REMARKS CONCERNING THE FUNCTIONS OF THE DEPUTY CHAIRMEN OF THE COUNCIL OF PEOPLE'S COMMISSARS

To Comrade Stalin with the request to pass it on (do not duplicate it—to do so would give publicity to polemics) to members of the Political Bureau and Comrade Tsyurupa (asking them to sign it and give the date when they have read it)

I am sorry for replying belatedly, but the delay was caused by the removal of the bullet.[109]

Comrade Rykov's remarks are "critical", but not concrete and do not require an answer.

I consider Comrade Tomsky's remarks on the bonus system incorrect. The collapse of the trade union bonus system, which, according to Comrade Tomsky, has degenerated into "robbery of the state", must force us to be more persevering in studying and improving the methods of applying the bonus system, but we must not reject it.

Some of Comrade Trotsky's remarks are likewise vague (for example, the "apprehensions" in paragraph 4) and do not require an answer; other remarks made by him renew old disagreements, that we have repeatedly observed in the Political Bureau. I shall reply to these on two main points: a) the Workers' and Peasants' Inspection and b) the State Planning Commission.

a) As regards the Workers' and Peasants' Inspection, Comrade Trotsky is fundamentally wrong. In view of the hidebound "departmentalism" that prevails even among the best Communists, the low standard of efficiency of the employees and the internal intrigues in the departments (worse than any Workers' and Peasants' Inspection intrigues), we cannot at the moment dispense with the Workers' and Peasants Inspection. A lot of hard and systematic work has to be put in to convert it into an apparatus for investigating and improving all government work. We have no other practical means of investigating, improving and giving instruction in this work. If the Workers' and Peasants' Inspection now has an inefficient and underpaid staff of 12,000, that staff should be reduced and improved; for example, reduce it to one-sixth and the payroll by half, i.e., raise salaries threefold; at first select a few dozen and later hundreds of the best, absolutely honest and most efficient employees, who are now available but not registered, not selected, not put in any group and not organised. This can and must be done; if not, it will be impossible to combat departmentalism and red tape, it will be impossible to teach non-Party workers and peasants the art of administration, which is a task that at the present time we cannot shirk either in principle or in practice.

b) As regards the State Planning Commission, Comrade Trotsky is not only absolutely wrong but is judging something on which he is amazingly ill-informed. The State Planning Commission does not suffer from academic methods. On the contrary, it suffers from an overload of much too much petty, routine "vermicelli". Comrade Krzhizhanovsky, because he is soft-hearted, gives way much too easily to those who ask him for urgent assistance. Pyatakov, the new Deputy Chairman of the State Planning Commission, will, I hope, be "stricter" and help to rid the State Planning Commission of its shortcoming, which is quite the opposite of "academic methods".

Since I know full well the real shortcomings of the State Planning Commission, and in order to provide the members of the Political Bureau with factual, objective material and not with figments of the imagination, I asked Comrade Krzhizhanovsky if his work suffered from "abstractness" and what the exact facts about it were. Comrade Krzhizhanovsky sent me a list of the questions that have piled up before the Presidium of the State Planning Commission in the course of two months: February and March 1922. Result: aa) questions concerning planning—17 per cent; bb) questions of an important economic nature—37 per cent; cc) "vermicelli"—46 per cent. I can send this material to any member of the Political Bureau who would like to see it.

The second paper from Comrade Trotsky, dated April 23, 1922, and addressed to the Deputy Chairmen with a copy to the Secretariat of the Political Bureau (the copy was evidently posted to me by mistake), contains, first, an extremely excited but profoundly erroneous "criticism" of the Political Bureau decree on setting up a financial triumvirate (Sokolnikov and two deputies) as of a brake between the Narrow and Full Councils of People's Commissars. The sending of this criticism to the Deputy Chairmen is not in conformity either with planned or, in general, with any organised state activity.

Secondly, this paper flings the same fundamentally wrong and intrinsically untrue accusations of academic method at the State Planning Commission, accusations which lead up to the next incredibly uninformed statement by Comrade Trotsky. "At present," he writes, "there neither is nor can be an economic plan without establishing the quantity of money issued and without distributing cash funds between the departments. Yet, *as far as I can judge*, the State Planning Commission *has nothing whatever to do* with these basic questions."

The underscored words only make me want to ask the question: Why "judge" something about which you are uninformed? Any member of the C.C. or the Council of Labour and Defence could easily get the information he needs, and if he tried he would learn that the State Planning Commission has a financial and economic section, which deals precisely with the above questions. There are shortcomings in this work, of course, but they must not be sought in academic methods but in exactly the opposite direction.

Lenin

Written on May 5, 1922
First published,
in abridged form,
in 1928 in *Lenin Miscellany VIII*

Published according to
the manuscript

DRAFT DECISION
OF THE ALL-RUSSIA CENTRAL EXECUTIVE COMMITTEE ON THE REPORT OF THE DELEGATION TO THE GENOA CONFERENCE

The All-Russia Central Executive Committee's draft resolution on Joffe's report should be drawn up approximately as follows:

1. The delegation of the All-Russia Central Executive Committee has carried out its task correctly in upholding the full sovereignty of the R.S.F.S.R., opposing attempts to force the country into bondage and restore private property, and in concluding a treaty with Germany.

2. The international political and economic situation is characterised by the following features.

Political: the absence of peace and the danger of fresh imperialist wars |Ireland, India, China and others; worsening of relations¯ between Britain and France, between Japan and the United States, *etc.*, *etc.* ((in greater detail))|.

3. Economic: the "victor" countries, exceedingly powerful and enriched by the war (=by plunder), have not been able to re-establish even the former capitalist relations three and a half years after the war |currency chaos; non-fulfilment of the Treaty of Versailles and the impossibility of its fulfilment; non-payment of debts to the United States, *etc.*, *etc.* (*in greater detail*)|.

4. Therefore, Article One of the Cannes resolutions, by recognising the *equality* of the two *property systems* (capitalist or private property, and communist property, *so far* accepted only in the R.S.F.S.R.), is thus compelled

to recognise, even if only indirectly, the collapse, the bankruptcy of the first property system and the inevitability of its coming to an *agreement* with the second, on terms of equality.

5. The other articles of the Cannes terms, as well as the memoranda, etc., of the powers at Genoa, are in contradiction to this and are, therefore, still-born.

6. True equality of the two property systems—*if only as a temporary state, until such time as the entire world abandons* private property and the *economic chaos* and wars engendered by it for the higher property system—is found only in the Treaty of Rapallo.[110]

The All-Russia Central Executive Committee, therefore:

welcomes the Treaty of Rapallo as the only correct way out of the difficulties, chaos and danger of wars (as long as there remain two property systems, one of them as obsolete as capitalist property);

recognises *only* this type of treaty as normal for relations between the R.S.F.S.R. and capitalist countries;

instructs the Council of People's Commissars and the People's Commissariat of Foreign Affairs to pursue a policy along these lines;

instructs the Presidium of the All-Russia Central Executive Committee to confirm it by agreement with all republics that are in federal relations with the R.S.F.S.R.;

instructs the People's Commissariat of Foreign Affairs and the Council of People's Commissars to permit deviations from the Rapallo-type treaty only in exceptional circumstances that gain very special advantages for the working people of the R.S.F.S.R., etc.

Written on May 15 or 16, 1922
Published for the first time

Published according to
the manuscript

LETTER TO D. I. KURSKY

May 17, 1922

Comrade Kursky,

Further to our conversation, I herewith enclose the draft of an article supplementary to the Criminal Code.[111] It is a rough draft and, of course, needs altering and polishing up. The main idea will be clear, I hope, in spite of the faulty drafting—to put forward publicly a thesis that is correct in principle and politically (not only strictly juridical), which explains the *substance* of terror, its necessity and limits, and provides *justification* for it.

The courts must not ban terror—to promise that would be deception or self-deception—but must formulate the motives underlying it, legalise it as a principle, plainly, without any make-believe or embellishment. It must be formulated in the broadest possible manner, for only revolutionary law and revolutionary conscience can more or less widely determine the limits within which it should be applied.

With communist greetings,

Lenin

VARIANT 1.

Propaganda or agitation, or membership of, or assistance given to organisations the object of which (propaganda and agitation) is to assist that section of the international bourgeoisie which refuses to recognise the rights of the communist system of ownership that is superseding capitalism, and is striving to overthrow that system by violence, either by means of foreign intervention or blockade, or by espionage, financing the press, and similar means, is an offence punishable by death, which, if mitigating circumstances are proved, may be commuted to deprivation of liberty, or deportation.

VARIANT 2.

a) Propaganda or agitation that objectively serves (variant 2b) the interests of that section of the international bourgeoisie which, etc., to the end.

b) Persons convicted of belonging to, or assisting, such organisations, or persons who conduct activities of the aforesaid character (whose activities bear the aforesaid character), shall be liable to the same penalty.

> Variant 2b:
> serves
> or is likely
> to serve.

First published in 1924

Published according to
the manuscript

LETTERS TO J. V. STALIN
FOR MEMBERS OF THE POLITICAL BUREAU
OF THE C.C., R.C.P.(B.)
ON THE PROMOTION OF RADIO ENGINEERING

1

To Comrade Stalin with the request to pass this round to
all members of the Political Bureau

Comrade Stalin,

Appended are two reports. The first from Professor Osad-
chy, an expert on electricity, about radio-telegraph and
telephone communication; the second is from Bonch-Bruyevich (who is not related to the well-known Bonch-Bruyevich brothers, one of whom was the Executive Secretary
of the Council of People's Commissars, and the other an
outstanding tsarist general). This Bonch-Bruyevich, whose
report I append, is a prominent specialist and inventor
in radio engineering and one of the principal figures at the
Nizhni-Novgorod Radio Laboratory.

These reports show that it is technically quite feasible
to broadcast human speech over any distance by wireless;
furthermore, it is also possible to use many hundreds of
stations that could broadcast speeches, reports and lectures
delivered in Moscow to many hundreds of places throughout
the Republic, situated hundreds and, under certain conditions, thousands of versts away from Moscow.

I think that from the standpoint of propaganda and
agitation, especially for those masses of the population
who are illiterate, and also for broadcasting lectures, it
is absolutely necessary for us to carry out this plan. Con-

sidering the unfitness of most of the bourgeois professors of social sciences whom we are using and even the harm caused by them, we have no other way out than to enable our few communist professors, who are capable of delivering lectures on social sciences, to deliver these lectures for hundreds of localities in all parts of the Federation.

I am, therefore, of the opinion that under no circumstances should we stint funds to complete the organisation of wireless communication and produce efficiently working loudspeakers.

I propose that we pass a decision to allocate, as an extraordinary measure, a sum of up to 100,000 rubles from the gold fund over and above the estimate to organise the work at the Nizhni-Novgorod Radio Laboratory in order to accelerate to the maximum the completion of the work it has begun to instal efficient loudspeakers and many hundreds of stations throughout the Republic, which can repeat for the broad masses the speeches, reports and lectures delivered in Moscow or some other centre.

The Council of Labour and Defence must be instructed to organise special supervision over the expenditure of this fund and, perhaps, if it proves to be expedient, to institute bonuses from the above fund for specially rapid and successful work.

Let me add that today's *Izvestia* carries a report about an English invention in radio-telegraphy that transmits radio-telegrams secretly. If we managed to buy this invention, radio-telephone and radio-telegraph communication would be of further tremendous significance for military purposes.

May 19, 1922   *Lenin*

First published in
Pravda No. 21,
January 21, 1949

Dictated by telephone
Published according to
a typewritten copy

2

Comrade Stalin,

Re today's paper from Bonch-Bruyevich I think that we cannot finance the Radio Laboratory from the gold fund without special assignments.

I therefore propose instructing the Council of Labour and Defence to find out what expenditures are necessary to enable the Radio Laboratory to accelerate to the maximum the improvement and production of loudspeaking telephones and receivers. This is the only thing for which we should, in my opinion, allocate a definite sum of gold over and above the estimate.

May 19, 1922   *Lenin*

First published in 1945
in *Lenin Miscellany* XXXV

Dictated by telephone
Published according to
a typewritten copy

"DUAL" SUBORDINATION AND LEGALITY[112]

To Comrade Stalin for the Political Bureau

The question of the procuratorship has given rise to disagreement on the commission appointed by the Central Committee to direct the proceedings of the All-Russia Central Executive Committee session. If these disagreements do not cause this question to be brought before the Political Bureau automatically, I propose, in view of its extreme importance, that it be brought up in any case.

In substance, the point at issue is the following: On the question of the procuratorship, the majority of the commission elected by the All-Russia Central Executive Committee expressed opposition to the proposal that local procurators should be appointed solely by the central authority and be subordinate solely to the latter. The majority demands what is called "dual" subordination, the system that applies to all local officials, i.e., subordination to the central authority in the shape of the respective People's Commissariat, and also to the Gubernia Executive Committee.

The same majority of the commission of the All-Russia Central Executive Committee denies the right of local procurators to challenge the legality of decisions passed by gubernia executive committees, and by local authorities generally.

I cannot imagine on what grounds this obviously fallacious decision of the majority of the commission of the All-Russia Central Executive Committee can be justified. The only argument I have neard in support of it is that defence of "dual" subordination in this case means legitimate opposition to bureaucratic centralism, defending the necessary independence of the local authorities, and protecting the officials of the gubernia executive committees from high-handed conduct by the central authorities. Is there anything high-handed in the view that law cannot be Kaluga law or Kazan law, but that it must be uniform all-Russia law, and even uniform for the entire federation of Soviet Republics? The underlying fallacy of the view which has prevailed among the majority of the commission of the All-Russia Central Executive Committee is that they wrongly apply the principle of "dual" subordination. "Dual" subordination is needed where it is necessary to allow for a really inevitable difference. Agriculture in Kaluga Gubernia differs from that in Kazan Gubernia. The same thing can be said about industry; and it can be said about administration, or management, as a whole. Failure to make allowances for local differences in all these matters would mean slipping into bureaucratic centralism, and so forth. It would mean preventing the local authorities from giving proper consideration to specific local features, which is the basis of all rational administration. Nevertheless, the law must be uniform, and the root evil of our social life, and of our lack of culture, is our pandering to the ancient Russian view and semi-savage habit of mind, which wishes to preserve Kaluga law as distinct from Kazan law. It must be borne in mind that, unlike the administration authorities, the procurator has no administrative powers, and has no power to decide any question of administration. His rights and duties are reduced to one function, viz., to see that the law is really uniformly interpreted throughout the Republic, notwithstanding differences in local conditions, and in spite of all local influences. The only right and duty of the procurator is to take the matter before the court. What sort of court? Our courts are local courts. Our judges are elected by the local Soviets. Hence, the authority to which the procurator submits a case of infringement of the law is a local authority which, on the one hand, must strictly abide by the laws uniformly established for the whole Federation and, on the other hand, in determining the penalty, must take all local circumstances into consideration. And it has the right to say that although there has been a definite infringement of the law in a given case, nevertheless, certain circumstances, with which local people are closely familiar, and which come to light in the local court, compel the court to mitigate the penalty to which the culprit is liable, or even acquit him. Unless we strictly adhere to this most elementary condition for maintaining the uniformity of the law for the whole Federation, it will be utterly impossible to protect the law, or to develop any kind of culture.

Similarly, it is wrong in principle to argue that procurators should not have the right to challenge the decisions of gubernia executive committees, or of other local authorities; that legally the latter come under the jurisdiction of the Workers' and Peasants' Inspection.

The Workers' and Peasants' Inspection judges not only from the viewpoint of the law, but also from the viewpoint of expediency. The procurator must see to it that not a single decision passed by any local authority runs counter to the law, and only from this aspect is it his duty to challenge every illegal decision. He has no right to suspend such a decision; he must only take measures to secure that the interpretation of the law is absolutely uniform throughout the Republic. Hence, the decision of the majority of the commission of the All-Russia Central Executive Committee is not only utterly wrong in principle, it not only applies the principle of "dual" subordination in an utterly fallacious manner, but it also hinders all efforts to establish uniformity of the law and develop at least the minimum of culture.

Further, in deciding this question, it is necessary to take into account the weight of local influence. Undoubtedly, we are living amidst an ocean of illegality, and local influence is one of the greatest, if not the greatest obstacle to the establishment of law and culture. There is scarcely anyone who has not heard that the purging of the Party revealed the prevalence, in the majority of local purging committees, of personal spite and local strife in the process of purging the Party. This fact is incontrovertible, and significant. Scarcely anyone will dare deny that it is easier for the Party to find half a score of reliable Communists who possess an adequate legal education and are capable of resisting all purely local influences than to find hundreds of them. And this is precisely what the question boils down to in discussing whether procurators should be subject to "dual" subordination, or to subordination solely to the central authorities. At the centre we must find about half a score of men to exercise the functions of the central procurator authority represented by the Procurator General, the Supreme Tribunal, and the Collegium of the People's Commissariat of Justice (I leave aside the question as to whether the Procurator General should be the sole authority, or whether he should share his authority with the Supreme Tribunal and the Collegium of the People's Commissariat of Justice, for this is purely a secondary question, and can be settled, one way or another, in accordance with whether the Party will delegate vast authority to one person, or divide that authority among the three aforesaid bodies). These ten should work at the centre, under the closest supervision of and in closest contact with the three Party bodies which provide the most reliable barrier against local and personal influences, viz., the Organising Bureau of the Central Committee, the Political Bureau of the Central Committee, and the Central Control Commission. The latter body, i.e., the Central Control Commission, is responsible only to the Party Congress, and is constructed in such a way that no member of it can hold a position in any People's Commissariat, government department, or any organ of the Soviet government. It is clear that under these circumstances we have the greatest guarantee so far devised that the Party will set up a small central collegium that will be really capable of resisting local influences and local, and all other, bureaucracy, and which will establish real uniformity in the application of the laws throughout the Republic, and throughout the Federation. Hence, any mistake that this central legal collegium may make can be at once rectified on the spot by the Party bodies, which determine all the fundamental concepts and lay down all the fundamental rules for all our Party and Soviet activities throughout the Republic.

To depart from this would mean dragging in on the sly a view which nobody can defend openly and frankly, viz., that culture and law, which is its necessary concomitant, are so highly developed in our country that we can guarantee to find hundreds of absolutely irreproachable procurators capable of resisting all local influences, and of establishing uniformity of the law throughout the Republic by their own efforts.

To sum up, I draw the conclusion that to defend the "dual" subordination of procurators, and to deprive them of the right to challenge any decision passed by the local authorities, is not only wrong in principle, not only hinders our fundamental task of constantly introducing respect for the law, but is also an expression of the interests and prejudices of local bureaucrats and local influences, i.e., the most pernicious wall that stands between the working people and the local and central Soviet authorities, as well as the central authority of the Russian Communist Party.

I therefore propose that the Central Committee should reject "dual" subordination in this matter, establish the subordination of local procurators solely to the *central authority*, and allow the procurator to retain the right and duty to challenge the legality of any decision or order passed by the local authorities with the proviso, however, that he shall have no right to suspend such decisions; he shall only have the right to bring them before the courts.

Lenin

Dictated by telephone
on May 20, 1922

First published
in *Pravda* No. 91,
April 23, 1925

Published according to
the stenographer's notes
(typewritten copy

A FLY IN THE OINTMENT

Citizen O. A. Yermansky has written a very good, useful book: *The Taylor System and the Scientific Organisation of Labour* (Gosizdat, 1922). It is a revised edition of his book, *The Taylor System*, which first appeared in 1918. The book has been substantially enlarged; very important supplements have been added: I. "Productive Labour and Culture"; II. "The Problem of Fatigue". One of the most important sections, earlier entitled "Labour and Leisure", only 16 pages long, has now been enlarged to 70 pages (Chapter III: "Human Labour").

The book gives a detailed exposition of the Taylor system and, this is especially important, both its positive and *negative aspects*, and also the principal scientific data on the physiological intake and output in the human machine. On the whole the book is quite suitable, I think, as a standard textbook for all trade union schools and for all secondary schools in general. To learn how to work is now the main, the truly national task of the Soviet Republic. Our primary and most important task is to attain universal literacy, but we should in no circumstances limit ourselves to this target. We must at all costs go beyond it and adopt everything that is truly valuable in European and American science.

Citizen Yermansky's book has one serious flaw which may make it unacceptable as a textbook. It is the author's verbosity. He repeats the same thing again and again without any conceivable need. I suppose the author may be vindicated to some extent by the fact that he was not trying to write a textbook. However, he says on p. VIII that he regards the popular exposition of scientific questions as one of the merits of his book. He is right. But popular exposition should also shun repetition. The people have no time to waste on bulky volumes. Without good reason, Citizen Yermansky's book is much too bulky. That is what prevents it from being a popular book....*

Written after
September 10, 1922
First published in 1928

Published according to
the manuscript

---

* Here the manuscript breaks off.—*Ed.*

LETTER TO THE FIFTH ALL-RUSSIA CONGRESS OF TRADE UNIONS[113]

September 17, 1922

Dear Comrades,

This is the first time since my long illness that I am able to address a Congress, even though in writing. Permit me, therefore, to confine myself to expressing to you my cordial greetings, and to a few brief remarks on the position and tasks of our industry and of our Republic. Our position is particularly difficult because we lack the means to restore our fixed assets, i.e., machinery, tools, buildings, etc.; and it is precisely that part of industry known as heavy industry which is the main basis of socialism. In capitalist countries these fixed assets are usually restored by means of loans. We are refused loans until we restore the property of the capitalists and landowners; but this we cannot and will not do. The only road open to us is the long and extremely arduous road of slowly accumulating our savings, of raising taxes in order to be able gradually to repair our destroyed railways, machinery, buildings, etc. So far, we are the only country in the world in which the working peasants, under the leadership of the workers, are building socialism, flatly rejecting the leadership of the bourgeoisie who, under cover of florid phrases about democracy, liberty, etc., are actually consolidating the private ownership of the capitalists and landowners and establishing the rule of a handful of rich men who have divided the entire globe among themselves and are fighting one another for its redivision, for the enslavement of hundreds of millions of people in the weaker and more backward nations.

As long as we remain in the field alone the task of restoring our economy will be an extremely heavy burden on our shoulders. All the peasants and all the workers will have to exert themselves to the very utmost; our machinery of state, which is still working very inefficiently, must be improved and made less costly so that we may improve the conditions of the working people, and, to some extent at least, restore our economy, which was destroyed by the imperialist and civil wars.

Let every politically conscious peasant and worker who may become despondent over our hard conditions of life, or over the extremely slow progress of our work of state construction, remember the recent past, when the capitalists and landowners were in power. This will give him new zest in his work. The only way to save the workers' and peasants' rule is to make every effort to intensify and improve our work in all fields.

With comradely greetings,

V. Ulyanov (Lenin)

Published in *Trud* on
September 18, 1922
and in *Pravda* No. 210
on September 19, 1922

Published according to
the manuscript

MEMO TO THE POLITICAL BUREAU ON COMBATING DOMINANT NATION CHAUVINISM

I declare war to the death on dominant nation chauvinism. I shall eat it with all my healthy teeth as soon as I get rid of this accursed bad tooth.

It must be *absolutely* insisted that the Union Central Executive Committee should be *presided over* in turn by a
Russian,
Ukrainian,
Georgian, etc.
Absolutely!

Yours,
Lenin

Written on October 6, 1922

First published in *Pravda*
No. 21 on January 21, 1937

Published according to
the manuscript

TO THE WORKERS OF BAKU

Moscow, October 6, 1922

Dear Comrades,

I have just heard Comrade Serebrovsky's brief report on the situation in the Azerbaijan oilfields. The difficulties of the situation are by no means small. I send you my cordial greetings and urge you to do all you can to hold on for the immediate future. Things are always particularly difficult at first. Later on it will be easier. We must win, and we shall do so at all costs.

Once more, my most cordial communist greetings.

V. Ulyanov (Lenin)

Published in *Bakinsky Rabochy*
No. 251, November 7, 1922

Published according to
the manuscript

TO THE FIFTH CONGRESS OF THE YOUNG
COMMUNIST LEAGUE OF RUSSIA[114]

Dear Friends,

I regret very much that I am unable to greet you in person. I wish your Fifth Congress every success in its work. I am convinced that the youth will make such good progress that when the next stage of the world revolution approaches they will be fully capable of coping with their tasks.

With cordial communist greetings,

V. Ulyanov (Lenin)

October 11, 1922

Pravda No. 230,
October 12, 1922

Published according to
the manuscript

LETTER TO J. V. STALIN FOR MEMBERS OF THE C.C., R.C.P.(B.) RE THE FOREIGN TRADE MONOPOLY[115]

To Comrade Stalin, Secretary of the C.C.

October 13, 1922

The decision of the Plenary Meeting of the C.C. of October 6 (Minutes No. 7, Point 3) institutes what seems to be an unimportant, partial reform: "implement a number of separate decisions of the Council of Labour and Defence on temporary permission for the import and export of individual categories of goods or on granting the permission for specific frontiers".

In actual fact, however, this wrecks the foreign trade monopoly. Small wonder that Comrade Sokolnikov has been trying to get this done and has succeeded. He has always been for it; he likes paradoxes and has always undertaken to prove that monopoly is not to our advantage. But it is surprising that people, who in principle favour the monopoly, have voted for this without asking for detailed information from any of the business executives.

What does the decision that has been adopted signify?

Purchasing offices are being opened for the import and export trade. The owner of such an office has the right to buy and sell *only* specially listed goods.

Where is the control over this? Where are the means of control?

In Russia flax costs 4 rubles 50 kopeks, in Britain it costs 14 rubles. All of us have read in *Capital* how capitalism changes internally and grows more daring when interest rates and profits rise quickly. All of us recall that capitalism is capable of taking deadly risks and that Marx recognised this long before the war and before capitalism began its "leaps".

What is the situation now? What force is capable of holding the peasants and the traders from extremely profitable deals? Cover Russia with a network of overseers? Catch the neighbour in a purchasing office and prove that his flax has been sold to be smuggled out of the country?

Comrade Sokolnikov's paradoxes are always clever, but one must distinguish between paradoxes and the grim truth.

No "legality" on such a question is at all possible in the Russian countryside. No comparison with smuggling in general ("All the same," they say, "smuggling is also flourishing in spite of the monopoly") is in any way correct; it is one thing to deal with the professional smuggler on the frontier and another with *all* the peasantry, who will *all* defend themselves and fight the authorities when they try to deprive them of the profit "belonging to them".

Before we have had an opportunity to test the monopoly system, which is only just beginning to bring us millions (and will give us tens of millions and more), we are introducing complete chaos; we are shaking loose the very supports that we have only just begun to strengthen.

We have begun to build up a system; the foreign trade monopoly and the co-operatives are both only in the process of being built up. Some results will be forthcoming in a year or two. The profit from foreign trade runs into hundreds per cent, and we are *beginning* to receive millions and tens of millions. We have *begun* to build up mixed companies; we have begun to learn to receive *half* of their (monstrous) profits. We can already see signs of very substantial state profits. We are giving this up in the hope of duties which cannot yield any comparable profit; we are giving everything up and chasing a spectre!

The question was brought up at the Plenary Meeting hastily. There was no serious discussion worth mentioning. We have no reason for haste. Our business executives are only just beginning to go into things. Is there anything like a correct approach to the matter when major questions of trade policy are decided in a slapdash manner, without collecting the pertinent material, without weighing the *pros* and *cons* with documents and figures? Tired people vote in a few minutes and that's the end of it. We have weighed less complicated political questions over and over again and frequently it took us several months to reach a decision.

I regret it very much that illness prevented me from attending the meeting on that day and that I am now compelled to seek an exception to the rule.

But I think that the question must be weighed and studied, that haste is harmful.

I propose that the decision on this question be deferred for two months, i.e., until the next Plenary Meeting; in the interim information and verified *documents* on the experience of our trade policy should be collected.

V. Ulyanov (Lenin)

P.S. In the conversation I had with Comrade Stalin yesterday (I did not attend the Plenary Meeting and tried to get my information from the comrades who were there), we spoke, incidentally, of the proposal temporarily to open the Petrograd and Novorossiisk ports. It seems to me that both examples show the extreme danger of such experiments even for a most restricted list of goods. The opening of the Petrograd port would intensify the smuggling of flax across the Finnish frontier to prodigious proportions. Instead of combating professional smugglers we shall have to combat *all the peasantry* of the flax-growing region. In this fight we shall almost assuredly be beaten, and beaten irreparably. The opening of the Novorossiisk port would quickly drain us of surplus grain. Is this a cautious policy at a time when our reserves for war are small? When a series of systematic measures to increase them have not yet had time to show results?

Then the following should be given consideration. The foreign trade monopoly has started a stream of gold into Russia. It is only just becoming possible to calculate; the first trip of such-and-such a merchant to Russia for six months has given him, say, hundreds per cent of profit; he increases his price for this right from 25 to 50 per cent in favour of the Commissariat of Foreign Trade. Further-

more, it has become possible for us to learn and to *increase*
this profit. Everything will at once collapse, the whole
work will stop, because if here and there various ports are
opened for a time, *not a single merchant will pay a penny
for this kind of "monopoly"*. That is obvious. Before taking
such a risk things have to be thought over and weighed
several times. Besides there is the political risk of letting
through not foreign merchants by name, which we check,
but the entire petty bourgeoisie in general.

With the start of foreign trade we have begun to reckon
on an influx of gold. I see no other settlement except for
a liquor monopoly, but here there are very serious moral
considerations, and also some business-like objections from
Sokolnikov.

Lenin

P.P.S. I have just been informed (1.30 hours) that some
business executives have applied for a postponement. I
have not yet read this application, but I whole-heartedly
support it. It is only a matter of two months.

Lenin

Published for the first time
according to the manuscript

TO THE ALL-RUSSIA CONGRESS
OF FINANCIAL WORKERS[116]

Dear Comrades,

The strengthening of Soviet finances is one of the most difficult problems before us; but at present it stands in the forefront, and unless it is solved it will be impossible to make any considerable progress either in safeguarding the independence of Soviet Russia from international capital or in developing our industry and culture. Our financial organisations must do their utmost to collect the taxes as quickly as possible and thereby ensure the resources that the workers' and peasants' state needs to enable all the organs of state power to function properly.

I greet the All-Russia Congress of Financial Workers and express the firm conviction that in the building up of our finances you will justify the hopes placed in you by the masses of the working people of Soviet Russia.

V. Ulyanov (Lenin)

October 20, 1922

Pravda No. 240,
October 24, 1922

Published according to
the *Pravda* text

TO THE SOCIETY OF FRIENDS OF SOVIET RUSSIA (IN THE UNITED STATES)[117]

October 20, 1922

Dear Comrades,

I have just verified by special inquiry to the Perm Gubernia Executive Committee the extremely favourable information that was published in our newspapers about the work of the members of your Society, headed by Harold Ware, with the tractor team at the Toikino State Farm, Perm Gubernia.

In spite of the immense difficulties, particularly in view of the extreme remoteness of that locality from the centre, and also the devastation caused by Kolchak during the Civil War, you have achieved successes that must be regarded as truly outstanding.

I hasten to express to you my profound gratitude and to ask you to publish this in your Society's journal, and, if possible, in the general press of the United States.

I am sending a recommendation to the Presidium of the All-Russia Central Executive Committee that it should recognise this state farm as a model farm, and render it special and extraordinary assistance in building and also in supplying petrol, metal, and other materials necessary for a repair shop.

Once again on behalf of our Republic I express to you our profound gratitude, and ask you to bear in mind that no form of assistance is as timely and as important for us as that which you are rendering.

Lenin,
Chairman of the Council of People's Commissars

Pravda No. 240,
October 24, 1922

Published according to
the *Pravda* text

TO THE SOCIETY FOR TECHNICAL AID
FOR SOVIET RUSSIA[118]

October 20, 1922

Dear Comrades,

Extremely favourable information has appeared in our press about the work of members of your Society at the state farms in Kirsanov Uyezd, Tambov Gubernia, and at Mitino Station, Odessa Gubernia, and also about the work of the group of miners in the Donets Basin.

In spite of the enormous difficulties, and particularly in view of the devastation caused by the Civil War, you have achieved successes that must be regarded as outstanding.

I hasten to express to you my profound gratitude and to ask you to publish this in your Society's journal, and, if possible, in the general press in the United States.

I am sending a recommendation to the Presidium of the All-Russia Central Executive Committee that it should recognise the most successful farms as model farms, and render them the special and extraordinary assistance necessary for the successful promotion of their work.

Once again on behalf of our Republic I express to you our profound gratitude, and ask you to bear in mind that the work you are doing to cultivate land with the aid of tractors is particularly timely and important for us.

It gives me particular satisfaction to be able to congratulate you on your proposal to organise 200 agricultural communes.

Lenin,
Chairman of the Council of People's Commissars

Pravda No. 240,
October 24, 1922

Published according to
the *Pravda* text

GREETINGS TO THE LIBERATED PRIMORYE TERRITORY[119]

To the Chairman of the Council of Ministers of the Far Eastern Republic, Chita[120]

On the fifth anniversary of the victorious October Revolution the Red Army has taken another decisive step towards completely clearing the territory of the R.S.F.S.R. and of its allied republics of foreign troops of occupation. The capture of Vladivostok by the People's Revolutionary Army of the Far Eastern Republic unites with the masses of the working people of Russia the Russian citizens who have borne the heavy yoke of Japanese imperialism. I congratulate all the working people of Russia and our valiant Red Army on this new victory, and I request the Government of the Far Eastern Republic to convey to all the workers and peasants in the liberated regions, and in Vladivostok, the greetings of the Council of People's Commissars of the R.S.F.S.R.

V. Ulyanov (*Lenin*),
Chairman of the Council of People's
Commissars of the R.S.F.S.R.

Moscow, October 26, 1922

Pravda No. 243,
October 27, 1922

Published according to
the *Pravda* text

INTERVIEW GIVEN TO MICHAEL FARBMAN, *OBSERVER* AND *MANCHESTER GUARDIAN* CORRESPONDENT

1. *Question.* The anti-Russian press describes Herriot's reception in Moscow and the Franco-Russian negotiations as a definite change in Soviet Russia's foreign policy.

Is that true? Is it true that Russia regards British policy in the Middle East as a challenge and is ready to conclude an agreement with France directed against Britain?

Answer. I consider it absolutely incorrect to describe Herriot's reception in Moscow and the Franco-Russian negotiations as a change, even a slight one, in Soviet Russia's policy in general, or as being anti-British in particular.[121] We certainly value very highly both Herriot's reception in Moscow and the step taken towards a rapprochement with France or towards negotiations with her, which have now become possible, probable and, I should like to believe, essential. Any rapprochement with France is something we very much desire, especially in view of the fact that Russia's commercial interests imperatively demand closer relations with this strong continental power. But we are convinced that this rapprochement does not in the least imply that some change must necessarily take place in our policy towards Britain. We believe fully friendly relations with both powers to be quite possible, and that is our aim. We believe that the development of commercial relations will inevitably go a very long way towards achieving this aim. We believe that the interests of Britain and France, rightly understood, will likewise operate in that direction. We believe that the mutual interests of both Britain and France, insofar as they have points of contact

with Russia, do not under any circumstances contain elements of inevitable hostility between Britain and France.
On the contrary, we even think that peaceful and friendly
relations between these powers and Russia are a guarantee
(I am almost prepared to say—the strongest guarantee)
that peace and friendship between Britain and France will
last a long time, and that all possible, and under present
circumstances probable, differences between France and
Britain will most speedily and truly find a happy solution.

2. *Question*. Is not the virtual termination of the Greco-Turkish
War, a war supported by Britain, an opportune moment for the conclusion of an Anglo-Russian agreement?

Answer. Of course, the termination of the Greco-Turkish
War, which had Britain's support, is a factor that, to a
certain extent, improves the chances of an Anglo-Russian
agreement being concluded. We looked for such an agreement even before that war ended and shall now continue to
seek it with the utmost energy. True, some of the problems
connected with the termination of that war are objects
of our disagreement with Britain. But, first of all, the peace
which has followed the Greco-Turkish War is in our opinion
such an advantage to international politics as a whole that
we hope for an improvement in the general conditions under
which they are conducted, thanks to the Greco-Turkish
peace. Secondly, we do not consider the differences between
Britain and ourselves to be in any way insurmountable.
On the contrary, we expect that, with the Middle
East problem entering various stages, the near future will
show us to what extent we are right in hoping that the end
of the Greco-Turkish War will also be the end of the conflicts and differences which placed that war in the forefront
of international politics. We are doing everything in our
power to make the end of that war also the end of all friction
and disagreement with Britain, and we hope that the
interests of the British Government will rise on this occasion,
too, above any promptings and the frequently insincere
utterances of the anti-Russian press.

3. *Question*. Do you consider Russia's participation in the eastern
question a matter of prestige alone, or do you proceed **exclusively**
from Russia's real interests? Does the Russian Government agree

to the French proposal to permit Russia's participation in only that part of the Conference that will decide the question of the Straits?

Answer. I consider Russia's participation in the settlement of the Middle East question[122] to have nothing to do with prestige. I hope that our international politics as a whole over a period of five years have shown completely that we are quite indifferent to questions of prestige and that we are incapable of putting forward any demand whatsoever or of worsening the real chances of peace between states solely on account of prestige. I am confident that in no other country are the masses so indifferent to prestige and even so prepared to treat the question of prestige as such with happy ridicule. We are of the opinion that modern diplomacy will rapidly come to regard questions of prestige precisely in this way.

Our Middle East policy is a matter of Russia's most real, immediate and vital interest and of the interest of a number of states federated with her. If all these states did not succeed in getting their demand to participate in the Middle East Conference satisfied, there would remain a huge mass of elements of hostility, conflict and discontent; their non-participation would involve such difficulties in purely commercial affairs between Eastern Europe on the one hand, and all other states on the other, that either there would remain no grounds whatever for peaceful coexistence or that such existence would be extraordinarily difficult.

The Russian Government, therefore, is not satisfied with the proposal from Paris to allow Russia to participate only in that part of the Conference which will settle the problem of the Straits. We are of the opinion that such a limitation would inevitably lead to a number of very practical, immediate inconveniences, in particular economic inconveniences, from which France and Britain would themselves suffer, most probably in the near future.

4. *Question.* What is the Russian programme for the solution of the Straits problem?

Answer. Our Straits programme (still only approximate, of course) contains, among other things, the following:

First, the satisfaction of Turkey's national aspirations.

We consider this essential, and not only in the interests of national independence. Our five years' experience in settling the national question in a country that contains a tremendous number of nationalities such as could hardly be found in any other country, gives us the full conviction that under such circumstances the only correct attitude to the interests of nations is to meet those interests in full and provide conditions that exclude any possibility of conflicts on that score. Our experience has left us with the firm conviction that only exclusive attention to the interests of various nations can remove grounds for conflicts, can remove mutual mistrust, can remove the fear of any intrigues and create that confidence, especially on the part of workers and peasants speaking different languages, without which there absolutely cannot be peaceful relations between peoples or anything like a successful development of everything that is of value in present-day civilisation.

Secondly, our programme includes the closing of the Straits to all warships in times of peace and of war. This is in the direct commercial interests of all powers, not only of those whose territory is in the immediate vicinity of the Straits, but of all others, too. It must be remembered that all over the world there has been an inordinate amount of pacifist talk, an unusual number of pacifist phrases and assurances, and even vows against war and against peace,[123] although there is usually little preparedness on the part of the majority of states, especially on the part of the modern civilised states, to take any realistic steps, even the most simple, to ensure peace. On this, and on similar questions, we should like to see a minimum of general assurances, solemn promises and grandiloquent formulas, and the greatest possible number of the simplest and most obvious decisions and measures that would certainly lead to peace, if not to the complete elimination of the war danger.

Thirdly, our programme on the Straits includes complete freedom of commerce by sea. After what I have said above I do not think it at all necessary to explain this point or make it more concrete.

5. *Question*. Would the Russian Government agree to the League of Nations controlling the Straits if the League were to include in

its composition Russia, Turkey, Germany and the United States?

Or would Russia insist on the establishment of a special commission to control the Straits?

Answer. We are, of course, opposed to the League of Nations, and I do not think that it is only our economic and political system with its specific features that accounts for our negative attitude towards the League; the interests of peace, regarded from the point of view of the concrete conditions of modern international politics in general, also fully justify that negative attitude. The League of Nations bears so many marks of its world war origin, it is so intimately bound up with the Versailles Treaty and is so marked by the absence of anything resembling the establishment of the real equality of rights between nations, anything resembling a real chance of their peaceful coexistence, that I think our negative attitude to the League can be appreciated and does not stand in need of further comment.

6. *Question.* Does the refusal to ratify the agreement with Urquhart mean a victory of the "Left Communists"? What are the objective conditions which would make possible a resumption of negotiations and the ratification of the agreement with Urquhart?

Answer. The question of concluding an agreement with Urquhart[124] was raised by our government when I was ill and was unable to take part in affairs of state. Therefore I am not yet fully informed of all the details of this matter. Nevertheless I can assert quite definitely that there is not, nor can there now be, any question of a victory for the Left Communists. I know this from my direct observation of the course of government affairs.

The fact of the matter is that Britain's act of injustice, expressed in her unwillingness to admit us to the Conference, was so unexpected, aroused such indignation in Russia and so firmly united not only the Right with the Left Communists but also united the huge mass of the non-Party population of Russia, the workers and peasants, that things did not and could not reach the point of disagreement between the Left and Right Communists.

The reason given for our rejection of the Urquhart agreement was a direct expression, one may say, not only of the general Party sentiment but of that of the entire people, i.e., the sentiment of the entire mass of the workers and peasants.

The resumption of negotiations and the subsequent ratification of an agreement with Urquhart depend primarily on the elimination of the flagrant injustices committed against Russia by Britain in curtailing her right to participate in the Middle East Conference. As far as the concrete terms submitted to us by Urquhart are concerned, I have not yet had time to look into this matter in sufficient detail, and can only say that the government has decided to let the supporters and opponents of this agreement have their say in our press as soon as possible, in order to obtain, from the most objective and motivated discussion, material for the overall verification of all the pros and cons and for a decision on the issue in a manner that best accords with Russia's interests.

7. *Question.* To what extent are the accusations of the anti-Russian press in Britain justified when they assert that the recent arrests of industrialists in Moscow signify the end of the New Economic Policy and a reversion to the policy of nationalisation and confiscation?

Answer. As to your question concerning the accusations made against us in the British anti-Russian press that "Moscow industrialists" were being arrested, I must say that I have today just read in our newspaper (*Izvestia*) an item headed "Arrests of Black Marketeers". None other than Comrade Z. B. Katsnelson, chief of the Economic Division of the State Political Administration, tells us in this article that there was no question of arrests of industrialists, and that "rumours circulated by enemies of Soviet power, both within the R.S.F.S.R. and abroad, that the arrests are infringements on the freedom to trade are actually nothing but *nonsensical* inventions that have the definite counter-revolutionary intent of disrupting the economic relations that are being established with Western Europe".

Indeed, those arrested were exclusively profiteers on the so-called black market and our authorities are in possession of evidence establishing connection between these black-market currency profiteers and certain employees of foreign missions in Moscow. This evidence shows not only the sale of platinum and of gold bars but also the *organisation of contraband shipments of these valuables abroad.*

From this you can see how absolutely unfounded are the rumours that we are putting an end to the New Economic Policy and how utterly false are the accusations made by the anti-Russian press in Britain, which is trying by the most unheard-of distortion and deception to present our policy in a false light. Actually, there has never been any mention in any government circles whatsoever of discontinuing the New Economic Policy and returning to the old. Incidentally, the whole work of the government during the session of the All-Russia Central Executive Committee now in progress is aimed at obtaining the widest possible legislative sanction for what is known as the New Economic Policy, so as to eliminate all possibility of any deviation from it.

October 27, 1922

Pravda No. 254,
November 10, 1922

Published according to
a typewritten copy
corrected by Lenin

SPEECH AT THE FOURTH SESSION
OF THE ALL-RUSSIA
CENTRAL EXECUTIVE COMMITTEE,
NINTH CONVOCATION
OCTOBER 31, 1922[125]

(*Stormy, prolonged applause. All rise.*) Comrades, permit me to confine myself to a few words of greeting. We should first of all, of course, send our greetings to the Red Army, which has recently given further proof of its valour by capturing Vladivostok and clearing the entire territory of the last of the republics linked with Soviet Russia. I am sure that I am expressing the general opinion when I say that we all welcome this new feat of the Red Army, and also the fact that apparently a very important step has been taken towards bringing the war to a close; the last of the whiteguard forces have been driven into the sea. (*Applause.*) I think that our Red Army has rid us for a long time of the possibility of another whiteguard attack on Russia or on any of the republics that are directly or indirectly, closely or more or less remotely, connected with us.

At the same time, however, in order to avoid adopting a tone of inordinate self-adulation, we must say that the strength of the Red Army and its recent victory were not the only factors in this; other factors were the international situation and our diplomacy.

Some time ago Japan and the United States signed a pact to support Kolchak. But that was so long ago that many people have probably forgotten it completely. But that was the case. We have made such pacts impossible now, and, due to our efforts, the Japanese, in spite of their military strength, declared that they would withdraw, and have kept their promise; our diplomacy must also be given credit for this. I shall not drag out my brief greeting by saying what brought us that success. I shall only say that in the near future our diplomats will once again have to display their skill in a matter of immense importance, and one in which we are vitally interested. I have in mind the Middle East Conference that Great Britain is convening in Lausanne on November 13. I am sure that there, too, our diplomats will prove their mettle, and that we shall be able to vindicate the interests of all our federated republics, and of the R.S.F.S.R. At all events, we shall succeed in revealing to the masses where and what the obstacle is, and to what extent it is an obstacle to the legitimate desires and aspirations not only of ourselves, but of all countries interested in the question of the Straits.

I shall limit my utterances on foreign politics to these brief remarks and shall now deal with the proceedings of this session.

I think that here we have achieved no small success in spite of the fact that to some people the questions dealt with may at first sight appear to be not so very important. Take the first code of laws that you have already passed— the Code of Labour Laws. Our adoption of a code of laws which firmly lays down the principles of labour legislation such as the eight-hour day at a time when in all other countries the working class is being heavily attacked is a tremendous achievement for Soviet rule. True, there are people who, perhaps, would desire something more from this code; but I think that such a desire would be totally unjustified.

We must bear in mind that compared with all the countries where fierce capitalist competition is raging, where there are millions and tens of millions of unemployed, and where the capitalists are forming vast combinations and are launching an offensive against the working class—if we compare ourselves with those countries, we are the least cultured, our productivity of labour is the lowest, and we are the least efficient. This is, I would say, a very unpleasant thing to have to admit. I think, however, that precisely because we do not disguise such things with platitudes and stereotyped catchwords, but candidly admit them, precisely because we all admit, and are not afraid to proclaim from this rostrum, that we are exerting more efforts than any other country to rectify all this, we shall succeed in catching up with these countries faster than they ever dreamed possible.

This will not be done at a fantastic speed, of course, it will naturally take us several years of laborious effort to achieve it. It goes without saying that nothing can be done overnight. We have been in existence for five years, we have seen at what speed social relations change, and have learned to appreciate what time means; and we must go on learning what it means. Nobody believes that any important change can be achieved at a fantastic speed; but we do believe in real speed, speed compared with the rate of development in any period in history you like to take—especially if progress is guided by a genuinely revolutionary party; and this speed we shall achieve at all costs.

I will now touch upon the Land Code that you have passed. You are aware that in the very first days after the famous 25th of October, 1917, our laws, unlike any other laws, propounded a land principle[126] which, though very imperfect from the technical and perhaps also from the juridical point of view, nevertheless, provided the peasants with all that was vital and essential for them, and ensured their alliance with the workers. From that time onwards, difficult as it has been for us to pull through these five years of continuous war, we have never relaxed our efforts to satisfy to the utmost the peasants' desire for land. And if it turns out that the law which you have just passed also needs amending in some way or other, we shall adopt such amendments and improvements as readily as you have just adopted amendments and improvements to our Criminal Code. We regard the land question, the question of improving the living conditions of the peasants, who constitute the overwhelming majority of the population, as one of fundamental importance. In this respect we have already succeeded in convincing the Russian peasants that in our supreme legislative body every proposal to change the old laws will always meet, not with opposition, but with the most favourable consideration and support.

You have also had before you for your consideration the Civil Code and the Law on the Judicial System. You know that in the light of the policy which we have firmly adopted, and concerning which there can be no wavering in our ranks, this is a most important question for the vast masses of the population. You know also that here, too, we have tried to maintain the dividing line between what can satisfy the ordinary citizen's legitimate needs in present-day economic conditions, and what is abuse of the New Economic Policy—the things that are legal in all other countries, but which we do not want to legalise. The future will show to what extent the amendments you have approved of and adopted specifically for this purpose are effective. We shall leave ourselves a perfectly free hand in this matter. If everyday experience reveals abuses which we have not foreseen, we shall forthwith introduce the necessary amendments. As far as this is concerned, you are all well aware, of course, that, unfortunately, no other country can as yet vie with us in the speed with which we legislate. We shall see whether events in the near future will not compel them to try to catch up with Soviet Russia a little in this matter.

Further, I must speak about another important matter that you have finally settled here, and that is the question of the local congresses of Soviets and of the gubernia executive committees. This is a question that was always kept in the background under all previous legislative systems and in all constitutions. It was regarded as a matter of no importance; the opinion was that the local government bodies could continue to follow the old rut. We are of a contrary opinion. We are convinced that the successes our revolution has achieved are due to our having always devoted most of our attention to the local government bodies and to local experiences. The revolution of October 1917 at one stroke achieved such successes that it seemed to us in the spring of 1918 that the war had drawn to a close— actually, it had only just started in its worst form, the form of civil war; actually, peace with the Germans meant that they assisted the worst elements in the Civil War; actually, the peace treaty we then signed with the Germans and which collapsed in the autumn, in many cases meant

that assistance was given to these worst elements by the
Allied Powers who blamed us for concluding peace with
the Germans—and, I say, our revolution accomplished its
task so quickly in a few months, a few weeks even, because
we relied entirely on the forces in the localities, we gave
them full scope for their activities, and we looked to the
localities for the enthusiasm that made our revolution
swift and invincible. I am aware that since then our
localities have undergone many different perturbations, so
to say. The problem of the relations between the localities
and the centre has been one of no little difficulty, and I
do not want to suggest that we have always found the ideal
solution for it. Considering our general level of culture,
it was useless dreaming of an ideal solution. But we may
confidently say that we have solved it more sincerely,
justly and durably than it has been solved in any other
country.

In conclusion I shall touch only upon one other question
that particularly interests me, and which, I think, should
interest you, although officially it does not appear either
on your agenda or in the list of questions. This is the question of our machinery of state; an old and eternally new
question.

In August 1918 we took a census of public officials in
Moscow. We obtained a total of 231,000 state and Soviet
employees; this figure covered the number employed both in
central government offices and in the local, Moscow munic-
ipal offices. Recently, in October 1922, we took another
census in the belief that we had cut down these inflated
staffs and that they would certainly be smaller. The figure
obtained, however, was 243,000. This, then, was the result
of all the reductions of staffs that we carried through. A
great deal of effort will still have to be spent on investigating
and comparing these figures. When we took the first census
in 1918, in the first flush of reforms, we, to put it bluntly,
could make next to nothing of the returns. We had no time
for that sort of thing. The Civil War did not leave us a
minute to spare. Now, however, we hope that this work will be
done. We are convinced that our machinery of state, which
suffers from many defects, is inflated to far more than twice
the size we need, and often works not for us, but against

us—we need not be afraid to admit this truth even from the rostrum of the supreme legislative body of our Republic —we are convinced that this machinery of state will be improved. Much effort and skill will be required to improve it. We have made a beginning in the serious study of the problem of how to improve it, but this is only a beginning—a few essays and material from local research. If we all leave this session determined to devote more attention to this problem than we have done up to now, determined to spend less time on bustle and fuss—and all too often we spend a vast amount of time on this—if we really make a thorough study of our machinery of state and work for a number of years to improve it, that will be a great asset and a guarantee of success. We must have the courage to say that up to now we have built up our machinery of state spontaneously. Our best workers undertook the most arduous duties in both the civil and military fields, and very often they went about them in the wrong way, but they learned to rectify their mistakes and get things done. The proportion of these, perhaps, scores of courageous men and women, relative to the hundreds of those who sabotaged—or half-sabotaged, floundering among their voluminous papers— this proportion was very often such that our vital affairs became submerged in a deluge of paper. We have not been able to study this question up to now, but henceforth we must study it in the most comprehensive manner. This will take years and years; we shall have to study hard for years, for the cultural standard of our workers is low, they find it difficult to undertake the new tasks of production, but it is only on their sincerity and enthusiasm that we can rely. It will take us years and years to secure an improvement in our machinery of state, to raise it—not merely individuals, but as a whole—to a higher cultural level. I am sure that if we continue to devote our efforts to such work, we shall certainly and inevitably achieve better and better results. (*Prolonged applause.*)

Pravda No. 247,
November 1, 1922

Published according to
the *Pravda* text
checked with the verbatim report

TO *PETROGRADSKAYA PRAVDA*[127]

November 1, 1922

Dear Comrades,

I greet you from the bottom of my heart on the occasion of the fifth anniversary of the October Revolution and wish that during the next five years our fight on the peace front will be as successful as it has been hitherto on the war front.

With best greetings and wishes,
Yours,

V. Ulyanov (Lenin)

Petrogradskaya Pravda No. 251, November 5, 1922

Published according to the manuscript

TO *PRAVDA*

Dear Comrades,

I cordially greet you on the occasion of the fifth anniversary of the October Revolution. My desire is that we should in the next five years gain by peaceful efforts no less than we have gained up to now by force of arms.

November 2, 1922

Yours,
Lenin

Pravda No. 252,
November 7, 1922

Published according to
the manuscript

TO THE FIRST INTERNATIONAL CONFERENCE OF COMMUNIST CO-OPERATORS[128]

I welcome the very timely convocation of the International Conference of Communist Co-operators and wish you every success in your work.

Like the delegates at the conference, I fully appreciate the complexity and difficulty of the task you have undertaken, that of capturing the machinery of the co-operative movement in order to further the world revolution.

I shall be very glad if the experience we have gained in our work in Russia can be of use to the common cause.

Written on November 2, 1922

Published in *Pravda* No. 249,
November 3, 1922

Published according to
the newspaper text

TO THE ALL-RUSSIA CONGRESS OF STATISTICIANS[129]

November 4, 1922

From the bottom of my heart I thank you for your message of greetings and ask you to accept my gratitude and best wishes for success in your work.

V. Ulyanov (Lenin),
Chairman of the Council of People's Commissars

Pravda No. 251,
November 5, 1922

Published according to
the original signed
by Lenin

INTERVIEW WITH ARTHUR RANSOME, *MANCHESTER GUARDIAN* CORRESPONDENT[130]

FIRST VERSION

1. *Question.* I find considerable economic activity; everybody is buying and selling, and evidently, a new trading class is arising. My question is—*how is it that the Nepman is not, and shows no signs of aspiring to become, a political force?*

Answer. Your first question reminded me of a conversation I had long, long ago, in London. It was on a Saturday night. I was taking a stroll with a friend; that was some twenty years ago.[131] The streets were thronged. Traders were lined all along the curbs, and their stalls were lit up by small metal tubes, filled with naphtha, or something of that sort. The lights were very pretty. The traffic in the streets was really extraordinary. Everybody was buying or selling.

In Russia at that time there was a trend that we called Economism. By this rather slangy term we meant the childish vulgarisation of Marx's views on historical materialism. My friend was an Economist, and he at once began to show off his knowledge. This extraordinary economic activity, he argued, should create a desire for political power. I laughed at this interpretation of Marx. The abundance of small traders and their extremely lively activities, I said, do not prove in the least that this class is a great economic force, from which one could infer a desire for "political power". London, probably, became the world's commercial centre, both economic and political, in a somewhat more complicated way than my friend imagined, and the London street traders, their remarkable activity notwithstanding, were rather far from being a "political" force, and even from the desire to become one.

I am afraid that your question as to why our Nepmen (i.e., street traders? petty hucksters?) "show no signs of aspiring to become a political force" will raise a smile here; and our answer will be—for the very same reason that the Saturday night crowd buying and selling in the streets of London did not, in Britain, "show signs of aspiring to become a political force".

2. *Question.* I get the impression that in Russia, today, buying and selling and barter are highly profitable, whereas production is possible only in very rare cases. Buying and selling and barter are in the hands of the Nepmen. In most cases profitable production is conducted on a small scale, and is in the hands of private individuals. *Unprofitable* production is in the hands of the state. My question is—*does this not presage a continuous increase in the economic power of the Nepmen and a continuous dimiution of the power of the state?*

Answer. I am afraid that you formulate your second question also from an almost Economist angle in the sense indicated above. It was Bastiat, I think, who seriously held the opinion that "the ancient Greeks and Romans lived by plunder". The "economic" question as to where the loot obtained by the people who lived by plunder came from did not trouble him very much.

You "get the impression that in Russia, today, buying and selling and barter are highly profitable, whereas production is possible only in very rare cases".

I was very surprised to read such a conclusion drawn from observation of what goes on in the streets of Moscow. I thought to myself—what about the millions and millions of Russian peasants? The fact that they sow crops is not a rare, or very rare case, but the commonest case in Russia, is it not? Is it not "even" commoner than the "buying and selling" of the Nepmen? And, probably, peasant production is not only "possible" in Russia, but extremely "profitable", is it not? If it were not so, how could our peasants have obtained the means to pay the tax in kind, amounting to hundreds of millions of poods of grain, which they have already delivered to the government so very quickly and easily? How is one to explain the universal acceleration of building activity observed by everybody, both in town and country, throughout boundless Russia?

Does not the questioner take for "highly profitable selling and barter" the petty trade in which a small trader sometimes makes millions and millions of profits in depreciated Russian currency, when on the free market a million rubles is worth less than a ruble was before? It is scarcely possible to slip into such an error, for our government is now—has been for the last few months already— striking out the "superfluous" noughts of our paper currency.[132] One day the figure is a million million; four noughts are struck out and it becomes a hundred million. The state does not become richer as a result of this operation, but it is very strange to assume that it "becomes weaker", for this operation is an obvious step towards stabilising the currency, and the Nepmen are beginning to see that the ruble is becoming stabilised; this was to be seen in the summer, for example. The Nepmen are beginning to understand that the "striking out" of noughts will continue, and I doubt whether their "aspiration to become a political force" will hinder it.

To return to the question of production. In this country the land belongs to the state. The small peasants who occupy the land are paying the tax splendidly. Industrial production—in so-called light industry—is obviously reviving; and this production is partly in the hands of the state and managed by its employees, and partly in the hands of lessees.

Thus, there are no grounds for anticipating "a continuous diminution of the power of the state".

You must draw a distinction not between production and trade, but between production in light industry and that in heavy industry. The latter is really unprofitable, and this is actually creating serious difficulties for the country Of this, more below.

3. *Question*. It is being hinted that an attempt is to be made (by means of taxation) to compel the Nepmen to subsidise industry. My question is—*will not this merely result in a rise in prices and increased profits for the Nepmen, which will indirectly create the necessity of raising wages—thus causing a return to the former situation?*

Answer. The government has at its command hundreds of millions of poods of grain. That being the case, it is wrong to anticipate that taxes will "*merely*" result in a rise in prices. The taxes will also provide us with revenues, obtained from the Nepmen and manufacturers, which will be used for industry, particularly heavy industry.

4. *Question.* Judging by usual capitalist standards, the economic situation should be worse. Judging by communist standards, the situation should also be worse (decline of heavy industry). And yet, everybody I meet admits that his conditions are better than they were a year ago. Evidently, something is taking place that neither capitalist nor communist ideology allows for. Both presuppose progress. But what if, instead of progressing, we are receding? My question is—*is it not possible that we are not marching forward to new prosperity, but are reverting to the old conditions?* Is it not possible that Russia is going back to the period of agricultural production approximately commensurate with her needs, and to a brisk home trade only slightly affected by foreign imports? Is not such a period conceivable under the proletarian dictatorship as it was formerly under the feudal dictatorship?

Answer. Let us first "judge" by "usual capitalist standards". Throughout the summer our ruble remained stable. This is an obvious sign of improvement. Furthermore, the revival of peasant production and of light industry is beyond doubt. This, too, is an improvement. Lastly, the State Bank has obtained a net revenue of no less than 20,000,000 gold rubles (this is at the lowest estimate; actually, it obtained a larger sum). A small sum, but the improvement is beyond doubt. A small sum, but it undoubtedly marks the beginning of an increase in the funds available for heavy industry.

To proceed. Let us now judge by communist standards. All the three circumstances enumerated above are assets also from the communist viewpoint, for in this country political power is in the hands of the workers. The *step* towards the stabilisation of the ruble, the revival of peasant production and light industry and the *first* profits obtained by the State Bank (i.e., the state) are all assets from the communist viewpoint *too*.

How is it that although capitalism is the antithesis of communism, certain circumstances are *assets* from *the two opposite viewpoints*? It is because one possible way to proceed to communism is through state capitalism, provided the state is controlled by the working class. This is exactly the position in the "present case".

The decline of heavy industry is a loss to us. The first profits obtained by the State Bank and the People's Commissariat of Foreign Trade mark the beginning of an improvement in this field, too. The difficulties here are enormous; but the situation is by no means hopeless.

Let us proceed further. Is it possible that we are receding to something in the nature of a "feudal dictatorship"? It is utterly impossible, for although slowly, with interruptions, taking steps backward from time to time, we are still making progress along the path of state capitalism, a path that leads us forward to socialism and communism (which is the highest stage of socialism), and certainly not back to feudalism.

Foreign trade is growing; the ruble is becoming more stable, although the process is not altogether without interruptions; there is an obvious revival of industry in Petrograd and Moscow; a small, a very small beginning has been made in accumulating state funds for the purpose of assisting heavy industry, and so on, and so forth. All this shows that Russia is not receding, but advancing, although, I repeat, very slowly, and not without interruption.

5. *Question*. Or are we witnessing a deplorable *squandering of capital that should be utilised in production*?

Answer. This question has already been answered in the foregoing.

6. *Question*. In addition to these questions *The Manchester Guardian* would be interested to obtain direct from you a refutation of the rumours now freely circulating in Moscow that the ration system will be reintroduced this winter and that all Nepman stocks are to be requisitioned.

Answer. I readily affirm that the rumours to the effect that we intend to revert to the ration system or that we intend to "requisition all Nepman stocks" are groundless.

They are fairy-tales, nothing more. We are not contemplating anything of the sort.

Nothing of the sort is conceivable in present-day Russia.

These rumours are being maliciously circulated by people who are very angry with us, but are not very clever.

7. *Question*. Lastly, am I right in assuming that the agreement with Urquhart has not been finally rejected, but has only been shelved until normal, friendly relations have been established with the British Government?

Answer. You are absolutely right about Urquhart. I shall repeat what I recently told Farbman.* We have not finally rejected the proposal for a concession to Urquhart. We have rejected it only for the political reasons we have publicly announced. In our press we have started a discussion of all the *pros* and *cons*. And we hope that after this discussion we shall arrive at a definite opinion on both the political and economic aspects.

Yours,
Lenin

November 5, 1922

Published in *The Manchester Guardian* No. 23797, November 22, 1922

First published in Russian in 1930

Translated from the manuscript

---

* See pp. 383-89 of this volume.—*Ed.*

SECOND VERSION (UNFINISHED)

In reply to your questions:

1. I think that the "Nepman", i.e., the representative of the trading system developing under the "New Economic Policy", would like to become a political force, but shows no signs of this, or shows them in such a way as to conceal his aspirations. He is compelled to conceal his aspirations, for otherwise he would run the risk of meeting with the stern opposition of our state authorities, or perhaps even worse than opposition, i.e., downright hostility.

I am of the opinion that with the concentration of the bulk of the means of production in the hands of our state, what the petty bourgeoisie actually needs, economically, is freedom to buy and sell consumer goods. Our laws grant the petty bourgeoisie this freedom.

The term "Nepman" that you use leads to some misunderstanding. This word is made up of the abbreviation NEP, which stands for "New Economic Policy", and the word "man". Together it means "a man, or representative, of this New Economic Policy". This term first arose as a journalese nickname for the small huckster, or individual who took advantage of the free market for all sorts of abuses.

Outwardly, what strikes the eye most in the New Economic Policy is that people like the "Nepmen", that is, people of all sorts who "buy and sell", as you say, come to the fore.

But the actual economic activities of the actual majority of the population by no means consist in this. For example, it is sufficient to point to the activities of the vast masses of the peasantry who, precisely at the present time, are displaying tremendous energy and self-sacrifice in restoring their tillage, their agricultural implements, their houses, farm buildings, etc. On the other hand, at this very moment the industrial workers are displaying equal energy in improving their tools, in replacing worn out tools by new ones, in restoring wrecked, dilapidated or damaged buildings, etc.

The "Nepmen", if we are to employ this term, which belongs rather to the realm of journalese than to the realm of serious political economy, make more noise than their economic power warrants. I am therefore afraid that anybody who in a vulgarised way applied to our "Nepmen" the proposition of historical materialism that economic power must be followed by political power, is in danger of falling into serious error, and even of becoming the victim of a series of ridiculous misunderstandings.

The real nature of the New Economic Policy is this — firstly, the proletarian state *has given small producers freedom to trade*; and secondly, in respect of the *means of production in large-scale industry, the proletarian state is applying a number of the principles of what in capitalist economics is called "state capitalism"*.

I think that the "Nepmen" who draw from this the conclusion that they should aspire to become a political force are in danger not only of falling into error, but also of becoming a butt for newspaper quips about their vulgar conception of Marxism.

2. It seems to me that your impression that in Russia today buying and selling are highly profitable, "whereas production is possible only in very rare cases" is likely to call forth well-deserved ridicule over Mister Nepman's political economy.

If I am not mistaken, the overwhelming majority of the population of Russia are small peasants, who have now thrown themselves into production with extraordinary zeal, and have achieved (partly due to the assistance the government has given them by way of seed, etc.) enormous, almost incredible success, particularly if we bear in mind the unprecedented devastation caused by the Civil War, the famine, and so forth. The small peasants have been so successful that they delivered the state tax amounting to hundreds of millions of poods of grain with extraordinary ease, and almost without any coercion.

I therefore think that it would be more true to say that the overwhelming majority of the population, whose production is conducted on a very small scale and is concentrated in private hands, obtains very large profits. This applies to peasant farming as a whole. The same, or slightly smaller, profits are obtained from industrial production—part of which is in private hands and part in the hands of lessees from the state or state factories producing consumer goods for the rural population.

The only really unprofitable production in the hands of the state is that part which, to employ the scientific terminology of political economy, should be called the production of means of production (ores, metals, etc.), or the production of fixed capital. Under capitalist economy the renewal of this form of capital usually requires government loans, which at one stroke provide extremely large sums (hundreds of millions of rubles, or even dollars) for the reorganisation of a number of enterprises capable of restoring damaged means of production.

In our case, the restoration of the damaged means of production promises no profit whatever for a long time to come, and is "unprofitable", as you express it. For a long time we shall have to resort to revenues obtained from concessions, or state subsidies, for the purpose of restoring our fixed capital.

Such is the actual economic situation at present. As you see, my view of this situation is quite different from yours. I am afraid that your opinion that in this country there is a "continuous increase in the economic power of the Nepmen" and a "continuous diminution of the power of the state" would probably have prompted Marx to make some caustic remarks about vulgar political economy.

I still stick to my old idea that after Marx you can drag in non-Marxian political economy only for the purpose of fooling philistines, even if they are "highly civilised" philistines.

I am rounding off on the question of "political power". The basis of political power in Russia is the workers and peasants. In all capitalist countries the peasants are robbed by the landowners and capitalists. As the peasants become more politically educated they understand this better. That is why the bulk of the population will not follow the lead of the "buying and selling" Nepmen.

3. Will not the tax on the "Nepmen" merely result in increased wages and prices, instead of providing funds for production?

No, because prices will be based on grain. A certain part of this grain is in the hands of the state, collected in the form of a tax. The Nepmen cannot directly influence prices because they are not producers. The foreign trade monopoly, I must say in passing, will help us to keep the Nepmen in hand, for, without consulting them, prices will be determined by the price of production abroad plus the extra charge imposed by the state for the purpose of subsidising production.

I am afraid that you sometimes imagine that the Nepmen are forcing up prices although the rise in prices is actually due to the depreciation of our paper currency, caused by increased issues. That would be a mistake.

Written between October 27
and November 5, 1922

First published
in *Pravda* No. 17,
January 21, 1926

Published according to
a typewritten copy
with corrections
and additions by Lenin

TO THE NON-PARTY CONFERENCE OF WOMEN WORKERS AND PEASANTS OF MOSCOW CITY AND MOSCOW GUBERNIA[133]

Dear Comrades,

I thank you cordially for your kind wishes and greetings. I am very sorry that I am unable to attend in person.

Congratulations on the occasion of the fifth anniversary of the revolution and all best wishes for the success of your Conference.

Yours,
Lenin

November 6, 1922

Rabochaya Moskva No. 227,
November 9, 1922

Published according to
the *Rabochaya Moskva* text

TO THE WORKERS OF THE FORMER MICHELSON PLANT[134]

Dear Comrades,

I regret very much that precisely today a slight indisposition has forced me to stay indoors. I send you my warmest greetings and wishes on the occasion of the fifth anniversary. I wish you success in your work for the next five years.

Yours,
V. Ulyanov (Lenin)

November 7, 1922

First published in 1942

Published according to
the manuscript

TO THE WORKERS AND EMPLOYEES
AT THE STATE ELEKTROPEREDACHA
POWER STATION[135]

Dear Comrades,

Today, on the fifth anniversary of the revolution, it gives me particular pleasure to welcome the opening of your club. I express the hope that by joint efforts you, workers and employees at the State Elektroperedacha Power Station, will turn that club into one of the most important centres of education for workers.

V. Ulyanov (Lenin)

November 7, 1922

First published in 1945
in *Lenin Miscellany XXXV*

Published according to
the original corrected
and signed by Lenin

TO THE WORKERS AT THE STODOL CLOTH MILL IN KLINTSI[136]

November 8, 1922

Dear Comrades,

I thank you most heartily for your greetings and your gift. I will tell you as a secret that you ought not to send me any gifts. I earnestly request you to spread this secret among the workers as widely as possible.

Please accept my best thanks, greetings and wishes.

Yours,
V. Ulyanov (Lenin)

First published in 1924

Published according to
the manuscript

FOURTH CONGRESS OF THE
COMMUNIST INTERNATIONAL[137]

NOVEMBER 5-DECEMBER 5, 1922

1

TO THE FOURTH CONGRESS OF THE COMMUNIST INTERNATIONAL
AND TO THE PETROGRAD SOVIET OF WORKERS' AND RED ARMY DEPUTIES

I regret very much that I cannot be present at the first session of the Congress and that I must confine myself to greetings in writing.

Notwithstanding the enormous obstacles confronting the Communist Parties, the Communist International is growing and becoming strong. The main goal is still to win over the majority of the workers. We *shall attain* this goal in spite of everything.

The amalgamation of the Second and Two-and-a-Half Internationals will benefit the proletarian revolutionary movement: less fiction and less fraud is always to the benefit of the working class.

To the Petrograd workers and their newly-elected Soviet who are hosts to the Fourth Congress of the Communist International, I send my best wishes and cordial greetings.

The Petrograd workers must be in the foremost ranks on the economic front, too. We rejoice to hear about the beginning of the economic revival of Petrograd. I hope to be able to accept your invitation to visit Petrograd in the near future.

Soviet rule in Russia is celebrating its fifth anniversary. It is now sounder than ever. The Civil War is over. The first successes in the economic field have been achieved. Soviet Russia considers it a matter of the greatest pride to help the workers of the whole world in their difficult struggle to overthrow capitalism. Victory will be ours.

Long live the Communist International!

V. Ulyanov (Lenin)

Moscow, November 4, 1922

Pravda No. 253,
November 9, 1922

Published according to
the *Pravda* text

2

FIVE YEARS OF THE RUSSIAN REVOLUTION
AND THE PROSPECTS OF THE WORLD REVOLUTION

REPORT TO THE FOURTH CONGRESS OF THE COMMUNIST
INTERNATIONAL, NOVEMBER 13, 1922

(*Comrade Lenin is met with stormy, prolonged applause and a general ovation. All rise and join in singing "The Internationale".*) Comrades, I am down in the list as the main speaker, but you will understand that after my lengthy illness I am not able to make a long report. I can only make a few introductory remarks on the key questions. My subject will be a very limited one. The subject, "Five Years of the Russian Revolution and the Prospects of the World Revolution", is in general too broad and too large for one speaker to exhaust in a single speech. That is why I shall take only a small part of this subject, namely, the question of the New Economic Policy. I have deliberately taken only this small part in order to make you familiar with what is now the most important question—at all events, it is the most important to me, because I am now working on it.

And so, I shall tell you how we launched the New Economic Policy, and what results we have achieved with the aid of this policy. If I confine myself to this question, I shall, perhaps, succeed in giving you a general survey and a general idea of it.

To begin with how we arrived at the New Economic Policy, I must quote from an article I wrote in 1918.[138] At the beginning of 1918, in a brief polemic, I touched on the question of the attitude we should adopt towards state capitalism. I then wrote:

"State capitalism would be a *step forward* as compared with the present state of affairs (i.e., the state of affairs

at that time) in our Soviet Republic. If in approximately
six months' time state capitalism became established in our
Republic, this would be a great success and a sure guarantee
that within a year socialism will have gained a permanently
firm hold and will have become invincible in our country."

Of course, this was said at a time when we were more
foolish than we are now, but not so foolish as to be unable
to deal with such matters.

Thus, in 1918, I was of the opinion that with regard to
the economic situation then obtaining in the Soviet
Republic, state capitalism would be a step forward. This
sounds very strange, and perhaps even absurd, for already
at that time our Republic was a socialist republic and we
were every day hastily—perhaps too hastily—adopting
various new economic measures which could not be described
as anything but socialist measures. Nevertheless, I then
held the view that in relation to the economic situation
then obtaining in the Soviet Republic state capitalism
would be a step forward, and I explained my idea simply by
enumerating the elements of the economic system of Russia.
In my opinion these elements were the following: "(1)
patriarchal, i.e., the most primitive form of agriculture;
(2) small commodity production (this includes the majority
of the peasants who trade in grain); (3) private capitalism;
(4) state capitalism, and (5) socialism." All these economic
elements were present in Russia at that time. I set myself
the task of explaining the relationship of these elements
to each other, and whether one of the non-socialist elements, namely, state capitalism, should not be rated higher
than socialism. I repeat: it seems very strange to everyone
that a non-socialist element should be rated higher than,
regarded as superior to, socialism in a republic which
declares itself a socialist republic. But the fact will become
intelligible if you recall that we definitely did not regard
the economic system of Russia as something homogeneous
and highly developed; we were fully aware that in Russia
we had patriarchal agriculture, i.e., the most primitive
form of agriculture, alongside the socialist form. What
role could state capitalism play in these circumstances?

I then asked myself which of these elements predominated?
Clearly, in a petty-bourgeois environment the petty-

bourgeois element predominates. I recognised then that
the petty-bourgeois element predominated; it was impossible
to take a different view. The question I then put to myself—
this was in a specific controversy which had nothing to do
with the present question—was: what is our attitude towards
state capitalism? And I replied: although it is not a
socialist form, state capitalism would be for us, and for Russia, a more favourable form than the existing one. What
does that show? It shows that we did not overrate either
the rudiments or the principles of socialist economy,
although we had already accomplished the social revolution.
On the contrary, at that time we already realised to a certain extent that it would be better if we first arrived at
state capitalism and only after that at socialism.

I must lay special emphasis on this, because I assume
that it is the only point of departure we can take, firstly,
to explain what the present economic policy is; and, secondly, to draw very important practical conclusions for
the Communist International. I do not want to suggest that
we had then a ready-made plan of retreat. This was not the
case. Those brief lines set forth in a polemic were not by
any means a plan of retreat. For example, they made no
mention whatever of that very important point, freedom to
trade, which is of fundamental significance to state capitalism. Yet they did contain a general, even if indefinite, idea of
retreat. I think that we should take note of that not only
from the viewpoint of a country whose economic system
was, and is to this day, very backward, but also from the
viewpoint of the Communist International and the advanced
West-European countries. For example, just now we are
engaged in drawing up a programme. I personally think that
it would be best to hold simply a general discussion on all
the programmes, to make the first reading, so to speak, and
to get them printed, but not to take a final decision now,
this year. Why? First of all, of course, because I do not
think we have considered all of them in sufficient detail,
and also because we have given scarcely any thought to
possible retreat, and to preparations for it. Yet that is a
question which, in view of such fundamental changes in the
world as the overthrow of capitalism and the building of
socialism with all its enormous difficulties, absolutely

requires our attention. We must not only know how to act when we pass directly to the offensive and are victorious. In revolutionary times this is not so difficult, nor so very important; at least, it is not the most decisive thing. There are always times in a revolution when the opponent loses his head; and if we attack him at such a time we may win an easy victory. But that is nothing, because our enemy, if he has enough endurance, can rally his forces beforehand, and so forth. He can easily provoke us to attack him and then throw us back for many years. For this reason, I think, the idea that we must prepare for ourselves the possibility of retreat is very important, and not only from the theoretical point of view. From the practical point of view, too, all the parties which are preparing to take the direct offensive against capitalism in the near future must now give thought to the problem of preparing for a possible retreat. I think it will do us no harm to learn this lesson together with all the other lessons which the experience of our revolution offers. On the contrary, it may prove beneficial in many cases.

Now that I have emphasised the fact that as early as 1918 we regarded state capitalism as a possible line of retreat, I shall deal with the results of our New Economic Policy. I repeat: at that time it was still a very vague idea, but in 1921, after we had passed through the most important stage of the Civil War—and passed through it victoriously—we felt the impact of a grave—I think it was the gravest—internal political crisis in Soviet Russia. This internal crisis brought to light discontent not only among a considerable section of the peasantry but also among the workers. This was the first and, I hope, the last time in the history of Soviet Russia that feeling ran against us among large masses of peasants, not consciously but instinctively. What gave rise to this peculiar, and for us, of course, very unpleasant, situation? The reason for it was that in our economic offensive we had run too far ahead, that we had not provided ourselves with adequate resources, that the masses sensed what we ourselves were not then able to formulate consciously but what we admitted soon after, a few weeks later, namely, that the direct transition to purely socialist forms, to purely socialist distribution,

was beyond our available strength, and that if we were
unable to effect a retreat so as to confine ourselves to easier
tasks, we would face disaster. The crisis began, I think,
in February 1921. In the spring of that year we decided
unanimously—I did not observe any considerable disagreement among us on this question—to adopt the New Economic Policy. Now, after eighteen months have elapsed,
at the close of 1922, we are able to make certain comparisons.
What has happened? How have we fared during this period
of over eighteen months? What is the result? Has this
retreat been of any benefit to us? Has it really saved us,
or is the result still indefinite? This is the main question
that I put to myself, and I think that this main question is
also of first-rate importance to all the Communist Parties;
for if the reply is in the negative, we are all doomed. I think
that all of us can, with a clear conscience, reply to this
question in the affirmative, namely, that the past eighteen
months provide positive and absolute proof that we have
passed the test.

I shall now try to prove this. To do that I must briefly
enumerate all the constituent parts of our economy.

First of all I shall deal with our financial system and
our famous Russian ruble. I think we can say that Russian
rubles are famous, if only for the reason that their number
now in circulation exceeds a quadrillion. (*Laughter.*) That
is something! It is an astronomical figure. I am sure that
not everyone here knows what this figure signifies. (*General
laughter.*) But we do not think that the figure is so very
important even from the point of view of economic science,
for the noughts can always be crossed out. (*Laughter.*) We
have achieved a thing or two in this art, which is likewise
of no importance from the economic point of view, and I am
sure that in the further course of events we shall achieve
much more. But what is really important is the problem of
stabilising the ruble. We are now grappling with this problem, our best forces are working on it, and we attach decisive importance to it. If we succeed in stabilising the
ruble for a long period, and then for all time, it will prove
that we have won. In that case all these astronomical figures, these trillions and quadrillions, will not have mattered
in the least. We shall then be able to place our economy

on a firm basis, and develop it further on a firm basis. On
this question I think I can cite some fairly important and
decisive data. In 1921 the rate of exchange of the paper
ruble remained stable for a period of less than three months.
This year, 1922, which has not yet drawn to a close, the
rate remained stable for a period of over five months. I
think that this proof is sufficient. Of course, if you demand
scientific proof that we shall definitely solve this problem,
then it is not sufficient; but in general, I do not think it
is possible to prove this entirely and conclusively. The
data I have cited show that between last year, when we
started on the New Economic Policy, and the present day,
we have already learned to make progress. Since we have
learned to do this, I am sure we shall learn to achieve further successes along this road, provided we avoid doing
anything very foolish. The most important thing, however, is trade, namely, the circulation of commodities,
which is essential for us. And since we have successfully
coped with this problem for two years, in spite of having
been in a state of war (for, as you know, Vladivostok was
recaptured only a few weeks ago), and in spite of the fact
that only now we are able to proceed with our economic
activities in a really systematic way—since we have succeeded in keeping the rate of the paper ruble stable for
five months instead of only three months, I think I can say
that we have grounds to be pleased. After all, we stand
alone. We have not received any loans, and are not receiving
any now. We have been given no assistance by any of the
powerful capitalist countries, which organise their capitalist economy so "brilliantly" that they do not know to
this day which way they are going. By the Treaty of Versailles they have created a financial system that they themselves cannot make head or tail of. If these great capitalist
countries are managing things in this way, I think that
we, backward and uneducated as we are, may be pleased
with the fact that we have grasped the most important
thing—the conditions for the stabilisation of the ruble.
This is proved not by theoretical analysis but by practical
experience, which in my opinion is more important than
all the theoretical discussions in the world. Practice shows
that we have achieved decisive results in that field, namely,

we are beginning to push our economy towards the stabilisation of the ruble, which is of supreme importance for trade, for the free circulation of commodities, for the peasants, and for the vast masses of small producers.

Now I come to our social objectives. The most important factor, of course, is the peasantry. In 1921 discontent undoubtedly prevailed among a vast section of the peasantry. Then there was the famine. This was the severest trial for the peasants. Naturally, all our enemies abroad shouted: "There, that's the result of socialist economy!" Quite naturally, of course, they said nothing about the famine actually being the terrible result of the Civil War. All the landowners and capitalists who had begun their offensive against us in 1918 tried to make out that the famine was the result of socialist economy. The famine was indeed a great and grave disaster which threatened to nullify the results of all our organisational and revolutionary efforts.

And so, I ask now, after this unprecedented and unexpected disaster, what is the position today, after we have introduced the New Economic Policy, after we have granted the peasants freedom to trade? The answer is clear and obvious to everyone; in one year the peasants have not only got over the famine, but have paid so much tax in kind that we have already received hundreds of millions of poods of grain, and that almost without employing any measures of coercion. Peasant uprisings, which previously, before 1921, were, so to speak, a common occurrence in Russia, have almost completely ceased. The peasants are satisfied with their present position. We can confidently assert that. We think that this evidence is more important than any amount of statistical proof. Nobody questions the fact that the peasants are a decisive factor in our country. And the position of the peasantry is now such that we have no reason to fear any movement against us from that quarter. We say that quite consciously, without exaggeration. This we have already achieved. The peasantry may be dissatisfied with one aspect or another of the work of our authorit es. They may complain about this. That is possible, of course, and inevitable, because our machinery of state and our state-operated economy are still too inefficient to avert it; but any serious dissatisfaction with us on the part of the peasantry as a whole is quite out of the question. This has been achieved in the course of one year. I think that is already quite a lot.

Now I come to our light industry. In industry we have to make a distinction between heavy and light industry because the situation in them is different. As regards light industry, I can safely say that there is a general revival. I shall not go into details. I did not set out to quote a lot of statistics. But this general impression is based on facts, and I can assure you that it is not based on anything untrue or inaccurate. We can speak of a general revival in light industry, and, as a result, of a definite improvement in the conditions of the workers in Petrograd and Moscow. In other districts this is observed to a lesser degree, because heavy industry predominates in them. So this does not apply generally. Nevertheless, I repeat, light industry is undoubtedly on the upgrade, and the conditions of the workers in Petrograd and Moscow have unquestionably improved. In the spring of 1921 there was discontent among the workers in both these cities. That is definitely not the case now. We, who watch the conditions and mood of the workers from day to day, make no mistake on that score.

The third question is that of heavy industry. I must say that the situation here is still grave. Some turn for the better occurred in 1921-22, so that we may hope that the situation will improve in the near future. We have already gathered some of the resources necessary for this. In a capitalist country a loan of hundreds of millions would be required to improve the situation in heavy industry. No improvement would be possible without it. The economic history of the capitalist countries shows that heavy industry in backward countries can only be developed with the aid of long-term loans of hundreds of millions of dollars or gold rubles. We did not get such loans, and so far have received nothing. All that is now being written about concessions and so forth is not worth much more than the paper it is written on. We have written a great deal about this lately and in particular about the Urquhart concession. Yet I think our concessions policy is a very good one. However, we have not concluded a single profitable concession agreement so far. I ask you to bear that in mind.

Thus, the situation in heavy industry is really a very grave problem for our backward country, because we cannot count on loans from the wealthy countries. In spite of that, we see a tangible improvement, and we also see that our trading has brought us some capital. True, it is only a very modest sum as yet—a little over twenty million gold rubles. At any rate, a beginning has been made; our trade is providing us with funds which we can employ for improving the situation in heavy industry. At the present moment, however, our heavy industry is still in great difficulties. But I think that the decisive circumstance is that we are already in a position to save a little. And we shall go on saving. We must economise now though it is often at the expense of the population. We are trying to reduce the state budget, to reduce staffs in our government offices. Later on, I shall have a few words to say about our state apparatus. At all events, we must reduce it. We must economise as much as possible. We are economising in all things, even in schools. We must do this, because we know that unless we save heavy industry, unless we restore it, we shall not be able to build up an industry at all; and without an industry we shall go under as an independent country. We realise this very well.

The salvation of Russia lies not only in a good harvest on the peasant farms—that is not enough; and not only in the good condition of light industry, which provides the peasantry with consumer goods—this, too, is not enough; we also need *heavy* industry. And to put it in a good condition will require several years of work.

Heavy industry needs state subsidies. If we are not able to provide them, we shall be doomed as a civilised state, let alone as a socialist state. In this respect, we have taken a determined step. We have begun to accumulate the funds that we need to put heavy industry on its feet. True, the sum we have obtained so far barely exceeds twenty million gold rubles; but at any rate this sum is available, and it is earmarked exclusively for the purpose of reviving our heavy industry.

I think that, on the whole, I have, as I have promised, briefly outlined the principal elements of our economy, and feel that we may draw the conclusion from all this that the

New Economic Policy has already yielded dividends. We already have proof that, as a state, we are able to trade, to maintain our strong positions in agriculture and industry, and to make progress. Practical activity has proved it. I think this is sufficient for us for the time being. We shall have to learn much, and we have realised that we still have much to learn. We have been in power for five years, and during these five years we have been in a state of war. Hence, we have been successful.

This is understandable, because the peasantry were on our side. Probably no one could have supported us more than they did. They were aware that the whiteguards had the landowners behind them, and they hate the landowners more than anything in the world. That is why the peasantry supported us with all their enthusiasm and loyalty. It was not difficult to get the peasantry to defend us against the whiteguards. The peasants, who had always hated war, did all they possibly could in the war against the whiteguards, in the Civil War against the landowners. But this was not all, because in substance it was only a matter of whether power would remain in the hands of the landowners or of the peasants. This was not enough for us. The peasants know that we have seized power for the workers and that our aim is to use this power to establish the socialist system. Therefore, the most important thing for us was to lay the economic foundation for socialist economy. We could not do it directly. We had to do it in a roundabout way. The state capitalism that we have introduced in our country is of a special kind. It does not agree with the usual conception of state capitalism. We hold all the key positions. We hold the land; it belongs to the state. This is very important, although our opponents try to make out that it is of no importance at all. That is untrue. The fact that the land belongs to the state is extremely important, and economically it is also of great practical purport. This we have achieved, and I must say that all our future activities should develop only within that framework. We have already succeeded in making the peasantry content and in reviving both industry and trade. I have already said that our state capitalism differs from state capitalism in the literal sense of the term in that our proletarian state not only owns the land, but also all the vital branches of industry. To begin with, we have leased only a certain number of the small and medium plants, but all the rest remain in our hands. As regards trade, I want to re-emphasise that we are trying to found mixed companies, that we are already forming them, i.e., companies in which part of the capital belongs to private capitalists—and foreign capitalists at that—and the other part belongs to the state. Firstly, in this way we are learning how to trade, and that is what we need. Secondly, we are always in a position to dissolve these companies if we deem it necessary, and do not, therefore, run any risks, so to speak. We are learning from the private capitalist and looking round to see how we can progress, and what mistakes we make. It seems to me that I need say no more.

I should still like to deal with several minor points. Undoubtedly, we have done, and will still do, a host of foolish things. No one can judge and see this better than I. (*Laughter*.) Why do we do these foolish things? The reason is clear: firstly, because we are a backward country; second-ly, because education in our country is at a low level; and thirdly, because we are getting no outside assistance. Not a single civilised country is helping us. On the contrary, they are all working against us. Fourthly, our machinery of state is to blame. We took over the old machinery of state, and that was our misfortune. Very often this machinery operates against us. In 1917, after we seized power, the government officials sabotaged us. This fright-ened us very much and we pleaded: "Please come back." They all came back, but that was our misfortune. We now have a vast army of government employees, but lack sufficiently educated forces to exercise real control over them. In practice it often happens that here at the top, where we exercise political power, the machine functions somehow; but down below government employees have arbitrary control and they often exercise it in such a way as to counteract our measures. At the top, we have, I don't know how many, but at all events, I think, no more than a few thousand, at the outside several tens of thousands of our own people. Down below, however, there are hundreds of thousands of old officials whom we got from the tsar and from bourgeois society and who, partly deliberately and partly unwittingly, work against us. It is clear that nothing can be done in that respect overnight. It will take many years of hard work to improve the machinery, to remodel it, and to enlist new forces. We are doing this fairly quickly, perhaps too quickly. Soviet schools and Workers' Faculties have been formed; a few hundred thousand young people are studying; they are studying too fast perhaps, but at all events, a start has been made, and I think this work will bear fruit. If we do not work too hurriedly we shall, in a few years' time, have a large body of young people capable of thoroughly overhauling our state apparatus.

I have said that we have done a host of foolish things, but I must also say a word or two in this respect about our enemies. If our enemies blame us and say that Lenin himself admits that the Bolsheviks have done a host of foolish things, I want to reply to this: yes, but you know, the foolish things we have done are nonetheless very different from yours. We have only just begun to learn, but are learning so methodically that we are certain to achieve good results. But since our enemies, i.e., the capitalists and the heroes of the Second International, lay stress on the foolish things we have done, I take the liberty, for the sake of comparison, to cite the words of a celebrated Russian author, which I shall amend to read as follows: if the Bolsheviks do foolish things the Bolshevik says, "Twice two are five", but when their enemies, i.e., the capitalists and the heroes of the Second International, do foolish things, they get, "Twice two make a tallow candle".[139] That is easily proved. Take, for example, the agreement concluded by the U.S.A., Great Britain, France and Japan with Kolchak. I ask you, are there any more enlightened and more powerful countries in the world? But what has happened? They promised to help Kolchak without calculation, without reflection, and without circumspection. It ended in a fiasco, which, it seems to me, is difficult for the human intellect to grasp.

Or take another example, a closer and more important one: the Treaty of Versailles. I ask you, what have the "great" powers which have "covered themselves with glory" done? How will they find a way out of this chaos and confusion? I don't think it will be an exaggeration to repeat that the foolish things we have done are nothing compared with those done in concert by the capitalist countries, the capitalist world and the Second International. That is why I think that the outlook for the world revolution—a subject which I must touch on briefly—is favourable. And given a certain definite condition, I think it will be even better. I should like to say a few words about this.

At the Third Congress, in 1921, we adopted a resolution on the organisational structure of the Communist Parties and on the methods and content of their activities. The resolution is an excellent one, but it is almost entirely Russian, that is to say, everything in it is based on Russian conditions. This is its good point, but it is also its failing. It is its failing because I am sure that no foreigner can read it. I have read it again before saying this. In the first place, it is too long, containing fifty or more points. Foreigners are not usually able to read such things. Secondly, even if they read it, they will not understand it because it is too Russian. Not because it is written in Russian—it has been excellently translated into all languages—but because it is thoroughly imbued with the Russian spirit. And thirdly, if by way of exception some foreigner does understand it, he cannot carry it out. This is its third defect. I have talked with a few of the foreign delegates and hope to discuss matters in detail with a large number of delegates from different countries during the Congress, although I shall not take part in its proceedings, for unfortunately it is impossible for me to do that. I have the impression that we made a big mistake with this resolution, namely, that we blocked our own road to further success. As I have said already, the resolution is excellently drafted; I am prepared to subscribe to every one of its fifty or more points. But we have not learnt how to present our Russian experience to foreigners. All that was said in the resolution has remained a dead letter. If we do not realise this, we shall be unable to move ahead. I think that after five years of the Russian revolution the most important thing for all of us, Russian and foreign comrades alike, is to sit down and study. We have only now obtained the opportunity to do so. I do not know how long this opportunity will last. I do not know for how long the capitalist powers will give us the opportunity to study in peace. But we must take advantage of every moment of respite from fighting, from war, to study, and to study from scratch.

The whole Party and all strata of the population of Russia prove this by their thirst for knowledge. This striving to learn shows that our most important task today is to study and to study hard. Our foreign comrades, too, must study. I do not mean that they have to learn to read and write and to understand what they read, as we still have to do. There is a dispute as to whether this concerns proletarian or bourgeois culture. I shall leave that question open. But one thing is certain: we have to begin by learning to read and write and to understand what we read. Foreigners do not need that. They need something more advanced: first of all, among other things they must learn to understand what we have written about the organisational structure of the Communist Parties, and what the foreign comrades have signed without reading and understanding. This must be their first task. That resolution must be carried out. It cannot be carried out overnight; that is absolutely impossible. The resolution is too Russian, it reflects Russian experience. That is why it is quite unintelligible to foreigners, and they cannot be content with hanging it in a corner like an icon and praying to it. Nothing will be achieved that way. They must assimilate part of the Russian experience. Just how that will be done, I do not know. The fascists in Italy may, for example, render us a great service by showing the Italians that they are not yet sufficiently enlightened and that their country is not yet ensured against the Black Hundreds.[140] Perhaps this will be very useful. We Russians must also find ways and means of explaining the principles of this resolution to the foreigners. Unless we do that, it will be absolutely impossible for them to carry it out. I am sure that in this connection we must tell not only the Russians, but the foreign comrades as well, that the most important thing

in the period we are now entering is to study. We are studying in the general sense. They, however, must study in the
special sense, in order that they may really understand
the organisation, structure, method and content of revolutionary work. If they do that, I am sure the prospects
of the world revolution will be not only good, but excellent. (*Stormy, prolonged applause. Shouts of* "Long live
our Comrade Lenin!" *evoke a fresh stormy ovation.*)

Pravda No. 258,
November 15, 1922

Published according to the text
in   *Bulleten   Chetvyortogo
Kongressa   Kommunisticheskogo
Internatsionala* (Bulletin of the
Fourth Congress of the Communist International) No. 8, November 16, 1922, checked with the
verbatim report in German corrected by Lenin

GREETINGS TO THE ALL-RUSSIA
AGRICULTURAL EXHIBITION[141]

I attach great importance to this Exhibition; I am sure that all organisations will co-operate with it in every way. With all my heart I wish you the best success.

V. Ulyanov (Lenin)

November 14, 1922

Published in 1922

Published according to the manuscript

TO THE *CLARTÉ* GROUP[142]

November 15, 1922

Dear Friends,

I take this opportunity to send you best greetings. I have been seriously ill, and for over a year I have not been able to see a single one of the productions of your group. I hope that your organisation *"des anciens combattants"** still exists and is growing stronger not only numerically, but also spiritually, in the sense of intensifying and spreading the struggle against imperialist war. It is worth devoting one's whole life to the struggle against this kind of war; it is a struggle in which one must be ruthless and chase to the furthermost corners of the earth all the sophistry that is uttered in its defence.

Best greetings.

Yours,
Lenin

First published in 1925
in French in *Clarté* No. 71

First published in Russian
in 1930

Published according to
the manuscript

---

* Ex-servicemen.—*Ed.*

SPEECH AT A PLENARY SESSION
OF THE MOSCOW SOVIET
NOVEMBER 20, 1922[143]

(*Stormy applause. "The Internationale" is sung*.) Comrades, I regret very much and apologise that I have been unable to come to your session earlier. As far as I know you intended a few weeks ago to give me an opportunity of attending the Moscow Soviet. I could not come because after my illness, from December onwards, I was incapacitated, to use the professional term, for quite a long time, and because of this reduced ability to work had to postpone my present address from week to week. A very considerable portion of my work which, as you will remember, I had first piled on Comrade Tsyurupa, and then on Comrade Rykov, I also had to pile additionally on Comrade Kamenev. And I must say that, to employ a simile I have already used, he was suddenly burdened with two loads. Though, to continue the simile, it should be said that the horse has proved to be an exceptionally capable and zealous one. (*Applause.*) All the same, however, nobody is supposed to drag two loads, and I am now waiting impatiently for Comrades Tsyurupa and Rykov to return, and we shall divide up the work at least a little more fairly. As for myself, in view of my reduced ability to work it takes me much more time to look into matters than I should like.

In December 1921, when I had to stop working altogether, it was the year's end. We were effecting the transition to the New Economic Policy, and it turned out already then that, although we had embarked upon this transition in the beginning of 1921, it was quite a difficult, I would say a very difficult, transition. We have now been effecting this transition for more than eighteen months, and one would think that it was time the majority took up new places and disposed themselves according to the new conditions, particularly those of the New Economic Policy.

As to foreign policy, we had the fewest changes in that field. We pursued the line that we had adopted earlier, and I think I can say with a clear conscience that we pursued it quite consistently and with enormous success. There is no need, I think, to deal with that in detail; the capture of Vladivostok, the ensuing demonstration and the declaration of federation which you read in the press[144] the other day have proved and shown with the utmost clarity that no changes are necessary in this respect. The road we are on is absolutely clearly and well defined, and has ensured us success in face of all the countries of the world, although some of them are still prepared to declare that they refuse to sit at one table with us. Nevertheless, economic relations, followed by diplomatic relations, are improving, must improve, and certainly will improve. Every country which resists this risks being late, and, perhaps in some quite substantial things, it risks being at a disadvantage. All of us see this now, and not only from the press, from the newspapers. I think that in their trips abroad comrades are also finding the changes very great. In that respect, to use an old simile, we have not changed to other trains, or to other conveyances.

But as regards our home policy, the change we made in the spring of 1921, which was necessitated by such extremely powerful and convincing circumstances that no debates or disagreements arose among us about it—that change continues to cause us some difficulties, great difficulties, I would say. Not because we have any doubts about the need for the turn—no doubts exist in that respect—not because we have any doubts as to whether the test of our New Economic Policy has yielded the successes we expected. No doubts exist on that score—I can say this quite definitely—either in the ranks of our Party or in the ranks of the huge mass of non-Party workers and peasants.

In this sense the problem presents no difficulties. The difficulties we have stem from our being faced with a task whose solution very often requires the services of new people, extraordinary measures and extraordinary methods. Doubts still exist among us as to whether this or that is correct. There are changes in one direction or another. And it should be said that both will continue for quite a long time. "The New Economic Policy!" A strange title. It was called a New Economic Policy because it turned things back. We are now retreating, going back, as it were; but we are doing so in order, after first retreating, to take a running start and make a bigger leap forward. It was on this condition alone that we retreated in pursuing our New Economic Policy. Where and how we must now regroup, adapt and reorganise in order to start a most stubborn offensive after our retreat, we do not yet know. To carry out all these operations properly we need, as the proverb says, to look not ten but a hundred times before we leap. We must do so in order to cope with the incredible difficulties we encounter in dealing with all our tasks and problems. You know perfectly well what sacrifices have been made to achieve what has been achieved; you know how long the Civil War has dragged on and what effort it has cost. Well now, the capture of Vladivostok has shown all of us (though Vladivostok is a long way off, it is after all one of our own towns) (*prolonged applause*) everybody's desire to join us, to join in our achievements. The Russian Soviet Federative Socialist Republic now stretches from here to there. This desire has rid us both of our civil enemies and of the foreign enemies who attacked us. I am referring to Japan.

We have won quite a definite diplomatic position, recognised by the whole world. All of you see it. You see its results, but how much time we needed to get it! We have now won the recognition of our rights by our enemies both in economic and in commercial policy. This is proved by the conclusion of trade agreements.

We can see why we, who eighteen months ago took the path of the so-called New Economic Policy, are finding it so incredibly difficult to advance along that path. We live in a country devastated so severely by war, knocked

out of anything like the normal course of life, in a country
that has suffered and endured so much, that willy-nilly
we are beginning all our calculations with a very, very
small percentage—the pre-war percentage. We apply this
yardstick to the conditions of our life, we sometimes do
so very impatiently, heatedly, and always end up with
the conviction that the difficulties are vast. The task we
have set ourselves in this field seems all the more vast
because we are comparing it with the state of affairs in any
ordinary bourgeois country. We have set ourselves this
task because we understood that it was no use expecting
the wealthy powers to give us the assistance usually
forthcoming under such circumstances.* After the Civil
War we have been subjected to very nearly a boycott, that
is, we have been told that the economic ties that are customary and normal in the capitalist world will not be maintained in our case.

Over eighteen months have passed since we undertook
the New Economic Policy, and even a longer period has
passed since we concluded our first international treaty.
Nonetheless, this boycott of us by all the bourgeoisie and
all governments continues to be felt. We could not count
on anything else when we adopted the new economic
conditions; yet we had no doubt that we had to make the
change and achieve success single-handed. The further we go,
the clearer it becomes that any aid that may be rendered
to us, that will be rendered to us by the capitalist powers,
will, far from eliminating this condition, in all likeli-
hood and in the overwhelming majority of cases intensify
it, accentuate it still further. "Single-handed"—we told
ourselves. "Single-handed"—we are told by almost every
capitalist country with which we have concluded any
deals, with which we have undertaken any engagements,

---

* In the verbatim report the text reads further: "and that even
if we took into consideration the extremely high, say such-and-such
a rate of interest, that is imposed in these circumstances on a country that, to use the accepted term, is rendered aid. Properly speaking, these rates of interest are very far from being aid. To put it bluntly, they would deserve a far less polite term than the word aid,
but even these usual conditions would have been onerous for us."—Ed.

with which we have begun any negotiations. And that is where the special difficulty lies. We must realise this difficulty. We have built up our own political system in more than three years of work, incredibly hard work that was incredibly full of heroism. In the position in which we were till now we had no time to see whether we would smash something needlessly, no time to see whether there would be many sacrifices, because there were sacrifices enough, because the struggle which we then began (you know this perfectly well and there is no need to dwell on it) was a life-and-death struggle against the old social system, against which we fought to forge for ourselves a right to existence, to peaceful development. And we have won it. It is not we who say this, it is not the testimony of witnesses who may be accused of being partial to us. It is the testimony of witnesses who are in the camp of our enemies and who are naturally partial—not in our favour, however, but against us. These witnesses were in Denikin's camp. They directed the occupation. And we know that their partiality cost us very dear, cost us colossal destruction. We suffered all sorts of losses on their account, and lost values of all kinds, including the greatest of all values—human lives—on an incredibly large scale. Now we must scrutinise our tasks most carefully and understand that the main task will be not to give up our previous gains. We shall not give up a single one of our old gains. (*Applause.*) Yet we are also faced with an entirely new task; the old may prove a downright obstacle. To understand this task is most difficult. Yet it must be understood, so that we may learn how to work when, so to speak, it is necessary to turn ourselves inside out. I think, comrades, that these words and slogans are understandable, because for nearly a year, during my enforced absence, you have had in practice, handling the jobs on hand, to speak and think of this in various ways and on hundreds of occasions, and I am confident that your reflections on that score can only lead to one conclusion, namely, that today we must display still more of the flexibility which we employed till now in the Civil War.

We must not abandon the old. The series of concessions that adapt us to the capitalist powers is a series of concessions that enables them to make contact with us, ensures them a profit which is sometimes bigger, perhaps, than it should be. At the same time, we are conceding but a little part of the means of production, which are held almost entirely by our state. The other day the papers discussed the concession proposed by the Englishman Urquhart, who has hitherto been against us almost throughout the Civil War. He used to say: "We shall achieve our aim in the Civil War against Russia, against the Russia that has dared to deprive us of this and of that." And after all that we had to enter into negotiations with him. We did not refuse them, we undertook them with the greatest joy, but we said: "Beg your pardon, but we shall not give up what we have won Our Russia is so big, our economic potentialities are so numerous, and we feel justified in not rejecting your kind proposal, but we shall discuss it soberly, like businessmen." True, nothing came of our first talk, because we could not agree to his proposal for political reasons. We had to reject it. So long as the British did not entertain the possibility of our participating in the negotiations on the Straits, the Dardanelles, we had to reject it, but right after doing so we had to start examining the matter in substance. We discussed whether or not it was of advantage to us, whether we would profit from concluding this concession agreement, and if so, under what circumstances it would be profitable. We had to talk about the price. That, comrades, is what shows you clearly how much our present approach to problems should differ from our former approach. Formerly the Communist said: "I give my life", and it seemed very simple to him, although it was not always so simple. Now, however, we Communists face quite another task. We must now take all things into account, and each of you must learn to be prudent. We must calculate how, in the capitalist environment, we can ensure our existence, how we can profit by our enemies, who, of course, will bargain, who have never forgotten how to bargain and will bargain at our expense. We are not forgetting that either, and do not in the least imagine commercial people anywhere turning into lambs and, having turned into lambs, offering us blessings of all sorts for nothing. That does not happen, and we do not expect

it, but count on the fact that we, who are accustomed to
putting up a fight, will find a way out and prove capable
of trading, and profiting, and emerging safely from difficult economic situations. That is a very difficult task.
That is the task we are working on now. I should like us
to realise clearly how great is the abyss between the old
and the new tasks. However great the abyss may be, we
learned to manoeuvre during the war, and we must understand that the manoeuvre we now have to perform, in the
midst of which we now are, is the most difficult one. But
then it seems to be our last manoeuvre. We must test our
strength in this field and prove that we have learned more
than just the lessons of yesterday and do not just keep
repeating the fundamentals. Nothing of the kind. We have
begun to relearn, and shall relearn in such a way that we
shall achieve definite and obvious success. And it is for
the sake of this relearning, I think, that we must again
firmly promise one another that under the name of the
New Economic Policy we have turned back, but turned
back in such a way as to surrender nothing of the new,
and yet to give the capitalists such advantages as will
compel any state, however hostile to us, to establish contacts and to deal with us. Comrade Krasin, who has had
many talks with Urquhart, the head and backbone of the
whole intervention, said that Urquhart, after all his
attempts to foist the old system on us at all costs, throughout
Russia, seated himself at the same table with him, with
Krasin, and began asking: "What's the price? How much?
For how many years?" (*Applause.*) This is still quite far
from our concluding concession deals and thus entering
into treaty relations that are perfectly precise and binding—from the viewpoint of bourgeois society—but we can
already see that we are coming to it, have nearly come to
it, but have not quite arrived. We must admit that, comrades, and not be swell-headed. We are still far from having
fully achieved the things that will make us strong, self-
reliant and calmly confident that no capitalist deals can
frighten us, calmly confident that however difficult a deal
may be we shall conclude it, we shall get to the bottom of
it and settle it. That is why the work—both political and
Party—that we have begun in this sphere must be

continued, and that is why we must change from the old methods to entirely new ones.

We still have the old machinery, and our task now is to remould it along new lines. We cannot do so at once, but we must see to it that the Communists we have are properly placed. What we need is that they, the Communists, should control the machinery they are assigned to, and not, as so often happens with us, that the machinery should control them. We should make no secret of it, and speak of it frankly. Such are the tasks and the difficulties that confront us—and that at a moment when we have set out on our practical path, when we must not approach socialism as if it were an icon painted in festive colours. We need to take the right direction, we need to see that everything is checked, that the masses, the entire population, check the path we follow and say: "Yes, this is better than the old system." That is the task we have set ourselves. Our Party, a little group of people in comparison with the country's total population, has tackled this job. This tiny nucleus has set itself the task of remaking everything, and it will do so. We have proved that this is no utopia but a cause which people live by. We have all seen this. This has already been done. We must remake things in such a way that the great majority of the masses, the peasants and workers, will say: "It is not you who praise yourselves, but we. We say that you have achieved splendid results, after which no intelligent person will ever dream of returning to the old." We have not reached that point yet. *That is why NEP remains the main, current, and all-embracing slogan of today.* We shall not forget a single one of the slogans we learned yesterday. We can say that quite calmly, without the slightest hesitation, say it to anybody, and every step we take demonstrates it. But we still have to adapt ourselves to the New Economic Policy. We must know how to overcome, to reduce to a definite minimum all its negative features, which there is no need to enumerate and which you know perfectly well. We must know how to arrange everything shrewdly. Our legislation gives us every opportunity to do so Shall we be able to get things going properly? That is still far from being settled. We are making a study of things. Every issue of our Party newspaper offers you a dozen articles which tell you that at such-and-such a factory, owned by so-and-so, the rental terms are such-and-such, whereas at another, where our Communist comrade is the manager, the terms are such-and-such. Does it yield a profit or not, does it pay its way or not? We have approached the very core of the everyday problems, and that is a tremendous achievement. Socialism is no longer a matter of the distant future, or an abstract picture, or an icon. Our opinion of icons is the same—a very bad one. We have brought socialism into everyday life and must here see how matters stand. That is the task of our day, the task of our epoch. Permit me to conclude by expressing confidence that difficult as this task may be, new as it may be compared with our previous task, and numerous as the difficulties may be that it entails, we shall all—not in a day, but in a few years—all of us together fulfil it whatever the cost, so that NEP Russia will become socialist Russia. (*Stormy, prolonged applause.*)

Pravda No. 263,
November 21, 1922

Published according to
the *Pravda* text
checked with
the verbatim report

TO THE PRESIDIUM OF THE FIFTH ALL-RUSSIA CONGRESS OF THE SOVIET EMPLOYEES' UNION[145]

November 22, 1922

Dear Comrades,

The primary, immediate task of the present day, and of the next few years, is systematically to reduce the size and the cost of the Soviet machinery of state by cutting down staffs, improving organisation, eliminating red tape and bureaucracy, and by reducing unproductive expenditure. In this field your union has a great deal of work before it.

Wishing the Fifth All-Russia Congress of the Soviet Employees' Union success and fruitful work, I hope that it will especially deal with the question of the Soviet machinery of state.

V. Ulyanov (Lenin),
Chairman of the Council of People's Commissars

Izvestia No. 267,
November 25, 1922

Published according to
a typewritten copy checked
and signed by Lenin

TO THE EDUCATIONAL WORKERS' CONGRESS[146]

Thank you for your greetings, comrades. I wish you success in grappling with the great and responsible task before you of training the rising generation for the work of building up our new society.

Lenin

Written on November 26, 1922

Published in *Rabotnik Prosveshcheniya* No. 10, December 1922

Published according to the *Rabotnik Prosveshcheniya* text

TO THE THIRD CONGRESS
OF THE YOUNG COMMUNIST INTERNATIONAL,
MOSCOW[147]

December 4, 1922

Dear Comrades,

I regret that I cannot greet you in person. I send you my best wishes for success in your work. I hope that notwithstanding your lofty title you will not forget the main thing, namely, that it is necessary to promote in a practical manner the training and education of young people.

With best communist greetings,

V. Ulyanov (Lenin)

Pravda No. 275,
December 5, 1922

Published according to
a typewritten copy   corrected
and signed by Lenin

NOTES ON THE TASKS OF OUR DELEGATION AT THE HAGUE[148]

On the question of combating the danger of war, in connection with the Conference at The Hague, I think that the greatest difficulty lies in overcoming the prejudice that this is a simple, clear and comparatively easy question.

"We shall retaliate to war by a strike or a revolution"— that is what all the prominent reformist leaders usually say to the working class. And very often the seeming radicalness of the measures proposed satisfies and appeases the workers, co-operators and peasants.

Perhaps the most correct method would be to start with the sharpest refutation of this opinion; to declare that particularly now, after the recent war, only the most foolish or utterly dishonest people can assert that such an answer to the question of combating war is of any use; to declare that it is impossible to "retaliate" to war by a strike, just as it is impossible to "retaliate" to war by revolution in the simple and literal sense of these terms.

We must explain the real situation to the people, show them that war is hatched in the greatest secrecy, and that the ordinary workers' organisations, even if they call themselves revolutionary organisations, are utterly helpless in face of a really impending war.

We must explain to the people again and again in the most concrete manner possible how matters stood in the last war, and why they could not have been otherwise.

We must take special pains to explain that the question of "defence of the fatherland" will inevitably arise, and that the overwhelming majority of the working people will inevitably decide it in favour of their bourgeoisie.

Therefore, first, it is necessary to explain what "defence of the fatherland" means. Second, in connection with this, it is necessary to explain what "defeatism" means. Lastly, we must explain that the only possible method of combating war is to preserve existing, and to form new, illegal organisations in which all revolutionaries taking part in a war carry on *prolonged* anti-war activities—all this must be brought into the forefront.

Boycott war—that is a silly catch-phrase. Communists must take part in every war, even the most reactionary.

Examples from, say, pre-war German literature, and in particular, the example of the Basle Congress of 1912, should be used as especially concrete proof that the theoretical admission that war is criminal, that socialists cannot condone war, etc., turn out to be empty phrases, because there is nothing concrete in them. The masses are not given a really vivid idea of how war may and will creep up on them. On the contrary, every day the dominant press, in an infinite number of copies, obscures this question and weaves such lies around it that the feeble socialist press is absolutely impotent against it, the more so that even in time of peace it propounds fundamentally erroneous views on this point. In all probability, the communist press in most countries will also disgrace itself.

I think that our delegates at the International Congress of Co-operators and Trade Unionists should distribute their functions among themselves and expose all the sophistries that are being advanced at the present time in justification of war.

These sophistries are, perhaps, the principal means by which the bourgeois press rallies the masses in support of war; and the main reason why we are so impotent in face of war is either that we do not expose these sophistries beforehand, or still more that we, in the spirit of the Basle Manifesto of 1912, waive them aside with the cheap, boastful and utterly empty phrase that we shall not allow war to break out, that we fully understand that war is a crime, etc.

I think that if we have several people at The Hague Conference who are capable of delivering speeches against war in various languages, the most important thing would be to refute the opinion that the delegates at the Conference are opponents of war, that they understand how war may and will come upon them at the most unexpected moment, that they to any extent understand what methods should be adopted to combat war, that they are to any extent in a position to adopt reasonable and effective measures to combat war.

Using the experience of the recent war to illustrate the point, we must explain what a host of both theoretical and practical questions will arise on the morrow of the declaration of war, and that the vast majority of the men called up for military service will have no opportunity to examine these questions with anything like clear heads, or in a conscientious and unprejudiced manner.

I think that this question must be explained in extraordinary detail, and in two ways:

First, by relating and analysing what happened during the last war and telling all those present that they are ignorant of this, or pretend that they know about it, but actually shut their eyes to what is the very pivot of the question which must be understood if any real efforts are to be made to combat war. On this point I think it is necessary to examine all the opinions and shades of opinion that arose among Russian socialists concerning the last war. We must show that those shades of opinion did not emerge accidentally, but out of the very nature of modern wars in general. We must prove that without an analysis of these opinions, without ascertaining why they inevitably arise and why they are of decisive significance in the matter of combating war—without such an analysis it is utterly impossible to make any preparations for war, or even to take an intelligent stand on it.

Secondly, we must take the present conflicts, even the most insignificant, to illustrate the fact that war may break out any day as a consequence of a dispute between Great Britain and France over some point of their treaty with Turkey, or between the U.S.A. and Japan over some trivial disagreement on any Pacific question, or between any of the big powers over colonies, tariffs, or general commercial policy, etc., etc. It seems to me that if there is the slightest doubt about being able at The Hague to say all we want to say against war with the utmost freedom, we should consider various stratagems that will enable us to say at least what is most important and to publish in pamphlet form what could not be said. We must take the risk of our speaker being stopped by the chairman.

I think that for the same purpose the delegation should consist not only of speakers who are able, and whose duty it shall be, to make speeches against war as a whole, i.e., to enlarge on all the main arguments and all the conditions for combating war, but also of people who know all the three principal foreign languages, whose business it shall be to enter into conversation with the delegates and to ascertain how far they understand the main arguments, what need there is to advance certain arguments and to quote certain examples.

Perhaps on a number of questions the mere quoting of facts of the last war will be sufficient to produce serious effect. Perhaps on a number of other questions serious effect can be produced only by explaining the conflicts that exist today between the various countries and how likely they are to develop into armed collisions.

Apropos of the question of combating war, I remember that a number of declarations have been made by our Communist deputies, in parliament and outside parliament, which contain monstrously incorrect and monstrously thoughtless statements on this subject. I think these declarations, particularly if they have been made since the war, must be subjected to determined and ruthless criticism, and the name of each person who made them should be mentioned. Opinion concerning these speakers may be expressed in the mildest terms, particularly if circumstances require it, but not a single case of this kind should be passed over in silence, for thoughtlessness on this question is an evil that outweighs all others and cannot be treated lightly.

A number of decisions have been adopted by workers' congresses which are unpardonably foolish and thoughtless.

All material should be immediately collected, and all the separate parts and particles of the subject, and the whole "strategy" to be pursued should be thoroughly discussed at a congress.

On such a question, not only a mistake, but even lack of thoroughness on our part will be unpardonable.

December 4, 1922

First published in *Pravda* No. 96,
April 26, 1924
Signed: *Lenin*

Published according to
a typewritten copy
corrected and signed by Lenin

A FEW WORDS ABOUT N. Y. FEDOSEYEV[149]

My recollections of Nikolai Yevgrafovich Fedoseyev go back to the beginning of the nineties. I cannot vouch for their accuracy.

At that time I was living in the provinces—namely, in Kazan and in Samara. I heard about Fedoseyev while I was in Kazan, but I never met him. In the spring of 1889 I went to live in Samara Gubernia, where, at the end of the summer, I heard of the arrest of Fedoseyev and of other members of study circles in Kazan—including the one to which I belonged. I think that I, too, might easily have been arrested had I remained in Kazan that summer. Soon after this, Marxism, as a trend, began to spread, merging with the Social-Democratic trend initiated in Western Europe very much earlier by the Emancipation of Labour group.[150]

Fedoseyev was one of the first to proclaim his adherence to the Marxist trend. I remember that this was the grounds of his polemics with N. K. Mikhailovsky, who in *Russkoye Bogatstvo*[151] replied to one of his secretly circulated letters. This, too, prompted me to start corresponding with Fedoseyev. I remember that the go-between in our correspondence was Hopfenhaus, whom I met once, and through whom I made an unsuccessful attempt to arrange a meeting with Fedoseyev in Vladimir. I went to that town in the hope that he would succeed in getting out of the prison, but I was disappointed.[152]

Later, Fedoseyev was exiled to Eastern Siberia. This was at the time I was in exile there; and it was in Siberia that he committed suicide, because, I think, of certain tragic incidents in his private life connected with the exceptionally unhappy conditions under which he lived.

As far as I remember, my correspondence with Fedoseyev was concerned with the problems that then arose about the Marxist or Social-Democratic world outlook. I particularly remember that Fedoseyev enjoyed the affection of all those who knew him, and was regarded as a typical old-time revolutionary, entirely devoted to his cause, who, perhaps, had made his conditions worse by certain statements, or unguarded actions towards the gendarmes.

Probably I have some fragments of Fedoseyev's letters or manuscripts somewhere, but I cannot say definitely whether they have been preserved or may be found.

At all events, Fedoseyev played a very important role in the Volga area and in certain parts of Central Russia during that period; and the turn towards Marxism at that time was, undoubtedly, very largely due to the influence of this exceptionally talented and exceptionally devoted revolutionary.

December 6, 1922

Published in *N. Y. Fedoseyev, a Pioneer of Revolutionary Marxism in Russia (A Collection of Reminiscences)*, Moscow-Petrograd, 1923
Signed: *Lenin*

Published according to the text in the collection

TO THE ALL-UKRAINE CONGRESS OF SOVIETS[153]

I welcome the opening of the All-Ukraine Congress of Soviets.

One of the most important problems which the Congress has to solve is that of uniting the republics. The proper solution of this problem will determine the future organisation of our machinery of state, the glaring defects of which were so vividly and strikingly revealed by the recent census of Soviet employees in Moscow, Petrograd and Kharkov.

The second problem to which the Congress must devote special attention is that of our heavy industry. To raise the output of the Donbas and of the oil and iron and steel industries to pre-war level is the fundamental problem of our entire economy; and we must concentrate all our efforts on solving this problem.

I am firmly convinced that the Congress will find the correct solutions for these problems, and with all my heart I wish you success in your work.

Lenin

December 10, 1922

Kommunist (Kharkov) No. 285,
December 12, 1922

Published according to
the *Kommunist* text
checked with
a typewritten copy

RE THE MONOPOLY OF FOREIGN TRADE[154]

TO COMRADE STALIN FOR THE PLENARY MEETING OF THE CENTRAL COMMITTEE

I think it is most important to discuss Comrade Bukharin's letter. His first point says that "neither Lenin nor Krasin says a word about the incalculable losses that are borne by the economy of the country as a consequence of the inefficiency of the People's Commissariat of Foreign Trade, due to the 'principles' on which it is organised; they do not say a word about the losses incurred because we ourselves are unable (and will not be able for a long time for quite understandable reasons) to mobilise the peasants' stocks of goods and use them for international trade".

This statement is positively untrue, for in his § 2 Krasin clearly discusses the formation of mixed companies as a means, firstly, of mobilising the peasants' stocks of goods, and secondly, of obtaining for our Exchequer no less than half the profits accruing from this mobilisation. Thus it is Bukharin who is trying to evade the issue, for he refuses to see that the profits accruing from the "mobilisation of the peasants' stocks of goods" will go wholly and entirely into the pockets of the Nepmen. The question is: will our People's Commissariat of Foreign Trade operate for the benefit of the Nepmen or of our proletarian state? This is a fundamental question over which a fight can and should be put up at a Party Congress.

Compared with this primary, fundamental question of principle, the question of the inefficiency of the People's Commissariat of Foreign Trade is only a minor one, for this inefficiency is only part and parcel of the inefficiency of all our People's Commissariats, and is due to their general social structure; to remedy this we shall require many years of persistent effort to improve education and to raise the general standard.

The second point in Bukharin's theses says that "points like § 5 of Krasin's theses, for example, are fully applicable to concessions in general". This, too, is glaringly untrue, for Krasin's 5th thesis states that "the most pernicious exploiter, the merchant, profiteer, the agent of foreign capital, operating with dollars, pounds and Swedish crowns, will be artificially introduced into the rural districts". Nothing of the kind will happen in the case of concessions, which not only stipulate territory, but also envisage special permission to trade in specified articles; and what is most important, we control the trade in the articles specified in the concession. Without saying a single word in opposition to Krasin's argument that we shall be unable to keep free trade within the limits laid down by the decision of the Plenary Meeting of October 6, that trade will be torn out of our hands by pressure brought to bear not only by smugglers, but also by the entire peasantry—without saying a word in answer to this fundamental economic and class argument, Bukharin hurls accusations against Krasin that are amazingly groundless.

In the third point of his letter Bukharin writes "§3 of Krasin's theses". (By mistake he mentions § 3 instead of § 4.) "We are maintaining our frontiers", and he asks: "What does this mean? In reality, this means that we are doing nothing. It is exactly like a shop with a splendid window, but with nothing on its shelves (the 'shut the shops system')." Krasin very definitely says that we are maintaining our frontiers not so much by tariffs, or frontier guards, as by means of our monopoly of foreign trade. Bukharin does not say a word to refute this obvious, positive and indisputable fact, nor can he do so. His sneering reference to the "shut the shops system" belongs to the category of expressions to which Marx, in his day, retorted with the expression "free-trader *vulgaris*", for it is nothing more than a vulgar free-trader catch-phrase.

Further, in his fourth point, Bukharin accuses Krasin

of failing to realise that we must improve our tariff system, and at the same time he says that I am wrong in talking about having inspectors all over the country, because export and import bases are the only point under discussion. Here, too, Bukharin's objections are amazingly thoughtless and quite beside the point; for Krasin not only realises that we must improve our tariff system and not only fully admits it, but says so with a definiteness that leaves no room for the slightest doubt. This improvement consists, firstly, in our adopting the monopoly of foreign trade, and secondly, in the formation of mixed companies.

Bukharin does not see—this is his most amazing mistake, and a purely theoretical one at that—that no tariff system can be effective in the epoch of imperialism when there are monstrous contrasts between pauper countries and immensely rich countries. Several times Bukharin mentions tariff barriers, failing to realise that under the circumstances indicated any of the wealthy industrial countries can completely break down such tariff barriers. To do this it will be sufficient for it to introduce an export bounty to encourage the export to Russia of goods upon which we have imposed high import duties. All of the industrial countries have more than enough money for this purpose, and by means of such a measure any of them could easily ruin our home industry.

Consequently, all Bukharin's arguments about the tariff system would in practice only leave Russian industry entirely unprotected and lead to the adoption of free trading under a very flimsy veil. We must oppose this with all our might and carry our opposition right to a Party Congress, for in the present epoch of imperialism the only system of protection worthy of consideration is the monopoly of foreign trade.

Bukharin's accusation (in his fifth point) that Krasin fails to appreciate the importance of increasing circulation is utterly refuted by what Krasin says about mixed companies, for these mixed companies have no other purpose than to increase circulation and to provide real protection for our Russian industry and not the fictitious protection of tariff barriers.

Further, in point six, in answer to me, Bukharin writes that he attaches no importance to the fact that the peasants will enter into profitable transactions, and that the struggle will proceed between the Soviet government and the exporters and not between the peasants and the Soviet government. Here, too, he is absolutely wrong, for with the difference in prices that I have indicated (for example, in Russia the price of flax is 4 rubles 50 kopeks, while in Britain it is 14 rubles), the exporter will be able to mobilise all the peasants around himself in the swiftest and most certain manner. In practice, Bukharin is acting as an advocate of the profiteer, of the petty bourgeois and of the upper stratum of the peasantry in opposition to the industrial proletariat, which will be totally unable to build up its own industry and make Russia an industrial country unless it has the protection, not of tariffs, but of the monopoly of foreign trade. In view of the conditions at present prevailing in Russia, any other form of protection would be absolutely fictitious; it would be merely paper protection, from which the proletariat would derive no benefit whatever. Hence, from the viewpoint of the proletariat and of its industry, the present fight rages around fundamental principles. The mixed company system is the only system that can be really effective in improving the defective machinery of the People's Commissariat of Foreign Trade; for under this system foreign and Russian merchants will be operating side by side. If we fail to learn the business thoroughly even under such circumstances, it will prove that ours is a nation of hopeless fools.

By talking about "tariff barriers" we shall only be concealing from ourselves the dangers which Krasin points out quite clearly, and which Bukharin has failed to refute in the slightest degree.

I will add that the partial opening of the frontiers would be fraught with grave currency dangers, for in practice we should be reduced to the position of Germany; there would be the grave danger that the petty-bourgeoisie and all sorts of agents of émigré Russia would penetrate into Russia, without our having the slightest possibility of exercising control over them.

The utilisation of mixed companies as a means of obtaining serious and long tuition is the only road to the restoration of our industry.

Lenin

Dictated by telephone
on December 13, 1922

First published, in abridged
form, in *Izvestia* No. 21,
January 26, 1924

First published in full in 1930
in the journal *Proletarskaya
Revolutsia* No. 2-3

Published according to
the stenographer's
notes (typewritten copy)

LETTER TO J. V. STALIN FOR MEMBERS
OF THE C.C., R.C.P.(B.)

I have now finished winding up my affairs and can leave with my mind at peace.[155] I have also come to an agreement with Trotsky on the defence of my views on the monopoly of foreign trade. Only one circumstance still worries me very much; it is that it will be impossible for me to speak at the Congress of Soviets.[156] My doctors are coming on Tuesday and we shall see if there is even a small chance of my speaking. I would consider it a great inconvenience to miss the opportunity of speaking, to say the least. I finished preparing the summary a few days ago. I therefore propose that the writing of a report which somebody will deliver should go ahead and that the possibility be left open until Wednesday that I will perhaps personally make a speech, a much shorter one than usual, for example, one that will take three-quarters of an hour. Such a speech would in no way hinder the speech of my deputy (whoever you may appoint for this purpose), but would be useful politically and from the personal angle as it would eliminate cause for great anxiety. Please have this in mind, and if the opening of the Congress is delayed, inform me in good time through my secretary.[157]

Lenin

December 15, 1922

I am emphatically against any procrastination of the question of the monopoly of foreign trade. If any circumstance (including the circumstance that my participation is desirable in the debate over this question) gives rise to the idea to postpone it to the next Plenary Meeting, I would most emphatically be against it because, firstly, I am sure Trotsky will uphold my views as well as I; secondly, the statements that you, Zinoviev and, according to rumours, Kamenev have made prove that some members of the C.C. have already changed their minds; thirdly, and most important, any further vacillation over this extremely important question is absolutely impermissible and will wreck all our work.

Lenin

December 15, 1922

Dictated by telephone

First published, in abridged form,
in 1930 in Vol. XXVII of the 2nd
and 3rd Russian language editions
of Lenin's *Works*

Published in full according to
the stenographer's notes
(typewritten copy)

PAGES FROM A DIARY

The recent publication of the report on literacy among the population of Russia, based on the census of 1920 (*Literacy in Russia*, issued by the Central Statistical Board, Public Education Section, Moscow, 1922), is a very important event.

Below I quote a table from this report on the state of literacy among the population of Russia in 1897 and 1920.

	Literates per thousand males		Literates per thousand females		Literates per thousand population	
	1897	1920	1897	1920	1897	1920
1. European Russia	326	422	136	255	229	330
2. North Caucasus	241	357	56	215	150	281
3. Siberia (Western)	170	307	46	134	108	218
Overall average	318	409	131	244	223	319

At a time when we hold forth on proletarian culture and the relation in which it stands to bourgeois culture, facts and figures reveal that we are in a very bad way even as far as bourgeois culture is concerned. As might have been expected, it appears that we are still a very long way from attaining universal literacy, and that even compared with tsarist times (1897) our progress has been far too slow. This should serve as a stern warning and reproach to those who have been soaring in the empyreal heights of "proletarian culture". It shows what a vast amount of urgent spade-work we still have to do to reach the standard of an ordinary West-European civilised country.

It also shows what a vast amount of work we have to do today to achieve, on the basis of our proletarian gains, anything like a real cultural standard.

We must not confine ourselves to this incontrovertible but too theoretical proposition. The very next time we revise our quarterly budget we must take this matter up in a practical way as well. In the first place, of course, we shall have to cut down the expenditure of government departments other than the People's Commissariat of Education, and the sums thus released should be assigned for the latter's needs. In a year like the present, when we are relatively well supplied, we must not be chary in increasing the bread ration for schoolteachers.

Generally speaking, it cannot be said that the work now being done in public education is too narrow. Quite a lot is being done to get the old teachers out of their rut, to attract them to the new problems, to rouse their interest in new methods of education, and in such problems as religion.

But we are not doing the main thing. We are not doing anything—or doing far from enough—to raise the schoolteacher to the level that is absolutely essential if we want any culture at all, proletarian or even bourgeois. We must bear in mind the semi-Asiatic ignorance from which we have not yet extricated ourselves, and from which we cannot extricate ourselves without strenuous effort—although we have every opportunity to do so, because nowhere are the masses of the people so interested in real culture as they are in our country; nowhere are the problems of this culture tackled so thoroughly and consistently as they are in our country; in no other country is state power in the hands of the working class which, in its mass, is fully aware of the deficiencies, I shall not say of its culture, but of its literacy; nowhere is the working class so ready to make, and nowhere is it actually making, such sacrifices to improve its position in this respect as in our country.

Too little, far too little, is still being done by us to adjust our state budget to satisfy, as a first measure, the requirements of elementary public education. Even in our People's Commissariat of Education we all too often find disgracefully inflated staffs in some state publishing establishment, which is contrary to the concept that the state's first concern should not be publishing houses but that there should be people to read, that the number of people able to read is greater, so that book publishing should have a wider political field in future Russia. Owing to the old (and bad) habit, we are still devoting much more time and effort to technical questions, such as the question of book publishing, than to the general political question of literacy among the people.

If we take the Central Vocational Education Board, we are sure that there, too, we shall find far too much that is superfluous and inflated by departmental interests, much that is ill-adjusted to the requirements of broad public education. Far from everything that we find in the Central Vocational Education Board can be justified by the legitimate desire first of all to improve and give a practical slant to the education of our young factory workers. If we examine the staff of the Central Vocational Education Board carefully we shall find very much that is inflated and is in that respect fictitious and should be done away with. There is still very much in the proletarian and peasant state that can and must be economised for the purpose of promoting literacy among the people; this can be done by closing institutions which are playthings of a semi-aristocratic type, or institutions we can still do without and will be able to do without, and shall have to do without, for a long time to come, considering the state of literacy among the people as revealed by the statistics.

Our schoolteacher should be raised to a standard he has never achieved, and cannot achieve, in bourgeois society. This is a truism and requires no proof. We must strive for this state of affairs by working steadily, methodically and persistently to raise the teacher to a higher cultural level, to train him thoroughly for his really high calling and—mainly, mainly and mainly—to improve his position materially.

We must systematically step up our efforts to organise the schoolteachers so as to transform them from the bulwark of the bourgeois system that they still are in all capitalist countries without exception, into the bulwark of

the Soviet system, in order, through their agency, to divert
the peasantry from alliance with the bourgeoisie and to
bring them into alliance with the proletariat.

I want briefly to emphasise the special importance in
this respect of regular visits to the villages; such visits,
it is true, are already being practised and should be regularly promoted. We should not stint money—which we
all too often waste on the machinery of state that is almost
entirely a product of the past historical epoch—on measures
like these visits to the villages.

For the speech I was to have delivered at the Congress
of Soviets in December 1922 I collected data on the patron-
age undertaken by urban workers over villagers. Part of
these data was obtained for me by Comrade Khodorovsky,
and since I have been unable to deal with this problem and
give it publicity through the Congress, I submit the matter
to the comrades for discussion now.

Here we have a fundamental political question—the
relations between town and country—which is of decisive
importance for the whole of our revolution. While the
bourgeois state methodically concentrates all its efforts
on doping the urban workers, adapting all the literature
published at state expense and at the expense of the tsarist
and bourgeois parties for this purpose, we can and must
utilise our political power to make the urban worker an
effective vehicle of communist ideas among the rural proletariat.

I said "communist", but I hasten to make a reservation
for fear of causing a misunderstanding, or of being taken
too literally. Under no circumstances must this be understood to mean that we should immediately propagate
purely and strictly communist ideas in the countryside.
As long as our countryside lacks the material basis for
communism, it will be, I should say, harmful, in fact,
I should say, fatal, for communism to do so.

That is a fact. We must start by establishing contacts
between town and country without the preconceived aim
of implanting communism in the rural districts. It is an
aim which cannot be achieved at the present time. It is
inopportune, and to set an aim like that at the present
time would be harmful, instead of useful, to the cause.

But it is our duty to establish contacts between the urban workers and the rural working people, to establish between them a form of comradeship which can easily be created. This is one of the fundamental tasks of the working class which holds power. To achieve this we must form a number of associations (Party, trade union and private) of factory workers, which would devote themselves regularly to assisting the villages in their cultural development.

Is it possible to "attach" all the urban groups to all the village groups, so that every working-class group may take advantage regularly of every opportunity, of every occasion to serve the cultural needs of the village group it is "attached" to? Or will it be possible to find other forms of contact? I here confine myself solely to formulating the question in order to draw the comrades' attention to it, to point out the available experience of Western Siberia (to which Comrade Khodorovsky drew my attention) and to present this gigantic, historic cultural task in all its magnitude.

We are doing almost nothing for the rural districts outside our official budget or outside official channels. True, in our country the nature of the cultural relations between town and village is automatically and inevitably changing. Under capitalism the town introduced political, economic, moral, physical, etc., corruption into the countryside. In our case, towns are automatically beginning to introduce the very opposite of this into the countryside. But, I repeat, all this is going on automatically, spontaneously, and can be improved (and later increased a hundredfold) by doing it consciously, methodically and systematically.

We shall begin to advance (and shall then surely advance a hundred times more quickly) only after we have studied the question, after we have formed all sorts of workers' organisations—doing everything to prevent them from becoming bureaucratic—to take up the matter, discuss it and get things done.

January 2, 1923

Pravda No. 2,
January 4, 1923
Signed: *N. Lenin*

Published according to
the *Pravda* text
checked with
the stenographer's notes

ON CO-OPERATION

I

It seems to me that not enough attention is being paid to the co-operative movement in our country. Not everyone understands that now, since the time of the October Revolution and quite apart from NEP (on the contrary, in this connection we must say—because of NEP), our co-operative movement has become one of great significance. There is a lot of fantasy in the dreams of the old co-operators. Often they are ridiculously fantastic. But why are they fantastic? Because people do not understand the fundamental, the rock-bottom significance of the working-class political struggle for the overthrow of the rule of the exploiters. We have overthrown the rule of the exploiters, and much that was fantastic, even romantic, even banal in the dreams of the old co-operators is now becoming unvarnished reality.

Indeed, since political power is in the hands of the working class, since this political power owns all the means of production, the only task, indeed, that remains for us is to organise the population in co-operative societies. With most of the population organised in co-operatives, the socialism which in the past was legitimately treated with ridicule, scorn and contempt by those who were rightly convinced that it was necessary to wage the class struggle, the struggle for political power, etc., will achieve its aim automatically. But not all comrades realise how vastly, how infinitely important it is now to organise the population of Russia in co-operative societies. By adopting NEP we made a concession to the peasant as a trader, to the principle of private trade; it is precisely for this reason (contrary to what some people think) that the co-operative movement is of such immense importance. All we actually need under NEP is to organise the population of Russia in co-operative societies on a sufficiently large scale, for we have now found that degree of combination of private interest, of private commercial interest, with state supervision and control of this interest, that degree of its subordination to the common interests which was formerly the stumbling-block for very many socialists. Indeed, the power of the state over all large-scale means of production, political power in the hands of the proletariat, the alliance of this proletariat with the many millions of small and very small peasants, the assured proletarian leadership of the peasantry, etc.—is this not all that is necessary to build a complete socialist society out of co-operatives, out of co-operatives alone, which we formerly ridiculed as huckstering and which from a certain aspect we have the right to treat as such now, under NEP? Is this not all that is necessary to build a complete socialist society? It is still not the building of socialist society, but it is all that is necessary and sufficient for it.

It is this very circumstance that is underestimated by many of our practical workers. They look down upon our co-operative societies, failing to appreciate their exceptional importance, first, from the standpoint of principle (the means of production are owned by the state), and, second, from the standpoint of transition to the new system by means that are the *simplest, easiest and most acceptable to the peasant*.

But this again is of fundamental importance. It is one thing to draw up fantastic plans for building socialism through all sorts of workers' associations, and quite another to learn to build socialism in practice in such a way that *every* small peasant could take part in it. That is the very stage we have now reached. And there is no doubt that, having reached it, we are taking too little advantage of it.

We went too far when we introduced NEP, but not because we attached too much importance to the principle of free enterprise and trade—we went too far because we lost sight of the co-operatives, because we now underrate the co-operatives, because we are already beginning to forget the vast importance of the co-operatives from the above two points of view.

I now propose to discuss with the reader what can and must at once be done practically on the basis of this "co-operative" principle. By what means can we, and must we, start at once to develop this "co-operative" principle so that its socialist meaning may be clear to all?

Co-operation must be politically so organised that it will not only generally and always enjoy certain privileges, but that these privileges should be of a purely material nature (a favourable bank-rate, etc.). The co-operatives must be granted state loans that are greater, if only by a little, than the loans we grant to private enterprises, even to heavy industry, etc.

A social system emerges only if it has the financial backing of a definite class. There is no need to mention the hundreds of millions of rubles that the birth of "free" capitalism cost. At ·present we have to realise that the co-operative system is the social system we must now give more than ordinary assistance, and we must actually give that assistance. But it must be assistance in the real sense of the word, i.e., it will not be enough to interpret it to mean assistance for any kind of co-operative trade; by assistance we must mean aid to co-operative trade in which *really large masses of the population actually take part*. It is certainly a correct form of assistance to give a bonus to peasants who take part in co-operative trade; but the whole·point is to verify the nature of this participation, to verify the awareness behind it, and to verify its quality. Strictly speaking, when a co-operator goes to a village and opens a co-operative store, the people take no part in this whatever; but at the same time guided by their own interests they will hasten to try to take part in it.

There is another aspect to this question. From the point of view of the "enlightened" (primarily, literate) European there is not much left for us to do to induce absolutely everyone to take not a passive, but an active part in co-operative operations. Strictly speaking, there is *"only"* one thing we have left to do and that is to make our people so "enlightened" that they understand all the advantages of everybody participating in the work of the co-operatives, and organise this participation. *"Only"* that. There are now no other devices needed to advance to socialism. But to achieve this "only", there must be a veritable revolution—the entire people must go through a period of cultural development. Therefore, our rule must be: as little philosophising and as few acrobatics as possible. In this respect NEP is an advance, because it is adjustable to the level of the most ordinary peasant and does not demand anything higher of him. But it will take a whole historical epoch to get the entire population into the work of the co-operatives through NEP. At best we can achieve this in one or two decades. Nevertheless, it will be a distinct historical epoch, and without this historical epoch, without universal literacy, without a proper degree of efficiency, without training the population sufficiently to acquire the habit of book-reading, and without the material basis for this, without a certain sufficiency to safeguard against, say, bad harvests, famine, etc.—without this we shall not achieve our object. The thing now is to learn to combine the wide revolutionary range of action, the revolutionary enthusiasm which we have displayed, and displayed abundantly, and crowned with complete success—to learn to combine this with (I am almost inclined to say) the ability to be an efficient and capable trader, which is quite enough to be a good co-operator. By ability to be a trader I mean the ability to be a cultured trader. Let those Russians, or peasants, who imagine that since they trade they are good traders, get that well into their heads. This does not follow at all. They do trade, but that is far from being cultured traders. They now trade in an Asiatic manner, but to be a good trader one must trade in the European manner. They are a whole epoch behind in that.

In conclusion: a number of economic, financial and banking privileges must be granted to the co-operatives—this is the way our socialist state must promote the new principle on which the population must be organised. But this is only the general outline of the task; it does not define and depict in detail the entire content of the practi-

cal task, i.e., we must find what form of "bonus" to give
for joining the co-operatives (and the terms on which we
should give it), the form of bonus by which we shall assist
the co-operatives sufficiently, the form of bonus that will
produce the civilised co-operator. And given social ownership of the means of production, given the class victory
of the proletariat over the bourgeoisie, the system of civilised co-operators is the system of socialism.

January 4, 1923

II

Whenever I wrote about the New Economic Policy I always quoted the article on state capitalism[158] which I wrote in 1918. This has more than once aroused doubts in the minds of certain young comrades. But their doubts were mainly on abstract political points.

It seemed to them that the term "state capitalism" could not be applied to a system under which the means of production were owned by the working class, a working class that held political power. They did not notice, however, that I used the term "state capitalism", *firstly*, to connect historically our present position with the position adopted in my controversy with the so-called Left Communists; also, I argued at the time that state capitalism would be superior to our existing economy. It was important for me to show the continuity between ordinary state capitalism and the unusual, even very unusual, state capitalism to which I referred in introducing the reader to the New Economic Policy. *Secondly*, the practical purpose was always important to me. And the practical purpose of our New Economic Policy was to lease out concessions. In the prevailing circumstances, concessions in our country would unquestionably have been a pure type of state capitalism. That is how I argued about state capitalism.

But there is another aspect of the matter for which we may need state capitalism, or at least a comparison with it. It is the question of co-operatives.

In the capitalist state, co-operatives are no doubt collective capitalist institutions. Nor is there any doubt that under our present economic conditions, when we combine private capitalist enterprises—but in no other way than on nationalised land and in no other way than under the control of the working-class state—with enterprises of a consistently socialist type (the means of production, the land on which the enterprises are situated, and the enterprises as a whole belonging to the state), the question arises about a third type of enterprise, the co-operatives, which were not formerly regarded as an independent type differing fundamentally from the others. Under private capitalism, co-operative enterprises differ from capitalist enterprises as collective enterprises differ from private enterprises. Under state capitalism, co-operative enterprises differ from state capitalist enterprises, firstly, because they are private enterprises, and, secondly, because they are collective enterprises. Under our present system, co-operative enterprises differ from private capitalist enterprises because they are collective enterprises, but do not differ from socialist enterprises if the land on which they are situated and the means of production belong to the state, i.e., the working class.

This circumstance is not considered sufficiently when co-operatives are discussed. It is forgotten that owing to the special features of our political system, our co-operatives acquire an altogether exceptional significance. If we exclude concessions, which, incidentally, have not developed on any considerable scale, co-operation under our conditions nearly always coincides fully with socialism.

Let me explain what I mean. Why were the plans of the old co-operators, from Robert Owen onwards, fantastic? Because they dreamed of peacefully remodelling contemporary society into socialism without taking account of such fundamental questions as the class struggle, the capture of political power by the working class, the overthrow of the rule of the exploiting class. That is why we are right in regarding as entirely fantastic this "co-operative" socialism, and as romantic, and even banal, the dream of transforming class enemies into class collaborators and class war into class peace (so-called class truce) by merely organising the population in co-operative societies.

Undoubtedly we were right from the point of view of the fundamental task of the present day, for socialism cannot be established without a class struggle for political power in the state.

But see how things have changed now that political power is in the hands of the working class, now that the political power of the exploiters is overthrown and all the means of production (except those which the workers' state voluntarily abandons on specified terms and for a certain time to the exploiters in the form of concessions) are owned by the working class.

Now we are entitled to say that for us the mere growth of co-operation (with the "slight" exception mentioned above) is identical with the growth of socialism, and at the same time we have to admit that there has been a radical modification in our whole outlook on socialism. The radical modification is this; formerly we placed, and had to place, the main emphasis on the political struggle, on revolution, on winning political power, etc. Now the emphasis is changing and shifting to peaceful, organisational, "cultural" work. I should say that emphasis is shifting to educational work, were it not for our international relations, were it not for the fact that we have to fight for our position on a world scale. If we leave that aside, however, and confine ourselves to internal economic relations, the emphasis in our work is certainly shifting to education.

Two main tasks confront us, which constitute the epoch—to reorganise our machinery of state, which is utterly useless, and which we took over in its entirety from the preceding epoch; during the past five years of struggle we did not, and could not, drastically reorganise it. Our second task is educational work among the peasants. And the economic object of this educational work among the peasants is to organise the latter in co-operative societies. If the whole of the peasantry had been organised in co-operatives, we would by now have been standing with both feet on the soil of socialism. But the organisation of the entire peasantry in co-operative societies presupposes a standard of culture among the peasants (precisely among the peasants as the overwhelming mass) that cannot, in fact, be achieved without a cultural revolution.

Our opponents told us repeatedly that we were rash in undertaking to implant socialism in an insufficiently cultured country. But they were misled by our having started from the opposite end to that prescribed by theory (the theory of pedants of all kinds), because in our country the political and social revolution preceded the cultural revolution, that very cultural revolution which nevertheless now confronts us.

This cultural revolution would now suffice to make our country a completely socialist country; but it presents immense difficulties of a purely cultural (for we are illiterate) and material character (for to be cultured we must achieve a certain development of the material means of production, must have a certain material base).

January 6, 1923

First published in *Pravda*
Nos. 115 and 116,
May 26 and 27, 1923
Signed: *N. Lenin*

Published according to
the *Pravda* text
checked with
the stenographer's notes

OUR REVOLUTION

(APROPOS OF N. SUKHANOV'S NOTES)

I

I have lately been glancing through Sukhanov's notes on the revolution. What strikes one most is the pedantry of all our petty-bourgeois democrats and of all the heroes of the Second International. Apart from the fact that they are all extremely faint-hearted, that when it comes to the minutest deviation from the German model even the best of them fortify themselves with reservations—apart from this characteristic, which is common to all petty-bourgeois democrats and has been abundantly manifested by them throughout the revolution, what strikes one is their slavish imitation of the past.

They all call themselves Marxists, but their conception of Marxism is impossibly pedantic. They have completely failed to understand what is decisive in Marxism, namely, its revolutionary dialectics. They have even absolutely failed to understand Marx's plain statements that in times of revolution the utmost flexibility[159] is demanded, and have even failed to notice, for instance, the statements Marx made in his letters—I think it was in 1856—expressing the hope of combining a peasant war in Germany, which might create a revolutionary situation, with the working-class movement[160]—they avoid even this plain statement and walk round and about it like a cat around a bowl of hot porridge.

Their conduct betrays them as cowardly reformists who are afraid to deviate from the bourgeoisie, let alone break with it, and at the same time they disguise their cowardice with the wildest rhetoric and braggartry. But what strikes one in all of them even from the purely theoretical point of view is their utter inability to grasp the following Marxist considerations: up to now they have seen capitalism and bourgeois democracy in Western Europe follow a definite path of development, and cannot conceive that this path can be taken as a model only *mutatis mutandis*, only with certain amendments (quite insignificant from the standpoint of the general development of world history).

First—the revolution connected with the first imperialist world war. Such a revolution was bound to reveal new features, or variations, resulting from the war itself, for the world has never seen such a war in such a situation. We find that since the war the bourgeoisie of the wealthiest countries have to this day been unable to restore "normal" bourgeois relations. Yet our reformists—petty bourgeois who make a show of being revolutionaries—believed, and still believe, that normal bourgeois relations are the limit (thus far shalt thou go and no farther). And even their conception of "normal" is extremely stereotyped and narrow.

Secondly, they are complete strangers to the idea that while the development of world history as a whole follows general laws it is by no means precluded, but, on the contrary, presumed, that certain periods of development may display peculiarities in either the form or the sequence of this development. For instance, it does not even occur to them that because Russia stands on the border-line between the civilised countries and the countries which this war has for the first time definitely brought into the orbit of civilisation—all the Oriental, non-European countries—she could and was, indeed, bound to reveal certain distinguishing features; although these, of course, are in keeping with the general line of world development, they distinguish her revolution from those which took place in the West-European countries and introduce certain partial innovations as the revolution moves on to the countries of the East.

Infinitely stereotyped, for instance, is the argument they learned by rote during the development of West-

European Social-Democracy, namely, that we are not yet ripe for socialism, that, as certain "learned" gentlemen among them put it, the objective economic premises for socialism do not exist in our country. It does not occur to any of them to ask: but what about a people that found itself in a revolutionary situation such as that created during the first imperialist war? Might it not, influenced by the hopelessness of its situation, fling itself into a struggle that would offer it at least some chance of securing conditions for the further development of civilisation that were somewhat unusual?

"The development of the productive forces of Russia has not attained the level that makes socialism possible." All the heroes of the Second International, including, of course, Sukhanov, beat the drums about this proposition. They keep harping on this incontrovertible proposition in a thousand different keys, and think that it is the decisive criterion of our revolution.

But what if the situation, which drew Russia into the imperialist world war that involved every more or less influential West-European country and made her a witness of the eve of the revolutions maturing or partly already begun in the East, gave rise to circumstances that put Russia and her development in a position which enabled us to achieve precisely that combination of a "peasant war" with the working-class movement suggested in 1856 by no less a Marxist than Marx himself as a possible prospect for Prussia?

What if the complete hopelessness of the situation, by stimulating the efforts of the workers and peasants tenfold, offered us the opportunity to create the fundamental requisites of civilisation in a different way from that of the West-European countries? Has that altered the general line of development of world history? Has that altered the basic relations between the basic classes of all the countries that are being, or have been, drawn into the general course of world history?

If a definite level of culture is required for the building of socialism (although nobody can say just what that definite "level of culture" is, for it differs in every West-European country), why cannot we begin by first achieving the prerequisites for that definite level of culture in a revolutionary way, and *then*, with the aid of the workers' and peasants' government and the Soviet system, proceed to overtake the other nations?

January 16, 1923

———

II

You say that civilisation is necessary for the building of socialism. Very good. But why could we not first create such prerequisites of civilisation in our country as the expulsion of the landowners and the Russian capitalists, and then start moving towards socialism? Where, in what books, have you read that such variations of the customary historical sequence of events are impermissible or impossible?

Napoleon, I think, wrote: *"On s'engage et puis ... on voit."* Rendered freely this means: "First engage in a serious battle and then see what happens." Well, we did first engage in a serious battle in October 1917, and then saw such details of development (from the standpoint of world history they were certainly details) as the Brest peace, the New Economic Policy, and so forth. And now there can be no doubt that in the main we have been victorious.

Our Sukhanovs, not to mention Social-Democrats still farther to the right, never even dream that revolutions cannot be made otherwise. Our European philistines never even dream that the subsequent revolutions in Oriental countries, which possess much vaster populations and a much vaster diversity of social conditions, will undoubtedly display even greater distinctions than the Russian revolution.

It need hardly be said that a textbook written on Kautskian lines was a very useful thing in its day. But it is time, for all that, to abandon the idea that it foresaw all the forms of development of subsequent world history. It would be timely to say that those who think so are simply fools.

January 17, 1923

First published
in *Pravda* No. 117,
May 30, 1923
Signed: *Lenin*

Published according to the newspaper text, with additional corrections in the stenographer's notes on Lenin's instructions

HOW WE SHOULD REORGANISE THE WORKERS' AND PEASANTS' INSPECTION

(RECOMMENDATION TO THE TWELFTH PARTY CONGRESS)[161]

It is beyond question that the Workers' and Peasants' Inspection is an enormous difficulty for us, and that so far this difficulty has not been overcome. I think that the comrades who try to overcome the difficulty by denying that the Workers' and Peasants' Inspection is useful and necessary are wrong. But I do not deny that the problem presented by our state apparatus and the task of improving it is very difficult, that it is far from being solved, and is an extremely urgent one.

With the exception of the People's Commissariat of Foreign Affairs, our state apparatus is to a considerable extent a survival of the past and has undergone hardly any serious change. It has only been slightly touched up on the surface, but in all other respects it is a most typical relic of our old state machine. And so, to find a method of really renovating it, I think we ought to turn for experience to our Civil War.

How did we act in the more critical moments of the Civil War?

We concentrated our best Party forces in the Red Army; we mobilised the best of our workers; we looked for new forces at the deepest roots of our dictatorship.

I am convinced that we must go to the same source to find the means of reorganising the Workers' and Peasants' Inspection. I recommend that our Twelfth Party Congress adopt the following plan of reorganisation, based on some enlargement of our Central Control Commission.

The Plenary Meetings of the Central Committee of our Party are already revealing a tendency to develop into a

kind of supreme Party conference. They take place, on the
average, not more than once in two months, while the routine work is conducted, as we know, on behalf of the Central
Committee by our Political Bureau, our Organising Bureau,
our Secretariat, and so forth. I think we ought to follow
the road we have thus taken to the end and definitely transform the Plenary Meetings of the Central Committee into
supreme Party conferences convened once in two months
jointly with the Central Control Commission. The Central
Control Commission should be amalgamated with the main
body of the reorganised Workers' and Peasants' Inspection
on the following lines.

I propose that the Congress should elect 75 to 100 new
members to the Central Control Commission. They should
be workers and peasants, and should go through the same
Party screening as ordinary members of the Central Committee, because they are to enjoy the same rights as the
members of the Central Committee.

On the other hand, the staff of the Workers' and Peasants'
Inspection should be reduced to three or four hundred
persons, specially screened for conscientiousness and
knowledge of our state apparatus. They must also undergo
a special test as regards their knowledge of the principles
of scientific organisation of labour in general, and of
administrative work, office work, and so forth, in particular.

In my opinion, such an amalgamation of the Workers'
and Peasants' Inspection with the Central Control Commission will be beneficial to both these institutions. On the one
hand, the Workers' and Peasants' Inspection will thus
obtain such high authority that it will certainly not be
inferior to the People's Commissariat of Foreign Affairs.
On the other hand, our Central Committee, together with
the Central Control Commission, will definitely take the
road of becoming a supreme Party conference, which in
fact it has already taken, and along which it should proceed
to the end so as to be able to fulfil its functions properly
in two respects: in respect to *its own* methodical, expedient
and systematic organisation and work, and in respect to
maintaining contacts with the broad masses through the
medium of the best of our workers and peasants.

I foresee an objection that, directly or indirectly, may come from those spheres which make our state apparatus antiquated, i.e., from those who urge that its present utterly impossible, indecently pre-revolutionary form be preserved (incidentally, we now have an opportunity which rarely occurs in history of ascertaining the period necessary for bringing about radical social changes; we now see clearly *what* can be done in five years, and what requires much more time).

The objection I foresee is that the change I propose will lead to nothing but chaos. The members of the Central Control Commission will wander around all the institutions, not knowing where, why or to whom to apply, causing disorganisation everywhere and distracting employees from their routine work, etc., etc.

I think that the malicious source of this objection is so obvious that it does not warrant a reply. It goes without saying that the Presidium of the Central Control Commission, the People's Commissar of the Workers' and Peasants' Inspection and his collegium (and also, in the proper cases, the Secretariat of our Central Committee) will have to put in years of persistent effort to get the Commissariat properly organised, and to get it to function smoothly in conjunction with the Central Control Commission. In my opinion, the People's Commissar of the Workers' and Peasants' Inspection, as well as the whole collegium, can (and should) remain and guide the work of the entire Workers' and Peasants' Inspection, including the work of all the members of the Central Control Commission who will be "placed under his command". The three or four hundred employees of the Workers' and Peasants' Inspection that are to remain, according to my plan, should, on the one hand, perform purely secretarial functions for the other members of the Workers' and Peasants' Inspection and for the supplementary members of the Central Control Commission; and, on the other hand, they should be highly skilled, specially screened, particularly reliable, and highly paid, so that they may be relieved of their present truly unhappy (to say the least) position of Workers' and Peasants' Inspection officials.

I am sure that the reduction of the staff to the number

I have indicated will greatly enhance the efficiency of the
Workers' and Peasants' Inspection personnel and the quality of all its work, enabling the People's Commissar and
the members of the collegium to concentrate their efforts
entirely on organising work and on systematically and
steadily improving its efficiency, which is so absolutely
essential for our workers' and peasants' government, and
for our Soviet system.

On the other hand, I also think that the People's Commissar of the Workers' and Peasants' Inspection should
work on partly amalgamating and partly co-ordinating those
higher institutions for the organisation of labour (the Central
Institute of Labour, the Institute for the Scientific Organisation of Labour, etc.), of which there are now no fewer
than twelve in our Republic. Excessive uniformity and
a consequent desire to amalgamate will be harmful. On the
contrary, what is needed here is a reasonable and expedient
mean between amalgamating all these institutions and
properly delimiting them, allowing for a certain independence for each of them.

Our own Central Committee will undoubtedly gain no
less from this reorganisation than the Workers' and Peasants' Inspection. It will gain because its contacts with
the masses will be greater and because the regularity and
effectiveness of its work will improve. It will then be possible (and necessary) to institute a stricter and more responsible procedure of preparing for the meetings of the
Political Bureau, which should be attended by a definite
number of members of the Central Control Commission
determined either for a definite period or by some organisational plan.

In distributing work to the members of the Central Control Commission, the People's Commissar of the Workers'
and Peasants' Inspection, in conjunction with the Presidium of the Central Control Commission, should impose on
them the duty either of attending the meetings of the Political Bureau for the purpose of examining all the documents appertaining to matters that come before it in one
way or another; or of devoting their working time to theoretical study, to the study of scientific methods of organising
labour; or of taking a practical part in the work of super-

vising and improving our machinery of state, from the higher state institutions to the lower local bodies, etc.

I also think that in addition to the political advantages accruing from the fact that the members of the Central Committee and the Central Control Commission will, as a consequence of this reform, be much better informed and better prepared for the meetings of the Political Bureau (all the documents relevant to the business to be discussed at these meetings should be sent to all the members of the Central Committee and the Central Control Commission not later than the day before the meeting of the Political Bureau, except in absolutely urgent cases, for which special methods of informing the members of the Central Committee and the Central Control Commission and of settling these matters must be devised), there will also be the advantage that the influence of purely personal and incidental factors in our Central Committee will diminish, and this will reduce the danger of a split.

Our Central Committee has grown into a strictly centralised and highly authoritative group, but the conditions under which this group is working are not commensurate with its authority. The reform I recommend should help to remove this defect, and the members of the Central Control Commission, whose duty it will be to attend all meetings of the Political Bureau in a definite number, will have to form a compact group which should not allow anybody's authority without exception, neither that of the General Secretary nor of any other member of the Central Committee, to prevent them from putting questions, verifying documents, and, in general, from keeping themselves fully informed of all things and from exercising the strictest control over the proper conduct of affairs.

Of course, in our Soviet Republic, the social order is based on the collaboration of two classes: the workers and peasants, in which the "Nepmen", i.e., the bourgeoisie, are now permitted to participate on certain terms. If serious class disagreements arise between these classes, a split will be inevitable. But the grounds for such a split are not inevitable in our social system, and it is the principal task of our Central Committee and Central Control Commission, as well as of our Party as a whole, to watch very closely over such circumstances as may cause a split, and to forestall them, for in the final analysis the fate of our Republic will depend on whether the peasant masses will stand by the working class, loyal to their alliance, or whether they will permit the "Nepmen", i.e., the new bourgeoisie, to drive a wedge between them and the working class, to split them off from the working class. The more clearly we see this alternative, the more clearly all our workers and peasants understand it, the greater are the chances that we shall avoid a split, which would be fatal for the Soviet Republic.

January 23, 1923

Pravda No. 16,
January 25, 1923
Signed: *N. Lenin*

Published according to the stenographer's notes (typewritten
copy) checked with the text
in the newspaper

BETTER FEWER, BUT BETTER

In the matter of improving our state apparatus, the Workers' and Peasants' Inspection should not, in my opinion, either strive after quantity or hurry. We have so far been able to devote so little thought and attention to the efficiency of our state apparatus that it would now be quite legitimate if we took special care to secure its thorough organisation, and concentrated in the Workers' and Peasants' Inspection a staff of workers really abreast of the times, i.e., not inferior to the best West-European standards. For a socialist republic this condition is, of course, too modest. But our experience of the first five years has fairly crammed our heads with mistrust and scepticism. These qualities assert themselves involuntarily when, for example, we hear people dilating at too great length and too flippantly on "proletarian" culture. For a start, we should be satisfied with real bourgeois culture; for a start, we should be glad to dispense with the cruder types of pre-bourgeois culture, i.e., bureaucratic culture or serf culture, etc. In matters of culture, haste and sweeping measures are most harmful. Many of our young writers and Communists should get this well into their heads.

Thus, in the matter of our state apparatus we should now draw the conclusion from our past experience that it would be better to proceed more slowly.

Our state apparatus is so deplorable, not to say wretched, that we must first think very carefully how to combat its defects, bearing in mind that these defects are rooted in the past, which, although it has been overthrown, has not yet been overcome, has not yet reached the stage of a culture that has receded into the distant past. I say culture deliberately, because in these matters we can only regard as achieved what has become part and parcel of our culture, of our social life, our habits. We might say that the good in our social system has not been properly studied, understood, and taken to heart; it has been hastily grasped at; it has not been verified or tested, corroborated by experience, and not made durable, etc. Of course, it could not be otherwise in a revolutionary epoch, when development proceeded at such breakneck speed that in a matter of five years we passed from tsarism to the Soviet system.

It is time we did something about it. We must show sound scepticism for too rapid progress, for boastfulness, etc. We must give thought to testing the steps forward we proclaim every hour, take every minute and then prove every second that they are flimsy, superficial and misunderstood. The most harmful thing here would be haste. The most harmful thing would be to rely on the assumption that we know at least something, or that we have any considerable number of elements necessary for the building of a really new state apparatus, one really worthy to be called socialist, Soviet, etc.

No, we are ridiculously deficient of such an apparatus, and even of the elements of it, and we must remember that we should not stint time on building it, and that it will take many, many years.

What elements have we for building this apparatus? Only two. First, the workers who are absorbed in the struggle for socialism. These elements are not sufficiently educated. They would like to build a better apparatus for us, but they do not know how. They cannot build one. They have not yet developed the culture required for this; and it is culture that is required. Nothing will be achieved in this by doing things in a rush, by assault, by vim or vigour, or in general, by any of the best human qualities. Secondly, we have elements of knowledge, education and training, but they are ridiculously inadequate compared with all other countries.

Here we must not forget that we are too prone to compensate (or imagine that we can compensate) our lack of knowledge by zeal, haste, etc.

In order in renovate our state apparatus we must at all costs set out, first, to learn, secondly, to learn, and thirdly, to learn, and then see to it that learning shall not remain a dead letter, or a fashionable catch-phrase (and we should admit in all frankness that this happens very often with us), that learning shall really become part of our very being, that it shall actually and fully become a constituent element of our social life. In short, we must not make the demands that are made by bourgeois Western Europe, but demands that are fit and proper for a country which has set out to develop into a socialist country.

The conclusions to be drawn from the above are the following: we must make the Workers' and Peasants' Inspection a really exemplary institution, an instrument to improve our state apparatus.

In order that it may attain the desired high level, we must follow the rule: "Measure your cloth seven times before you cut."

For this purpose, we must utilise the very best of what there is in our social system, and utilise it with the greatest caution, thoughtfulness and knowledge, to build up the new People's Commissariat.

For this purpose, the best elements that we have in our social system—such as, first, the advanced workers, and, second, the really enlightened elements for whom we can vouch that they will not take the word for the deed, and will not utter a single word that goes against their conscience—should not shrink from admitting any difficulty and should not shrink from any struggle in order to achieve the object they have seriously set themselves.

We have been bustling for five years trying to improve our state apparatus, but it has been mere bustle, which has proved useless in these five years, or even futile, or even harmful. This bustle created the impression that we were doing something, but in effect it was only clogging up our institutions and our brains.

It is high time things were changed.

We must follow the rule: Better fewer, but better. We must follow the rule: Better get good human material in two or even three years than work in haste without hope of getting any at all.

I know that it will be hard to keep to this rule and apply it under our conditions. I know that the opposite rule will force its way through a thousand loopholes. I know that enormous resistance will have to be put up, that devilish persistence will be required, that in the first few years at least work in this field will be hellishly hard. Nevertheless, I am convinced that only by such effort shall we be able to achieve our aim; and that only by achieving this aim shall we create a republic that is really worthy of the name of Soviet, socialist, and so on, and so forth.

Many readers probably thought that the figures I quoted by way of illustration in my first article* were too small. I am sure that many calculations may be made to prove that they are. But I think that we must put one thing above all such and other calculations, i.e., our desire to obtain really exemplary quality.

I think that the time has at last come when we must work in real earnest to improve our state apparatus and in this there can scarcely be anything more harmful than haste. That is why I would sound a strong warning against inflating the figures. In my opinion, we should, on the contrary, be especially sparing with figures in this matter. Let us say frankly that the People's Commissariat of the Workers' and Peasants' Inspection does not at present enjoy the slightest authority. Everybody knows that no other institutions are worse organised than those of our Workers' and Peasants' Inspection, and that under present conditions nothing can be expected from this People's Commissariat. We must have this firmly fixed in our minds if we really want to create within a few years an institution that will, first, be an exemplary institution, secondly, win everybody's absolute confidence, and, thirdly, prove to all and sundry that we have really justified the work of such a highly placed institution as the Central Control Commission. In my opinion, we must immediately and irrevocably reject all general figures for the size of office staffs. We must select employees for the Workers' and Peasants' Inspection with particular care and only on the basis of the strictest test. Indeed, what is the use of establishing a People's Commissariat which carries on anyhow, which does not enjoy the slightest confidence, and whose

---

* See pp. 481-86 of this volume.—*Ed.*

word carries scarcely any weight? I think that our main object in launching the work of reconstruction that we now have in mind is to avoid all this.

The workers whom we are enlisting as members of the Central Control Commission must be irreproachable Communists, and I think that a great deal has yet to be done to teach them the methods and objects of their work. Furthermore, there must be a definite number of secretaries to assist in this work, who must be put to a triple test before they are appointed to their posts. Lastly, the officials whom in exceptional cases we shall accept directly as employees of the Workers' and Peasants' Inspection must conform to the following requirements:

First, they must be recommended by several Communists.

Second, they must pass a test for knowledge of our state apparatus.

Third, they must pass a test in the fundamentals of the theory of our state apparatus, in the fundamentals of management, office routine, etc.

Fourth, they must work in such close harmony with the members of the Central Control Commission and with their own secretariat that we could vouch for the work of the whole apparatus.

I know that these requirements are extraordinarily strict, and I am very much afraid that the majority of the "practical" workers in the Workers' and Peasants' Inspection will say that these requirements are impracticable, or will scoff at them. But I ask any of the present chiefs of the Workers' and Peasants' Inspection, or anyone associated with that body, whether they can honestly tell me the practical purpose of a People's Commissariat like the Workers' and Peasants' Inspection. I think this question will help them recover their sense of proportion. Either it is not worth while having another of the numerous reorganisations that we have had of this hopeless affair, the Workers' and Peasants' Inspection, or we must really set to work, by slow, difficult and unusual methods, and by testing these methods over and over again, to create something really exemplary, something that will win the respect of all and sundry for its merits, and not only because of its rank and title.

If we do not arm ourselves with patience, if we do not devote several years to this task, we had better not tackle it at all.

In my opinion we ought to select a minimum number of the higher labour research institutes, etc., which we have baked so hastily, see whether they are organised properly, and allow them to continue working, but only in a way that conforms to the high standards of modern science and gives us all its benefits. If we do that it will not be utopian to hope that within a few years we shall have an institution that will be able to perform its functions, to work systematically and steadily on improving our state apparatus, an institution backed by the trust of the working class, of the Russian Communist Party, and the whole population of our Republic.

The spade-work for this could be begun at once. If the People's Commissariat of the Workers' and Peasants' Inspection accepted the present plan of reorganisation, it could now take preparatory steps and work methodically until the task is completed, without haste, and not hesitating to alter what has already been done.

Any half-hearted solution would be extremely harmful in this matter. A measure for the size of the staff of the Workers' and Peasants' Inspection based on any other consideration would, in fact, be based on the old bureaucratic considerations, on old prejudices, on what has already been condemned, universally ridiculed, etc.

In substance, the matter is as follows:

Either we prove now that we have really learned something about state organisation (we ought to have learned something in five years), or we prove that we are not sufficiently mature for it. If the latter is the case, we had better not tackle the task.

I think that with the available human material it will not be immodest to assume that we have learned enough to be able systematically to rebuild at least one People's Commissariat. True, this one People's Commissariat will have to be the model for our entire state apparatus.

We ought at once to announce a contest in the compilation of two or more textbooks on the organisation of labour in general, and on management in particular. We can take as a basis the book already published by Yerman-sky, although it should be said in parentheses that he obviously sympathises with Menshevism and is unfit to compile textbooks for the Soviet system. We can also take as a basis the recent book by Kerzhentsev, and some of the other partial textbooks available may be useful too.

We ought to send several qualified and conscientious people to Germany, or to Britain, to collect literature and to study this question. I mention Britain in case it is found impossible to send people to the U.S.A. or Canada.

We ought to appoint a commission to draw up the preliminary programme of examinations for prospective employees of the Workers' and Peasants' Inspection; ditto for candidates to the Central Control Commission.

These and similar measures will not, of course, cause any difficulties for the People's Commissar or the collegium of the Workers' and Peasants' Inspection, or for the Presidium of the Central Control Commission.

Simultaneously, a preparatory commission should be appointed to select candidates for membership of the Central Control Commission. I hope that we shall now be able to find more than enough candidates for this post among the experienced workers in all departments, as well as among the students of our Soviet higher schools. It would hardly be right to exclude one or another category beforehand. Probably preference will have to be given to a mixed composition for this institution, which should combine many qualities, and dissimilar merits. Consequently, the task of drawing up the list of candidates will entail a considerable amount of work. For example, it would be least desirable for the staff of the new People's Commissariat to consist of people of one type, only of officials, say, or for it to exclude people of the propagandist type, or people whose principal quality is sociability or the ability to penetrate into circles that are not altogether customary for officials in this field, etc.

*　*　*

I think I shall be able to express my idea best if I compare my plan with that of academic institutions. Under the guidance of their Presidium, the members of the Central

Control Commission should systematically examine all the papers and documents of the Political Bureau. Moreover, they should divide their time correctly between various jobs in investigating the routine in our institutions, from the very small and privately-owned offices to the highest state institutions. And lastly, their functions should include the study of theory, i.e., the theory of organisation of the work they intend to devote themselves to, and practical work under the guidance either of older comrades or of teachers in the higher institutes for the organisation of labour.

I do not think, however, that they will be able to confine themselves to this sort of academic work. In addition, they will have to prepare themselves for work which I would not hesitate to call training to catch, I will not say rogues, but something like that, and working out special ruses to screen their movements, their approach, etc.

If such proposals were made in West-European government institutions they would rouse frightful resentment, a feeling of moral indignation, etc.; but I trust that we have not become so bureaucratic as to be capable of that. NEP has not yet succeeded in gaining such respect as to cause any of us to be shocked at the idea that somebody may be caught. Our Soviet Republic is of such recent construction, and there are such heaps of the old lumber still lying around that it would hardly occur to anyone to be shocked at the idea that we should delve into them by means of ruses, by means of investigations sometimes directed to rather remote sources or in a roundabout way. And even if it did occur to anyone to be shocked by this, we may be sure that such a person would make himself a laughing-stock.

Let us hope that our new Workers' and Peasants' Inspection will abandon what the French call *pruderie*, which we may call ridiculous primness, or ridiculous swank, and which plays entirely into the hands of our Soviet and Party bureaucracy. Let it be said in parentheses that we have bureaucrats in our Party offices as well as in Soviet offices.

When I said above that we must study and study hard in institutes for the higher organisation of labour, etc., I did not by any means imply "studying" in the schoolroom way, nor did I confine myself to the idea of studying only in the schoolroom way. I hope that not a single genuine revolutionary will suspect me of refusing, in this case, to understand "studies" to include resorting to some semi-humorous trick, cunning device, piece of trickery or something of that sort. I know that in the staid and earnest states of Western Europe such an idea would horrify people and that not a single decent official would even entertain it. I hope, however, that we have not yet become as bureaucratic as all that and that in our midst the discussion of this idea will give rise to nothing more than amusement.

Indeed, why not combine pleasure with utility? Why not resort to some humorous or semi-humorous trick to expose something ridiculous, something harmful, something semi-ridiculous, semi-harmful, etc.?

It seems to me that our Workers' and Peasants' Inspection will gain a great deal if it undertakes to examine these ideas, and that the list of cases in which our Central Control Commission and its colleagues in the Workers' and Peasants' Inspection achieved a few of their most brilliant victories will be enriched by not a few exploits of our future Workers' and Peasants' Inspection and Central Control Commission members in places not quite mentionable in prim and staid textbooks.

* *
*

How can a Party institution be amalgamated with a Soviet institution? Is there not something improper in this suggestion?

I do not ask these questions on my own behalf, but on behalf of those I hinted at above when I said that we have bureaucrats in our Party institutions as well as in the Soviet institutions.

But why, indeed, should we not amalgamate the two if this is in the interests of our work? Do we not all see that such an amalgamation has been very beneficial in the case of the People's Commissariat of Foreign Affairs, where it was brought about at the very beginning? Does not the Political Bureau discuss from the Party point of view many questions, both minor and important, concerning the "moves" we should make in reply to the "moves" of foreign powers in order to forestall their, say, cunning, if we are not to use a less respectable term? Is not this flexible amalgamation of a Soviet institution with a Party institution a source of great strength in our politics? I think that what has proved its usefulness, what has been definitely adopted in our foreign politics and has become so customary that it no longer calls forth any doubt in this field, will be at least as appropriate (in fact, I think it will be much more appropriate) for our state apparatus as a whole. The functions of the Workers' and Peasants' Inspection cover our state apparatus as a whole, and its activities should affect all and every state institution without exception: local, central, commercial, purely administrative, educational, archive, theatrical, etc.—in short, all without any exception.

Why then should not an institution, whose activities have such wide scope, and which moreover requires such extraordinary flexibility of forms, be permitted to adopt this peculiar amalgamation of a Party control institution with a Soviet control institution?

I see no obstacles to this. What is more, I think that such an amalgamation is the only guarantee of success in our work. I think that all doubts on this score arise in the dustiest corners of our government offices, and that they deserve to be treated with nothing but ridicule.

* *
*

Another doubt: is it expedient to combine educational activities with official activities? I think that it is not only expedient, but necessary. Generally speaking, in spite of our revolutionary attitude towards the West-European form of state, we have allowed ourselves to become infected with a number of its most harmful and ridiculous prejudices; to some extent we have been deliberately infected with them by our dear bureaucrats, who counted on being able again and again to fish in the muddy waters of these prejudices. And they did fish in these muddy waters to so great an extent that only the blind among us failed to see how extensively this fishing was practised.

In all spheres of social, economic and political relationships we are "frightfully" revolutionary. But as regards precedence, the observance of the forms and rites of office management, our "revolutionariness" often gives way to the mustiest routine. On more than one occasion, we have witnessed the very interesting phenomenon of a great leap forward in social life being accompanied by amazing timidity whenever the slightest changes are proposed.

This is natural, for the boldest steps forward were taken in a field which was long reserved for theoretical study, which was promoted mainly, and even almost exclusively, in theory. The Russian, when away from work, found solace from bleak bureaucratic realities in unusually bold theoretical constructions, and that is why in our country these unusually bold theoretical constructions assumed an unusually lopsided character. Theoretical audacity in general constructions went hand in hand with amazing timidity as regards certain very minor reforms in office routine. Some great universal agrarian revolution was worked out with an audacity unexampled in any other country, and at the same time the imagination failed when it came to working out a tenth-rate reform in office routine; the imagination, or patience, was lacking to apply to this reform the general propositions that produced such brilliant results when applied to general problems.

That is why in our present life reckless audacity goes hand in hand, to an astonishing degree, with timidity of thought even when it comes to very minor changes.

I think that this has happened in all really great revolutions, for really great revolutions grow out of the contradictions between the old, between what is directed towards developing the old, and the very abstract striving for the new, which must be so new as not to contain the tiniest particle of the old.

And the more abrupt the revolution, the longer will many of these contradictions last.

*   *
*

The general feature of our present life is the following: we have destroyed capitalist industry and have done our best to raze to the ground the medieval institutions and landed proprietorship, and thus created a small and very small peasantry, which is following the lead of the proletariat because it believes in the results of its revolutionary work. It is not easy for us, however, to keep going until the socialist revolution is victorious in more developed countries merely with the aid of this confidence, because economic necessity, especially under NEP, keeps the productivity of labour of the small and very small peasants at an extremely low level. Moreover, the international situation, too, threw Russia back and, by and large, reduced the labour productivity of the people to a level considerably below pre-war. The West-European capitalist powers, partly deliberately and partly unconsciously, did everything they could to throw us back, to utilise the elements of the Civil War in Russia in order to spread as much ruin in the country as possible. It was precisely this way out of the imperialist war that seemed to have many advantages. They argued somewhat as follows: "If we fail to overthrow the revolutionary system in Russia, we shall, at all events, hinder its progress towards socialism." And from their point of view they could argue in no other way. In the end, their problem was half-solved. They failed to overthrow the new system created by the revolution, but they did prevent it from at once taking the step forward that would have justified the forecasts of the socialists, that would have enabled the latter to develop the productive forces with enormous speed, to develop all the potentialities which, taken together, would have produced socialism; socialists would thus have proved to all and sundry that socialism contains within itself gigantic forces and that mankind had now entered into a new stage of development of extraordinarily brilliant prospects.

The system of international relationships which has now taken shape is one in which a European state, Germany, is enslaved by the victor countries. Furthermore, owing to their victory, a number of states, the oldest states in the West, are in a position to make some insignificant concessions to their oppressed classes—concessions which, insignificant though they are, nevertheless retard the revolutionary movement in those countries and create some semblance of "class truce .

At the same time, as a result of the last imperialist war, a number of countries of the East, India, China, etc., have been completely jolted out of the rut. Their development has definitely shifted to general European capitalist lines. The general European ferment has begun to affect them, and it is now clear to the whole world that they have been drawn into a process of development that must lead to a crisis in the whole of world capitalism.

Thus, at the present time we are confronted with the question—shall we be able to hold on with our small and very small peasant production, and in our present state of ruin, until the West-European capitalist countries consummate their development towards socialism? But they are consummating it not as we formerly expected. They are not consummating it through the gradual "maturing" of socialism, but through the exploitation of some countries by others, through the exploitation of the first of the countries vanquished in the imperialist war combined with the exploitation of the whole of the East. On the other hand, precisely as a result of the first imperialist war, the East has been definitely drawn into the revolutionary movement, has been definitely drawn into the general maelstrom of the world revolutionary movement.

What tactics does this situation prescribe for our country? Obviously the following. We must display extreme caution so as to preserve our workers' government and to retain our small and very small peasantry under its leadership and authority. We have the advantage that the whole world is now passing to a movement that must give rise to a world socialist revolution. But we are labouring under the disadvantage that the imperialists have succeeded in splitting the world into two camps; and this split is made more complicated by the fact that it is extremely difficult for Germany, which is really a land of advanced, cultured, capitalist development, to rise to her feet. All the capitalist powers of what is called the West are pecking at her and preventing her from rising. On the other hand, the entire East, with its hundreds of millions of exploited working people, reduced to the last degree of human suffering, has been forced into a position where its physical and material strength cannot possibly be compared with the physical, material and military strength of any of the much smaller West-European states.

Can we save ourselves from the impending conflict with these imperialist countries? May we hope that the internal antagonisms and conflicts between the thriving imperialist countries of the West and the thriving imperialist countries of the East will give us a second respite as they did the first time, when the campaign of the West-European counter-revolution in support of the Russian counter-revolution broke down owing to the antagonisms in the camp of the counter-revolutionaries of the West and the East, in the camp of the Eastern and Western exploiters, in the camp of Japan and the U.S.A.?

I think the reply to this question should be that the issue depends upon too many factors, and that the outcome of the struggle as a whole can be forecast only because in the long run capitalism itself is educating and training the vast majority of the population of the globe for the struggle.

In the last analysis, the outcome of the struggle will be determined by the fact that Russia, India, China, etc., account for the overwhelming majority of the population of the globe. And during the past few years it is this majority that has been drawn into the struggle for emancipation with extraordinary rapidity, so that in this respect there cannot be the slightest doubt what the final outcome of the world struggle will be. In this sense, the complete victory of socialism is fully and absolutely assured.

But what interests us is not the inevitability of this complete victory of socialism, but the tactics which we, the Russian Communist Party, we, the Russian Soviet Government, should pursue to prevent the West-European counter-revolutionary states from crushing us. To ensure our existence until the next military conflict between the counter-revolutionary imperialist West and the revolutionary and nationalist East, between the most civilised countries of the world and the Orientally backward countries which, however, comprise the majority, this majority must become civilised. We, too, lack enough civilisation to enable us to pass straight on to socialism, although we do have the political requisites for it. We should adopt the following tactics, or pursue the following policy, to save ourselves.

We must strive to build up a state in which the workers retain the leadership of the peasants, in which they retain the confidence of the peasants, and by exercising the greatest economy remove every trace of extravagance from our social relations.

We must reduce our state apparatus to the utmost degree of economy. We must banish from it all traces of extravagance, of which so much has been left over from tsarist Russia, from its bureaucratic capitalist state machine.

Will not this be a reign of peasant limitations?

No. If we see to it that the working class retains its leadership over the peasantry, we shall be able, by exercising the greatest possible thrift in the economic life of our state, to use every saving we make to develop our large-scale machine industry, to develop electrification, the hydraulic extraction of peat, to complete the Volkhov Power Project,[162] etc.

In this, and in this alone, lies our hope. Only when we have done this shall we, speaking figuratively, be able to change horses, to change from the peasant, muzhik horse of poverty, from the horse of an economy designed for a ruined peasant country, to the horse which the proletariat is seeking and must seek—the horse of large-scale machine industry, of electrification, of the Volkhov Power Station, etc.

That is how I link up in my mind the general plan of our work, of our policy, of our tactics, of our strategy, with the functions of the reorganised Workers' and Peasants' Inspection. This is what, in my opinion, justifies the exceptional care, the exceptional attention that we must devote to the Workers' and Peasants' Inspection in raising it to an exceptionally high level, in giving it a leadership with Central Committee rights, etc., etc.

And this justification is that only by thoroughly purging our government machine, by reducing to the utmost everything that is not absolutely essential in it, shall we be certain of being able to keep going. Moreover, we shall be able to keep going not on the level of a small-peasant country, not on the level of universal limitation, but on a level steadily advancing to large-scale machine industry.

These are the lofty tasks that I dream of for our Workers' and Peasants' Inspection. That is why I am planning for it the amalgamation of the most authoritative Party body with an "ordinary" People's Commissariat.

March 2, 1923

Pravda No. 49,
March 4, 1923
Signed: *N. Lenin*

Published according to the stenographer's notes (type-written copy) checked with the newspaper text

NOTES

[1] The *Mensheviks* were adherents of the petty-bourgeois opportunist trend in the Russian Social-Democratic movement and instruments of bourgeois influence over the working class. They received their name at the close of the Second R.S.D.L.P. Congress in August 1903, when at the elections to the Party's central organs they found themselves in the minority (*menshinstvo*), and the revolutionary Social-Democrats headed by Lenin won the majority (*bolshinstvo*); hence the names Bolsheviks and Mensheviks. The Mensheviks sought to secure agreement between the proletariat and the bourgeoisie and pursued an opportunist line in the working-class movement. In the period of dual power after the bourgeois-democratic revolution of February 1917, when the dictatorship of the bourgeoisie as represented by the Provisional Government intertwined with the dictatorship of the proletariat and peasants as represented by the Soviets, the Mensheviks and the Socialist-Revolutionaries accepted posts in the Provisional Government, supported its imperialist policy and opposed the mounting proletarian revolution. In the Soviets the Mensheviks pursued the same policy of supporting the Provisional Government and diverting the masses from the revolutionary movement.

After the October Revolution, they became an openly counter-revolutionary party, organising and participating in conspiracies and revolts against Soviet power.   p. 21

[2] The *Socialist-Revolutionaries* were members of a petty-bourgeois party in Russia, which emerged at the end of 1901 and beginning of 1902.

After the February bourgeois-democratic revolution in 1917 they were, together with the Mensheviks, the mainstay of the counter-revolutionary Provisional Government of the bourgeoisie and landowners, while their leaders held posts in that government. Far from supporting the peasants' demand for the abolition of landlordism, the Socialist-Revolutionary Party pressed for its preservation. The Socialist-Revolutionary Ministers of the Provisional Government sent punitive detachments against peasants who seized landed estates.

At the close of November 1917, the Left Socialist-Revolutionaries formed an independent party.

During the years of foreign military intervention and the Civil War the Socialist-Revolutionaries carried on counter-revolutionary subversive activities, vigorously supported the interventionists and whiteguards, took part in counter-revolutionary plots and organised terrorist acts against leaders of the Soviet Government and the Communist Party. After the Civil War they continued their hostile activities within the country and among whiteguard émigrés.   p. 21

[3] The *Two-and-a-Half International* (whose official name was the International Association of Socialist Parties) was an international organisation of Centrist socialist parties and groups that had been forced out of the Second International by the revolutionary masses. It was formed at a conference in Vienna in February 1921. While criticising the Second International, the leaders of the Two-and-a-Half International pursued an opportunist, splitting policy on all key issues of the proletarian movement and sought to utilise their association to offset the growing influence of the Communists among the working-class masses.

In May 1923, the Second and Two-and-a-Half Internationals merged into the so-called Socialist Labour International. p. 21

[4] The *Communist Workers Party of Germany* was formed in April 1920 by "Left" Communists, who had been expelled from the Communist Party of Germany at the Heidelberg Congress in 1919. In November 1920, in order to facilitate the unification of all communist forces in Germany and satisfy the wishes of the best proletarian elements within it, the C.W.P.G. was temporarily admitted to the Comintern with the rights of a sympathising member on the condition that it merged with the United Communist Party of Germany and supported its actions. The C.W.P.G. leadership did not fulfil the instructions of the Comintern Executive Committee. For the sake of the workers still supporting the C.W.P.G., the Third Comintern Congress decided to give it two or three months in which to convene a congress and settle the question of unification. The C.W.P.G. leadership failed to fulfil the decision of the Third Congress and continued their splitting tactics with the result that the Comintern Executive Committee was compelled to break off relations with the party. The C.W.P.G. found itself outside the Comintern and subsequently degenerated into an insignificant sectarian group that had no proletarian support whatever and was hostile to the working class of Germany.   p. 21

[5] The *Workers' Opposition* was an anti-Party faction formed in the Russian Communist Party in 1920 by Shlyapnikov, Medvedyev, Kollontai and others. It took final shape during the debates on the role of the trade unions in 1920-21. Actually there was nothing of the working class about this opposition, which expressed the mood and aspirations of the petty bourgeoisie. It counterposed the trade unions to the Soviet Government and the Communist

Party, considering them the highest form of working-class organisation.

After the Tenth Party Congress, which found the propagation of the ideas of the Workers' Opposition incompatible with membership in the Communist Party, a large number of rank-and file members of that opposition broke away from it. p. 21

⁶ This is a reference to the counter-revolutionary mutiny, which broke out in Kronstadt on February 28, 1921. Organised by Socialist-Revolutionaries, Mensheviks and whiteguards, it involved a considerable number of sailors, most of whom were raw recruits from the villages, who had little or no knowledge of politics and voiced the peasants' dissatisfaction with the requisitioning of surplus food. The economic difficulties in the country and the weakening of the Bolshevik organisation at Kronstadt facilitated the mutiny.

Hesitating to oppose the Soviet system openly, the counter-revolutionary bourgeoisie adopted new tactics. With the purpose of deceiving the masses, the leaders of the revolt put forward the slogan "Soviets without Communists", hoping to remove the Communists from the leadership of the Soviets, destroy the Soviet system and restore the capitalist regime in Russia.

On March 2, the mutineers arrested the fleet command. They contacted foreign imperialists, who promised them financial and military aid. The seizure of Kronstadt by the mutineers created a direct threat to Petrograd.

Regular Red Army units commanded by Mikhail Tukhachevsky were sent by the Soviet Government to crush the mutiny. The Communist Party reinforced these units with more than 300 delegates of the Tenth Party Congress; all these men, with Kliment Voroshilov at their head, had had fighting experience. The mutiny was snuffed out on March 18. p. 21

⁷ The elections to the Constituent Assembly were held on November 12 (25), 1917 according to lists drawn up before the October Revolution. Most of the seats were held by Right Socialist-Revolutionaries and other counter-revolutionary elements. Though it did not mirror the new alignment of forces that took shape in the country as a result of the revolution, the Communist Party and the Soviet Government felt the necessity of convening it because backward sections of the working population still believed in bourgeois parliamentarism. The Assembly opened in Petrograd on January 5 (18), 1918, but was dissolved on the next day by a decree of the All-Russia Central Executive Committee when the counter-revolutionary majority in it rejected the Declaration of Rights of the Working and Exploited People submitted by the All-Russia Central Executive Committee and refused to endorse the decrees of the Second Congress of Soviets on peace, land and the transfer of power to the Soviets. The decision to dissolve the

Assembly was whole-heartedly approved by broad masses of workers, soldiers and peasants. p. 22

⁸ This peace treaty was signed between Soviet Russia and the Quadruple Alliance (Germany, Austria-Hungary, Bulgaria and Turkey) on March 3, 1918. It was ratified on March 15 by the Extraordinary Fourth All-Russia Congress of Soviets. The terms were extremely onerous for Soviet Russia. They gave Germany and Austria-Hungary control over Poland, almost the whole Baltic area and part of Byelorussia; the Ukraine was separated from Soviet Russia and became dependent upon Germany. Turkey received the towns of Kars, Batum and Ardagan.

The signing of the Brest Treaty was preceded by a vehement struggle against Trotsky and the anti-Party group of "Left Communists". The treaty was signed thanks to a huge effort on Lenin's part. It was a wise political compromise, for it gave Soviet Russia a peaceful respite and enabled her to demobilise the old, disintegrating army and create the new, Red Army, start socialist construction and muster her forces for the coming struggle against internal counter-revolution and foreign intervention. This policy promoted the further intensification of the struggle for peace and the growth of revolutionary sentiments among the troops and the masses of all belligerent countries. After the monarchy in Germany was overthrown by the revolution of November 1918, the All-Russia Central Executive Committee abrogated the predatory Brest Treaty. p. 22

⁹ Lenin refers to the counter-revolutionary mutiny of the Czechoslovak Corps inspired by the Entente with the connivance of the Mensheviks and Socialist-Revolutionaries. The Corps, consisting of Czech and Slovak war prisoners, was formed in Russia before the Great October Socialist Revolution. In the summer of 1918 it had more than 60,000 men (altogether in Russia there were about 200,000 Czech and Slovak prisoners of war). After Soviet rule was established, the financing of the Corps was undertaken by the Entente powers, who decided to use it against the Soviet Republic. Tomas Masaryk, President of the Czechoslovak National Council, proclaimed the Corps part of the French Army, and Entente representatives raised the question of evacuating it to France. The Soviet Government agreed to its evacuation on condition that the Russian soldiers in France were allowed to return home. Under an agreement signed on March 26, 1918, the Corps was given the possibility of leaving Russia via Vladivostok, provided it surrendered its weapons and removed the counter-revolutionary Russian officers from its command. But the counter-revolutionary command of the Corps perfidiously violated the agreement with the Soviet Government on the surrender of weapons and, acting on orders from the Entente imperialists, provoked an armed mutiny at the close of May. Operating in close contact with the whiteguards and kulaks, the White Czechs occupied

considerable territory in the Urals, the Volga country and Siberia, everywhere restoring bourgeois rule.

On June 11, soon after the mutiny broke out, the Central Executive Committee of the Czechoslovak communist groups in Russia appealed to the soldiers of the Corps, exposing the counter-revolutionary objectives of the mutiny and calling upon the Czech and Slovak workers and peasants to end the mutiny and join the Czechoslovak units of the Red Army. Most of the Czech and Slovak war prisoners were favourably disposed to Soviet power and did not succumb to the anti-Soviet propaganda of the Corps' reactionary command. Many of the soldiers refused to fight Soviet Russia after they realised that they were being deceived. Nearly 12,000 Czechs and Slovaks joined the Red Army.

The Volga country was liberated by the Red Army in the autumn of 1918. The White Czechs were finally routed early in 1920.

p. 23

[10] *Wrangel*—baron, tsarist general and rabid monarchist. During the foreign military intervention and Civil War he was a puppet of the British, French and U.S. imperialists. In April-November 1920 he was commander-in-chief of the whiteguard armed forces in South Russia. He fled abroad after his forces were defeated by the Red Army.

p. 23

[11] The *mistakes of the "Lefts" in the Communist Party of Germany* were that they incited the working class to premature actions. The German bourgeoisie utilised these mistakes to provoke the workers into armed action at an unpropitious time. A workers' revolt broke out in Central Germany in March 1921. That revolt was not supported by the workers of other industrial regions with the result that despite a heroic struggle it was quickly crushed. For Lenin's assessment of this revolt and criticism of the mistakes of the "Lefts" see his "Speech in Defence of the Tactics of the Communist International" at the Third Comintern Congress and his "A Letter to the German Communists" (see present edition, Vol. 32, pp. 468-77 and 512-23).

p. 25

[12] *Ekonomicheskaya Zhizn*—a daily newspaper published in Moscow from November 1918 to November 1937.

p. 30

[13] From December 1920 the *Council of Labour and Defence* was a permanent organ of the Council of People's Commissars. It existed until 1937. It emerged in April 1920 on the basis of the Council of Workers' and Peasants' Defence, set up by decision of the All-Russia Central Executive Committee of November 30, 1918, with the purpose of mobilising manpower and means for the country's defence. The Council of Labour and Defence was also headed by Lenin.

p. 32

[14] Lenin has in mind the Eighth All-Russia Congress of Soviets (December 22-29, 1920) decision "On Soviet Construction".

p. 35

[15] The purge was undertaken in the second half of 1921 on the basis of the Tenth R.C.P.(B.) Congress resolution "On Problems of Party Development". It was preceded by long and careful preparation.

Under the purge nearly 170,000 people, i.e. almost 25 per cent of the membership, were expelled from the Party. This improved the Party's social composition, strengthened discipline, gave the Party greater prestige among the non-Party worker and peasant masses and freed the Party from elements who discredited it. The Party's ideological and organisational unity was enhanced.
p. 39

[16] The idea of convening a so-called *labour congress*, proposed by P.B. Axelrod and supported by other Mensheviks, was aimed at getting representatives of various workers' organisations together and founding a legal "broad labour party", which would include Social-Democrats, Socialist-Revolutionaries and anarchists. Actually, it would have meant the dissolution of the R.S.D.L.P. and its replacement by a non-Party organisation.
p. 40

[17] *Cadets*—members of the Constitutional-Democratic Party, the chief political organisation of the liberal-monarchist bourgeoisie in Russia. It was founded in October 1905, its membership including representatives of the bourgeoisie, Zemstvo leaders from among the landowners, and bourgeois intellectuals. In order to deceive the working people the Cadets falsely called themselves the "Party of People's Freedom", but in reality they never went beyond the demand for a constitutional monarchy. They considered their main task to be the fight against the revolutionary movement and aspired to share power with the tsar and the feudal landowners. During the First World War they actively supported the tsarist government's foreign policy of conquest, and in the period of the bourgeois-democratic revolution of February 1917 they tried to save the monarchy. After the Great October Socialist Revolution they became irreconcilable enemies of Soviet rule and actively participated in all the armed counter-revolutionary actions and campaigns of the interventionists. When the interventionists and whiteguards were defeated, the Cadets fled abroad, where they continued their anti-Soviet, counter-revolutionary activity.   p. 40

[18] Lenin wrote this letter to J. V. Stalin, who was at that time People's Commissar of Workers' and Peasants' Inspection, after receiving a preliminary report from Loginov, head of the fuel section at the industrial department of the Workers' and Peasants' Inspection, on the fuel situation and on the work of fuel enterprises.

The ideas in this letter were further developed by Lenin in a series of articles, including "How We Should Reorganise the

Workers' and Peasants' Inspection" and "Better Fewer, But Better" (see present volume, pp. 481-86, 487-502). p. 42

[19] *Sazhen*—a Russian linear measure equal to 2.13 metres, used in the U.S.S.R. before the introduction of the metric system. p. 46

[20] This Congress, convened on Lenin's initiative, was held in Moscow on October 1-9, 1921. It was attended by nearly 900 scientists, engineers and technicians as well as workers from various industrial enterprises.

Lenin was elected honorary chairman of the Congress, and his letter of greetings was read at the morning sitting on October 9, 1921. p. 49

[21] The Extraordinary International Socialist Congress that sat in Basle on November 24-25, 1912, adopted a manifesto on war, which warned the peoples that an imperialist world war was imminent, showed the predatory objectives of that war and called upon the workers of all countries to make a determined stand for peace. It included a point, contributed by Lenin to the resolution of the Stuttgart Congress of 1907, that if an imperialist war broke out the socialists should utilise the economic and political crisis stemming from it to accelerate the downfall of capitalist class domination and to work for a socialist revolution. p. 57

[22] Held in Moscow on October 17-22, 1921, this Congress was attended by 307 delegates.

Its main object was to endorse a plan of work for 1922 and work out the forms and methods of agitation and propaganda in the situation called forth by the New Economic Policy.

Lenin, who was given an ovation by the delegates, spoke at the evening session on October 17.

The *Political Education Departments* were formed by local (volost, uyezd and gubernia) public education bodies in conformity with a decree issued on February 23, 1920. Their work was guided by the Central Political Education Committee at the People's Commissariat of Education. p. 60

[23] The All-Russia Central Executive Committee passed its decision of April 29, 1918 on the basis of Lenin's report "On the Immediate Tasks of the Soviet Government". The propositions in that report and in the article "The Immediate Tasks of the Soviet Government" were summed up by Lenin in six theses, which, with some additions, were unanimously endorsed by the Party Central Committee on May 3, 1918. See "Six Theses on the Immediate Tasks of the Soviet Government" (present edition, Vol. 27, pp. 314-17). p. 61

[24] *Gubernia economic conferences* were local organs of the Council of Labour and Defence. They were set up by the Executive

Committees of the gubernia Soviets in conformity with the decision passed by the Eighth All-Russia Congress of Soviets in December 1920.   p. 76

[25] This Conference was held on October 29-31, 1921, and was attended by 637 delegates.

It debated 1) the international and domestic situation, 2) the report of the gubernia economic conference, 3) the report on the work of the Moscow Committee of the R.C.P.(B.), 4) the report of the Auditing Commission, and 5) the report of the Control Commission. Moreover, it heard a report on the purging of the Party in Moscow and Moscow Gubernia, and on other questions.

Lenin delivered his report on the New Economic Policy at the first sitting on October 29.   p. 81

[26] Lenin has in mind his articles: "The Chief Task of Our Day", "The Immediate Tasks of the Soviet Government", "'Left-Wing' Childishness and the Petty-Bourgeois Mentality" and others (see present edition, Vol. 27, pp. 159-63, 235-77, 323-54).   p. 87

[27] See Lenin, *Collected Works*, Vol. 27, pp. 314-17.   p. 88

[28] *Listok Obyavleni (Moskovsky Listok Obyavleni* [Moscow Advertising Sheet]) was published privately in Moscow from October 1921 to February 1922.   p. 89

[29] See Engels's letters to A. Bebel of March 18-28, 1875 and December 11, 1884 (Marx and Engels, *Selected Correspondence*, Moscow, 1965, pp. 291, 381).   p. 110

[30] Engels, *Emigré Literature* (see Marx/Engels, *Werke*, Bd. 18, S. 534. Dietz Verlag. Berlin).   p. 111

[31] See Lenin, *Collected Works*, Vol. 27, p. 274.   p. 112

[32] This meeting, attended by 2,000 workers, was organised as an evening of reminiscences.

Lenin spoke in his capacity of Deputy to the Moscow Soviet elected by the workers of the Prokhorov Textile Mills.

p. 117

[33] This pamphlet was not published. Lenin's pamphlet *The Problem of the New Economic Policy*, which included the articles "Fourth Anniversary of the October Revolution" and "The Importance of Gold Now and After the Complete Victory of Socialism", was published in 1921 (see present volume, pp. 51-59, 109-116). p. 121

[34] See Lenin, *Collected Works*, Vol. 29, pp. 55-88.   p. 121

[35] The *First Moscow Gubernia Agricultural Congress*, held on November 28-30, 1921, was attended by more than 300 delegates

from peasants and land offices. Lenin spoke on November 29, 1921. p. 128

[36] *La Voix Paysanne*—weekly organ of the Central Association of Working Peasants, was published in Paris by the Communist Party of France in 1920-37. p. 131

[37] Lenin refers to Engels's article "The Peasant Question in France and Germany" (see Marx and Engels, *Selected Works* in Two Volumes, Vol. II, Moscow, 1958, pp. 420-40). p. 134

[38] This letter was written in connection with the drawing up of a resolution on Party purge for the Eleventh All-Russia Conference of the R.C.P.(B.). Illness prevented Lenin from attending the Conference. His recommendations on stricter conditions for admission into the Party were incorporated in the resolution adopted by the Party Conference (see *KPSS v rezolyutsiakh i resheniyakh syezdov, konferentsi i plenumov Ts.K.* [C.P.S.U. in Resolutions and Decisions of Congresses, Conferences and C.C. Plenary Meetings], Part I, 1954, p. 597). p. 138

[39] Lenin's recommendation that the Ninth All-Russia Congress of Soviets adopt a special resolution against the adventurist policy of the bourgeois governments of Poland, Finland and Rumania was approved by the Political Bureau of the C.C., R.C.P.(B.), at a meeting on December 22, 1921. p. 139

[40] The *Ninth All-Russia Congress of Soviets* sat in Moscow on December 23-28, 1921. It was attended by 1,993 delegates, of whom 1,631 had a casting vote and 362 a consultative voice.

This Congress summed up the first results of activities under the New Economic Policy, fully approving the home and foreign policy of the workers' and peasants' government. In its "Declaration on the International Position of the R.S.F.S.R.", the Congress made the proposal to the governments of neighbouring and all other states to found their foreign policy on the principle of peaceful coexistence, on "peaceful and friendly coexistence with the Soviet republics".

The Congress devoted its main attention to finding ways of rapidly restoring agriculture as a key condition for the development of the country's entire economy. It also gave much of its attention to famine relief, calling upon workers and peasants to bend every effort to help the people, particularly children, stricken by famine along the Volga. The Congress expressed its "warm appreciation to the workers of all countries who came to the assistance of the famine-stricken gubernias of Soviet Russia".

The Congress decisions stated that the restoration and development of large-scale industry "is, in addition to the restoration of agriculture, the cardinal task of the Republic".

Lenin was very active in preparing for the Congress and directed its work.

He wrote the "Instructions on Questions of Economic Management", which were adopted by the Congress, and also a number of documents on which the Congress decisions were based.

The Congress elected a new All-Russia Central Executive Committee consisting of 386 members and 127 alternate members.

p. 141

[41] This Conference on restricting naval armaments and on Pacific and Far Eastern problems was convened on the initiative of the U.S.A. It sat in Washington from November 12, 1921 to February 6, 1922 and was attended by representatives of the U.S.A., Britain, Japan, France, Italy, China, Belgium, Portugal and the Netherlands. Soviet Russia was not invited, nor was the Far Eastern Republic, which was in existence at the time. Without the Soviet Republic's participation, the Conference examined a number of problems concerning Soviet Russia. In this connection, the People's Commissariat of Foreign Affairs lodged two protests—on July 19 and November 2, 1921—with the governments concerned, stating it would not recognise decisions taken by the Conference without the participation of one of the principal interested parties. On December 8, 1921, the People's Commissariat of Foreign Affairs protested against the discussion at the Washington Conference of the problem of the Chinese-Eastern Railway, which solely concerned Russia and China.

The decisions of the Conference were a supplement to the Versailles Treaty; under pressure brought to bear by the U.S.A. and Britain, Japan was compelled to relinquish some of the positions she had captured in China, but at the same time she consolidated her rule in South Manchuria. p. 155

[42] *Yugostal*—a mining metallurgical trust founded in September 1921. It embraced some large iron and steel plants in the Ukraine, the Northern Caucasus and the Crimea and played an important part in rehabilitating the country's iron and steel industry. It existed until 1929. p. 168

[43] The first section (capacity—5,000 kw) of the State Shatura District Power Station, a project started in 1918, was commissioned on July 25, 1920. The station was completed in 1925 and was named after Lenin.

The building of the Kashira Power Station was started in February 1919, and it was expected that it would be completed by the end of 1921, when the Ninth All-Russia Congress of Soviets was due to open. Lenin attached great importance to this station as a power source for some of the largest factories and mills in Moscow and as the first project under the electrification plan. He kept a close watch on the course of the project, directly participating in the solution of many of its problems and checking how it was being supplied with the necessary materials, manpower, fuel and equipment.

The first section (12,000 kw) of this power station became operational on June 4, 1922.   p. 169

44 The Krasny Oktyabr (formerly Utkina Zavod) Power Station was
completed in 1922, its first section (10,000 kw) becoming operational on October 8, 1922.   p. 170

45 This is a reference to the trial of 35 private businessmen—owners
of tea-and-dining rooms, bakeries, shoemaking establishments,
etc.—in Moscow on December 15-18, 1921. They were charged
with violating the Labour Code, namely, exploiting the labour
of children, juveniles and women, lengthening the working day,
and so on. Workers of large enterprises, both members and non-
members of the Party, acted as prosecutors. The court sentenced
ten of the accused to large fines or to forced labour without
imprisonment.   p. 171

46 Lenin has in mind the fable *Geese* by the well-known Russian
writer Ivan Krylov.   p. 173

47 The role and tasks of the trade unions under the conditions created
by the New Economic Policy were examined at a Plenary Meeting of the C.C., R.C.P.(B.) on December 28, 1921. The draft of
the decision on the trade unions adopted by the C.C., R.C.P.(B.)
was written by Lenin.
    The theses of January 12, 1922 were examined by the Political
Bureau of the Central Committee which unanimously approved
them and submitted them without amendments to the Eleventh
Party Congress. They were unanimously passed at that Congress
(see *KPSS v rezolyutsiakh i resheniyakh syezdov, konferentsi i
plenumov Ts.K.* [C.P.S.U. in Resolutions and Decisions of Congresses, Conferences and C.C. Plenary Meetings], Part I, 1954,
pp. 603-12).   p. 184

48 The *Draft Directive of the Political Bureau on the New Economic
Policy* was debated at a meeting of the Political Bureau of the
Central Committee on January 12, 1922 and accepted as a basis;
it was endorsed on January 16, 1922.   p. 197

49 Lenin's greeting to the working people of Daghestan was written
in reply to a letter from Comrade Karkmasov, Chairman of the
Council of People's Commissars of the Daghestan Soviet Socialist Republic, in which he reported that a start had been made
in tapping mineral resources. Two poods of mercury extracted
in Daghestan were sent to Lenin as a production gift.   p. 199

50 This letter was written on the eve of the First Congress of Soviets
of Georgia, which was held on February 25-March 3, 1922.
    Lenin's suggestion to strengthen the Georgian Red Army was
called forth by the aggressive stand of the British imperialists

and by the campaign of slander started against the Soviet Republic by the reactionary imperialist press together with the leaders
of the Second and Two-and-a-Half Internationals and the Georgian Mensheviks. They demanded the withdrawal of the Red
Army from Georgia with the objective of wresting that territory
away from Soviet Russia.

The First Congress of Soviets of Georgia adopted statement
"On the Red Army", which declared that the strengthening of the
existing nucleus of the Georgian Red Army was the cardinal task
and requested the Government of the fraternal Russian Soviet
Republic not to withdraw the Red Army from Georgian territory.

Lenin's suggestion on strengthening the Georgian Red Army
was accepted by the Political Bureau on February 25, 1922.

p. 200

[51] The Civil Code was revised on the basis of Lenin's directives
in the letter to D. I. Kursky. It was examined at the Third and
Fourth Sessions of the Ninth All-Russia Central Executive Committee (in May and October 1922). The Fourth Session passed
a decision to give effect to the Civil Code as of January 1, 1923
(see Lenin's speech at the Fourth Session of the Ninth All-Russia
Central Executive Committee in the present volume, pp. 390-95).

p. 202.

[52] The *International Economic and Financial Conference* was held
in Genoa on the initiative of the Soviet Government expressed
in Notes to Britain, Italy, the U.S.A., France and Japan on October 28, 1921. The Soviet Notes stated that the Conference should
examine the establishment of peace and economic co-operation
in Europe and also the question of Russian debts. The decision
to convene the Conference was taken by the Supreme Entente
Council at a conference in Cannes on January 6, 1922.

The Allied countries invited Soviet Russia to the Conference
in the hope of compelling her to make a number of political and
economic concessions and, at the same time, establishing economic relations with her.

The Soviet delegation to the Genoa Conference was named
by the All-Russia Central Executive Committee at an extraordinary meeting on January 27. Lenin was appointed to lead the
delegation, and G. V. Chicherin was named as his deputy. The
question of Lenin going to Genoa was widely discussed by the
people of the Soviet republics. Many of them expressed apprehen-
sion for his life and safety and opposed his going to the Conference.
The Central Committee of the Russian Communist Party (Bolsheviks) passed a special decision on this question, under which
Lenin's plenary powers as head of the delegation were passed to
Chicherin.

Lenin directed the work of the delegation, drew up the Central
Committee's directives to it and also other important documents
connected with Soviet Russia's participation in the Genoa Conference.

The Conference sat from April 10 to May 19, 1922. It was attended by representatives of 29 countries. At the Conference the Soviet delegation reiterated the need for peaceful coexistence between states with different social and economic systems. Its statement, approved by Lenin and endorsed by the Council of People's Commissars, declared: "While remaining true to the principles of communism, the Russian delegation recognises that in the present epoch, which makes the parallel existence of the old and the emergent social system possible, economic co-operation between states representing the two systems of ownership is imperatively necessary for universal economic reconstruction (see *Materialy Genuezskoi konferentsii. Polny stenograficheskhy otchot* [Materials of the Genoa Conference. Complete Verbatim Report], Moscow, 1922, p. 78).

The Genoa Conference failed to settle the problems that confronted it. The Soviet delegation emphatically rejected the attempts of the imperialist powers to impose a colonial status upon Soviet Russia (the establishment of control over Soviet finances and so forth). By proposing talks on a general reduction of armaments and the banning of the most barbarous means of warfare (poison gases, military aircraft), the Soviet delegation demonstrated the peace-loving nature of Soviet Russia's Leninist foreign policy to the whole world. p. 203

[53] This article was not completed. p. 204

[54] *Smena Vekh*—the title of a collection of articles published in Prague in 1921, and then the name of a journal published in Paris from October 1921 to March 1922. It was the mouthpiece of advocates of a socio-political trend that emerged among White émigré intellectuals in 1921 and was supported by part of the old, bourgeois intelligentsia that did not emigrate for various reasons.

A certain revival of capitalist elements in Soviet Russia following the implementation of the New Economic Policy served as the social foundation for this trend. When its adherents saw that foreign military intervention could not overthrow Soviet rule they began advocating co-operation with the Soviet government, hoping for a bourgeois regeneration of the Soviet state. They regarded the New Economic Policy as an evolution of Soviet rule towards the restoration of capitalism. Some of them were prepared loyally to co-operate with the Soviet government and promote the country's economic rejuvenation. Subsequently, most of them openly sided with the counter-revolution.

A characteristic of this trend is given by Lenin in this volume (see pp. 285-86). p. 205

[55] *Judas Golovlyov*—a landowner and main personage of M. Y. Saltykov-Shchedrin's *The Golovlyov Family*. He was called Judas for his bigotry, hypocrisy and callousness. The name Judas Golovlyov has become a synonym for these negative traits. p. 205

[56] This is a reference to the fable *The Eagle and the Hens* by Ivan
Krylov. p. 210

[57] In the Reichstag on August 4, 1914, the Social-Democratic faction
voted with the bourgeois representatives in favour of granting the
imperial government war credits amounting to 5,000 million marks,
thereby approving Wilhelm II's imperialist policy. p. 210

[58] This Congress, held in Moscow on March 3-7, 1922, was attended
by 318 delegates representing more than half a million members
of the metalworkers' union. Lenin spoke at a meeting of the Communist group at the Congress on the morning of March 6. p. 212

[59] *Oblomov*—the main personage in the novel of the same name
by I. A. Goncharov. The name Oblomov has become a synonym
of narrow-mindedness, stagnation and immobility. p. 214

[60] The *All-Russia Democratic Conference* was convened in September 1917 in Petrograd by the Menshevik and Socialist-Revolutionary Central Executive Committee of Soviets to decide the question of power. Actually, the conference was called with the purpose
of distracting the people's attention from the mounting revolution.
More than 1,500 persons attended the conference. The Menshevik
and Socialist-Revolutionary leaders did their utmost to reduce
representation from the Soviets of Workers' and Peasants' Deputies
and increase the number of delegates from various petty-bourgeois and bourgeois organisations and thereby ensure a majority.
The Bolsheviks went to the conference to use its rostrum for
exposing the Mensheviks and Socialist-Revolutionaries.
The conference passed a resolution on the formation of a Pre-
Parliament (Provisional Council of the Republic). This was an
attempt to create the illusion that a parliamentary system had
been instituted in Russia. However, the rules endorsed by the Provisional Government reduced the Pre-Parliament to the status
of a consultative body. Lenin categorically insisted on a boycott
of the Pre-Parliament, because to remain in it would give the
impression that that body could resolve the tasks of the revolution.
The Central Committee debated Lenin's suggestion and, despite
the opposition of Kamenev and other capitulators, adopted a
decision to recall Bolsheviks from the Pre-Parliament. On October 7 (20), the day the Pre-Parliament opened, the Bolsheviks
made the Central Committee Declaration public and walked out.
p. 219

[61] Lenin refers to the "Speech on the Attitude Towards the Provisional Government" at a sitting of the First All-Russia Congress
of Soviets of Workers' and Soldiers' Deputies on June 4 (17),
1917 (see present edition, Vol. 25, p. 20). p. 219

[62] *Officer cadets*—students of military academies in tsarist Russia.
p. 219

[63] This is a reference to Vladimir Mayakovsky's *Incessant Meeting Sitters*.   p. 223

[64] Lenin refers to words used by Engels in *Emigré Literature* (Marx/Engels, *Werke*, Bd. 18, S. 534. Dietz Verlag. Berlin.)   p. 223

[65] *Istpart* (Commission for Collecting and Studying Materials on the History of the October Revolution and the History of the Russian Communist Party) was set up at the People's Commissariat of Education by a decree passed by the Council of People's Commissars on September 21, 1920. On December 1, 1921, by a decision passed by the C.C., R.C.P.(B.), Istpart became a department of the Party Central Committee. In 1928 it was merged with the Lenin Institute at the C.C., C.P.S.U.(B.).   p. 224

[66] *Pod Znamenem Marksizma*—a philosophical and socio-economic journal published in Moscow from January 1922 to June 1944 with the purpose of popularising materialism and atheism.
                                                   p. 227

[67] *N. G. Chernyshevsky* (1828-1889)—a Russian revolutionary democrat, an outstanding predecessor of Russian Social-Democracy, economist, philosopher and writer.   p. 228

[68] *Popular Socialists* were members of the petty-bourgeois Popular Socialist Labour Party, which stemmed from the Right wing of the Socialist-Revolutionary Party in 1906. The Popular Socialists advocated a bloc with the Constitutional-Democrats. During the First World War they preached social-chauvinistic views.

After the bourgeois-democratic revolution of February 1917 the Popular Socialists actively supported the bourgeois Provisional Government, accepting portfolios in it. After the October Socialist Revolution they took part in counter-revolutionary conspiracies and in armed action against the Soviet government. They ceased to exist as a party during the period of the foreign military intervention and the Civil War.   p. 228

[69] *Josef Dietzgen* (1828-1888)—a German tannery worker, who independently arrived at dialectical materialism.   p. 228

[70] See Engels, *Emigré Literature* (Marx/Engels, *Werke*, Bd. 18, S. 532. Dietz Verlag. Berlin).   p. 229

[71] Lenin borrowed this expression from *A Story of a Town* by M. Y. Saltykov-Shchedrin, the well-known Russian satirist.   p. 234

[72] *Ekonomist*—a journal published in Petrograd in 1921-22 by the Department of Industry and Economy of the Russian Technical Society.

The *Russian Technical Society* was a scientific body founded in St. Petersburg in 1866. It had branches in other towns and its purpose was to help promote industry and popularise technical knowledge.

After the October Revolution most of the Society's members, who, in addition to engineers and technicians, included office employees, lawyers, merchants and former owners of industrial enterprises, were hostile to Soviet rule. The Society was closed in 1929.   p. 234

[73] On March 10, 1922, E. A. Preobrazhensky's theses "Fundamental Principles of the Policy of the R.C.P. in the Present-Day Country-side", prepared by him for the Eleventh Party Congress, were circulated to all members of the Organising Bureau and the Political Bureau of the C.C., R.C.P.(B.). Lenin wrote the letter published in this volume after reading these theses. The Political Bureau discussed Preobrazhensky's theses on March 18 and endorsed the proposals formulated by Lenin in Paragraph 15 of his letter.
                                                                          p. 237

[74] *Poor Peasants' Committees* were instituted by the All-Russia Central Executive Committee in conformity with its decree "On Organising and Supplying the Village Poor" of June 11, 1918. The functions of these committees were to register the food reserves of the peasant farms, bring to light food surpluses at the kulak farms, help Soviet food organs to requisition these surpluses, supply the poor peas-ants with food at the expense of the kulak farms, distribute farm implements and manufactured goods, and so forth. However, their practical activities embraced all aspects of the work in the countryside and they became centres and organs of the proletarian dictatorship in the countryside. The organisation of these commit-tees ushered in the further development of the socialist revolution in the countryside. At the end of 1918, having fulfilled their tasks, the Poor Peasants' Committees were merged with volost and village Soviets.   p. 238

[75] The decree of the State Political Administration committing members of the C.C. and active members of the Socialist-Revolu-tionary Party for trial before the Supreme Revolutionary Tri-bunal for counter-revolutionary, terrorist acts against Soviet rule, was published on February 28, 1922. In reply to this decree, a group of Socialist-Revolutionaries living abroad and calling them-selves "Delegation of Socialist-Revolutionaries Living Abroad", published an appeal "To Socialist Parties Throughout the World" in issue No. 913 of their newspaper *Golos Rossii* (Voice of Russia) (published in Berlin) on March 11, 1922. In this appeal they pro-tested against what they alleged was a predetermined death sen-tence for the accused. The appeal was supported by the parties of the Second and Two-and-a-Half Internationals and also by reformist trade unions and bourgeois intellectuals.

The document published in this volume was written in connec-tion with telegrams sent to Lenin and Chicherin by the National Council of the Independent Labour Party of Britain, T. Stauning,

Chairman of the Danish Social-Democratic Party, E. Vandervelde, a leader of the Second International, and by the Presidium of the General German Workers' Union, who demanded that the trial of the Socialist-Revolutionaries be postponed until the Berlin Conference of the three Internationals.

The *trial of the Socialist-Revolutionaries* was held in Moscow on June 8-August 7, 1922. Thirty-four persons were tried: members of the Central Committee and of the Moscow Bureau of the Central Committee, and individual members of the Socialist-Revolutionary Party who acted on the strength of directives from that party's Central Committee. The trial fully bore out the indictment and revealed the counter-revolutionary activity of the Central Committee of the Socialist-Revolutionary Party: conspiracies and the organisation of uprisings against Soviet rule, the murder of workers' leaders, support for the foreign intervention. The Supreme Tribunal sentenced twelve of the main accused to death. The Presidium of the All-Russia Central Executive Committee endorsed this sentence and ordered it to be executed if the Socialist-Revolutionary Party did not relinquish its armed struggle against Soviet rule and continued its terrorist acts and organising uprisings. Some of the accused were sentenced to imprisonment of from two to ten years. A number of the accused, who repented and exposed the criminal activities of the Central Committee of the Socialist-Revolutionary Party, were released from custody.

p. 243

[76] See Note No. 3   p. 243

[77] The reference is to the resolution on electrification adopted by the Eighth All-Russia Congress of Soviets, which sat on December 22-29, 1920 (see present edition, Vol. 31, p. 532).   p. 246

[78] Lenin refers to the People's Commissariat of Workers' and Peasants' Inspection.

The *Workers' and Peasants' Inspection* was set up in February 1920 on Lenin's initiative through the reorganisation of the People's Commissariat of State Control, which began functioning in the first months after the establishment of Soviet rule.   p. 247

[79] Lenin wrote this greeting at the request of *Bednota*'s editor V. A. Karpinsky.

Lenin took a keen interest in the work of this newspaper and required Karpinsky to send him regular reports on the number of letters received by the newspaper from peasants and Red Army men, on the general mood expressed in these letters and the main questions raised in them.

Bednota, whose publication was started in Moscow on March 27, 1918, was a newspaper for peasants. On February 1, 1931 it was merged with the newspaper *Sotsialisticheskoye Zemledeliye*.

p. 249

[80] This letter was discussed on March 25, 1922 at a Plenary Meeting of the C.C., R.C.P.(B.), which endorsed the plan of the report proposed by Lenin.   p. 251

[81] The *Narrow Council of People's Commissars* was organised in December 1917. It had the rights of a commission of the Council of People's Commissars and its task was to relieve the Council of People's Commissars of minor affairs. Its decisions had to be endorsed by the Chairman of the Council of People's Commissars.
                                                                 p. 252

[82] The *Eleventh Congress of the R.C.P.(B.)* was held in Moscow on March 27-April 2, 1922.

It was convened a year after the Civil War ended and the country went over to peaceful economic development. Its purpose was to sum up the results of the first year of the New Economic Policy and map out the further plan of socialist construction.

This was the last Party Congress in which Lenin participated. It was attended by 522 delegates with a casting vote and 165 delegates with a consultative voice. It discussed 1) the political report of the Central Committee, 2) the organisation report of the Central Committee, 3) the report of the Auditing Commission, 4) the report of the Central Control Commission, 5) the report of the Communist International, 6) the trade unions, 7) the Red Army, 8) the financial policy, 9) the results of the Party purge and the accompanying strengthening of the Party ranks, and the co-reports on work with young people and on the press and propaganda, and 10) elections to the Central Committee and the Central Control Commission.

Lenin opened the Congress, delivered the political report of the C.C., R.C.P.(B.), a closing speech on the report and a speech closing the Congress.   p. 259

[83] Here Lenin refers to Mátyás Rakosi's article "The New Economic Policy in Soviet Russia", which analyses Otto Bauer's pamphlet *"Der neue Kurs" in Sowjetrussland* ("The New Policy" in Soviet Russia), published in Vienna in 1921. Rakosi's article appeared in March 1922 in the magazine *Communist International* No. 20.

Communist International, organ of the Executive Committee of the Communist International, was published in Russian, German, French, English, Spanish and Chinese. The first issue was put out on May 1, 1919. Publication was stopped in June 1943 following the decision of the Presidium of the Comintern Executive Committee of May 15, 1943 to dissolve the Communist International.   p. 282

[84] Lenin has in mind the struggle waged abroad between the Bolsheviks and the Mensheviks.   p. 282

[85] The Commission for Mixed Companies under the Council of Labour and Defence. This Commission was set up by a decision of the

Council of Labour and Defence on February 15, 1922. Its Chairman was Sokolnikov.   p. 283

[86] The *Northern Timber Trust* was a special administrative body of the timber industry of the North White Sea area. It was established in 1921.   p. 283

[87] *Persuader-in-Chief* was the nickname given by the soldiers to A. F. Kerensky, then the War and Navy Minister of the Provisional Government, for trying to persuade the soldiers to start an offensive when he toured the front in the summer of 1917. This attempt was made on orders from the Anglo-French imperialists and the Russian bourgeoisie.   p. 284

[88] Alexander Todorsky's book *A Year With a Rifle and a Plough* was published in 1918 by the Vesyegonsk Uyezd Executive Committee of Soviets, Tver Gubernia. Lenin speaks of this book in his article "A Little Picture in Illustration of Big Problems" (see present edition, Vol. 28, pp. 386-89).   p. 289

[89] The *Central Verification Commission* was set up on June 25, 1921 by the C.C., R.C.P. (B.) to direct the work of local verification commissions during the period of the Party purge. It consisted of five men.   p. 305

[90] At the Congress E. A. Preobrazhensky suggested that another organ of the Central Committee, an Economic Bureau, should be set up in addition to the Political Bureau and the Organising Bureau.

He accused the Central Committee of violating that part of the Party Programme dealing with bourgeois specialists, which stated that while creating a comradely atmosphere for the work of these people and showing concern for their material welfare no political concessions should be made to them and their counter-revolutionary impulses should be curbed. He alleged that the C.C. had made a political concession to the professors who had taken part in the strikes at institutions of higher learning in Moscow, Kazan, Petrograd and other cities in 1921-22. One of their basic demands was that the new Rules of Institutions of Higher Learning, drawn up by the Central Administration of Vocational and Political Schools and Institutions of Higher Learning and endorsed in the autumn of 1921 by the Council of People's Commissars, should be revised. They objected to the Workers Faculties at institutions of higher learning and to the procedure, laid down in the new Rules, of forming the boards of these institutions with the participation of representatives of the students, trade unions and the Central Administration of Vocational and Political Schools and Institutions of Higher Learning. They demanded that the latter right be transferred to the teachers' boards, and also made a number of economic demands. The Central Administration of Vocational and Political Schools and Institutions of Higher Learning, which was at that time headed by Preobrazhensky, made the mistake of insisting on stern measures, including detention, against the striking instructors. The same stand was taken by the Communist cells and Workers' Faculties of some institutions of higher learning.

The Political Bureau of the C.C., R.C.P.(B.) took this question up several times. In view of the need for a flexible approach to specialists, it rectified the mistake of the Central Administration of Vocational and Political Schools and Institutions of Higher Learning, instructing A. V. Lunacharsky, M. N. Pokrovsky and other leading officials of the People's Commissariat of Public Education to examine the teachers' demands and, without making any fundamental, political concessions, to reach agreement with them. In February 1922 the Political Bureau set up a commission consisting of representatives of the People's Commissariat of Public Education, the Central Committee of the Trade Union of Public Education Workers and teachers to examine the economic position of institutions of higher learning and recognised the need for new Rules of Institutions of Higher Learning. After repeated conferences between the teachers and the commission, and a number of other measures that were taken by the People's Commissariat of Public Education on instructions from the Party C.C., the strikes were stopped.   p. 313

[91] J. V. Stalin was People's Commissar of Nationalities from the time the People's Commissariat of Nationalities was set up on October 26 (November 8), 1917 to its dissolution in July 1923. As from March 1919, he was also People's Commissar of State Control, and after the reorganisation of this Commissariat in February 1920, he was People's Commissar of Workers' and Peasants' Inspection until April 25, 1922.   p. 315

[92] N. Osinsky (V. V. Obolensky), speaking at the Congress, proposed that a "Cabinet" of Commissars be set up. His suggestion was that it should be formed not by the All-Russia Central Executive Committee but unilaterally by its Chairman, who would be responsible to A.R.C.E.C.

While Osinsky spoke Lenin made the following entry in his notebook: *"(Set up a cabinet!)* one member should form the Cabinet" (*Lenin Miscellany XIII*, 1930, p. 22).   p. 317

[93] At the Congress Y. Larin alleged that an authorised body of the State Planning Commission had proposed that at the Genoa Conference the Soviet delegation should offer to lease (as a concession) three-quarters of the country's railways, the Petrograd-Rybinsk waterway, the iron and steel plants in the Urals with a railway network of 3,000 versts, and the power engineering industry. This allegation was refuted by G. M. Krzhizhanovsky.   p. 319

[94] The *Debating Club* at the Moscow Committee of the R.C.P.(B.) was organised in August 1921. Similar clubs were opened in various parts of Moscow. They debated Party and Soviet development, the

Soviet Republic's economic policy and other problems. However, the Debating Club soon began to be used by opposition groups as a forum for propagandising their views.

On February 20, 1922, the Central Committee of the R.C.P. (B.) examined the question of the Debating Club on the basis of a report from the Central Control Commission and instructed the Moscow Committee to reconsider the composition of the Club's board and to organise its work in conformity with the Party's tasks.   p. 320

[95] See present volume, pp. 237-42.   p. 321

[96] This anti-Party statement was sent on February 26, 1922 to the Presidium of the Extended Plenary Meeting of the Comintern Executive Committee by a group of members of the former Workers' Opposition (A. G. Shlyapnikov, S. P. Medvedyev, A. M. Kollontai, G. I. Myasnikov and others), which continued to exist as a faction despite the resolution "On Party Unity" passed by the Tenth Congress of the R.C.P.(B.). The statement claimed that "matters were unsatisfactory with regard to a united front in our country", that the leading Party bodies were ignoring the requirements and interests of the workers and that a split was impending in the Party.

The Comintern Executive Committee appointed a commission consisting of Clara Zetkin, Marcel Cachin, Jacob Friis, Vasil Kolarov, Karl Krejbich, Umberto Terracini and Arthur McManus to look into the Statement of the Twenty-Two. On March 4, on the basis of the report of this commission, a Plenary Meeting of the Comintern Executive Committee, with four abstentions, passed a resolution rejecting the accusations in the statement and censured the stand of the twenty-two as running counter to the decisions of the Tenth Congress of the R.C.P.(B.).

The Eleventh Congress of the R.C.P.(B.) appointed a commission of 19 persons to examine the Statement of the Twenty-Two. On April 2, on the basis of the report of this commission, a closed session of the Congress adopted a special resolution "On Certain Members of the Former Workers' Opposition", in which it stigmatised the anti-Party behaviour of members of the Workers' Opposition group, and warned the leaders of the group that they would be expelled from the Party if they renewed their factional activity.   p. 321

[97] On a motion proposed by Lenin, the joint sitting of the Plenary Meeting of the Central Committee and the Central Control Commission on August 9, 1921, examined the question of expelling A. Shlyapnikov from the Central Committee and from the Party for anti-Party activity.   p. 322

[98] In Motovilikha District, Perm Gubernia, G. I. Myasnikov organised an anti-Party group which opposed the Party's policy. On July 29, 1921, the Organising Bureau of the C.C., R.C.P.(B.)

examined Myasnikov's statements in the Perm organisation, found
that they were directed against the Party and set up a commission to investigate Myasnikov's activities. On August 22, acting on the basis of the report of this commission, the Organising
Bureau found Myasnikov's theses incompatible with Party interests, prohibited him from speaking of his theses at official Party
meetings, recalled him from the Perm organisation and placed
him at the disposal of the Central Committee. Myasnikov dis-
obeyed the Central Committee, returned to Motovilikha and continued his anti-Party activities. At the same time, he tried to
organise an anti-Party group in Petrograd. After investigating
his activities, the C.C., R.C.P.(B.) commission proposed that
he should be expelled from the Party for repeated violations of
Party discipline and for organising a special anti-Party group
in defiance of the Tenth Party Congress decision on Party unity.
On February 20, 1922, the Political Bureau approved the commission's decision on Myasnikov's expulsion from the Party, with
the provision that he should have the right to apply for Party
membership in a year (see *Eleventh Congress of the R.C.P.(B.).
Verbatim Report*, Moscow, 1961, pp. 748-49).   p. 323

[99] See present edition, Vol. 32, pp. 504-09.   p. 323

[100] The suggestions made in Lenin's letter were used as the basis for
the Eleventh Party Congress resolution "On Work in the Countryside". The Congress instructed the Central Committee to set up
a permanent commission at the C.C. to direct work in the countryside.   p. 327

[101] Workers' uprisings broke out in March 1922 in Johannesburg,
Benoni and Brakpan in South Africa.
   In order to preserve their profits following the drop of the price
of gold in the world market, the owners of the goldfields began
lowering the wages of European workers and discharging them
en masse. On January 9, 1922, this provoked a strike in the goldfields. In March the strike developed into an uprising. The workers
seized the towns of Benoni and Brakpan, and two workers'
suburbs (Fordsburg and Geppestown) of Johannesburg. The then
young Communist Party of South Africa was active in the uprising.
Many Communists heroically sacrificed their lives during the
armed struggle. On March 10, the reactionary government of
General Smuts declared the above towns in a state of siege, and
brought in troops, artillery and aircraft. On March 14, the uprising was suppressed and more than 10,000 persons were arrested.
Thousands of workers were tried by military tribunals.   p. 331

[102] This decree was the result of extensive work by Lenin, who drew
up new rules covering the functions of the Council of People's
Commissars and the Council of Labour and Defence.

A. D. Tsyurupa and A. I. Rykov, Deputy Chairmen of the Council of People's Commissars and the Council of Labour and Defence, helped to draft the decree.   p. 335

103 This book (*Documents on the History of Franco-Russian Relations for 1910-14*) was published by the People's Commissariat of Foreign Affairs in 1922. Changes were made in it on the basis of suggestions from Lenin.   p. 344

104 Lenin's pamphlet *Old Articles on Almost New Subjects. On the Question of the New Economic Policy (Two Articles and a Speech, 1918)* was published in 1922 by the Moscow branch of the State Publishing House. The pamphlet included the Preface to the 1922 Edition, the article "The Immediate Tasks of the Soviet Government", report on the immediate tasks of the Soviet Government at the session of the All-Russia C.E.C. on April 29, 1918, and the article "'Left-Wing' Childishness and the Petty-Bourgeois Mentality" (see present edition, Vol. 27, pp. 235-77, 281-305, 323-54).
p. 345

105 See present edition, Vol. 27, pp. 306-13.   p. 346

106 *Iskra* (old) was the first Russian illegal Marxist newspaper. Founded by Lenin in 1900, it played the decisive role in the formation of a revolutionary Marxist party of the working class of Russia.
    Soon after the Second Party Congress (1903), control of the newspaper was seized by Menshevik opportunists. With the publication of its 52nd issue *Iskra* ceased to be an organ of revolutionary Marxism.   p. 349

107 Lenin refers to the Second Congress of the R.S.D.L.P., which was held on July 17-August 10 (July 30-August 23), 1903. The first thirteen sessions took place in Brussels. Owing to police persecution, the Congress was moved to London.   p. 351

108 Here Lenin means the cash collections that were undertaken by workers for their newspaper *Pravda*.   p. 351

109 One of the bullets that struck Lenin during the assassination attempt on August 30, 1918, was removed on April 23, 1922 at the Soldatenkovskaya Hospital (now the Botkin Hospital).   p. 353

110 The treaty signed by Soviet Russia and Germany on April 16, 1922 at Rapallo (near Genoa) at the time of the Genoa Conference.
    Under this treaty the signatories renounced all claims arising from the First World War. On the condition that the Soviet Government would not meet similar claims of other states, the German Government renounced its demand for the return to former German owners of enterprises nationalised by the Soviet Government. At the same time the two countries established diplomatic relations and most favoured nation treatment in economic questions.

The signing of the Rapallo Treaty was a major achievement of Soviet diplomacy. It strengthened the Soviet state's international position and wrecked the attempts to form a united anti-Soviet front. This treaty showed the Soviet Government's desire to normalise relations with bourgeois states solely on the basis of recognition of the equality of the two systems of ownership. p. 357

[111] The revised draft Criminal Code, in which Lenin's recommendations were used for Articles 57, 58, 61 and 70, was examined and endorsed by the Third Session of the Ninth All-Russia Central Executive Committee (May 12-26, 1922). p. 358

[112] Lenin wrote this letter in connection with the drawing up of the Rules of the Procurator's office. On May 24, 1922 the Political Bureau discussed Lenin's letter and accepted the recommendations in it. On May 26, acting on the report of the special commission, the Third Session of the Ninth All-Russia Central Executive Committee approved the Rules in accordance with Lenin's recommendations. p. 363

[113] The *Fifth All-Russia Congress of Trade Unions* was held in Moscow on September 17-22, 1922. It was attended by 970 delegates representing 5,100,000 trade union members. The Congress elected Lenin an honorary member of its presidium. Lenin's letter was read at the first sitting on September 17, 1922. The Congress sent Lenin greetings in reply. p. 370

[114] This Congress was held in Moscow on October 11-17, 1922. It elected Lenin its honorary chairman. Lenin's greetings were read at the first (ceremonial) sitting on October 11. In their greetings in reply, the Y.C.L.ers pledged themselves to surmount all the difficulties standing in the way of the working class and its youth, and asked for help in the communist education of young people. p. 374

[115] This letter was written after the Plenary Meeting of the C.C., R.C.P. (B.), at its October 6, 1922 sitting, which Lenin did not attend, acted on a report by G. Y. Sokolnikov and passed a decision to relax the monopoly of foreign trade.

Lenin disagreed with this decision, holding that it would wreck that monopoly.

In his letter to the C.C., R.C.P. (B.), the first part of which was written on October 12 and the postscript on October 13, he showed that the decision on foreign trade was wrong and proposed postponing a decision on this question for two months, until the next Plenary Meeting of the Central Committee.

On October 13, the Central Committee Secretariat sent the members of the C.C. the letter from Lenin and also the Theses of the People's Commissariat of Foreign Trade on the Foreign Trade System drawn up by L. B. Krasin. The members of the C.C., with few exceptions, supported Lenin's recommendations. N. I. Bukharin, for example, wrote to Stalin on October 15, trying to give grounds for the demand to annul the foreign trade monopoly. Stalin wrote to members of the Central Committee: "Comrade Lenin's letter has not persuaded me that the decision of the C.C. Plenary Meeting of October 6 on foreign trade was wrong.... Nonetheless, in view of Comrade Lenin's insistence that fulfilment of the C.C. Plenary Meeting decision be delayed, I shall vote *for* a postponement so that the question may be again raised for discussion at the next Plenary Meeting which Comrade Lenin will attend." On October 16, on the basis of a questionnaire proposed by Lenin, the members of the Central Committee, by fourteen votes against one, decided to postpone a decision on this question until the next Plenary Meeting.   p. 375

116 The *All-Russia Congress of Financial Workers* was held in Moscow on October 22-28, 1922. Lenin was elected honorary chairman. His letter was read on October 22.   p. 379

117 The *Friends of Soviet Russia (in the United States)* was founded in June 1921. It had over 200 local organisations, each of which had an Executive Committee or Committee of Action, which was directly linked up with the Society's National Executive. The National Executive and the Consultative Committee directed all organisational and propaganda work and also concentrated all cash donations into a single fund. The aim of the Society was to help the workers and peasants of Soviet Russia, tell the people of the U.S.A. the truth about Soviet Russia and secure the lifting of the U.S. economic blockade of Russia.

In May 1922, the Society sent to Russia a tractor team, which began working at the Toikino State Farm, Sarapul Uyezd, Perm Gubernia, on July 17. The team did much to raise production at the state farm and to show the peasants the advantages of large-scale farming with machines.

On Lenin's recommendation, Toikino was recognised as a model farm by the Presidium of the All-Russia Central Executive Committee on November 9, 1922.

Lenin's letter was translated into English and printed on November 15, 1922 in the magazine *Soviet Russia*, which was published in New York by Russian workers' organisations in the U.S.A.   p. 380

118 The *Society for Technical Aid for Soviet Russia* was organised by Russian émigrés in New York in May 1919. Similar societies sprang up elsewhere in the U.S.A. and also in Canada. These societies were founded with the active participation of Americans and Canadians. Their purpose was to help Soviet Russia restore her economy by sending skilled workers and technicians from the U.S.A. and Canada.

The work of the societies for Technical Aid for Soviet Russia and of Friends of Soviet Russia (in the United States) was

evaluated by Lenin as a striking manifestation of proletarian
internationalism and fraternal solidarity among working people.
    Lenin's letter was translated into English and printed in De-
cember 1922 in the magazine *Soviet Russia*, which was published
in New York by Russian workers' organisations in the U.S.A.
                                                                    p. 381

[119] Lenin sent his telegram of greetings to the liberated Primorye
Territory on the occasion of the liberation of Vladivostok on
October 25, 1922, by troops of the Far Eastern Republic, who
acted jointly with guerillas in clearing out the whiteguards and
Japanese interventionists. In their reply, the working people
of Primorye Territory sent greetings to the Soviet Government
and thanked it for its assistance.   p. 382

[120] The *Far Eastern Republic* was established in April 1920. It
embraced the Trans-Baikal Area, Amur, Primorye and Kamchatka
regions, and the northern part of the Sakhalin Island. The formation of this "buffer" state as a bourgeois-democratic republic
that pursued an essentially Soviet policy suited the interests
of Soviet Russia, which sought to secure a prolonged respite
on the Eastern Front and avoid war with Japan.
    On November 14, 1922, after the interventionists and the white-
guards were driven out of the Far East (with the exception of
the northern part of the Sakhalin Island), the People's Assembly
of the Far Eastern Republic passed a decision to unite with the
R.S.F.S.R. ·   p. 382

[121] Edouard Herriot, leader of the Radical Socialist Party, member
of Parliament and Mayor of Lyons, visited Russia unofficially on
September 20-October 10, 1922. He toured the country with the
aim of elucidating economic and political possibilities for establishing relations between France and the R.S.F.S.R.   p. 383

[122] The Lausanne Conference, which took place on November 20,
1922-July 24, 1923.   p. 385

[123] The Versailles Peace Treaty.   p. 386

[124] Talks on the leasing of a mining concession in the Urals and
Siberia were held with John Leslie Urquhart, a leading British
industrialist. During the discussion of the draft agreement, Trotsky, Zinoviev and Kamenev insisted on the acceptance of the
fettering terms proposed by Urquhart. On October 6, 1922, the
Council of People's Commissars rejected the draft agreement
with Urquhart because of the hostile policy of the British Government towards Soviet Russia and the shackling terms of the agreement.   p. 387

[125] The *Fourth Session of the Ninth All-Russia Central Executive
Committee* was held on October 23-31, 1922. Lenin spoke at the
closing sitting.   p. 390

126 The Decree on Land adopted by the Second All-Russia Congress of Soviets of Workers' and Soldiers' Deputies (see present edition, Vol. 26, pp. 258-60).   p. 392

127 *Petrogradskaya Pravda*—a daily newspaper which started publication on April 2, 1918 as the organ of the Central and Petrograd Committees of the R.C.P.(B.). In January 1924 the newspaper's name was changed to *Leningradskaya Pravda*.   p. 396

128 The *First International Conference of Communist Co-operators* took place in Moscow on November 1-6, 1922. It was attended by representatives from Armenia, Australia, Austria, Azerbaijan, Bulgaria, Denmark, Estonia, the Far Eastern Republic, Finland, France, Georgia, Germany, Italy, Latvia, Lithuania, Norway, Poland, the R.S.F.S.R., Sweden, Switzerland and the Ukraine.

The cardinal question before the conference was that of the tactics of Communists in the co-operative movement. The resolution adopted by the conference rejected the principle that co-operatives should be neutral in politics and underlined the need for establishing a close bond between co-operative work and the political and economic tasks of the proletariat, and for carrying on this work in closer co-operation with Communist Parties and revolutionary trade unions. The conference elected Lenin its honorary chairman and sent him greetings. Lenin's greetings in reply were read on November 2, 1922.   p. 398

129 The *Fourth All-Russia Congress of Statisticians* was held in Moscow on November 3-12, 1922. Lenin was elected honorary chairman of the Congress and sent a telegram of greetings. His reply was read at the second sitting on November 5.   p. 399

130 Arthur Ransome, *Manchester Guardian* correspondent, came to Soviet Russia in October 1922 with the express purpose of interviewing Lenin. On October 26 he was asked to write down the questions that he wanted answered. On the next day Ransome wrote seven questions which he sent to Lenin.

Lenin received Ransome in the evening of November 3. They spoke of the parliamentary elections in Britain and the fascist coup in Italy, but mostly the talk was around the questions submitted by Ransome. Lenin said that he had not yet answered all the questions, but promised to do so before Ransome left the country. On Sunday, November 5, Lenin wrote his answers to all of Ransome's seven questions.   p. 400

131 Lenin and his wife Nadezhda Krupskaya lived in London from April 1902 to April 1903. The friend that Lenin mentions is K. M. Takhtarev, a Social-Democrat, member of the St. Petersburg League of Struggle for the Emancipation of the Working Class and one of the leaders of Economism.

The *Economists* were representatives of an opportunist trend in the Russian Social-Democratic movement of the close of the

19th and beginning of the 20th century. The Economists incorrectly assessed the relation between economics and politics and belittled the role of the political revolutionary struggle. They said that the working class should confine itself to an economic struggle for higher wages, better working conditions and so forth, maintaining that the political struggle was a matter for the liberal bourgeoisie. They rejected the idea that the party of the working class plays the leading role, that socialist political consciousness must be brought into the working-class movement. They thereby cleared the road for bourgeois ideology. Economism held out the threat of steering the proletariat away from the road of revolution and making it politically dependent on the bourgeoisie. This trend was completely routed ideologically by Lenin.   p. 400

[132] On October 24, 1922, the Council of People's Commissars passed a decision to put into circulation banknotes dated 1923. Under the new decision, signed by Lenin, one 1923 ruble was equal to a million rubles of the banknotes that had been removed from circulation or one hundred 1922 rubles.   p. 402

[133] This conference was held on November 6, 1922. It was attended by over 2,000 delegates.
Lenin handed his letter of greetings to the delegates who were sent to him to ask him to speak at the conference.   p. 410

[134] In August 1922 the workers of this factory requested the Moscow Soviet to name their factory after Lenin. This request was granted on September 9, 1922. In connection with the renaming of the factory and the approaching fifth anniversary of the October Revolution, a general meeting of workers decided to hold a rally on November 7. The workers invited Lenin to attend the rally.
Unable to do so because of his illness, Lenin wrote this letter.
                    p. 411

[135] Lenin's letter of greetings to the workers and employees of the Elektroperedacha Power Station (now the Klasson Station, named after the engineer who built it) was written in reply to an invitation to speak at the opening of the club on the occasion of the fifth anniversary of the October Revolution.   p. 412

[136] This letter was written in reply to greetings from the Stodol Mill workers of November 3, 1922, when the mill was named after Lenin. Together with greetings, the workers sent Lenin a gift—a suit-length made at the mill.   p. 413

[137] The *Fourth Congress of the Communist International* took place on November 5-December 5, 1922. It opened in Petrograd and then, from November 9 onwards, the sittings were held in Moscow. It was attended by 408 delegates, 343 of whom had a casting vote, representing 58 Communist organisations in various countries. Also present were representatives of the Italian Socialist Party,

the Iceland Workers' Party, the Mongolian People's Revolutionary Party, the Young Communist International, the Profintern, the International Women's Secretariat, the International Workers' Aid and U.S. Negro Organisation. The Congress endorsed the theses on a united workers' front, drawn up by the R.C.P. (B.), approved the theses on the tactics of the Communist International, on the tasks of Communists in the trade union movement, and on the Eastern question, and adopted a resolution on the socialist revolution in Russia, on the Young Communist International and other questions.

Lenin read his report "Five Years of the Russian Revolution and the Prospects of the World Revolution" in German at the morning sitting on November 13.   p. 415

138 Lenin refers to the article "'Left-Wing' Childishness and the Petty-Bourgeois Mentality" (see present edition, Vol. 27, pp. 323-54).
                                                                  p. 418

139 This expression was used in Ivan Turgenev's *Rudin* by Pigasov, who was a woman-hater. Refusing to credit women with the ability to think logically, Pigasov maintained: "A man may, for example, say that twice two make not four but five or three and a half; but a woman will say that twice two make a tallow candle."   p. 429

140 *Black Hundreds* were monarchist gangs that were formed by the tsarist police to combat the revolutionary movement. They murdered revolutionaries, attacked progressive intellectuals and organised Jewish pogroms.   p. 431

141 The *All-Russia Agricultural Exhibition* was, according to a decision of the Ninth All-Russia Congress of Soviets, scheduled to open in the autumn of 1922. However, on account of the large volume of work that went into organising the exhibition and into surmounting the consequences of a crop failure, the opening was postponed until 1923. Great importance was attached to the foreign section at the exhibition, and many foreign businessmen were eager to take part in it. In the press it was emphasised that the exhibition "must be not only Russian but also, to some extent, international".

The First Agricultural and Crafts Exhibition in the Soviet Union was opened in Moscow on August 19, 1923. Lenin took a keen interest in the exhibition. On October 19, during his last stay in Moscow, Lenin drove across the territory of the exhibition despite being gravely ill.   p. 433

142 The *Clarté* group of progressive writers and cultural workers was organised by Henri Barbusse in 1919 on the basis of *l'Association Républicaine des Anciens Combattants*. Similar groups were set up in other countries, and together they formed the War Veterans International, whose main motto was: War on war. The *Clarté*

group included supporters of the Third International—Henri Barbusse, Anatole France, Paul Vaillant-Couturier—and pacifist writers—Romain Rolland, Stefan Zweig, H. G. Wells, Thomas Hardy, Upton Sinclair, Jules Romain, and others. The group published a monthly magazine of the same name (in Paris from October 1919 to January 1928), which in its first years was quite popular in France and abroad. However, the ideological disagreements within the group and its organisational weakness did not permit it to become a large and influential organisation. Soon after Barbusse resigned as editor (in April 1924), the magazine lost its progressive significance. It ceased publication in 1928 and the group disintegrated. p. 434

[143] Lenin spoke at the Plenary Meeting of the Moscow Soviet, which held a joint sitting with all the district Soviets in Moscow, in the evening of November 20, 1922. This was his last public speech. p. 435

[144] The decision adopted by the People's Assembly of the Far Eastern Republic on November 14, 1922, to join the R.S.F.S.R. This decision was published on November 15, 1922. The full text of the decision was published in the newspapers on November 21, 1922, after Lenin had made his speech. p. 436

[145] The *Fifth All-Russia Congress of the Soviet Employees' Union* was held in Moscow on November 16-21, 1922. Lenin was elected an honorary delegate to the congress by the Sixth Tver Gubernia Congress of the Soviet Employees' Union. Electing Lenin its honorary chairman, the Fifth All-Russia Congress sent him a message of greetings. p. 444

[146] The *Fourth All-Russia Educational Workers' Congress* took place in Moscow on November 21-26, 1922. It elected Lenin its honorary chairman and sent him a message of greetings. Lenin's reply was read at the morning sitting on November 26. p. 445

[147] The *Third Congress of the Young Communist International* took place in Moscow on December 4-16, 1922. It was attended by 121 delegates from 38 youth organisations in different countries. Lenin's letter of greetings was read at the opening session. The congress sent him a message in reply. p. 446

[148] The *Hague International Peace Congress*, December 10-15, 1922, was convened by the Amsterdam International Federation of Trade Unions as a result of pressure brought to bear by the working class with the purpose of combating the threat of another world war. The Soviet delegation, invited to the congress on the demand of revolutionary trade unions and co-operatives in face of the resistance of the opportunist majority at the congress, set forth the tasks of the proletariat with regard to war. It spoke in the spirit of the instructions given to it by Lenin. The congress

rejected the programme of action proposed by the Soviet delegation.   p. 447

149 This article was written at the request of the Party History Commission for a special volume dedicated to the revolutionary activity of N. Y. Fedoseyev. Fedoseyev wrote a number of Marxist
works directed against the Narodniks, primarily against
N. K. Mikhailovsky. The correspondence with Fedoseyev mentioned by Lenin has not been found.   p. 452

150 *Emancipation of Labour* was the first Russian Marxist group. It
was formed in Switzerland in 1883 by G. V. Plekhanov. The
group did much to popularise Marxism in Russia.   p. 452

151 *Russkoye Bogatstvo*—a monthly magazine published in St. Petersburg from 1876 to mid-1918. Early in the 1890s it became the
organ of liberal Narodniks. It preached conciliation with the
tsarist government and was savagely opposed to Marxism and
the Russian Marxists.   p. 452

152 Lenin went to Vladimir at the beginning of October 1893 with the
intention of meeting N. Y. Fedoseyev.   p. 452

153 The *Seventh All-Ukraine Congress of Soviets* was held in Kharkov
on December 10-14, 1922. One of its principal decisions, adopted
on the basis of a report delivered by M. V. Frunze, was on the
union federation of the Soviet republics. Lenin's telegram was
read at the opening session on December 10. The congress elected
Lenin an honorary member of the All-Ukraine Central Executive
Committee and sent him a telegram of greetings in reply. p. 454

154 On October 16, 1922 (see Note No. 115), the Central Committee
decided that the question of the monopoly on foreign trade would
be re-examined at a Plenary Meeting of December 15 (then the
date of the meeting was postponed to December 18). Lenin had
prepared carefully for the meeting.

However, on December 13, Lenin's illness took a turn for the
worse and he was not permitted to work by his doctors. Unable
to take part in the C.C. Plenary Meeting, he wrote this letter of
December 13, in which he analysed and rejected Bukharin's arguments against the monopoly of foreign trade in a letter to the
Central Committee of October 15, 1922.

The December Plenary Meeting of the Central Committee unanimously passed a decision revoking the decision of the preceding
Plenary Meeting held in October, and confirmed that it was "unquestionably necessary to preserve and organisationally strength-
en the foreign trade monopoly". Nonetheless Lenin attached
such great importance to the question of the monopoly of foreign
trade that he intended to speak about it to the Communist group
at the forthcoming Tenth All-Russia Congress of Soviets and
to bring it up for discussion at the Twelfth Party Congress.

Acting on Lenin's instructions, the Twelfth Party Congress, which was held on April 17-25, 1923, examined the question of the foreign trade monopoly. Its resolution, passed on the report of the C.C., R.C.P.(B.), stated: "The Congress categorically affirms that the monopoly of foreign trade is immutable and that no one is permitted to bypass it or to waver in implementing it. The new Central Committee is instructed to take systematic measures to strengthen and promote the monopoly of foreign trade" (*KPSS v resolyutsiakh i resheniyakh syezdov, konferentsi i plenumov Ts.K.* [C.P.S.U. in Resolutions and Decisions of Congresses, Conferences and C.C. Plenary Meetings], Part I, 1954, p. 682).
p. 455

[155] When Lenin's health deteriorated his doctors ordered him to move to Gorki, a suburb of Moscow. p. 460

[156] The *Tenth All-Russia Congress of Soviets*, which opened in Moscow on December 23, 1922. It was attended by 2,215 delegates, of whom 488 were representatives from the Transcaucasian Soviet Federative Socialist Republic, the Ukrainian Soviet Socialist Republic and the Byelorussian Soviet Socialist Republic. Lenin was elected honorary chairman. A message of greetings to Lenin was adopted amidst stormy applause and the singing of *The Internationale*.

The Congress discussed the report of the All-Russia Central Executive Committee and the Council of People's Commissars on the home and foreign policy of the Soviet Republic, and also the reports of the Supreme Economic Council, the People's Commissariat of Education, the People's Commissariat of Finance and the People's Commissariat of Agriculture. Fully endorsing the work of the Soviet Government, the Congress passed decisions mapping out a series of measures aimed at further promoting industry, agriculture and finances. On December 26 the Congress heard a report on the unification of the Soviet republics, and on the next day, at its last sitting, it passed a decision on this question, finding it necessary to form the Union of Soviet Socialist Republics.

Moreover, the Congress adopted an address to all the peoples of the world, in which on behalf of the workers and peasants of Russia it solemnly reaffirmed its desire for peace and called upon the working people of all countries to combine their efforts with those of the peoples of the Soviet Union in order to secure peace and save mankind from monstrous wars of extermination. p. 460

[157] Due to a further deterioration of his health, Lenin was unable to attend the Tenth All-Russia Congress of Soviets. p. 460

[158] Lenin refers to his article "'Left-Wing' Childishness and the Petty-Bourgeois Mentality" (see present edition, Vol. 27, pp. 323-54). p. 472

[159] This, evidently, is a reference to the Paris Commune as a supremely flexible political system in Marx's *The Civil War in France*

(see Karl Marx and Frederick Engels, *Selected Works in 2 Volumes*, Vol. I, pp. 473-90) and the high appraisal of the "flexibility of the Parisians" given by Marx in a letter to L. Kugelmann on April 12, 1871 (see Karl Marx and Frederick Engels, *Selected Works in 2 Volumes*, Vol. II, pp. 463-64). p. 476

[160] Lenin has in mind the following excerpt from a letter from Marx to Engels on April 16, 1856: "The whole thing in Germany will depend on the possibility of backing the proletarian revolution by some second edition of the Peasant War. Then the affair will be splendid" (see Marx and Engels, *Selected Correspondence*, p. 92). p. 476

[161] This article and its continuation, *Better Fewer, But Better*, were written by Lenin for the Twelfth Party Congress.

The decisions adopted by that Congress, April 17-25, 1923, took into account all of the instructions in Lenin's last articles and letters. It passed a special resolution "On the Tasks of the Workers' and Peasants' Inspection and the Central Control Commission" and also a decision on amalgamating these two bodies. p. 481

[162] The power project on the Volkhov River was the first of the large hydropower stations in the Soviet Union. Construction on this project was started in 1918, but the work really got under way only in 1921, after the Civil War. The station became operational in 1926. p. 501

THE LIFE AND WORK
OF
V. I. LENIN

Outstanding Dates
(August 1921-January 1924)

1921

August 16 and September 1	Lenin writes to the Central Statistical Board, instructing it on the organisation of current industrial and agricultural statistics.
August 20	Lenin writes the article "New Times and Old Mistakes in a New Guise".
August 31	Lenin instructs the Commission for the Hydraulic Extraction of Peat to check up on the invention of an industrial method of dehydrating peat.
August-September	Lenin directs the preparations for the Eighth All-Russia Congress of Electrical Engineers.
August-December	Lenin instructs the Supreme Economic Council, the People's Commissariat of Railways, the People's Commissariat of Finance, the People's Commissariat of Food and other People's Commissariats to provide the Kashira and Volkhov power projects with labour and all the necessary materials.
September 1	Lenin writes a letter to *Ekonomicheskaya Zhizn* on the newspaper's basic tasks in dealing with economic problems.
September 3	In a letter to the People's Commissariat of Justice Lenin instructs it on measures to combat bureaucracy.
September 5	Lenin writes a letter to the Statistical Department of the C.C., R.C.P.(B.), instructing it how to keep an account of the distribution of leading Party cadres working in the Soviet apparatus.
September 15	Lenin submits to the C.C., R.C.P.(B.) a draft circular on the procedure of giving recommendations in connection with the Party purge.
September 19	Lenin talks with representatives of U.S. workers, who came to Russia with the purpose of rendering production and technical aid; he writes a letter

to V. V. Kuibyshev, Secretary of the C.C., R.C.P.(B.), instructing him to organise a production colony for them in the Kuznetsk Basin.

September 20   Lenin writes the article "Purging the Party".

September 27   Lenin writes the letter "Tasks of the Workers' and Peasants' Inspection and How They Are to Be Understood and Fulfilled".

September 30   Lenin presides over a meeting of the Council of Labour and Defence commission on the supply of fuel to the railways.

Lenin presides over a meeting of the Council of Labour and Defence, which discusses: the plan of distributing grain reserves for 1921-22; the measures to rehabilitate and develop the Donbas coal industry and the Baku and Grozny oil industries; land improvement at the state farms in Moscow Gubernia, and other questions.

October 4   Lenin presides over a meeting of the Council of People's Commissars, which discusses: measures to be taken to collect the tax in kind; the procedure and time-limit for putting the new ruble in circulation; the institution of the State Bank of the R.S.F.S.R., and other questions.

October 8   Lenin writes a greeting "To the Presidium of the Eighth All-Russia Congress of Electrical Engineers".

Lenin directs the work of the Plenary Meeting of the C.C., R.C.P.(B.), which discusses: the financial policy; commodity exchange and co-operatives; the Party purge; the registration of responsible workers and the procedure for their distribution (Lenin submits a draft proposal); the People's Commissariat of Public Education; the Comintern; and the international situation.

Lenin writes directives of the Political Bureau on giving factories in the Ukraine land for sowing sugar-beet.

October 14   Lenin writes the article "Fourth Anniversary of the October Revolution".

October 17   Lenin delivers a report on "The New Economic Policy and the Tasks of the Political Education Departments" to the Second All-Russia Congress of Political Education Departments.

Lenin instructs the People's Commissariat of Finance to prepare for a monetary reform.

October 21   Lenin presides over a meeting of the Council of Labour and Defence, which discusses: Lenin's draft "Atlas of Diagrams for the Council of Labour and Defence" with statistics on industry, agriculture, transport and so forth; a loan to the Azerbaijanian Soviet Republic for land improvement in Mugan; the Murmansk and Petrograd ports, and other questions.

October 22   Lenin witnesses the testing of an electric plough at the experiment farm of the Moscow Zootechnical Institute at Butyrsky Khutor.

October 24   Lenin sends N. A. Semashko, People's Commissar of Public Health, directives on the procedure of holding a household sanitary week and demands exemplary cleanliness in Moscow.

October 29   Lenin reports on the New Economic Policy to the Seventh Moscow Gubernia Party Conference and delivers the closing speech.

November 3   Lenin instructs the Narrow Council of People's Commissars urgently to examine the draft agreement with the Mongolian People's Republic.

November 4   Lenin presides over a meeting of the Council of Labour and Defence, which discusses: the work of the State Planning Commission departments on dividing Russia up into districts; the order for turbines for the Volkhov Power Station; the Kara Sea Expedition, and other questions.

November 5   Lenin writes the article "The Importance of Gold Now and After the Complete Victory of Socialism".

Lenin receives a delegation from the Mongolian People's Republic.

November 6   Lenin speaks at a meeting of the Prokhorov Textile Mills workers held to mark the fourth anniversary of the October Revolution.

November 7   Lenin speaks at a meeting of working men and women, Red Army men and young people of Khamovniki District, Moscow, held to mark the fourth anniversary of the October Revolution.

Lenin speaks at a workers' meeting at the Elektro-sila Plant No. 3 (formerly Dynamo Plant) held to mark the fourth anniversary of the October Revolution.

November 10   Lenin presides over a meeting of the Council of People's Commissars, which discusses: an improvement of the living conditions of scientists; the tariff policy, and other questions.

Lenin receives Wilhelm Pieck and Fritz Heckert and discusses with them the situation in the German Communist Party.

November 16   Lenin writes the preface to the pamphlet "The Problem of the New Economic Policy".

Not earlier than   Lenin sends greetings to the Council of People's
November 17   Commissars of the Azerbaijanian Soviet Republic on the occasion of the opening of the Azerbaijanian State Bank.

November 18   Lenin presides over a meeting of the Council of People's Commissars, which discusses: the financial plan and the emission plan for 1922 (Lenin submits additions to the draft decision); the composition of the commission for the systematisation of legislation in the sphere of the New Economic Policy, and other questions.

Lenin presides over a meeting of the Council of Labour and Defence, which discusses: the commissioning of the Kashira Power Station; the reserve food stocks, and other questions.

November 23   Lenin instructs the State Planning Commission to take steps to accelerate the building and commissioning of the Ivanovo-Voznesensk Power Station.

November 25   Lenin presides over a meeting of the Council of Labour and Defence, which discusses: the mining, and gold and platinum industries; the switch-over of the oil industry to a self-supporting basis; stepping up the work at the Urals and Siberian mines; supplies to miners in the Moscow Basin, and other questions.

November 28   Lenin writes a letter to A. D. Tsyurupa, setting forth a plan of work for the Deputy Chairmen of the Council of People's Commissars and the Council of Labour and Defence.

November 29   Lenin speaks at the First Moscow Gubernia Agricultural Congress.

November 30   Lenin signs a decision of the Council of Labour and Defence on organising a tree seed fund to ensure the planting of forests, fixing sands and ravines and setting up snow-retention zones.

December 5   Lenin writes a letter (in English) to American comrades, requesting them to inform him of their opinion of his book *New Data on the Laws Governing the Development of Capitalism in Agriculture. Part One. Capitalism and Agriculture in the United States of America* and asking them to send him the official publication of the U.S. census for 1920.

December 6   Lenin writes a letter to Maxim Gorky, asking him to request Bernard Shaw and H. G. Wells to take part in organising aid for the famine-stricken in Russia.

Lenin writes notes for the Comintern theses on a united front.

Lenin is given sick leave and moves to Gorki, a suburb of Moscow.

December 11   Lenin writes the article "The Theses on the Agrarian Question Adopted by the Communist Party of France".

December 16   Lenin instructs the People's Commissar of Public Education to set up a commission to examine the question of organising a film industry in Russia.

December 17   Lenin begins writing a report on the work of the government to the Ninth All-Russia Congress of Soviets, and asks the People's Commissariats for the necessary reference materials.

December 19   Lenin writes a letter to members of the Political Bureau of the C.C., R.C.P.(B.) on purging the Party and on the conditions of admission into the Party.

December 22   Lenin suggests that the Political Bureau draw up a special resolution for the Ninth All-Russia Congress of Soviets on the international situation.

December 23   Lenin delivers the report of the All-Russia Central Executive Committee and the Council of

People's Commissars on "The Home and Foreign Policy of the Republic" at the Ninth All-Russia Congress of Soviets.

December 25   Lenin writes his "Instructions on Questions of Economic Activities", which are adopted by the Ninth All-Russia Congress of Soviets on December 28, 1921.

December 26   Lenin attends the conference of non-Party delegates to the Ninth All-Russia Congress of Soviets, makes notes of the speeches and replies to questions by the delegates.

December 27   Lenin writes a letter to the C.C., R.C.P.(B.) on "British Labour Party Policy".

December 28   Lenin attends a Plenary Meeting of the C.C., R.C.P.(B.).

December 30-   Lenin writes a draft decision of the C.C., R.C.P.(B.)
January 4, 1922   on "The Role and Functions of the Trade Unions Under the New Economic Policy". The draft was endorsed by the Central Committee on January 12, 1922.

December 31   Lenin attends a meeting of the Political Bureau of the C.C., R.C.P.(B.).

The Political Bureau passes a decision to grant Lenin six weeks' leave as from January 1, 1922.

1922

January 3   Lenin instructs the Executive Secretary of the Council of People's Commissars to establish the procedure for accounting and the drawing up of balance-sheets by enterprises and offices to whom state supplies had been stopped, and for making all trade enterprises accountable to the State Bank.

Between Janu-   Lenin writes the "Draft Directive of the Political
ary 9 and 12   Bureau on the New Economic Policy".

January 17   Lenin writes a letter to D. I. Kursky on the fundamental principles of the Civil Code of the R.S.F.S.R. and on the struggle against abuses of the New Economic Policy.

January 17-   Lenin lives on a state farm near the village of
March 1   Kostino (near Moscow).

January 20	Lenin instructs the Executive Secretary of the Council of People's Commissars urgently to send all the People's Commissariats the Political Bureau directive on the New Economic Policy.
January 24, February 15, 20, 21 and 27	In letters to A. D. Tsyurupa Lenin issues directives on the reorganisation of the work of the Council of People's Commissars, the Council of Labour and Defence and the Narrow Council of People's Commissars.
January 27	Lenin writes a letter for members of the Political Bureau, suggesting that M. I. Kalinin be sent to the Ukraine to collect food for the famine-stricken areas. An extraordinary session of the Ninth All-Russia Central Executive Committee appoints Lenin head of the Soviet delegation to the Genoa Conference.
January-March	Lenin draws up the basic directives for the Soviet delegation to the Genoa Conference.
February 2	The Political Bureau passes a decision to prolong Lenin's leave until the Eleventh Party Congress.
February 13	Lenin writes his "Letter to G. K. Orjonikidze on the Strengthening of the Georgian Red Army".
February 15, 18, 22 and 28	Lenin writes letters to the People's Commissariat of Finance, A. D. Tsyurupa and the State Bank with instructions on the tasks of the State Bank under the New Economic Policy.
February 20 and 28	Lenin writes to D. I. Kursky, instructing him on the work of the People's Commissariat of Justice and on the drafting of the Civil Code.
February 22	Lenin writes a letter for members of the Political Bureau on the Civil Code of the R.S.F.S.R.
End of February	Lenin writes the article "Notes of a Publicist. On Ascending a High Mountain; the Harm of Despondency; the Utility of Trade; Attitude Towards the Mensheviks, etc."
March 1	In a letter to the Central Council of Co-operative Societies Lenin outlines the functions of the co-operatives under the New Economic Policy.
March 3	In a letter to members of the Political Bureau Lenin suggests rejecting Sokolnikov's proposal for

permitting the free import of food and demands decisive measures to strengthen the monopoly of foreign trade and an investigation into the delay over the purchase of tinned food abroad.

Lenin writes letters to V. M. Molotov for members of the Political Bureau in which he criticises Sokolnikov's theses for the Ninth Party Congress on the basic principles of the financial programme and proposes adopting the theses that the monopoly of foreign trade has to be strengthened.

March 6   Lenin speaks on "The International and Domestic Situation of the Soviet Republic" at a meeting of the Communist group at the Fifth All-Russia Congress of Metalworkers.

March 10   Lenin instructs the Executive Secretary of the Council of People's Commissars to take steps to create normal conditions of work for the Public Library in Moscow (now the Lenin State Library).

March 12   Lenin writes the article "On the Significance of Militant Materialism" for the magazine *Pod Znamenem Marksizma*.

March 16   In a letter to the Political Bureau Lenin criticises Preobrazhensky's theses on work in the countryside and proposes to reject them; he also proposes convening a conference of delegates to the Eleventh Party Congress to study the experience of work in the countryside.

Lenin instructs the Executive Secretary of the Council of People's Commissars to request the Central Statistical Board to submit statistical reports to the Council of People's Commissars under the established time-table.

March 17   Lenin writes a draft letter to E. Vandervelde in reply to the attempt of the leaders of the Second and Two-and-a-Half Internationals to intervene in the trial of Right Socialist-Revolutionaries.

Lenin instructs the Executive Secretary of the Council of People's Commissars to ensure the implementation of his directives on the promotion of the film industry and the building of a radio and telephone network.

March 18   Lenin writes a preface to I. I. Stepanov's *The Electrification of the R.S.F.S.R. and the Transitional Phase of World Economy*.

March 21	Lenin writes his "Letter to J.V. Stalin on the Functions of the Deputy Chairmen of the Council of People's Commissars and of the Council of Labour and Defence".
March 23	In a letter to the Plenary Meeting of the C.C., R.C.P.(B.) Lenin sets forth a plan for the political report for the Eleventh Party Congress.
	Lenin writes greetings to the newspaper *Bednota* on the occasion of its fourth anniversary.
March 24	Lenin submits to the Plenary Meeting of the C.C., R.C.P.(B.) suggestions on conditions for admitting new members to the Party.
March 26	Lenin writes a letter for members of the C.C., R.C.P.(B.) on the C.C. Plenary Meeting decision on the conditions for admitting new members to the Party.
March 31	Lenin writes a letter to D. I. Kursky, People's Commissar of Justice, on bureaucratic practices in the Committee for Inventions.
March 27-April 2	Lenin directs the work of the Eleventh Congress of the R.C.P.(B.).
March 27	Lenin opens the Congress and delivers the political report of the Central Committee.
March 28	Lenin delivers the closing speech on the Central Committee political report at the Congress.
April 1	Lenin writes to the Agricultural Section of the Eleventh Congress, giving directives on the draft resolution of the Congress on work in the countryside.
April 2	The Congress elects Lenin a member of the C.C., R.C.P.(B). Lenin speaks at the closing session of the Congress.
April 3	Lenin takes part in the work of the Plenary Meeting of the C.C., R.C.P.(B.).
	Lenin submits a draft decision on the work of the C.C. Secretariat.
April 6	Lenin instructs G. M. Krzhizhanovsky to take energetic measures to promote the development of the Kursk iron-ore deposits.

April 6, 10	In letters to V. V. Adoratsky, Lenin instructs the Marx and Engels Institute to publish selected correspondence by Marx and Engels.
April 9	Lenin writes the article "We Have Paid Too Much".
April 11	Lenin writes the draft "Decree on the Functions of the Deputy Chairmen of the Council of People's Commissars and of the Council of Labour and Defence".
April 12	Lenin writes a letter to the editorial boards of *Pravda* and *Izvestia* with instructions to organise the study of local experience and popularise the achievements of the localities and local workers.
April 15	In a letter to the Political Bureau Lenin draws attention to the slipshod publication of the book *Materialy po istorii franko-russkikh otnosheni za 1910-1914 gody* ("Documents on the History of Franco-Russian Relations for 1910-14").
April 23	Lenin undergoes an operation for the removal of a bullet at the Botkin Hospital.
April 28	Lenin writes "Preface to the pamphlet *Old Articles on Almost New Subjects.* Preface to the 1922 Edition".
	Lenin sends a telegram to the workers and engineers of the Azneft Trust in Baku thanking them for their courage in localising a fire at the Surakhan oilfields.
May 2	Lenin writes the article "On the Tenth Anniversary of *Pravda*".
	Lenin writes a letter to G. Y. Sokolnikov on the proposed internal grain loan, demanding "really revolutionary measures" to strengthen the country's financial position.
May 5	Lenin writes his "Reply to Remarks Concerning the Functions of the Deputy Chairmen of the Council of People's Commissars" for members of the Political Bureau.
May 15	Lenin studies the draft Criminal Code of the R.S.F.S.R. and suggests a wider use of the death penalty for Mensheviks and Socialist-Revolutionaries engaged in counter-revolutionary activities.

May 15 or 16	Lenin draws up the "Draft Decision of the All-Russia Central Executive Committee on the Report of the Delegation to the Genoa Conference"
May 16	Lenin takes part in the work of a Plenary Meeting of the C.C., R.C.P.(B.).
May 17	Lenin sends D. I. Kursky, People's Commissar of Justice, a draft of an additional paragraph for the Criminal Code on the use of terror with regard to counter-revolutionary parties.
	Lenin writes a letter to the People's Commissar of Public Education, saying that the price of books had to be reduced so that they could be bought by the broad masses.
May 19	Lenin writes two letters on the promotion of radio engineering for members of the Political Bureau.
May 23-October 1	Lenin resides at Gorki near Moscow.
May 20	Lenin writes a letter to the Political Bureau on "'Dual' Subordination and Legality".
May 26	Lenin has his first attack of illness.
Mid-June	There is some improvement in Lenin's health.
July 13	In a note to L. A. Fotieva, Lenin says his health is better and instructs her to send him books.
After September 10	Lenin writes the article "A Fly in the Ointment".
September 13	Lenin writes a draft letter to the Fifth All-Russia Congress of Trade Unions and sends it to members of the Political Bureau.
September 12, 18	In letters for members of the Political Bureau Lenin opposes an endorsement of an agreement to lease a concession to Urquhart.
September 17	Lenin writes to the Council of People's Commissars on financial aid to the Donbas and Baku.
	Lenin sends a letter of greetings to the Fifth All-Russia Trade Union Congress.

September 25   Lenin requests the People's Commissariat of Justice to inform him of the progress in preparing the Soviet Code of Laws for publication.

October 2   Lenin returns to Moscow and resumes work.

October 3   Lenin presides over a meeting of the Council of People's Commissars, which discusses: the wages fund for October; a one-day census of employees in Moscow; the organisation of a fish economy administration, and other questions.

October 5   Lenin attends a Plenary Meeting of the C.C., R.C.P.(B.).

October 6   Lenin writes a memo to the Political Bureau on combating dominant-nation chauvinism in connection with the discussion in the C.C., R.C.P.(B.) of the question of forming the Union of Soviet Socialist Republics.

Lenin signs a decision of the Council of People's Commissars rejecting the agreement to lease a concession to Urquhart.

Lenin writes a letter of greetings "To the Workers of Baku".

Lenin sends greetings to the editorial staff of *Put Molodezhi*, a newspaper published by the Bauman District Committee of the Young Communist League of Russia.

October 10   Lenin presides over a meeting of the Council of People's Commissars, which discusses: the code of land laws; the code of labour laws; the law on local budgets; the civil code; the rules of the judicial systems, and other questions.

Lenin sends greetings to the Fifth All-Russia Congress of Textile Workers.

October 11   Lenin sends greetings to the Fifth Congress of the Young Communist League of Russia.

October 13   Lenin writes a letter on the foreign trade monopoly.

October 17   Lenin presides over a meeting of the Council of People's Commissars, which discusses: the draft rules of gubernia congresses of Soviets and gubernia executive committees; the budget of the People's Commissariat of Railways, and other questions.

October 19   Lenin attends a meeting of the Political Bureau.

October 20   Lenin sends greetings to the All-Russia Congress of Financial Workers.

Lenin writes letters to the Society of Friends of Soviet Russia (in the United States) and to the Society for Technical Aid for Soviet Russia.

October 21   Lenin sends a telegram to the Central Committee of the Communist Party of Georgia categorically demanding the adoption of measures to stop the anti-Party struggle of the Mdivani group of national-deviators.

October 24   Lenin presides over a meeting of the Council of People's Commissars, which discusses: the trade agreement with Finland; the civil code, and other questions.

October 26   Lenin attends a meeting of the Political Bureau.

Lenin writes greetings to the liberated Primorye Territory.

October 27   Lenin writes answers to questions from Michael Farbman, *Observer* and *Manchester Guardian* correspondent.

October 28   Lenin writes a letter on measures to be taken to help and promote the economic revival of Soviet Armenia.

October 31   Lenin speaks at the Fourth Session of the Ninth All-Russia Central Executive Committee.

Lenin presides over a meeting of the Council of People's Commissars, which discusses: the issue of a state lottery-loan; a subsidy for the promotion of cotton-growing in Armenia, and other questions.

November 1   Lenin sends greetings to *Petrogradskaya Pravda* on the occasion of the fifth anniversary of the October Revolution.

November 2   Lenin attends a meeting of the Political Bureau.

Lenin sends greetings to *Pravda* on the occasion of the fifth anniversary of the October Revolution.

Lenin sends greetings to the First International Conference of Communist Co-operators.

November 3   Lenin presides over a meeting of the bureau of the R.C.P.(B.) delegation to the Fourth Congress of the Communist International. The meeting discusses questions connected with preparations for the Congress. Lenin proposes an amendment in the draft letter of greetings "To the Fourth Congress of the Communist International and to the Petrograd Soviet of Workers' and Red Army Deputies".

Lenin writes greetings to textile workers in Petrograd.

Lenin presides over a meeting of the Council of Labour and Defence, which discusses: the report of the authorised representative of the Council of Labour and Defence on the sale of new-harvested grain; electric ploughing; the minimum wages for November 1922; the provision of funds for the Donbas; the supply of firewood to the iron and steel plants in the Urals, and other questions.

Lenin receives Arthur Ransome, *Manchester Guardian* correspondent.

November 4   Lenin sends greetings to the All-Russia Congress of Statisticians.

November 5   Lenin finishes writing his answers to questions put by Arthur Ransome.

November 6   Lenin sends greetings to the Non-Party Conference of Women Workers and Peasants of Moscow City and Moscow Gubernia.

November 6, 8   Lenin requests information on the situation in the Donbas and on the implementation of the decision on the State Seed Board.

November 7   Lenin sends greetings to the workers of the former Michelson Plant on the occasion of the fifth anniversary of the October Revolution.

Lenin sends greetings to the workers and employees at the State Elektroperedacha Power Station on the opening of a club on the fifth anniversary of the October Revolution.

November 8   Lenin writes greetings to the workers at the Stodol Cloth Mill in Klintsi.

November 9   Lenin attends a meeting of the Political Bureau.

November 13   Lenin delivers a report on "Five Years of the Russian Revolution and the Prospects of the World Revolution" at the Fourth Congress of the Communist International.

November 14   Lenin writes greetings to the All-Russia Agricultural Exhibition.

November 15   Lenin writes greetings to foreign writer war-veterans, who had formed the *Clarté* group in France.

Lenin writes a letter to I. I. Skvortsov-Stepanov on Party policy with regard to bourgeois specialists under the dictatorship of the proletariat.

November 16   Lenin attends a meeting of the Political Bureau.

November 17   Lenin presides over a meeting of the Council of Labour and Defence, which discusses: the preparation of materials for the Tenth All-Russia Congress of Soviets; measures for the sale of new-harvested grain; the financing of the coal and oil industries, and other questions.

November 18   Lenin requests information on the work and experiments of I. V. Michurin; proposes to submit to the Council of Labour and Defence the question of the irrigation system in Turkestan.

November 20   Lenin speaks on foreign and home policy at a Plenary Meeting of the Moscow Soviet.

November 22   Lenin writes a letter to the Presidium of the Fifth All-Russia Congress of the Soviet Employees' Union.

November 23   Lenin attends a meeting of the Political Bureau.

November 25   Lenin asks that a letter of greetings be sent on his behalf to the Fourth All-Russia Educational Workers' Congress.

November   Lenin has a series of talks with delegates to the Fourth Congress of the Communist International on the organisational pattern of Communist Parties and on the methods and content of their work.

December 1   Lenin instructs the Executive Secretary of the Council of People's Commissars to request for summary data on the state of industry for the year and on the budget of industry in connection with the preparations for the Tenth All-Russia Congress of Soviets.

December 2

In a letter to the Secretary of the Central Committee of the International Workers' Aid Lenin appeals to the workers and working people of the whole world to launch a campaign for economic aid to Soviet Russia.

December 4

Lenin sends greetings to the Third Congress of the Young Communist International in Moscow.

Lenin writes his "Notes on the Tasks of Our Delegation at The Hague".

December 5

Lenin writes directives on the distribution of functions between the Deputy Chairmen of the Council of People's Commissars and the Council of Labour and Defence.

Lenin instructs the Executive Secretary of the Council of People's Commissars to ask the People's Commissariat of Agriculture what measures had been taken to help I. V. Michurin.

December 6

Lenin writes the article "A Few Words About N. Y. Fedoseyev".

December 7

Lenin attends a meeting of the Political Bureau.

December 7-12

Lenin lives at Gorki; he prepares for his report to the Tenth All-Russia Congress of Soviets.

December 9

Lenin draws up instructions on the functions of the Deputy Chairmen and Chairman of the Council of People's Commissars.

December 10

Lenin sends greetings to the All-Ukraine Congress of Soviets.

December 12

Lenin works in his study in the Kremlin for the last time.

December 13

Lenin dictates a letter to the C.C., R.C.P.(B.) on the foreign trade monopoly.

First half of December

Lenin prepares to speak at the Tenth All-Russia Congress of Soviets, drawing up an outline of his speech.

December 15   Lenin dictates a letter to J. V. Stalin for members of the Central Committee, on the speech for the Tenth All-Russia Congress of Soviets.

December 16   Lenin suffers the second attack of illness.

December 23   Lenin summons his secretary, dictates letters and demands books.

December 29   Lenin's doctors allow him to read.

1923

January 1, 2   Lenin dictates the article "Pages From a Diary"

January 4, 6   Lenin dictates the article "On Co-operation".

January 9, 13   Lenin dictates the first variant of the article "How We Should Reorganise the Workers' and Peasants' Inspection".

January 10   Lenin instructs the Executive Secretary of the Council of People's Commissars to request the Central Statistical Board to send him the figures of the census of Soviet employees.

January 16, 17   Lenin dictates the article "Our Revolution (Apropos of N. Sukhanov's Notes)".

January 19, 20 22, 23   Lenin dictates the second variant of the article "How We Should Reorganise the Workers' and Peasants' Inspection (Recommendation to the Twelfth Party Congress)" and has it sent to press.

February 2, 4 5, 6, 7, 8, 9   Lenin dictates the article "Better Fewer, But Better".

March 2   Lenin looks through his article "Better Fewer, But Better" and has it sent to press.

March 9   Lenin has another attack.

May 15   Lenin is moved to Gorki.

Second half of July   Lenin's health improves.

October 19   Lenin comes to Moscow for a few hours, goes to his study. On the way back to Gorki he visits the Agricultural Exhibition.

1924

January 21, *6.50 p.m.,* *Gorki*	Lenin dies.
Night of *January 21*	The Central Committee of the R.C.P.(B.) holds a Plenary Meeting in connection with Lenin's death.
January 22	M. I. Kalinin informs the Eleventh All-Russia Congress of Soviets of Lenin's death.
January 22-23	Members of the Central Committee and Central Control Commission of the R.C.P.(B.), members of the Council of People's Commissars, delegations from the Congress of Soviets and Moscow organisations, as well as peasants from the surrounding villages come to Gorki to take their leave of Lenin.
January 23, *10-11 a.m.*	The coffin with Lenin's body is carried from Gorki to the Gerasimovo (now Leninskaya) Station.
January 23, *1 p.m., Moscow*	The funeral train with Lenin's body arrives in Moscow. Lenin's immediate associates carry the coffin to the Hall of Columns of the House of Trade Unions.
January 26	The Second Congress of Soviets of the U.S.S.R. meets in memorial session. It adopts an address "To Working Mankind" and passes decisions to rename Petrograd into Leningrad, to erect monuments to Lenin, and to publish his works.
January 23-27	Hundreds of thousands of workers, peasants, Red Army men and employees of Moscow, and delegations from the working people of all parts of the Soviet Union file in endless day and night procession through the Hall of Columns to take their leave of Lenin.
January 27, *9.20 a.m.*	The coffin with Lenin's body is carried from the Hall of Columns to Red Square.
January 27, *4. p.m.*	The coffin with Lenin's body is installed in the mausoleum in Red Square.

В. И. ЛЕНИН

СОЧИНЕНИЯ

Том 33

На английском языке